NAVAL WARFARE

NAVAL WARFARE

AN ILLUSTRATED HISTORY

Edited by Richard Humble

With a foreword by Peter Kemp

FORMER HEAD OF THE ROYAL NAVAL HISTORICAL BRANCH

ORBIS PUBLISHING LONDON

Printed in Italy by SAGDOS SpA, Milan

ISBN 0-85613-285-3

Endpapers: The bombardment of Gibraltar, 1704.
Pages 2–3: Fireships threaten the Spanish
Armada, 1588.
Page 6: USS *Missouri* in action.

Contents

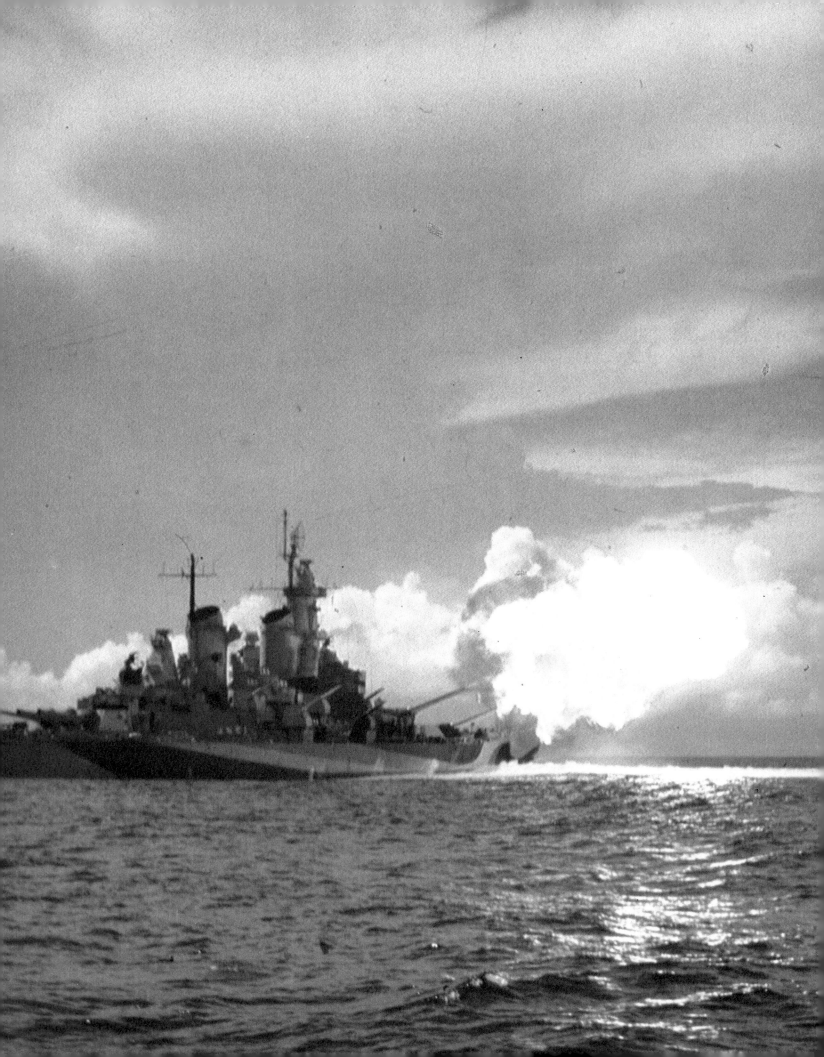

Foreword

Sea power has had a profound effect on the history of the world through its influence in the rise and fall of nations. It is won and maintained by ships, by seamen, by the acceptance and use of the developing technology of the time, and by prowess in battle, an amalgam of human courage and leadership. The despatch of the British task force to the Falkland Islands as recently as April 1982 served to highlight the continuing importance of conventional naval power even in this nuclear age.

This is a book about naval warfare which deals with the significant campaigns of naval history, the decisive battles in those campaigns, and includes biographical sketches of the principal naval leaders who directed and fought those battles. These are linked together with penetrating introductions to each new era of naval evolution, explaining the changes wrought in strategy and tactics by the development of new naval technology. The overall view is worldwide and it covers the story of sea warfare from the first days of the fighting galley to the first operational use in the Falklands of modern missile systems.

This is a big book, big in its conception and in its all-embracing treatment of this important subject. I know of few other books in which the full world story of naval warfare is told, and there is certainly none which tells it so vividly, and with such convincing authority.

Peter Kemp.

PART ONE

The Ancient World

Naval warfare in the ancient world was determined by the Mediterranean Sea and by the empires that rose and fell around its shores. The Mediterranean was a relatively calm sea with few strong prevailing winds and almost no tidal flow. These factors were vital in making the Mediterranean an important artery of trade and in determining the form of maritime warfare in the ancient world.

The first records we have of seagoing ships come from the Egyptians, though it is likely that boatbuilding techniques were equally, or more advanced in the East and Arabia. In 2700 BC the first naval engagement was recorded when an expeditionary force of eight Egyptian ships was sent on a raid along the Mediterranean. Despite this the Egyptians were not primarily a maritime power and it was the Minoans who first developed the concept of a warship, one specially designed to operate against other ships.

The Phoenician peoples, who occupied a region corresponding to present-day Lebanon, were masters of boatbuilding and seamanship, and controlled the eastern Mediterranean during the period 1100 to 800 BC. They were primarily bound together by commercial – rather than political – considerations, spreading their settlements westwards along Africa's north coast and establishing trading stations on Sicily, Sardinia, Malta and at the mineral-rich town of Cadiz. Contemporary illustrations depict the two distinct forms of vessel which they employed; the 'round ship' was used solely for trade, while the 'long ship' had a sharp ram at the bow, which was to revolutionize the tactics of the sea battle and emphasize the value of the ship as a fighting vessel and not merely as a troop transport. It was the 'long ship' or galley that became the dominant fighting vessel of the Mediterranean throughout the classical age and it was still in active use as late as the eighteenth century.

The galley was developed further by the Greeks who replaced the Phoenicians as the major maritime force, and by the Romans who in turn ousted the Greeks as the dominant naval power in the Mediterranean. Three of the great naval battles of the ancient world, Salamis, Mylae and Actium, were fought with galleys, and the design developed as the techniques of naval warfare became established.

The earliest galley of which we have any knowledge is the 'long ship' of the Mycenaean Greeks, who flourished from about 1300 to 1100 BC. However, the poet Homer, who described two main types of these vessels, belonged to a later period, c.800 BC, so his report may not be totally reliable. He describes the larger type of vessel as having twenty-five oars a side, including steering oars, and being about 27m (90ft) long. The smaller galley had only ten oars a side, again including steering oars, and was about 12m (40ft) in length.

The ships were built on a frame of ribs and keel, the long side planks being fitted edge-to-edge,

An oared vessel used by the Minoans, representing a forerunner of the galley. The model is based on the decoration of a vase excavated at Crete.

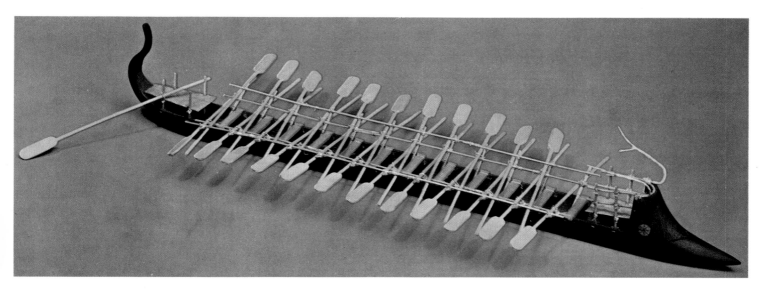

RIGHT The Egyptian pottery decoration pictured here dates from 3100 BC and is the earliest known representation of a vessel under sail.

FAR RIGHT A piece of Egyptian pottery of 3300 BC depicting a river boat.

carvel fashion, and sewn together with cords. A liberal coating of pitch was applied in an attempt to make the hull waterproof. Apart from small platforms at the bow and stern, these ships were undecked. The rowers, who rowed from the gunwale, sat at benches beneath which was stored any cargo the vessel might have to carry. Valuable stores such as wine-skins which the commander might wish to keep an eye on could be stowed under the after platform on which the commander and helmsman had their stations. The forward platform was occupied by the ship's lookout.

A single mast and sail were carried – a rig that remained unchanged for many centuries. The mast was supported by a pair of leather forestays, which were also used for hoisting and lowering it, and a single backstay. The yard was hoisted by means of halyards, also of leather, which were secured at the foot of the mast. Braces, which controlled the yard, were led aft to the helmsman's position. The sail, made up of several sections of linen sewn together, was controlled by sheets lashed to bronze rings set into the corners of the sail and led aft to the helmsman. The usual practice while under sail was that the helmsman made one sheet fast and retained hold of the other, thus allowing him instant control over the sail. Reefing was carried out by means of brailing-ropes, secured to the foot of the sail, led up its face and over the yard and joining into a single rope aft to the helmsman's position. The helmsman, having control over the sail and steering oar as he did, had to be an experienced seaman and usually acted as the second-in-command to the captain.

These vessels were fragile, leaky and dangerously unseaworthy, and so naval activity was correspondingly limited by the weather. The 'sailing season' usually commenced in April, when good weather could be expected. Sometime during the previous October the ships would have been hauled ashore and dismantled for the winter. Although Homer makes no mention of dockyard facilities, such as shipsheds or shipways, something of the sort must have existed as it is difficult to imagine the vessels being left exposed to the elements through the winter. In early April the ships would be carefully inspected, repaired where necessary and launched. The usual Mycenaean practice at sea was to keep within sight of the shore, navigating by landmarks and anchoring in some sheltered cove for the night. As the cramped galleys could carry very little food or water, meals were probably obtained ashore, when this was possible.

During the period from about 800 to 550 BC, the Greek city states were engaged in a long series of explorations and colonization, which took them the length and breadth of the Mediterranean and the Black Sea. The Phoenicians had already founded many trading posts in the western Mediterranean and the arrival of the Greeks sparked off a series of clashes during which the early 'Homeric' galley became refined into an efficient and deadly weapon.

The invention of the ram, some time during the eighth century BC, revolutionized naval warfare. Previously fighting at sea had been carried on between the crews of the respective vessels by boarding and fighting it out hand-to-hand. Now the galley itself could be used as a weapon to sink or cripple enemy ships.

Victory at sea became a matter of training. The commander whose crew was so well-trained as to respond instantly to his commands could quickly out-manoeuvre an ill-trained or clumsy enemy ship

and sink her. If, on the other hand, his crew was itself badly trained, or badly commanded, he stood a good chance of being sunk himself. Ramming was a tactic that required quick thinking and a good sense of timing. If the attacking vessel went in too fast the ram could be jammed in the enemy's hull, and the attacker ran the risk of going down with the other ship. If the attack was too slow the enemy could avoid it, in which case the attacking crew had to be able to back off quickly and work out another attack, always bearing in mind that the rowers would quickly become exhausted. The usual tactic was to attempt to run up alongside the enemy and snap off his oars, then to use the ram to sink him when he was unmanoeuvrable.

The new tactics, no less than the old, required large numbers of fighting men to be carried, mainly archers and spearmen. They could keep the enemies' heads down during the run-in and then, after impact, either act as boarders themselves or stand by to repel enemy boarders. Extra deck space had to be found to accommodate these men and it took the form of a fighting platform linking the fore and aft decks. Some authorities believe that platforms were also built along the gunwales, above the oars, and light breastworks erected to give protection to the rowers. The increase in missile fire accompanying these tactics meant that the oarsmen were now dangerously exposed and to give them some protection an additional set of rowing benches was fitted beneath the existing ones. Before the galley went into action the oarsmen moved onto the lower set of benches and rowed through oarports.

The fact that the galley could be rowed without difficulty from either position made the next step obvious – to row it from both positions at once. To obtain the additional bank of oars the existing one was split into two, so that the upper bank now consisted of thirteen oarsmen and the lower bank twelve. The banks were arranged in a staggered pattern that allowed each oar to move freely with a reduced chance of fouling the others.

The new arrangement allowed the hull to be shortened and strengthened, thus increasing its seaworthiness. On the other hand it did expose the rowers of the upper bank to enemy fire. This seems to have been accepted as the price of potentially greater power. Most probably some kind of temporary protection would have been erected before going into action. It may have been at this time that the gunwale fighting platforms were built.

It should not be imagined that these changes took place overnight, or even over a relatively short period of time. Both the ram and the two-banked galley, or bireme, are thought to have been invented between 800 and 700 BC, but the dates given are traditional and there is no real evidence. It is not even known which came first, as the invention of either could have set off a search for the other. For instance, the invention of the ram would have set off a search for increased power to be able to use it effectively. On the other hand, the invention of the bireme could have set men looking for a weapon to which this greater power could be applied.

By 700 BC the standard warship was the bireme. Fast and handy, it was capable of turning in its own length and moving at 7 knots in short bursts. The rig had remained unchanged from that of the earlier galleys: a single mast supporting one large sail. Both mast and sail were taken down before going into action. The disadvantages of the galley, which were never overcome during its long career up to the

A keel-less boat is portrayed upon this relief, which is dated 2500 BC. Longitudinal bracing was provided by a stout rope or hogging truss above the deck.

eighteenth century, were that its fragile construction rendered it incapable of facing heavy weather and that it could not carry sufficient stores for long cruises.

The search for increased power did not stop with the bireme, but there were considerable obstacles to overcome. The only way to obtain an increase in power was to increase the number of oarsmen. This meant either adding a third bank of oarsmen or extending the two existing banks. If the second alternative was adopted it meant lengthening and therefore weakening the hull. However, the addition of a third bank of oars would be even more dangerous because the height of the hull would have to be increased, and, unless this was accompanied by a relative increase in the length and beam, stability would be dangerously affected. These increases in

until 482 BC that Themistocles was able to persuade the Athenians to build a strong navy of 200 triremes.

The Athenian triremes differed little from those of other city states. Some, notably the Corinthian and Phoenician, were employed to carry large forces of fighting men and were fully decked for this purpose. The Athenian vessels were commanded, in theory at least, by the *treirarch*, a wealthy man who had agreed to be responsible for the building of a ship and its maintenance for a year. In return he received the nominal command although the vessel was actually run by his second-in-command, the *kybernetes*. This name and the names of the other officers derive from the days of the 'long ships' when the officers actually carried out duties from which their rank derived. *Kybernetes*,

Ramses III, the last of the great Pharaohs, won an important naval victory over 'the northerners of the isles' in about 1180 BC; the action is commemorated on the temple walls at Medinet Habu.

dimensions would increase the weight to be moved and therefore would cancel out the increased power.

The solution to the problem was both simple and extremely ingenious. Outriggers were built onto the existing hull on both sides and the third bank of oarsmen rowed from them, thus increasing the power considerably without any drastic alterations to the hull or increase in weight. Stability was also increased, and it became possible to build galleys longer, up to a length-to-beam ratio of 8:1, so making them even faster. The first galley with outriggers was probably built by the Phoenicians around 700 BC, as one is depicted in Assyrian reliefs of that period. Other states were soon to adopt the new invention, for Herodotus reports that the then ruler of Egypt, Necho, was building triremes before 593 BC, and it is certain that the new type of vessel was firmly established in Greece by 500 BC.

In view of her future naval supremacy it is interesting to note that at the time of the Ionian Revolt (494 BC) the navy of Athens consisted of only twenty ships, none of them triremes. It was not

for example, means helmsman, but he became the navigating officer, while the *proreus*, or bow officer, became the first lieutenant, the *keleustes* (timebeater) was responsible for the oarsmen, their equipment and training and the *pentecontarchos*, a later rank, was the junior officer on board.

The crew consisted of 170 oarsmen, all of whom had to be skilled rowers, divided into three grades. The 62 *thranite* oarsmen rowed from the upper bank and they had the most tiring stroke as their oars were at a steeper angle than the remainder. The 54 *zygite* oarsmen rowed from the gunwale and the 54 *thalamite* oarsmen from the lower bank. The recruitment of these oarsmen was a constant headache for the Athenian naval authorities. They were usually obtained from the poorest classes of citizens who were, however, reluctant to serve at sea and had to be paid high wages.

In the period of the battle of Salamis (480 BC), the Athenians embarked fourteen marines and twenty-five seamen as well as officers and oarsmen, making a total crew of 214 men in a single galley. The Athenian fleet at Salamis numbered 200 ships, so the

number of men needed was around 42,600 and, as a strong army had to be maintained in addition, the drain on resources is obvious.

The rig of the galley had remained unchanged, being still the single mast and sail, but the Athenians had added a smaller mast and sail which could be kept on board when going into action and hoisted if the need for a quick departure arose. Athenian triremes were divided into three classes. The first class consisted of the newest vessels which were not employed on routine duties, but were kept in reserve. The ships in the second and third classes were rated according to age and condition. When too old for the third class they were either sold or employed as horse transports.

Battle tactics consisted of two main manoeuvres. The *dieceplus* was first reported as being used by the Phoenicians at Artemisium (480 BC). It consisted of the attacking fleet, at a prearranged signal, suddenly dashing forward and using its speed to cut through the enemy line, after which it turned to attack their sterns. This attack demanded highly trained crews and could be very effective against opponents who

were slow to react. It failed at Artemisium because Themistocles, the Athenian and allied commander, formed up his fleet in a circle with their prows pointing outward. From here the highly trained Athenian crews launched devastating attacks. The Spartans tried the same defence at the battle of Patras (429 BC), where they outnumbered the Athenians by two to one, but their vessels were loaded down with troops and equipment. The Spartan commander formed up his fleet in a circle and waited for his chance to attack. The Athenian squadron was commanded by Phormio, an experienced officer. He had taken the trouble to study the area and, knowing that a wind usually came up at dawn, had commenced the action at first light. He ordered his fleet to circle the Spartan formation slowly, relying on his crews' speed of manoeuvre to avoid any sudden attacks. When the wind came up it threw the dense Spartan formation into confusion and, seizing their opportunity, the Athenians attacked, sinking several of the enemy and driving the remainder off in confusion.

The second manoeuvre was the *periplus*. Much

A Phoenician warship of about 700 BC, with two banks of oars. Archers were carried on the upper bridge, while the pointed bow ram was the galley's main offensive weapon.

ABOVE RIGHT A very detailed fresco provides evidence of Minoan seagoing ships in about 1500 BC.

BELOW A Tarshish ship, of the type employed by Phoenician traders, is pictured on a sarcophagus found in the harbour at Sidon.

simpler, it consisted of a fast run around the enemy's flank to take him in the rear. The usual defence was to anchor one flank in shallows, or against the shore.

Although the Athenians had carried fighting with the ram to heights never since equalled and thus dominated the eastern Mediterranean, they finally over-reached themselves. The Syracusan expedition, from 415 to 413 BC, cost over 210 ships and vast numbers of trained oarsmen who could not be replaced. Athens rebuilt her fleet, only to see it destroyed at the battle of Aergospotami in 405 BC. The Spartan admiral waited until the Athenians had beached their fleet and settled down to eat and then

attacked and burnt 171 ships. The nine that escaped raided the Spartan camp where they burned their enemy's rigging and sails to prevent pursuit.

A new development of this period was the introduction of the strengthened cathead or *epotides* by the Spartan admiral Polyanthes as a means of countering superior Athenian seamanship. The *epotides* was a structure built on the bows of a galley and used in close-quarters fighting to damage the bows of the enemy ship and break its oars. This new device was used to good effect by another Spartan commander, Gylippus, in the destruction of the Athenian blockading force in the Great Harbour at Syracuse in 413 BC.

It was mentioned previously that the problem in recruiting oarsmen led indirectly to the next stage of development. Dionysius, Tyrant of Syracuse, had ambitions to found an empire in southern Italy and Sicily. He had built up a large army and developed new types of siege artillery. His navy, however, consisted largely of triremes with their attendant problems in manpower. Dionysius solved this problem by the invention of the quadrireme – a single-banked galley in which four men rowed at a single oar. This resulted in a great saving of manpower. Where the triremes had required 170 skilled oarsmen, the quadrireme, assuming that it rowed twenty-five oars a side, required only fifty skilled oarsmen. The remaining 150 could be selected merely for their muscle. The new galleys were completely decked and as well as large forces of marines carried some of the recently developed artillery – the first warships ever to do so. There are no surviving descriptions of these Syracusan war-ships, so we have no idea what they looked like. We do know that in one of their actions they were dragged over a fairly wide neck of land, so they cannot have been very large vessels.

The cities of Greece kept an interested eye on the new developments but did not seem anxious to bring the new vessels into their fleets. Athens,

A reconstruction of
Phoenician war galleys
under sail. The galley had
by this time evolved from a
troop-carrier into a
formidable fighting ship.

probably suffering from excessive war-weariness, was very slow to use quadriremes. By 325 BC there were only fifty of them in service, plus seven quinqueremes, which were rowed by five men at each oar.

During the wars which followed the death of Alexander the Great in 323 BC, Demetrius Poliorcetes, son of Antigonus (one of Alexander's generals), emerged as a gifted naval officer and a talented ship designer. Being fully aware of the value of sea power, he decided to build a fleet that could not be matched by his main enemy, Egypt. To do this he needed bigger vessels than those in existence, the quadrireme and the quinquereme. During 315 BC his shipwrights produced galleys with six and seven men to the oar. Several years later, by 301 BC, he possessed galleys which are described as 'tens', 'elevens' and 'thirteens', and by 289 BC he had added a 'fifteen' and a 'sixteen'. The increase in size was carried on after his defeat in 285 BC, by his son Antigonus Gonatus, who built an 'eighteen'. To match this the Egyptian King Ptolemy II produced a 'twenty' and two 'thirties', but the limit was reached when Ptolemy IV built a 'forty'. As with Dionysius' vessels, we have no idea what these giant galleys looked like. There are plenty of ideas and inspired guesses, none of which is based upon authentic information. We know that the largest seagoing type, the 'twenty', must have been gigantic since it carried several hundred marines and needed over 2000 rowers to move it. We also know that the 'forty' was over 120m (400ft) long and 15m (50ft) wide and that it needed 4000 rowers, but it is generally believed to have been only a floating palace, which was not intended for sea duty.

Possibly the most convincing explanation is that these vessels were simply scaled-up versions of the single-banked galley, the bireme and the trireme. For instance a 'sixteen' could well have been a scaled-up trireme in which the number of rowers in

a 'room' – the vertical section of the three banks – totalled sixteen. An interesting theory that has recently been advanced is that the 'twenty' and the 'forty' could have been catamarans. Demetrius used this type of vessel during his attack on Rhodes in 306–305 BC. By building a platform on two large galleys he was able to mount siege towers and catapults on it and he may well have talked to his son about building a ship in that form.

A change that did occur as a result of the growth in size of vessels is that, for the first time, more than one mast was fitted. Ships now carried two masts and the largest possibly three, but each mast still carried a single square sail. These large galleys were so expensive to build and maintain that they could not be kept in commission for any length of time. Although the various countries building them tried all sorts of ideas, such as a special 'galley tax' imposed in Egypt, and the reintroduction of the system of *treirarchs*, the ships proved so expensive that they simply went out of use. The first was launched in 315 BC and by 260 BC they had gone, leaving the quinquereme as the standard warship.

The quinquereme was used by the navy of Carthage during the First Punic War (264–241 BC). Rome entered this war with no navy to speak of, but by a tremendous feat of organization and construction, the Romans built a hundred quinqueremes and twenty triremes in sixty days during 261 BC. Moreover, they manned this fleet, sailed it to Sicily and fought a victorious battle against the Carthaginian fleet at Mylae in 260 BC.

During the Second Punic War (219–203 BC) Rome's naval supremacy played a vital role in defeating the Carthaginians. Although Hannibal gained many great tactical victories in Italy, the Roman navy was able to cut his supply lines to North Africa and so prevent the Carthaginian general from taking Rome itself. Roman control of the western Mediterranean allowed the army of Scipio Africanus to land in Africa at will and in

ABOVE   Carving of a Greek
ship with steering oars in the
raised position, allowing it
to be beached stern first.

RIGHT   A somewhat less
detailed Roman galley
appears on this coin from
the second century BC.

204 BC achieve the decisive victory of the war at the battle of Zama.

The only new type of warship that Rome introduced was the *liburnian*, originally a light, fast, single-banked vessel. The Romans added a second bank of oars and used it for a variety of duties such as anti-piracy patrols and the carrying of despatches. The true contribution of Rome to naval warfare, however, was her genius for organization. The Romans had instituted a system of navy commissioners in 311 BC who were responsible for Roman maritime affairs on a full-time basis. In peacetime they acted in a regulatory capacity and in time of war they were sufficiently experienced to build up a naval fleet at short notice.

The first important technical development of the galley by the Romans was the introduction of the *corvus*, a wide plank of wood with a spike at one end which acted as a boarding bridge. Unlike the Athenians or Carthaginians the Romans were less concerned with the finer points of seamanship and concentrated on getting alongside and boarding the enemy ship, relying on the superior quality of their heavily armed soldiers in hand-to-hand fighting.

The Roman preoccupation with close-quarters combat was taken a stage further by the Roman admiral, Marcus Agrippa, who invented the *harpago*. The *harpago* was fired from a catapult and consisted of an iron-bound piece of timber with a grapnel attached to the parent ship by a length of rope. Once securely embedded in the enemy vessel, the Roman galley could be hauled alongside it, preparatory to boarding.

By the time of the Wars of the Second Triumvirate (43–34 BC) the tactic of hurling firebrands at the enemy ships was commonplace, and was used to good effect by Agrippa at the battle of Actium (31 BC) against Mark Antony's fleet. The Roman victory at Actium secured the entire Mediterranean for Rome, and until the barbarian invasion of the fourth century AD it became in effect a Roman lake.

Salamis

A VICTORY FOR SEAMANSHIP

The upper oarsmen of an Athenian trireme are depicted in this detail from a relief. Their oars extended through holes in the vessel's outrigger planking.

The battle of Salamis, which saved the Athenian republic and halted the Persian conquest of Greece on 23 September 480 BC, remains one of the classic examples of the inestimable value of sea power. Prior to the battle, the Athenians and their allies had proved quite unable to halt the advance of the massive Persian army through Greece. Athens itself had been abandoned to the invaders and the city's entire population had taken to flight. Within weeks of the sea victory off Salamis, however, the Persian host was retreating north to avoid being trapped in Greece, never to return.

The creation of the Persian Empire by Cyrus I, who ruled from 550 to 530 BC, and its expansion into Asia Minor (modern-day Turkey), caused friction with the flourishing Greek colonies on the mainland (Ionian) coast of Asia Minor. While Cyrus lived, the Ionian Greeks enjoyed a comparatively benevolent regime under their Persian overlords, but this changed under Cambyses (530–521 BC) and Darius I (521–486 BC) as the animosity between Greek and Persian grew. The Ionian Greeks' revolt in the 490s was crushed, but resulted in Darius' plan to root out further subversion on the part of Athens by invading Greece.

Darius made two attempts to subdue the Greek states, both of which ended in failure. The first expedition in 492 BC took the form of an overland march across the Dardanelles and around the northern edge of the Aegean Sea. The destruction of the Persian fleet in a storm off Mount Athos, however, left the Persian army unsupported from the seaward side, and the cautious Persian commander called off the invasion and retired across the Dardanelles. Two years later another Persian army advanced from Asia Minor but was soundly defeated by the Athenians and their allies at the Battle of Marathon. Both expeditions revealed to the Persians the necessity of gaining naval supremacy in the Aegean, for without a strong fleet the Persian land army was vulnerable to the flanking attacks of the Athenian navy.

The humiliation of Marathon only made Darius more determined than ever to crush Athens, but he was prevented from launching a third expedition by domestic squabbles over the Persian line of succession and the revolt of the province of Egypt. Darius died in 486 BC unable to complete his grand design. His successor, Xerxes, was forced to make his position secure throughout the empire and reconquered Egypt before resuming plans for the conquest of Greece. This third Persian attempt involved the army in an overland march with the fleet sailing in support. This time, however, the invasion was to be in overwhelming strength, a steamroller advance to force as many Greek cities as possible to forsake the Athenian cause. In order to give his fleet maximum protection during its voyage along the coast, Xerxes had a ship canal cut through the Mount Athos peninsula to avoid the chance of another mass shipwreck. By the spring of 480 BC the huge Persian invasion force – estimated at 180,000 men and 750 war galleys – was ready for the march on Athens.

In the face of such overwhelming numerical odds, the strategy of the Athenians was to slow down the advancing Persians as much as possible in order to encourage the states of southern Greece – the most powerful of which was Sparta, in the Peloponnese – to raise forces and march them north to reinforce the Athenian field army. In the years since Marathon, however, the Athenians had made a vital addition to their defence forces.

In 483 BC the state revenue of Athens had received an unexpected bonus: the opening of a rich new vein in the republic's silver mine at Laurium. Normally the profits would have been shared out among the ruling aristocracy and spent on improving social amenities to buy votes. But the statesman

Themistocles persuaded the Athenians to spend their financial windfall on building a new battle-fleet. The new fleet of 200 triremes was ready for action by the time of Xerxes' invasion in 480 BC. The other fifteen maritime states in alliance with Athens could together contribute rather less than 185 warships, yielding a combined Greek fleet with a maximum strength of about 385 warships.

Although the Athenian naval contingent was by far the largest, the touchy independence and rivalry which kept the Greek states at odds with each other, even in their hour of greatest communal danger, prevented the Athenians from wielding the supreme command at sea. The war effort on land depended on the cooperation of the superb Spartan army and, although the initial Spartan naval contribution was only ten ships, they refused to serve under an Athenian admiral. Wisely, the Athenians swallowed their pride and accepted a Spartan fleet commander, Eurybiades.

While Eurybiades was the nominal commander it was Themistocles who exercised effective control of the Greek fleet. In this task he was ably supported by his second-in-command, Cimon, a professional sailor who was to handle the tactical side of the great battle.

Themistocles' strategy was for the Greeks to engage the Persian armada as far north as possible, whittling away the Persian advantage in numbers by attacking in confined waters where the Persians would be unable to deploy their full strength. The Greeks were helped by a timely north-easterly gale which hit the Persian fleet on its way down the coast and wrecked about 400 warships and transports. By the time Xerxes' army approached the Greek force holding the Thermopylae Pass, Themistocles had persuaded Eurybiades to concentrate the Greek fleet at Artemisium. His plan was to fight a delaying action in the narrow bottleneck of sea between the northern tip of Euboea and the mainland, through which the Persian fleet would have to pass.

Leonidas and the 'Three Hundred' would never have been able to win immortality in the Pass of Thermopylae if the Greek fleet at Artemisium had not gallantly prevented the Persians from landing troops behind the defenders of the Pass. For three days the fleets engaged on virtually equal terms because of the narrow confines of the strait. Despite extensive damage to their own ships the Greeks stopped the Persians from forcing the strait, sinking at least thirty Persian ships on the first day alone and emerging with well-earned battle honours and vital combat experience. When the naval commanders heard that the Persians had stormed Thermopylae and that the road to Athens was open, they had no choice but to withdraw from Artemisium in order to prepare for the last-ditch defence of the city of Athens.

In this crisis Athens was left on her own, with the northern Greek states making their peace with the advancing Persians and the southern states opting for withdrawal into the Peloponnese. Themistocles persuaded the Athenians to abandon their city, migrate *en masse* to the offshore island of Salamis, and put their trust in the fleet. He then cajoled Eurybiades to remain with the Athenian fleet instead of decamping with the Peloponnesian ships. Withdrawal to Athenian waters had brought the Greek fleet welcome reinforcements; it now numbered about 380 warships, while the Persian fleet, depleted by shipwreck and the losses suffered at Artemisium, seems to have been barely a hundred vessels stronger.

The sprawling island of Salamis covers the Bay of Eleusis like an ill-fitting plug, so creating a channel or strait between Salamis and the mainland with entrances to the bay to the east and west of the island. Themistocles' plan was to lure the Persian ships up the strait in order to nullify their advantage in numbers: the narrowness of the strait would hem the Persians in and prevent them from turning the Greek's flank. While the Greeks were familiar with their home waters the Persians had little knowledge of the coastal region around Salamis.

A number of the Greek commanders opposed Themistocles and recommended that the Greek fleet disperse while it still had time. In order to prevent this Themistocles sent a false 'intelligence' report to Xerxes urging him to attack the Greeks as swiftly as possible. The Persians fell for the ruse and late on 22 September they began to prepare for action.

In order to trap the Greek fleet, Xerxes despatched his Egyptian squadrons to block the western passage while the bulk of the fleet would advance up the eastern sound. He then set up his golden throne on the mainland heights and prepared to watch the final destruction of the Greek navy, the penultimate obstacle to the Persian conquest of all Greece.

The battle commenced on 23 September 480 BC. Both sides watched while the Greek triremes came out in a flimsy-looking line-ahead, debouching across the eastern sound and sagging northward to form an arc across the entrance. Eurybiades with sixteen ships held the right flank while the Athenians held the left with the bulk of the fleet, and the centre came under the control of the Greek allies.

The Persian fleet was deployed in three lines but was forced to break into columns in order to pass the island of Psytallia which lay at the entrance to the eastern passage. This operation caused unexpected confusion and by the time the Persians had negotiated this obstacle their line was in disorder. The Greek ships then turned bows-on to face the confused masses of Xerxes' Phoenician and Ionian squadrons.

Themistocles had timed his deployment to coincide with the commencement of the daily sea breeze which sent a heavy swell rolling in through the

narrows. In the words of Plutarch: 'This breeze was
no disadvantage to the Greek ships, which were
comparatively small and lay low in the water, but it
caught the Persian vessels, which were difficult to
manoeuvre with their high decks and towering
sterns, and swung them round broadside-on to their
opponents.'

The Greek commanders launched their ships at
the now thoroughly disorganized Persian fleet in a
series of converging ramming attacks. The skilfully
handled Greek ships caused havoc in the broken
Persian line. At close quarters the Greeks had a
definite advantage; their ships were more strongly
built and were able to shear away the oars of the
Persian vessels if not ram and sink them outright.
Also, the eighteen well-armed marines aboard each
Athenian trireme overwhelmed the Persian archers
in boarding contests.

Attempts by the rearmost Persian ships to disengage only made this confusion worse and hastened the disintegration of their fleet. Nonetheless,
the Persians fought far more tenaciously than at
Artemisium – they were, after all, under the direct
eye of Xerxes – but despite hand-to-hand fighting
on the crippled hulks, the Persians could do more
than protract the one-sided action until sunset. The

Persians lost over 200 ships, the Greeks about forty.

Salamis left the rump of the Persian fleet facing
destruction and the Persian army facing isolation
and entrapment in Greece. Xerxes, having lost his
nerve, ordered an immediate retreat, leaving a
third of the army in token occupation under
Mardonius, but this force was destroyed at Plataea
in the following year. So ended the last Persian
invasion of Greece, whose citizens justly paid
tribute to Salamis, in the immortal words of
Simonides, as 'that noble and famous victory, the
most glorious exploit ever achieved at sea by Greek
or barbarian'.

Salamis was one of the most decisive battles in
history. Not only was it a great tactical victory for
the Greeks but strategically its consequences were
enormous. At one stroke Persian naval power in the
Aegean Sea was permanently destroyed, which in
turn made a Persian victory on land virtually
impossible as the Persian army could not survive
without the supportive functions of the fleet. The
western advance of the Persian Empire had been
halted and Greek civilization saved. The battle at
Salamis was the high-water mark of the Persian
Empire and heralded the rise of Greece as a great
Mediterranean sea power.

A nineteenth-century
representation of the battle
of Salamis. The Greek
triremes joined battle with
their sails furled, as shown
here, using oarpower to
generate speed for ramming.

19

Mylae

THE ROMAN ARMY TAKES TO THE SEA

Fought west of Messana (Messina) off the north-eastern tip of Sicily in 260 BC, the battle of Mylae was the first of a trio of Roman sea victories which ended the long rule of Carthage as mistress of the western Mediterranean. As well as signifying the Roman republic's coming of age as a sea power, Mylae also proved that a nation did not need to have centuries of experience at sea in order to win sea battles. Mylae was one of the earliest demonstrations of how a successful military power, by shrewd imitation and improvement on traditional techniques, can extend its prowess to the sea.

According to tradition Rome was founded in 753 BC, and had slowly expanded from a city state to an important Mediterranean power by the third century BC. Rome's victories over her neighbouring states gave her mastery of central and southern Italy and extended her rule to the Adriatic coast, but also brought her into conflict with the Greek urban colonies on the southern Italian coast. These called in the celebrated King Pyrrhus of Epirus to defend Greek interests in Italy and crush Rome (280–272 BC). Lacking a navy, Rome was unable to block this invasion; her armies, however, inflicted such losses on the Epirote expeditionary force (the original 'Pyrrhic victories') that Pyrrhus retreated to mainland Greece, never to return.

Down to and including the Pyrrhic War of the 270s, the great North African maritime republic of Carthage had welcomed and supported the rise of Rome in Italy. The growth of a new land power in the central Mediterranean was welcomed by Carthage who saw Rome as a buffer against the Greek states, Carthage's maritime rivals. Carthage's colonies gave her control of western Sicily, while Greek influence dominated the eastern half of the island. When Pyrrhus took his army to Sicily in 278–276 BC, he was confronted by a Roman–Carthaginian alliance. The invasion of Pyrrhus and new responsibilities in southern Italy made Rome increasingly sensitive about her sea communications, and this inevitably brought her into conflict with Carthage. In 264 BC a group of mercenaries in Syracuse called on Rome for military aid, which was readily supplied. From Rome's point of view the biggest menace in the south was now no longer the Greeks but Carthage. In 264 BC, therefore, Rome and Carthage went to war, the prize being the control and exploitation of Sicily.

This 'First Punic War' of 264–241 BC was a conflict between a sea power on the one hand and a land power on the other. Faced with an enemy hemmed in by the sea and presiding over a

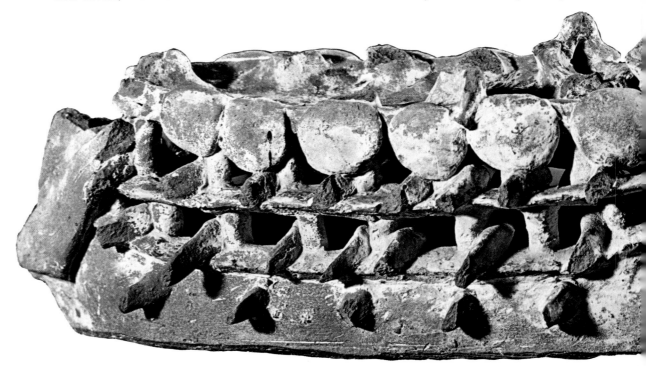

potentially rebellious group of subject peoples, Carthage had the advantage of mobility and surprise but failed to use them. Rome, on the other hand, snatched the initiative from the outset and successfully fought the only war of her long history to be decided mainly at sea.

The Romans seem to have had little trouble in building their first battle-fleet. Control of the Greek ports of southern Italy gave them all the examples and expertise they needed. As the Athenians had proved over 200 years before at Salamis, one of the most useful attributes of war galleys was that they could be built with great speed. This enabled losses due to battle or shipwreck to be made good rapidly. The Romans learned the art of building war galleys from a Carthaginian galley which ran ashore in southern Italy. Having acquired a pattern, they built a fleet of *penteres* – a form of quinquereme – to this specification, using wooden benches on shore to train the oarsmen.

After losing the consul Gnaeus Cornelius Scipio and seventeen ships off the Lipara Islands of northeast Sicily in 260 BC, Rome immediately sent a replacement fleet out to Sicilian waters under the command of the experienced general Gaius Duillius. Duillius had a simple objective: to stop the Carthaginians from severing Rome's sea links between the Italian mainland and the Roman armies attacking the Carthaginians in Sicily. The resultant action off Mylae was a total victory for the Romans because of the simple but deadly tactics used by Duillius.

War galleys in combat had a choice of three courses of action: they could sink enemy ships by ramming, cripple them by shearing off their oars or capture them by boarding. The first two courses demanded considerable seamanship, for which the Romans were never noted; as their troops were

A Phoenician trireme, modelled in about 300 BC. Carthage was founded by the Phoenicians, and the Carthaginians inherited their maritime ambitions.

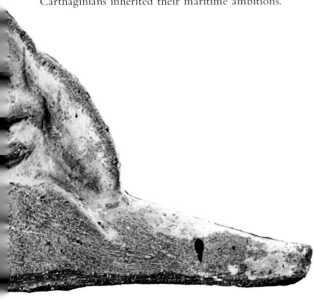

adept at hand-to-hand fighting, they relied heavily on closing and boarding. This was facilitated by the newly invented *corvus*, a weighted and spiked gangway, which stuck fast when dropped onto an enemy deck. This enabled the eighty soldiers who were carried as marines to run across and capture the ship.

The most serious problem facing Duillius when the Carthaginian fleet was sighted was how to get the enemy close enough to force a battle on the right lines. He seems to have done this by deliberately drawing up a textbook battle-line and inviting the Carthaginians to attack it. The Carthaginian commander, Hannibal (not the famous general), considered the Romans to be novices in sea warfare and attacked carelessly without adopting a compact formation. This absence of naval discipline enabled Duillius' well-trained force to pick off the Carthaginian vessels at will.

The Carthaginians were completely taken by surprise by the new Roman tactics and, having surrendered their advantage as the better seafarers, they were severely punished by the Romans' superiority in close-order fighting. After losing fifty ships, the remains of the Carthaginian fleet turned tail and fled.

Mylae confirmed Rome as a naval power and led directly to the invasion of Sardinia by the Romans and the evacuation of Corsica by the Carthaginians. Although Mylae was a great triumph the Romans were unable to win the war. After another sea victory three years later at Ecnomus, their subsequent landing in Africa was a fiasco and the war dragged on until 241 BC. Peace finally came after a third Roman sea victory, the Aegates Islands – fought, like Mylae and Ecnomus, in Sicilian waters. Sicily then became a province of Rome, which had proved itself as the dominant military and naval power in the Mediterranean.

The naval strength that Rome amassed during the First Punic War proved enough to overcome the Carthaginian fleet at Mylae, where the *corvus*, or boarding bridge, was employed with great success by the Romans.

Actium

THE LAST BATTLE OF ANTONY AND CLEOPATRA

Actium, fought on 2 September 31 BC, was the last great battle of the Roman Civil Wars and made Octavian – later known as the Emperor Augustus – the unchallanged master of the Roman world.

Following Julius Caesar's assassination on 15 March 44 BC his great-nephew and adopted heir Octavian, his most trusted lieutenant Antony, and Lepidus, governor of Gaul, formed a triumvirate. Their object was to defeat the republican conspirators and divide the rule of the Roman republic, with its extensive overseas colonies and dependencies. After Antony and Octavian had crushed the republicans at Philippi in 42 BC, Antony took over the eastern provinces while Octavian and Lepidus shared the west.

Antony's famous liaison with Cleopatra dated from 41 BC and was always far more political than is usually realized. Determined to survive as ruler of an independent Egypt, Cleopatra needed Antony's patronage and goodwill. As the first soldier of Rome, entrusted with the task of paying off old scores against the Parthian Empire, Antony needed the friendly subservience of Egypt. Soon, however, he also needed Egypt's wealth to pay his troops. Antony's growing financial dependence on Cleopatra inevitably strengthened her influence on him and slowly eroded the patience and loyalty of his own key officers.

For the first five years of the triumvirate, Octavian was compelled to solicit Antony's goodwill. Antony was the soldier of the trio; the only political asset enjoyed by Octavian was the influence of the family name of Caesar on the veteran Roman troops. Octavian therefore engineered a pact based on the marriage of his sister Octavia to Antony in 40 BC. Growing increasingly precarious as Antony's relationship with Cleopatra deepened, the alliance lasted eight years.

During this time Octavian's position steadily improved while that of Antony declined. The events of 36 BC formed the turning-point. At Naulochus, Octavian's brilliant admiral, Marcus Vipsanius Agrippa, shattered a marauding fleet commanded by Sextus Pompey, son of Julius Caesar's old enemy. This gave Octavian command of the central Mediterranean, and he went on to win over the twenty-two legions from Lepidus. Antony, meanwhile, had lost heavily in a disastrous Parthian campaign.

Biding his time, Octavian wanted to tackle Antony only as the leader of a just war against a traitor seeking to impose oriental domination on Rome. In 32 BC Antony formally divorced Octavia on the insistence of Cleopatra. Octavian procured and published what was purported to be his will (in favour of Cleopatra and her children), and used this as his *casus belli*.

A key objective for both sides was Greece, the natural buffer between Italy and Asia Minor. Although the initiative lay with Octavian in his role as Rome's avenger, the first trick went to Antony, who moved west to occupy Greece with nineteen legions in the summer of 32 BC. Cleopatra acted as chief paymaster, providing the war chest, supplies, Egyptian oarsmen for the fleet and 200 warships out of Antony's total of 500. Antony advanced to the western coast of Greece and set up a powerful base camp at Actium, on the southern shore of the bottleneck strait leading into the Gulf of Ambracia. The gulf provided a magnificent haven for the bulk of Antony's Egyptian fleet, while other naval detachments covered the long sea-lane leading east round the Greek coast to Asia Minor.

Although Antony's position at Actium could not be taken by direct assault, it was strategically weak. Antony was unable to prevent Octavian and Agrippa from crossing to Greece in the spring of 31 BC, driving back the Egyptian outposts north and south of Actium and putting Antony and Cleopatra under close blockade. By the middle of August their position was becoming desperate. Disease, desertions and slumping morale had remorselessly lowered the fighting potential of Antony's forces throughout the summer. Supplies were approaching starvation level, despite the requisitioning of the local harvest. Antony accepted that he was left with two alternatives: either to abandon the fleet and retreat overland to the Aegean, or to embark his best troops, break out with the fleet, and leave the remaining troops to escape as best they could. He decided on the naval breakout as the safer option.

As he no longer had enough oarsmen to man every ship in the fleet, Antony burned his surplus ships. This left him with about 230 warships against the 400 of Octavian and Agrippa.

Antony reckoned that his opponents would hardly throw away their numerical advantage by fighting in the confines of the strait: they would let him come out and try to overwhelm him at sea. But if the Egyptian fleet could get out just far enough,

ABOVE The battle of Actium, fought in 31 BC, saw the light and manoeuvrable galleys of Agrippa outflank the larger but slower ships of Mark Antony.

RIGHT A large Roman galley of the first century BC, probably a quadrireme. Note the heavily armed soldiers crowded on the upper deck.

their flanks protected by the widening shores of the bay, they could fight a delaying action until two o'clock in the afternoon, when they would pick up a favourable local wind, hoist their sails and escape.

Unfortunately Antony's friend Quintus Dellius deserted to Octavian on the eve of battle, taking with him full details of Antony's strength and battle-plan. Agrippa, whom Octavian had entrusted with the conduct of the coming battle, now knew his opponents' intentions. Agrippa's plan was to let Antony and his fleet move out of their safe haven and then overwhelm them, making escape impossible.

Antony's fleet was therefore permitted to debouch from the Gulf of Ambracia and form up in three squadrons, Antony commanding on the right with Cleopatra's own squadron lying behind them. Agrippa likewise deployed his forces in three squadrons and waited for Antony. Agrippa was in no hurry to engage and the two fleets lay on their oars for over an hour until the sea breeze began to blow around noon. While Antony's fleet had the larger, more powerful vessels, the fleet under Agrippa was largely made up of *liburnians*, light, fast and highly manoeuvrable war galleys.

Antony's left-wing squadron then advanced to bring on the action. As his strongest ships were on the flanks, his plan seems to have been to focus Agrippa's attention on his flanks in order to thin out the centre. For his part Agrippa gave Antony no further freedom of movement and attempted to outflank the Egyptian fleet. As each fleet tried to outflank the other the gaps between the ships increased and allowed the manoeuvrable galleys of Agrippa to bear down on Antony's ships. Although Antony's fleet fought resolutely his ships suffered grievously from the firebrands flung at them from catapults fitted in Agrippa's galleys.

In an attempt to reverse the desperate situation, Cleopatra hurled her reserve squadron into the fray but with no success. Disengaging her ships she fled the battle to Egypt and was closely followed by Antony who slipped away unnoticed.

Despite this defection the Egyptian fleet, now hopelessly out-numbered by Agrippa, fought on until nightfall when resistance ceased. The remaining Egyptian ships were put to the torch.

Although Antony and Cleopatra had managed to escape with between sixty and seventy ships, their position was hopeless. Antony's land army was isolated and short of supplies and had no chance against the well-trained legions of Octavian that were bearing down on them. Accepting the inevitable, Antony's army surrendered to Octavian.

A year later Octavian landed in Egypt to destroy the remaining power of Antony and Cleopatra who, realizing their position, committed suicide. Actium was the decisive battle in the campaign and left Octavian as the undisputed master of the Roman world; it also confirmed the city of Rome, rather than Alexandria, as the centre of the Roman Empire.

PART TWO

The Middle Ages

The barbarian invasions of the fourth and fifth century AD destroyed the Roman Empire in the west and with it Roman control of the Mediterranean. The seat of Roman power lay in the east at Constantinople, which had managed to stave off attacks from both Europe and Asia Minor. The Byzantine Empire, as it became, depended for its survival on a land army supported by a powerful fleet. A strong naval presence guaranteed the trade of the empire and held aggressors at bay. As long as her navy flourished so did Constantinople, and it was sound naval organization and the technical developments introduced by the Byzantines that gave them the edge over their warlike neighbours.

By AD 533 small, fast warships called *dromons* were escorting the Byzantine expedition to North Africa, and in AD 600 the name was being used for the largest type of warship in the Byzantine navy. By this time the dromon was a large, two-banked galley with fifty oars a side, divided into two banks of twenty-five. The upper banks were rowed by three men to an oar, the lower by one man to an oar. The outriggers had been dispensed with and the upper banks were rowed from the gunwale. The continuous deck had also been removed and three gangways connected the forward and after platforms, running down the centre and inside the gunwales. Fighting towers were built on the platforms, equipped with powerful catapults.

The Byzantines' main enemies were the Arabs, who by AD 643 had conquered Syria and Egypt and, appreciating the possibilities of sea power, had constructed a powerful fleet. Little is known of these Arab warships, but a large number of them were probably built in the imperial dockyards at Alexandria by the same shipwrights who had formerly built the Byzantines' vessels. Therefore it is probable that they resembled the Byzantine warships closely.

The Arabs inflicted a serious defeat upon the Byzantine fleet in the 'Battle of the Masts' in AD 655 and only the death of their ruler prevented an immediate attack on Constantinople. By AD 673 the Arabs had established a base on the promontory of Cyzicus on the south coast of the Sea of Marmara and were attempting to blockade the city. By AD 678 the fall of Constantinople seemed imminent, until the defenders produced a decisive weapon – Greek fire. Brought to Byzantium by a Syrian refugee named Callinicus, Greek fire was probably based on naphtha, which, when mixed with several other substances such as pitch, sulphur and saltpetre, was capable of spontaneous combustion. It was sealed in pottery containers and fired from cata-

The Byzantine dromon was developed from the light galleys first used in the Adriatic and adopted by the Romans. Here the crew of a dromon are spraying their enemies with Greek fire.

pults. It was almost impossible to extinguish even under water. Alternatively Greek fire could be discharged from tubes powered by a pump in the vessel in the form of a primitive flame-thrower.

Although the Mediterranean remained the focus of naval warfare in the Middle Ages, in the waters of northern Europe new forms of warfare were developing. The eighth century saw the emergence of the Scandinavian peoples as a great maritime force and for more than two centuries the Vikings became the scourge of Europe.

The word 'viking' originally meant a rover or raider by sea. In the course of time it became another name for the Scandinavian invaders – the Norsemen (later called Normans), the Danes (as the English called them), and the Rus or red-haired barbarians who carved out the principality of Kiev and gave their name to Russia. The more civilized Greeks of the Byzantine Empire recruited them as mercenaries in the tenth century, and referred to them as 'the axe-bearing barbarians'.

The early raiders from the sea, nosing their way up rivers in their longships to sack monasteries and towns in the ninth and tenth centuries, gave way to settlers and farmers, and rulers who demanded 'Danegeld' as a form of blackmail levied on tribes which wished to live in peace. Longer raiding trips became voyages of exploration, notably Leif Ericsson's claimed discovery of Newfoundland in 1001 and Eric the Red's island-hopping expeditions to Iceland and Greenland. When they settled down to form their own states, such as the Duchy of Normandy, and the Kingdoms of Sicily and England, the Normans exhibited unique qualities not only as warriors and shipbuilders, but also as administrators, scholars and architects.

Viking raiders in the Dark Ages possessed three great advantages. The chaotic state of Europe after the death of Charlemagne in 814 gave them the opportunity; in weapons and armour they were definitely superior to those they attacked; and a complete command of the sea gave them mobility, so that if they were repulsed in one place they could easily retreat to attack a weaker spot. The chronicler's description of the bands which invaded Ireland paints a fearsome picture: 'They formed a solid, skilful and firm rampart of strong coats of mail like a thick, dark stronghold of black iron, with a green polished wall of battle shields around their chiefs.' Their flexible coats of mail made from linked iron rings, their pointed shields, their helmets and axes and long swords made them invincible.

The Viking longship was one of the most functional warships ever built. A good deal is known about these ships because of the custom of using them for funeral purposes and placing them in burial mounds. Some of those excavated are in a remarkably good state of preservation, while many others have been reconstructed with scientific care.

A typical Viking longship was the one excavated at Gokstad near Oslo. Launched around AD 900, she was clinker-built with overlapping planks of pine held together by trenails and with the interstices caulked with sheep's wool. Just over 23 m (76 ft) long, she had a beam of 5.5 m (18 ft) and a draught of only 0.9 m (3 ft). This shallow draught, combined with the fact that such craft were double-ended and used a simple steering oar, enabled them to be beached easily and to penetrate up rivers in order to attack places as far from the sea as Paris and York.

While at sea a single square sail on a 12 m (40 ft) mast was used, the oars, varying between sixteen and twenty-four a side, being reserved for river work. The gaily-painted shields along the gunwales were placed there for show and convenience. Later on much larger 'dragon ships' (so-called because of

This well-preserved Viking longship was found at Oseberg Farm, near Tonsberg in Norway in 1904. She is smaller than the normal warship at 21.3 m (70 ft) and would have carried thirty oarsmen.

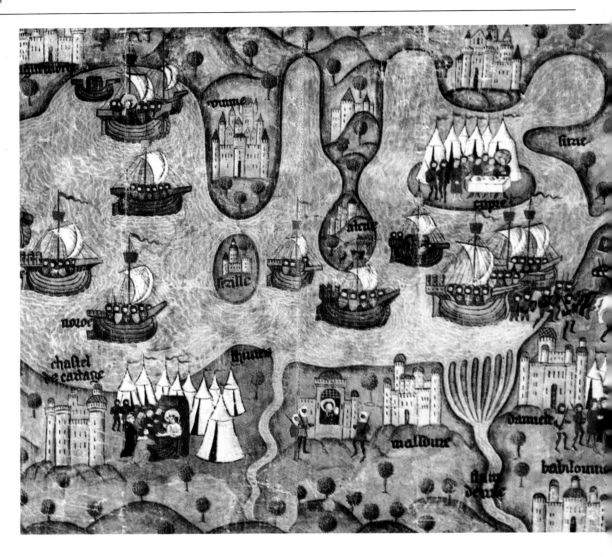

Led by Louis IX of France, a fleet of cogs sail in support of the Crusaders' bid to capture Jerusalem in 1248. Ships were borrowed from most of the Christian nations of western Europe for this purpose.

the serpent or dragon often carved as a figurehead) were built, some over 30m (100ft) long with sixty pairs of oars.

Longships with a broader beam were known as *knorrs* and were used for longer voyages including the expeditions to Greenland. The knorr was still in use in the thirteenth century when it was replaced for most peaceful purposes by the heavier cog.

In contrast to the galleys of the Mediterranean the Vikings rarely used their longships as war vessels. The longship was used either as a vehicle for plunder or for the simple transportation of troops across stretches of water. As their ships did not possess a ram, Viking naval tactics were based around hand-to-hand combat. When a sea battle did take place it was common for the longships to be lashed together in order to provide a stable fighting platform. The Viking naval engagement was a static affair affording little scope for tactical finesse.

The causes of the population pressure which impelled Scandinavian peoples to expand overseas remain obscure. The earliest known Viking raid was the sacking of Lindisfarne monastery in North-

umbria in AD 790. Many such monasteries, including Iona, were attacked in the next century. In 867 the city of York was captured and in 870 King Edmund was defeated and killed at the town of Bury St Edmunds. In the course of time the whole of the north and east of England became a colony called the Danelaw. Alfred the Great, King of Wessex, wrested London from the Danes and after many pitched battles built a fleet to defend the south and west.

The pressure continued and later invaders, now Christianized, came as immigrants rather than robbers to occupy so much of England that Canute (Cnut), who died in 1035, could call himself King of England, as well as King of Denmark and Norway. His fleet is described by a chronicler: 'Gold shone on the prows, silver flashed in the variously shaped ships. So great was the magnificence of the fleet that if its lord had desired to conquer any people, the ships alone would have terrified the enemy, before the warriors they carried joined battle.'

Other Viking bands invaded the rivers of northern Europe. Relics of their raids have been found up the Loire, the Seine and the Scheldt, while further south they raided Spain and even Pisa in Italy. So firm did their hold on the north become that the Duchy of Normandy was established in 911 by Rolf (or Rollo) who had entered France via the Loire after raiding Ireland.

At about the same time as the Vikings were invading France other hordes crossed the Baltic to capture Novgorod and establish the principality of Kiev. The more adventurous continued down the Dnieper to cross the Black Sea and they attacked Constantinople with 200 ships in 907. Here the emperor recruited them as his Varangian Guard, because of their fine physique and martial skills.

By the early eleventh century the force of the Viking expansion was spent. The decline of the Vikings also saw the slow decline of the longship and the rise of the cog as the major type of vessel in northern waters. The standard load-carrying vessel of medieval times was the round ship, which had a length-to-beam ratio of about $2\frac{1}{2}$:1. The cog was developed from this in the twelfth century in an attempt to improve its notoriously poor sailing qualities. The cog is mentioned in a number of medieval documents under a great variety of names such as *cocca*, *coccha*, *cocka*, *cogga*, *concha* and *coqua*. A document of 1226 mentions a fleet comprising six cogs and seven nefs (a large, French version of the round ship), and an engraving of a ship from the seal of the town of La Rochelle dated 24 August 1232 is said to represent a *cocha*.

Engravings of similar ships are found on the seals of the towns of Elbing and Stralsund and they were known as Hansa cogs. These vessels were used by the Hanseatic League to carry their goods. They had a single mast, carrying a single square sail, fitted with three rows of reef points. They were basically double-ended vessels, the stem being raked forward and running straight down to the keel, but curving slightly at the forefoot – the foremost part of the keel. The stern post raked aft and ran straight down to the keel and a rudder was suspended from it. Cogs were clinker-built boats, with the decks supported by beams within the hull. The forecastle was triangular-shaped and it projected high over the bows, but its after end was faired into the hull. The after castle was also a very high, angular structure.

At the battle of Sluys in 1340 the English king Edward II led his fleet into action in the cog *Thomas* against the French. Its cargo-carrying capacity made the cog a natural merchantman but it easily doubled as a warship, its after and forecastles being crammed with archers and men-at-arms. It was not, however, until the mid-fifteenth century that cannon began to be mounted on English cogs as an anti-ship weapon.

In his 'Glossaire Nautique' (1847) M. Jal, quoting from a thirteenth-century Florentine manuscript, relates the arrival in the Mediterranean of some *cogge* manned by pirates from Bayonne. It is alleged that this incident led to the adoption of vessels of this type by the merchants of Barcelona, Genoa and Venice, but there is evidence that the cog made its appearance in the Mediterranean much earlier. An anonymous history of Jerusalem dated 1177 refers to the presence of fifty ships 'commonly called cogges' and they are frequently mentioned in the contemporary chronicles of the Crusades (1095–1272). It has been suggested that the Bayonnaise cogs were of such superior construction to those in use in the Mediterranean that they caused

the shipbuilders in the Italian ports and also in Marseilles and Barcelona to adopt this improved design. The Mediterranean cogs, being carvel-built, were less robust than the clinker-built northern cogs, and in the Mediterranean ships the deck beams protruded through the side planking.

As regards size, it is estimated that in the fourteenth century the cog was a vessel with an overall length of 27m (90ft), a waterline length of 18m (60ft), a draught of 2.7m (9ft) and a sail area of about 170 sq m (1800 sq ft). She carried about 130 tons of cargo and had a crew of between twenty and thirty men. The sails were often treated with a dye made from red bark to prevent rotting, but old manuscripts also refer to red and white, white and green, and black sails. The Hansa cogs were amongst the first ships which were rigged with cordage made of hemp.

The remains of a ship, believed to have been a cog, were found near Bremen in 1962 and it was deduced that she was 21m (70ft) long, with a beam of 6m (20ft). In the course of time cogs were built larger, and the design changed considerably. The

The invention of the gunport in or around the year 1500 is attributed to a French shipwright. Mounting the guns lower in the ship's hull made for greater stability.

forecastle became smaller, possibly to improve the helmsman's view ahead, and the after castle gave place to a captain's cabin and accommodation for passengers. By the end of the fifteenth century, cogs are described as having three masts and of being capable of loading a thousand tons of grain. Ships of this type were used by the Genoese for their trade with England and they appear to have been the forerunners of the Venetian carrack, which incorporated a number of the features of the north European vessel.

The Crusades of the Middle Ages were a great stimulus to the Christian Mediterranean nations who ferried the Crusaders from western Europe to Palestine. As the power of Byzantium waned, that of the Italian maritime cities increased and in 1204 Constantinople was sacked by the Crusaders as part of a plan to reinstate a deposed Byzantine emperor. Without a strong fleet the Byzantines had been unable to oppose the Crusaders who had been transported to the city through a commercial deal with Venice.

During the thirteenth century the lucrative trade of the Mediterranean passed to the three Italian states of Venice, Genoa and Pisa, which fought out their rivalries over a period of nearly 200 years before the rise of the Ottoman Turks.

By the end of the thirteenth century the principal type of galley was the trireme, using three banks of oars. The rowing benches were fitted into the *telaro*, a long rectangular frame which was slightly wider than the hull. Gangways connecting the built-up poop and forecastle ran down the centre and sides of the *telaro*. The waterline ram had been discarded earlier and in its place had appeared a light beak, or spar, fitted well above the waterline. This was too lightly built to act as a true ram, so it was probably intended to break up the enemy oar banks and, possibly, to act as a boarding bridge. Most of the Italian galleys carried two masts, but the Venetians used only one which normally carried a lateen sail.

By the fifteenth century two important changes had taken place. First, the age-old method of steering by means of a steering oar had been replaced by a single centreline rudder, hung on the stern post and controlled by a tiller. This had first come into use in the Netherlands, probably about 1200, but had taken over a hundred years to be adopted in the Mediterranean. Secondly, it was around 1450 that the first anti-ship cannon appeared on board a galley. The only possible place that these weapons could be fitted was on the forecastle, firing directly ahead, although lighter guns could be fitted on the poop, and swivel guns on the broadside.

The galleasse was an attempt to combine the speed and handiness of the galley with the firepower and strength of the galleon. Developed from the large Venetian trading galleys, it was heavily armed but slow and clumsy and its fragile construction made it dangerous in heavy weather. The type was seldom used outside the Mediterranean, but, when it was, the three-masted lateen rig was exchanged for a square rig.

RIGHT The carrack is characterized by its rounded hull and high fore- and after castles. This is a Venetian vessel of the fifteenth century.

Svolde

THE BATTLE OF THE LONGSHIPS

ABOVE RIGHT This longship dates from around AD 900 and was unearthed at Gokstad, Norway, in 1880. It was the burial ship of a Norse chieftain and is a fine example of a Viking warship.

RIGHT A primitive carving of a longship found on the island of Gotland, an area rich in Viking relics.

Svolde was the most celebrated sea battle of the Viking era. It was fought in the western Baltic in the year 1000 between a combined Danish and Swedish fleet and a grossly outnumbered Norwegian fleet. The battle ended in a glorious fight to the death by the Norwegians under their king, Olaf Tryggveson. The real importance of Svolde, however, was the added stature it gave to Sweyn 'Forkbeard' of Denmark, afterwards conqueror and king of England, and father of the still more famous Canute.

Olaf's early career was the essence of Viking legend – the gallant young warrior winning fame and fortune by his prowess in battle. First seeing service with the Holy Roman Emperor Otto III, Olaf gained great prestige in a series of highly successful raids on the coasts of England and France. In alliance with Sweyn of Denmark he secured massive payments of Danegeld from the English. While in England Olaf was baptized a Christian and having vowed never to raid England again he returned to Scandinavia to claim the Norwegian crown in 996.

With all the zeal of a recent convert, Olaf was determined to force Christianity upon his subjects. In so doing he attacked and killed the Norwegian Viking Raud the Strong, whose *Little Serpent* was the biggest longship in Norway.

The Viking longship had by this time developed into the larger *drakkar*, with a reinforced hull and keel. A luff spar known as a *beitass* was invented around AD 900, and contributed greatly to the range and seaworthiness of the longship by enabling it to make way to windward. With the *Little Serpent* as his model, Olaf ordered the building of the *Long Serpent*. If the sagas are to be credited the *Long Serpent* was about 45m (150ft) long – nearly double the size of the longship found at Gokstad – and splendidly carved and ornamented. She was the pride of the new fleet with which Olaf planned to make Norway the hub of a new and ultimately Christian Scandinavia.

Olaf's biggest weakness, however, was his lack of any political finesse. Earl Eric, son of Hakon whom Olaf had killed and natural leader for all Norwegians who resented and opposed Olaf's policies, made common cause with Sweyn of Denmark against him. Instead of countering this dangerous combination by making sure of a Swedish alliance, Olaf alienated the Swedes as well. He tried to marry the widowed Queen Sigrid of Sweden but she angrily rejected him when he insisted that she would have to become a Christian. He finally married Sweyn's sister Thyri, who had deserted her pagan husband Burislav of Wendland – Sweyn's greatest ally south of the Baltic. Meanwhile, Sweyn had succeeded where Olaf had failed, by marrying Sigrid of Sweden. While she urged Sweyn to avenge the insult Olaf had paid her, Olaf launched an expedition to recover Thyri's lost estates at the mouth of the Oder.

This was a hopeless venture, for Olaf now faced a coalition of the Danes, Wends, Swedes and the followers of Earl Eric. Olaf's only allies were the formidable Jomsburg Vikings, who deserted him when Sweyn offered them more pay. The defection of the Jomsburg Vikings left Olaf with only eleven Norwegian ships when, returning empty-handed from his expedition against the Wends, he was intercepted off Svolde (probably off the coast of Rügen) by the enemy coalition fleet. The exact size of this is unknown but it seems to have been at least seventy vessels strong.

Olaf earned immortality in Viking legend for his decision to stand and fight, preferring death to dishonour, but the decision was almost certainly forced upon him. It seems that the battle was fought in a calm, and in a retreat under oars the giant *Long Serpent* – inevitably harder to row than the other lighter Norwegian ships – would soon have been isolated. Instead, Olaf ordered his ships to form line-abreast with the *Long Serpent* in the middle and lash themselves together. The floating fortress thus created could not be attacked by all the enemy ships at once, so reducing the combat to a battle of attrition.

The attackers concentrated on cutting out the outermost Norwegian ships and taking them piecemeal, thus accelerating the depletion of Olaf's hard-pressed 'floating garrison'. Each time the Norwegian formation shrank, the odds tipped further and further in the attackers' favour, until Olaf was left only with *Long Serpent* and her two flankers, one of which was *Little Serpent*. As the last boarding attack overwhelmed *Long Serpent*, Olaf escaped capture by leaping overboard to his death. Eric himself is credited with the last attack, launched from his ship *Iron Beard* with its distinctive bow sheathing of iron plates – one of the earliest ironclad warships mentioned in naval history.

RIGHT An artist's impression of the *Long Serpent* of Olaf Tryggveson, probably the best known of all Viking longships, which was lost at Svolde in 1000.

BELOW The prows of the Norse fleet are depicted on this thirteenth-century carving from Bergen. The figureheads are either wind-vanes or animal representations.

BELOW RIGHT An intricately engraved prow wind-vane from Heggen, fashioned from bronze-gilt.

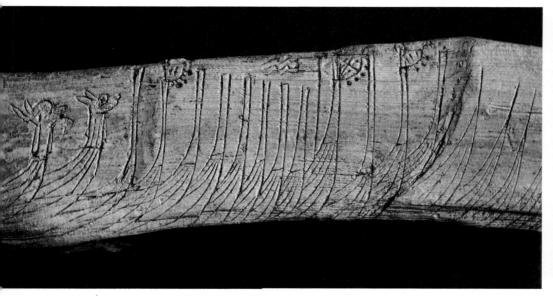

Dover

THE DEFEAT OF AN INVASION FLEET

The English victory at the battle of Dover was mainly due to the archers mounted in the castles of Hubert de Burgh's cogs. This fourteenth-century illustration shows the importance of the castles for both long-range archery and hand-to-hand fighting.

The battle of Dover, fought off Sandwich on 24 August 1217, St Bartholomew's Day, was one of the earliest English victories in six centuries of Anglo-French rivalry for control of the English Channel. This battle destroyed a crucial fleet carrying reinforcements and supplies for a French army in England, and ensured that they were trapped beyond hope. Within three weeks of the battle the French gladly signed a convention permitting them to withdraw from English soil.

The French landed in England in May 1216 to exploit the civil war which had broken out after King John's signing of the Magna Carta at Runnymede the previous year. Determined to wipe out the humiliation of Runnymede, John raised an army of mercenaries and took the field against his opponents. Equally determined to survive at all costs, even under a new French king, the rebel barons eagerly welcomed Prince Louis and his army of volunteer French knights. By the time John died at Newark on 19 October 1216 the French flag was flying over the Tower of London and the French and rebels had taken Lincoln, dominating most of south-east England.

On John's death the royalists rallied to the young King Henry III, only nine years old but championed by the Pope and the Regent, William the Marshal, the most respected knight in western Europe.

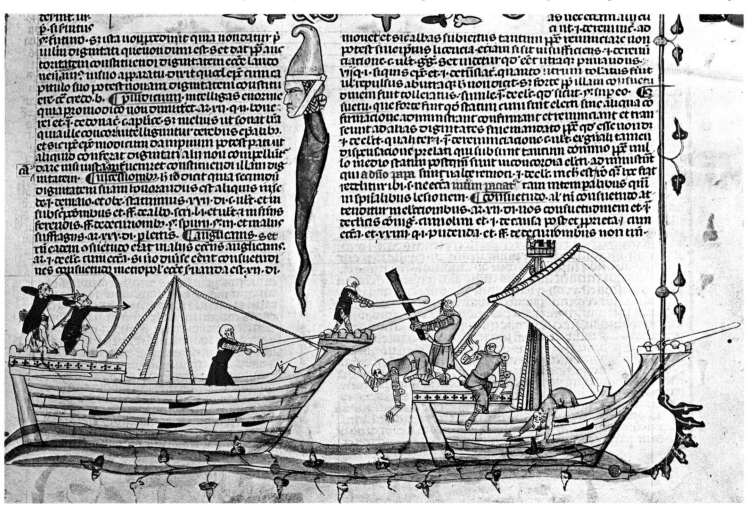

A detailed, though somewhat inaccurate representation of the ships of Henry III, the monarch who succeeded King John immediately prior to the battle of Dover.

the Monk, pirate, renegade, outlaw, and reputed black magician with the power of making himself invisible. The French had hired Eustace to command their fleets and he had directed the invasion of 1217; he was now to bring the reinforcement fleet across. He sailed from Calais on 24 August with seven troopships crammed with knights and men-at-arms, and seventy supply vessels. The plan was to cross the Dover Narrows and coast round to the Thames.

The English fleet numbered about forty ships and an indeterminate number of smaller craft. The basic simplicity of naval tactics is well illustrated by the fact that the seventy-three-year-old William the Marshal, who had never fought at sea in his life, wanted to command the English fleet in person. He was persuaded to stay ashore, however, and Hubert de Burgh, the royalist Governor of the Cinque Ports, took the English fleet out to battle.

On 24 August 1217, when the French sails were spotted by watchers on the cliffs of Dover, the wind was blowing from the south. This was ideal for a crossing from Calais and a cruise through the Downs, inshore of the Goodwin Sands, from the South Foreland to the North. The south-to-north lie of the land between Dover and Thanet meant that such a wind favoured the English as well. Hubert let the French pass Sandwich before deploying astern of the French ships and moving smoothly downwind into the attack. Forced to come up into the wind to meet the oncoming English, the French fleet was already disorganized and virtually immobile when the fleets collided.

With the wind behind them the English approached behind a cloud of powdered quicklime, released downwind to blind the defenders. The archers in the tops and bow 'castles' then took up the attack with the wind speeding their shafts. Although their ships were outnumbered two to one, the English troops immobilized the enemy by cutting their shrouds and halyards and then boarded them at will. The disorganized French put up a poor fight and were soon overwhelmed.

Two ships, Hubert's flagship and another, crashed into Eustace's flagship, which then fell to a ferocious boarding attack. Only the richer knights were spared for the sake of their ransoms. Eustace was found hiding in the bilges and was promptly beheaded, with the ship's gunwale acting as a block. The surviving troopships plus a few transports (some fifteen ships in all) ran for the open sea and put back to Calais, leaving the remaining transport to be looted by the exultant English.

Dover was a complete victory for the English royalists, leaving Louis with no choice but to negotiate for a phased withdrawal of the French from England. It is especially important in naval history in that it was the first battle to be fought by sailing-ship tactics; the superiority of English seamanship in gaining the weather gauge was the main factor in their victory.

Although on the surface things looked bleak for the royalist cause they held the trump card, namely control of the Cinque Ports. Prince Louis had failed to capture the vital ports of Rye, Winchelsea and above all Dover, which prevented him from securing a safe cross-Channel supply route.

One of the results of John's reign had been the loss of Normandy to France in 1204, which forced England to organize naval defences of her own for the first time since Duke William's conquest in 1066. Correctly, John had realized that sea power was a two-edged weapon, as useful for attack as for defence. When King Philip of France had prepared to invade England in 1213 and install Prince Louis as king, a combined English and Flemish fleet had wiped out a French invasion fleet of over three times its strength at Damme, the port of Bruges.

Preparing to meet another invasion attempt in 1216, John had concentrated the ships of twenty-one seaports off the mouth of the Thames, but the English fleet had been scattered by an untimely storm, leaving the Channel open to the French. Despite this setback the control of the Cinque Ports by the English royalists and the build-up of a new fleet enabled them to strike at any reinforcements which the French might try to send across. By the summer of 1217 the tide had turned and was running strongly in favour of the English royalists. On 20 May William the Marshal had thrown the French out of Lincoln and Louis had pulled back to make certain of holding London and as much of the south-east as possible. Though King Philip of France wanted to cut his losses and abandon the English enterprise, Louis's determined Princess, Blanche of Castile, urged the king not to give up. She raised another fleet and expeditionary force with which to reinforce Louis in England, and by the third week of August 1217 it was ready to sail.

The French fleet was commanded by one of the more colourful villains in maritime history: Eustace

The Venetian-Genoese Wars

EPIC STRUGGLE FOR THE MEDITERRANEAN

The sack of Constantinople in 1204 during the Fourth Crusade signalled the decline of the Byzantine Empire as a naval power and the emergence of the maritime republics of Pisa, Genoa and Venice. The intense rivalry between these states for trading concessions regularly broke out into war. Pisa, the weakest of the three, was destroyed as a sea-trader of any consequence by the Genoese in 1284 at the battle of Meloria. With her harbour silting up, and racked by internal dissension Pisa declined rapidly leaving the field open to Venice and Genoa.

The wars between Genoa and Venice were wars of commerce, the key to success being access to the rich markets of the east centred in the Levantine and in the remains of the Byzantine Empire. Both states acted as carriers, transporting precious goods from the Middle East to western Europe. Vast profits could be made from these trading ventures and both Venice and Genoa saw their commercial rivalry as a battle of survival.

The trade of the two states was carried in a variety of vessels including the round ship and later the cog but the warship remained the galley. The galley of the Middle Ages was a trireme with a forecastle and small poop. The waterline ram had been dispensed with and was replaced with a lighter spar for destroying the enemy ship's oars. The tactics of ramming and sinking the enemy had fallen out of

favour and instead the goal of the galley's captain would be to board and capture the opposing vessel.

The first major conflict between the two republics was the intermittent war that stretched from 1257 to 1271. Although no decisive battles were fought the Genoese came off worse and were forced to surrender the Levantine trade to Venice, but by way of compensation gained special agreements with the Byzantines for trade in the Black Sea.

War was renewed in 1291 after the surrender of the Kingdom of Jerusalem to the Turks and this time the Genoese gained the upper hand. The Genoese admiral, Lamba Doria, won a complete victory in 1298 against the Venetians at the battle of Curzola off the Dalmation coast. (Incidentally, it was at this battle that the young Marco Polo was taken prisoner by the Genoese.) A peace agreement was signed the following year which gave Genoa a virtual monopoly of commerce in the Black Sea while Venice concentrated on the Alexandrine trade with Egypt.

Although Venice fought a destructive and unsuccessful war against the Papal States and Ferrara (1306–1311), the rivalry between the two states was carried out on a merely commercial basis. By 1350, however, the Genoese attempts to gain a secure hold on the Levantine trade led to another outbreak of hostilities. Initially confined to the Levant, the war

The naval power of Pisa was dealt a destructive and ultimately fatal blow by the Genoese at the battle of Meloria in 1284. The surprise flank attack more usually associated with galley warfare proved decisive.

S. MARCU

A three-masted Venetian ship of the thirteenth century, depicted in a mosaic from St Mark's Cathedral, Rome. Note the twin steering oars projecting from the stern.

spread throughout the Mediterranean. The Venetians suffered a reverse in the Dardanelles in the opening phase of the war but in August 1353 at the battle of La Loiera, off the coast of Sardinia, the Genoese fleet was utterly defeated.

A year later the Genoese had their revenge at the battle of Modon where they crushed the Venetian fleet. The Genoese fleet commanded by Luciano Doria advanced against the Venetian anchorage off the island of Sapienza. Twelve Genoese galleys got between the Venetian fleet and the shore and attacked from the rear while the main fleet bore down on the disorganized Venetians from the front. The Venetians suffered heavy losses in both ships and men; 6000 men including their admiral were captured. The battle of Modon allowed the Genoese a virtual free hand in the Mediterranean, and according to one account they 'swept the coast of Barbary, assaulted and plundered Tripoli, and sold the city to a wealthy Saracen for 50,000 pieces of gold'.

Despite the military success of Genoa the Ven-

etians did well from the peace treaty formalized in 1355. This declared that each party respect the trade of the other in the Black Sea (like the Levant a bitter source of contention), and that Venetian warships were not to sail in the Gulf of Genoa, nor Genoese warships in the Adriatic. During the lapse in hostilities that followed the peace treaty, Venice found herself under constant pressure from King Louis of Hungary and was forced to cede Dalmatia to him, while in 1373 the Genoese were able to conquer Cyprus without Venetian opposition.

The last and decisive war between Venice and Genoa broke out in 1378 and involved rival claims to the island of Tenedos which the Venetians had gained from the Byzantine Empire. Genoa, strengthened by an alliance with two old enemies of Venice, Louis of Hungary and Francesco de Carrara of Padua, declared war.

The first engagement went in favour of the Venetians when Admiral Vittore Pisani defeated a Genoese force in the Tyrrhenian Sea. This victory was soon reversed at the battle of Pola (Pula) when

Pisani loaded a number of old vessels with rocks and sank them into the channels of the Lagoon which led to and from the Genoese in Chioggia. Consequently all means of reinforcement and escape were rendered impossible. Despite this the Genoese fleet and land forces were in a well-defended position and the Venetians were in no state to launch any major offensive.

The turning point in the war was the return of the Venetian Levantine fleet to the Adriatic. It forced a Genoese relief squadron to turn back and left the garrison at Chioggia isolated. The Levantine fleet arrived in Venice on 1 January 1380 with eighteen well-equipped galleys and a store of provisions. Venetian morale rose and plans were proposed for

Pisani's fleet was soundly defeated by the Genoese fleet under Luciano Doria. The Genoese commander was killed early in the battle, but inspired by his death the Genoese launched furious attacks on the Venetians and captured 1000 prisoners, many of whom were butchered in revenge for Doria's death.

The Genoese followed up their victory and with reinforcements under Pietro Doria they captured the island and city of Chioggia just south of Venice itself. The Venetians suffered heavy casualties at Chioggia and found themselves under a virtual state of siege. Abject peace terms were offered to the Genoese who, scenting complete victory, refused them and demanded an unconditional surrender.

Such a surrender would have destroyed Venice as a Mediterranean power and desperate measures were taken to effect a defence of the city. Pisani, who had been imprisoned as a result of his defeat off Pola, was recalled to service by popular demand. Through his expert knowledge of the shallow waters around Venice, Pisani realized that the Genoese were in a potentially vulnerable position.

the reduction of the fortifications at Chioggia. Although increasingly beleaguered, the Genoese fought on stubbornly throughout the spring of 1380 and it was only a shortage of food and supplies that forced them to surrender in June 1380.

The war had exhausted both republics and they were happy to accept the Peace of Turin in 1381. Venice lost some mainland territories to her neighbours but came through the war with her basic strength unimpaired. The Genoese, on the other hand, were half ruined: the war had drained the national coffers and the fierce internal strife that was such a characteristic feature of Genoese life was pulling the political fabric of city state apart. The defeat at Chioggia was the beginning of Genoa's decline to a second-rate power and by 1396 she had become a protectorate of France.

Venice was not slow to exploit Genoa's decline and establish herself as the leading maritime power in the Mediterranean, a position she held until the expansion of the Ottoman Turks at the end of the fifteenth century.

The Venetian galleasse was primarily a sailing ship, with oars a subsidiary source of motive power. It had a deeper hull than the galley, which made it a superior fighting ship in rough seas.

Sluys

EDWARD III LEADS A FLEET AGAINST THE FRENCH

The first set-piece battle of the 'Hundred Years' War' between England and France, Sluys was the only English naval victory since the time of Alfred the Great in which a reigning English king accompanied his fleet into battle. It was fought on 24 June 1340 and won undisputed command of the Channel for Edward III as he prepared to make good his claim to the French throne by force of arms.

Edward announced his claim in October 1337, but for the next two years he and his rival, Philip VI of France, were deeply engaged in raising funds and equipping ships and armies. It was, however, clear that the collision, when it came, would involve a naval fight. By launching a series of highly effective privateer raids, the French announced their determination to deny the English control of the Narrow Seas.

As one of the main issues at stake was England's flourishing trade with the weaving towns of Flan-

The battle of Sluys in June 1430 ranged the English fleet against a greater number of French ships. The French, however, surrendered the initiative and were defeated at anchor.

ders, which France tried in vain to dominate and detach from alliance with England, the war at sea was fought in Flemish rather than French waters. An English force made a successful raid on Cadsand in November 1337, but the French were not slow in hitting back and extending their operations into English waters. The French raided Portsmouth and Southampton, cruised in the Thames estuary and finally captured an entire English squadron off Walcheren in 1338–9. By 1340 the war at sea was running in France's favour.

As well as privateer cruising and small-scale operations, the French were building up a massive fleet to dominate the Flemish coast and defeat any invasion attempt by the English. The French fleet was led by Hué Quieret and his second-in-command Pierre Balmuchet. Lacking in both enterprise and seamanship the two French admirals refused to send their fleet out to sea to attack the English but instead kept it massed in the Zwin River, downstream of the port of Sluys and protected to the seaward side by sandbars and coastal shallows. The fleet included a squadron of Venetian galleys under the celebrated Admiral Barbanera, who failed to dissuade his French allies from keeping their ships penned in a narrow anchorage and thus yielding the initiative to the English.

If the English king had listened to his own naval advisers, this grave error by the French would hardly have mattered. English morale had suffered from the setbacks of the past two years and Edward's Commander of the Cinque Ports, Sir Robert Morley, had gloomily forecast total disaster if the English fleet were to assault the massed strength of the French. The French fleet numbered over 140 troop-carrying ships and a swarming armada of smaller vessels. By June 1340, however, Edward had gathered a fleet of 117 troop-carrying ships backed by around 250 transports. This fleet was made up of cogs, merchant ships taken over for the purpose of war. He was determined to cross to Flanders and open the war in earnest before his Flemish allies lost heart and defected to the French.

Edward saw at once that the French had thrown away their advantage in numbers by choosing to stay at their anchorage. He accepted that the French reserves of manpower were still enormous, but planned to remedy this by England's 'secret weapon' – the superior range and firepower of the

great care into three divisions with the most powerful ships at the head of the fleet. Men-at-arms were stationed in every third ship while the archers filled the two ships in between. This anticipated the formation which later English armies were to adopt at Crécy and Agincourt, the two famous land victories of the longbow. Edward also waited for the flood tide on 24 June, when the offshore sandbanks were safely under water, before heading in to attack with the sun at his archers' backs.

The ensuing fight was, as Froissart put it feelingly, 'right furious and horrible, for battles by sea are more dangerous and fiercer than battles by land, for at sea there is no retreat or fleeing; there is no remedy but to fight and abide the fortune'. The English tactics were simple, brutal, and effective. They approached the French first line downwind, behind dense flights of arrows which decimated the defenders. As the ships collided, grapples were flung and the men-at-arms boarded and took over the hand-to-hand fighting which cleared each French ship in succession. Both French admirals were killed; Balmuchet, who had led the raids on the English coast, was taken alive but promptly hanged from a yardarm.

ABOVE The French admirals lashed the ships of their fleet together, thus presenting a larger target to the English archers, who decimated the French from long range before overwhelming them in hand-to-hand fighting.

ABOVE RIGHT A gold noble commemorating the English victory at Sluys, on which Edward III is depicted standing in a stylized cog.

longbow. The lingering worry that the French might break out from their anchorage and overwhelm the English fleet by strength of numbers was dispelled when the English found that the French – like Olaf Tryggveson at Svolde, 300 years before – had lashed their ships together. Instead of converting the French fleet into an impregnable fortress, this created a floating killing-ground in which the English archers could not fail to inflict enormous casualties.

On Midsummer Eve 1340 the English got their first sight of the French fleet, 'so great a number of ships' it was said, 'that their masts seemed to be like a great wood'. There was nothing precipitate about the English attack. Edward deployed his fleet with

The toughest resistance was put up by the fourth and last line of the French fleet but by nightfall this line too had succumbed to the English. One of the French commanders managed to break out to the open sea with twenty-four ships, capturing two English ships as he went, and escaped after a running battle. The rest of the French fleet was annihilated.

The casualties at Sluys were immense: 25,000 French against 4000 English. The battle gave the English command of the Narrow Seas for the next two decades – the years of great land triumphs at Crécy and Poitiers. Furthermore, the destruction of the French fleet ensured that the battles of the Hundred Years' War were fought in France and not in England.

PART THREE

The Age of the Galleon

Naval warfare was revolutionized in the late fifteenth and sixteenth centuries. During the Middle Ages, maritime engagements were confined to the coastal waters of Europe and fought between ships that had changed little for hundreds of years. By 1600, however, the warship had been transformed into the cannon-armed galleon and the great European nations fought out their wars in every far corner of the globe.

The sixteenth century saw the rise of the nation state and the expansion of maritime trade to encompass the Far East and the New World. The wealth that could be gained from such trade was massive and rivalry between the European nations was correspondingly fierce. Spain's conquest of much of Central and South America fuelled this rivalry, which was the mainspring for the wars of this period. As the great trading routes began to bypass the Mediterranean the focus of maritime development travelled westwards to those nations

A late fifteenth-century caravel. The two masts were necessarily increased to three or four masts as vessels grew in size.

which bordered the Atlantic. The decline of Venice and the rise of Spain and then England reflected this change.

Although in decline, the Mediterranean was no backwater and the war between Islam and Christendom was the largest and most sustained conflict of the period. The Mediterranean remained a great battle-ground and the destruction of the Turkish fleet at the battle of Lepanto, fought off the Greek coast in 1571, was one of the most decisive in naval history.

The main warship in the Mediterranean remained the galley, with a length of 45m (150ft) and a combined crew of about 400 men. Most galleys had a few light cannon mounted on the bows, a development that led to the galleasse. Never a great success, the galleasse was an attempt to combine the speed of the galley and the seaworthiness and firepower of the galleon. Equipped with oars, it mounted a broadside of up to fifty guns, although these were small anti-personnel and not ship-sinking weapons. The Turks developed the galliot, a small, fast galley of from sixteen to twenty oars similar to the dromon of the Byzantine Empire.

These were all modifications; the main force of change came in western Europe with the development of ocean-going sailing ships from the cogs and nefs of the medieval period. The first new design of ship to emerge was the Portuguese caravel, followed a little later by the larger carrack.

Caravels were originally little craft of some 25 to 60 tons and sometimes larger. They were distinguishable by their two, three, or four masts with triangular 'fore-and-aft' lateen sails. Caravels could be decked or undecked. They were carvel-built — that is the planks met edge to edge and did not overlap, as was common in the north. They were steered with a rudder fixed centrally on a square transomed stern. The proportions of the hull were decided by a formula, which stated that the length of the keel was to be twice the beam and three times the height at the waist. In addition, the breadth of the bottom was one-third of the beam and the total length of the caravel was equal to the combined keel and beam. Shipwrights delighted in making every dimension a proportion of other dimensions, at this date and for many years later. In the case of the caravel, the formula produced an admirable sea-going vessel, which was very weatherly (capable of sailing close to the wind).

Considering how famous the caravel became in the history of maritime discovery during the fifteenth century, it is surprising how little is really known about this type of vessel. Caravels can be recognized in a number of contemporary illustrations, but seldom are two the same. The fifteenth-century caravel seems to have been predominantly based on a Portuguese type of fishing boat, which was admired for her seaworthiness and handiness under both sail and oars. The larger caravel was decked and could carry guns. It was eminently suitable for making long coastal voyages, as it was less endangered by currents and shoals than was the less handy fully square-rigged ship. Consequently it was considered to be a suitable vessel for exploration.

The caravel used for voyages of exploration was a *caravela redonda*, medium-sized, with square sails on fore and main masts and a lateen sail on the mizen. This gave her speed, handiness and a useful windward capability. The hull was not too beamy, was easily driven and the ship was small enough to be rowed in calm weather.

Sailing ships were always in danger near land, especially off the dreaded lee-shore. On occasions they could only anchor and trust to luck that the anchor would hold and the cable not part. The galley was no better, when caught in the open sea in heavy weather, as its length and narrow beam made it likely to founder or broach to. The caravel, however, stood a better chance under these conditions, although her cargo space was limited and she was not much of a fighting ship. Nevertheless, the armed caravel was well able to defend herself with her bombards against any hostile natives.

The carrack was a larger, beamy, round-hulled ship, with a fairly high forecastle and a very lofty after castle rising above the upper deck at each end. It carried three – or sometimes four – masts, of which the two foremost were rigged with square courses – lower sails – and topsails. A bowsprit, needed to take the strong forestays which supported the foretopmast, projected ahead of the bow, with a square spritsail spread beneath it. On the after mast, or masts – mizen and bonaventure – the lateen sail was retained.

The system of standing rigging was also taken, like the square-sail rig, from the northern European ships. The shrouds, which support the masts laterally, instead of being composed of short pendants to which tackles were attached and set up inside the hull, were made of single ropes and secured by means of lanyards and blocks known as 'dead-eyes' to 'chainwales' on the outside of the hull. This enabled the shrouds to be inter-connected by rope 'ratlines' at close intervals so as to form ladders, by which the sailors could go aloft on to the yards to 'hand' the square sails as necessary.

The square rig of the carrack, with its six or more sails, enabled a greater sail area to be spread than on the lateen-rigged caravel. Though the carrack could not beat to windward as well as the caravel, this was

Pieter Brueghel the Elder's impression of galleons at sea. It was the use of cannon in the galleon which was to revolutionize naval warfare from the sixteenth century onwards.

not a great disadvantage in ocean voyages, as sailing ships could make use of prevailing or seasonal winds to obtain a fair running passage for most of their voyages. In addition the area of square sail spread on the main sails on fore and main masts could be increased by lacing sections, known as bonnets, to the foot of each sail in light winds.

By 1500 the caravel and carrack were the established ships of the new Portuguese Empire and had pioneered the great voyages of discovery to Asia. It was three caravels, the *Santa Maria*, the *Niña* and the *Pinta*, which carried Columbus and his men on their historic voyage to the Americas. Despite their importance in opening up the new trade routes they were superseded in the sixteenth century by a new warship, the galleon.

The galleon derived directly from the carrack, being the result of an experiment by Sir John Hawkins around 1570. In his three voyages to Africa and the West Indies he had found that the high forecastle (common to all large ships at the time) caught the wind and prevented the ship from

heading to windward. Eliminating the forecastle made a ship more manoeuvrable and much more weatherly. The proportions of the galleon demonstrate how far ship design had advanced since the days of the round ship. While the round ship had a length-to-beam ratio of about $2\frac{1}{2}$:1, in the galleon the ratio was 4:1 or 5:1. The dimensions of a galleon given in one contemporary manuscript were an overall length of 37.5m (123ft), length of keel 27.5m (90ft) and a beam of 9m (30ft) which gave proportions of approximately 4:3:1.

The smaller galleons had only three masts, but four-masted galleons were quite usual. Contemporary pictures show galleons as square-rigged on the foremast and mainmast and lateen-rigged on the mizen mast and bonaventure mizen mast. They also had a long bowsprit which could carry a square sail above – when it was known as a spritsail topsail – and below – known as a square spritsail.

Curiously, although the galleon in its final form was essentially English, the term was never used by the English in describing their fighting vessels.

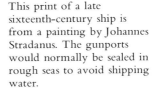

This print of a late sixteenth-century ship is from a painting by Johannes Stradanus. The gunports would normally be sealed in rough seas to avoid shipping water.

ABOVE Ferdinand Magellan lost his life attempting a voyage of world circumnavigation in 1519–22. The *Victoria*, pictured here, was the only surviving ship.

LEFT A model of a Venetian cog of the sixteenth century, with its characteristic bluff bow and full form amidships.

41

A sixteenth-century painting of a squadron of Portuguese carracks. These ships were used for both trade and war by Spain and Portugal.

Instead, these were known simply as 'King's Ships' although some, like the Ark Royal built by Sir Walter Raleigh in 1587, were privately owned. For most of the fifteenth and the early sixteenth centuries the suffix 'of the Tower' was added to the name of a warship to denote its naval status.

Large anti-ship cannon had been mounted on sailing ships since the mid-fifteenth century but it was the use of these weapons in the galleons of the sixteenth century that revolutionized naval warfare. The introduction of firearms had not changed the basic conception of the European warship as a floating fortress, it had merely extended the range and increased the firepower of the ship. Heavy cannon could not be mounted on the upper decks or the castles because of the danger of capsizing, but during the early sixteenth century the 'gunport' was introduced. This consisted of a simple hinged flap covering a hole in the ship's side which allowed heavy cannon to be mounted and run out from the lower decks of the ship.

The increase in size of the galleon allowed large numbers of cannon to be carried and, in effect, the warship became a floating battery. Naval tactics changed from ramming and boarding to longer-range engagements where the enemy ship could be virtually destroyed without coming into actual contact. That the English were the first nation to realize the implications of these new tactics was a large factor in explaining their rise to maritime power.

The fine sailing qualities of the English galleons played an important part in the famous battle between the English fleet and the Spanish Armada in 1588. The galleon design had not yet spread to Spain, and the Spanish fleet consisted of sixty-four large carracks, which were described as 'being of an huge bignesse and very stately built'. Their upperworks were capable of withstanding musket shot and the ribs and planking of the hulls were correspondingly stout. *San Martin*, the Duke of Medina Sidonia's flagship, displaced 1000 tons and carried fifty guns. Her complement was 177 sailors and 300 soldiers.

The Spanish still tended to arm their ships with a multitude of light-calibre weapons and pack them with soldiers, which reflected their belief in the primacy of boarding in naval engagements. The English, on the other hand, concentrated on improving the design of their ships and the quality of their seamanship; few soldiers were carried as the sailors were expected to carry out the military duties that might arise. The changing shape of the English galleon was partly determined by the emphasis on long-range gunnery. The fore and after castles were considered to be of less importance (now that soldiers were not needed to man them) and were lowered while the ship's beak – which corresponded to the galley's ram – remained only as a vestigial figurehead. These improvements were embodied in the *Revenge*, Sir Francis Drake's flagship against the Armada, considered the best and most beautiful galleon ever built in England. Her length was 33.5m (110ft) and her beam was 8.5m (28ft), giving a ratio of about 4:1. The *Revenge* was so much admired that other nations began to copy her and the English 'low-charged' ship became the model for the future. One of the *Revenge*'s important features was a deck devoted exclusively to guns and she was the first English ship to have this.

English galleons of this time mostly had a main armament of twenty large muzzle-loading culverins, which were about 3m (10ft) long and fired a ball weighing 8kg (18lb). They were mounted on the lower deck and were staggered on opposite sides, as the width of the deck – some 7.5m (25ft) – was insufficient to permit two guns to be run in and reloaded if they were mounted opposite one another. A battery of demi-culverins, which fired shots of about 4kg (9lb), was mounted on the upper deck and a number of smaller swivel guns (known as 'murderers') were carried in the fore and after castles. The supply of ammunition was a problem because of the different calibre of the various guns, as was found during the Armada battle in 1588.

The sixteenth century saw a steady improvement in the quality of the gunpowder used which previously had an unfortunate tendency to separate into its constituent parts. New methods of manufacture produced a stable 'corned' powder which consisted of unified grains. This new powder burned far more efficiently, which meant much greater power, giving longer ranges and higher muzzle velocity to the ball. The improved powder did pose one problem to the gunners, for it meant that, on breech-loading pieces, it was most important to have a really close fit between chamber and barrel, otherwise there was a heavy escape of gas from the gun. Hot escaping gases represented a loss of power and were a serious hazard to the gunners. One solution to this problem was to use cast-iron or brass cannon, which were muzzle-loading weapons like the earliest guns.

Cast cannon had several advantages, perhaps the greatest being that their thicker walls permitted the use of larger charges to give greater power. They were not, however, without fault, for they were heavy and, even more important, they were muzzle-loading. With the breech-loading weapon, a supply of loaded chambers could be prepared in advance, and consequently a fairly rapid rate of fire could be maintained. Muzzle loading meant a marked reduction in the rate of fire, because a somewhat lengthy reloading sequence had to be followed after the cannon had been fired. Cast guns also presented a problem for the loaders, since they had to be able to reach the muzzle. This problem was solved by attaching the gun to the ship's side

Although his fleet also included galleys, Henry VIII of England had some impressive sailing warships in his navy. Several of these are pictured here off Dover.

The fifty-five-gun *Ark Royal*, commanded by Lord Howard of Effingham, was the flagship of the fleet at the battle of the Spanish Armada in 1588.

with thick rope so that, when it was fired, it recoiled to the extent of the breeching rope, far enough inboard for it to be reloaded. When loaded, the carriage was hauled back to the gunport with a gun tackle.

The improvements in the construction of cannon and the introduction of gunports led to the development of broadside tactics which became the basic pattern of naval warfare for the next three centuries. Rows of cannon along each side of the ship allowed the simultaneous firing of all the guns on one side of the ship – the broadside. With the introduction of the naval tactic of the line of battle in the Second Dutch War in the 1660s most big naval actions became little more than slogging matches between lines of heavy, multi-gunned ships.

Although the size of cannon, tactics and other details changed over the centuries, the basic methods of naval gunnery remained the same. A drill sequence for loading and firing was worked out and soon became standardized. The first step was to ensure that no burning embers were left inside the cannon's bore from the previous shot. This was done by pushing down a scourer – a corkscrew-like device – which scraped any fouling from the bore. Next, a sponge was soaked in water and pushed down the bore, to extinguish any lingering sparks and also to cool the barrel. If this was not done, a spark could prematurely ignite the new charge, with disastrous results. A long, thin spike was pushed down the touch hole to ensure that it was clear and the cannon was then ready for loading. A charge of powder was pushed into the bore, either loose, or as a cartridge, with the powder wrapped in canvas, felt, or paper. Then a wad of oakum, yarn, felt or any other suitable material was rammed home on top of the powder with a heavy rod. This was followed by the ball and a second wad, which always received at least two extra thumps with the rammer, to ensure that it was firmly in place. Whilst the powder or cartridge was being inserted, the touch-hole, or vent, was covered by the gunner's finger to prevent its blockage by coarse powder. He then removed his finger and, if cartridges were being used, plunged a short, gimlet-like tool through the vent, to pierce the cartridge casing. Then, from a powder flask, he poured a quantity of fine-grained powder into the vent. The tip of a glowing piece of cord was touched to the powder in the vent to fire the cannon.

By the early seventeenth century the galleon was beginning to emerge as the ship-of-the-line; the

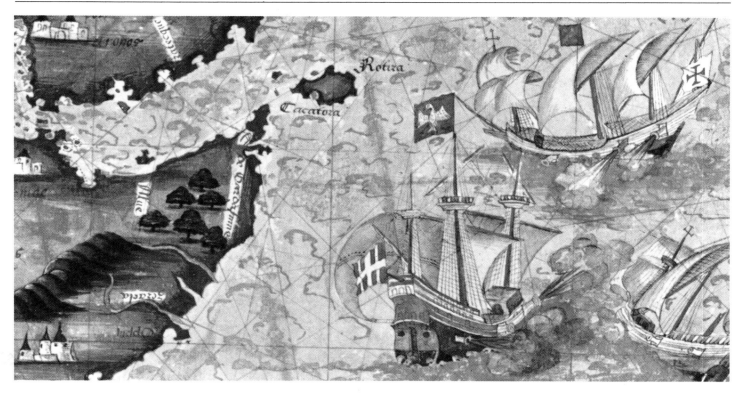

ABOVE The caravel was immensely popular with the Spanish and Portuguese explorers, since its shallow draught allowed it to sail close inshore. Two caravels here engage a carrack.

LEFT Launched in 1637, Charles I's *Sovereign of the Seas* carried 100 guns on three gun-decks and was the forerunner of the first-rate ship-of-the-line.

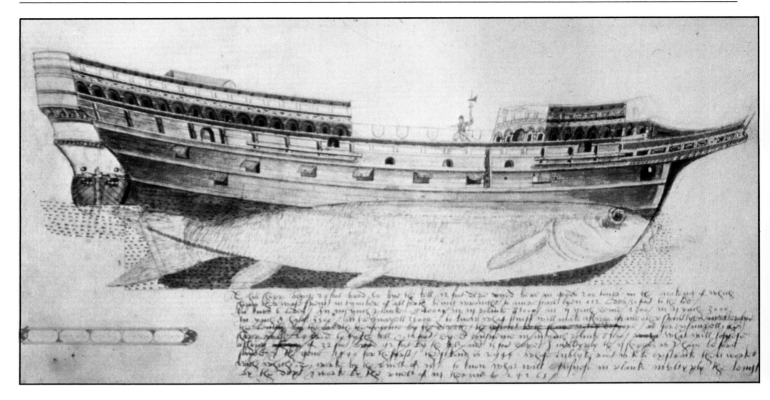

Produced in about 1585, this illustration from Matthew Baker's treatise on shipbuilding is the earliest existing technical drawing of an English ship. The outline of the fish is meant to illustrate the streamlined shape of the underwater hull.

pronounced 'sheer' – the rise of the deck – aft of the old galleon had disappeared; the sailing qualities of the vessel had been greatly improved and the weight of guns carried had increased. The richly decorated *Sovereign of the Seas*, launched in 1637, carried 100 guns on three decks and was the forerunner of the first-rate ship-of-the-line which was to form the backbone of the European navies until the mid-nineteenth century.

The sixteenth century was a turning point in naval strategy. Whereas in the Middle Ages naval strategy had been subordinate to land operations, by 1500 it was clear to a number of far-sighted individuals that naval power could be an effective instrument of national policy.

The great Portuguese admiral, Albuquerque, established a network of bases stretching from Africa to India in order to safeguard the Portuguese trade routes to the East Indies. Spain, too, began to see the merits of coordinating her naval activities as a means of exploiting the wealth of her new empire

and protecting it from interlopers. English economic policy was largely dictated by maritime activity. Large supplies of gold in the national coffers were considered essential for prosperity, and gold could be secured either from export trade or, more spectacularly but in fact less profitably, from plundering Spanish treasure ships and colonial possessions. This latter alternative found much favour with English naval commanders during the late sixteenth century.

The sixteenth century saw the beginnings of the national navy. Previously ships had been gathered together on an *ad hoc* basis in time of war and then disbanded on the cessation of hostilities. By the end of the century the idea of a permanent force of warships maintained during peacetime and expanded during war was universally accepted by the major naval powers. Warships had become specialized vessels, unsuited to anything but war; the age of the armed merchantman as a fighting ship was over.

Affonso de Albuquerque

1453–1515

Explorer and *conquistador* by sea in the name of his master, the King of Portugal, Affonso de Albuquerque stands out as perhaps the first genuine strategist in modern naval history. His vision and ruthless energy welded the handful of struggling trading-posts set up by the Portuguese east of the Cape of Good Hope into the first European empire, parts of which were still subject to Portuguese rule four-and-a-half centuries later.

The era of the great European voyages of exploration opened in January 1488, when Bartolomew Diaz of Portugal rounded the Cape of Good Hope and proved that the markets of India and the Far East could be reached by sea. Ten years later, Vasco da Gama and his small trading fleet carried the Portuguese flag as far as the west coast of India. In attaining the goal of decades of determined effort, da Gama and his men made another, less attractive discovery. Though the eastern seas now lay open to European merchants, the markets of the Orient did not. From the Red Sea to the South China Sea, the fleets of the Moslem world jealously guarded an absolute monopoly over trade. If Portugal was going to maintain the lead won by Diaz and da Gama – and above all obstruct other European rivals – this would have to be done by force.

Portugal approached her monumental task with one over-riding problem: she required sufficient manpower to garrison the fortified trading-posts between the costly sailings of armed fleets from home. Pedro Alvares Babral and Francisco de Almeida made a promising start, setting up bases at Cochin on the west coast of India and at Kilwa, Sofala and Mombasa on the east African coast. Grandiloquently entitled 'Viceroy of India', Almeida had added two more bases, Cananor and Calicut on the Indian west coast, by the time of his recall in 1509. He had also fought the first sea battle against the Moslems in the Indian Ocean, at Diu on 2 February 1509, temporarily securing Portuguese maritime supremacy in Indian waters.

Affonso de Albuquerque succeeded Almeida as Viceroy in 1509. Like his predecessors da Gama, Cabral and Almeida, Albuquerque was a tough soldier and courtier rather than a professional seaman; and fifty-five years old at the time of his appointment. Illegitimately connected with the Portuguese royal house, he had served as chief equerry to King João II, who had sent out Diaz on the voyage which first rounded the Cape. Under Almeida's rule, Albuquerque had served on punitive expeditions against the Moslems of the east African coast and Persian Gulf. By the time he embarked on his own vice-regency, Albuquerque was familiar with the waters he had to control and the enemy he had to fight. He had also worked out the only policy which offered Portugal a real chance of success.

Even if Portugal could have afforded the manpower to pattern the shores of the Indian Ocean with fortified bases, she could never have provided enough ships to keep all the garrisons supplied. Although Almeida had declared 'Avoid the annexation of territory; we can spare no men from the navy,' the new bases added under his command threatened to undermine such a strategy at birth. Albuquerque tackled the problem from the roots upward, starting with Portugal's objective: to break the Moslem stranglehold on oriental trade. As the sources of that trade lay not in India but in the East Indies, Portugal must command the seas in the East Indies as well as India. This could not be achieved by adding to a string of costly bases on the Indian coast.

In the space of six years, Albuquerque staked out an economical but resilient network of bases, all of them interdependent. Mombasa on the African east coast was the westernmost anchor, and Ormuz, at the mouth of the Persian Gulf, the north-western anchor. As Portugal's new stronghold on the west Indian coast, Albuquerque chose Goa, an island in a bay, and planted a Portuguese colony there in 1510. Goa was only the central link in the chain, however. In 1511 Albuquerque put all his strength into the capture of Malacca on the Malayan coast.

By the time of his recall in 1515 Albuquerque had proved that the new imperial outposts he had founded were capable of sending each other help in times of crisis: an essential quality required for any empire's survival. His tremendous expansion of the Portuguese zone of control had carried the first Portuguese explorers and traders to the Moluccas – the prized Spice Islands – and brought the coast of China within their grasp.

Enemies at court brought Albuquerque down, hinting at the vast personal fortune which he had amassed at the expense of the crown. The shock of the news of his supersession killed him and he was buried at Goa, cornerstone of the new empire which his pioneering grasp of naval strategy had bequeathed to his country.

The large trading empire established by Portugal in the early sixteenth century was largely attributable to the vision of Affonso de Albuquerque.

Andrea Doria

1466–1560

For centuries second only to Venice as the greatest seafaring republic in Italy, the city state of Genoa produced two great seamen in the late fifteenth century. One was Christopher Columbus, who discovered the Atlantic route to the New World. The other was Andrea Doria, admiral and champion of the Christian Mediterranean powers in their constant struggle against the Turks and Barbary pirates in the first half of the sixteenth century.

Born in 1466, Doria grew to manhood in a period which saw his city torn, like Florence, by the struggles of rival families, and increasingly subjected to a tug-of-war between France and the dukes of Milan. By 1500 the Republic of Genoa was a French puppet state in all but name, and the captains of her fleets sailed in French pay. Genoa's life-blood, however, remained her trade, and as the sixteenth century opened this was coming under increasing attack from fleets of Moslem corsairs based in North Africa. The most formidable of these corsairs were the brothers Barbarossa – a nickname bestowed by the apprehensive Italians. Of these the most famous was Khaireddin, who became the foremost admiral of the Moslem world and Andrea Doria's greatest foe.

Doria first saw action against the Barbarossas in 1510, when the brothers were attempting to set up their own corsair base in order to raid free of dependence on the Sultan of Tunis. This they had not yet achieved when they captured a richly laden Genoese trading ship.

The promptness of the Genoese reply caught the Barbarossas completely by surprise. Twelve war galleys commanded by Doria swept south for a reprisal raid, sacking the fortress of Galetta near Tunis, driving Khaireddin and his men back into Tunis itself and carrying off half of the Barbarossas' modest fleet of eight galleys.

The resounding success of Doria's first major command, though financed by France, made him more than a national hero in Genoa: it made him a national leader of the Genoese who were growing increasingly impatient with French rule. Most unwisely, the French neglected to make Doria secure by giving him such honour and wealth as might have made him a dependable 'vassal'. Doria chose his moment well. He struck on 9 September 1528 when the French had their hands full elsewhere in Italy, trying to hold off the Spanish and German troops of the Emperor Charles V. Expelling the French, Doria restored the Genoese republic with himself as *doge*. He then offered the services of the Genoese fleet to Charles V in a joint Christian effort to halt the further spread of Turkish power into the western Mediterranean basin.

The Turks were led by Khaireddin Barbarossa, now viceroy of Algiers and captain-general of the fleet to Sultan Suleiman the Magnificent in Constantinople. Seventy-eight years old but as vigorous as ever, Khaireddin sailed from Constantinople in the spring of 1534 with a fleet of eighty-four galleys, ravaged the Italian west coast and Sardinia, and finally seized Tunis in the name of Suleiman.

Charles V reacted by raising a massive fleet of 600 ships to carry an army and take Tunis from Khaireddin, thus smashing the latest Turkish bid to dominate the central Mediterranean. Charles accompanied the allied force, which amounted to a crusade, while Doria commanded the fleet. Assaulted in overwhelming strength, Tunis fell after a bloody siege, but Khaireddin escaped with twenty-seven galleys and successfully evaded Doria's pursuit. While Doria vainly scoured the seas, Khaireddin boldly sacked Puerto de Mahon – the modern Port Mahon – on Minorca before heading east to Constantinople for reinforcements.

The capture of Tunis and the momentary discomfiture of the Turkish fleet allowed Doria to patrol the Ionian Sea and raid the Turkish-held coast of Greece. Additionally the Venetian republic joined the allies against Turkey. By the summer of 1537, however, Khaireddin was back at sea with 135 galleys, despoiling the island colonies of Venice in the Ionian and Aegean Seas. To help Venice in the summer of 1538 came the massed fleets of Spain, the Papacy and Genoa under Doria's overall command. This force comprised 166 galleys plus sixty-four sailing ships armed with cannon broadsides.

What should have been the decisive showdown between these two redoubtable old men – Doria was seventy-two, Khaireddin about ten years older – was fought off Prevesa in the same area as the battle of Actium. Khaireddin positioned his outnumbered fleet of 122 galleys in the Gulf of Arta, but failed to persuade his impatient captains that Doria would be unable to maintain a prolonged blockade on a hostile coast; thus the fleets clashed on 27 September 1538.

Like Jutland, Prevesa remains one of the more controversial actions in naval history. It lasted three

days, and Doria was bitterly criticized for exposing the Venetian ships to the brunt of the Turkish attack, and for not forcing a close action on his outnumbered foe. It seems likely, however, that Doria was perplexed by the size of his multinational force, and especially by the tactical problem of integrating oared galleys with sailing ships. Another problem for Doria was the capricious wind patterns of the Gulf of Arta, which kept the Christian fleet scattered and favoured Khaireddin's breakout just as it had favoured the breakout of Mark Antony and Cleopatra at Actium. Taking two galleys and five sailing ships, Khaireddin got clean away, taunting Doria for his cowardice. Thus the Turks remained in command of Greek waters until the great battle of Lepanto, thirty-three years later.

A month after the battle of Prevesa, Doria's fleet took Castelnuovo on the south-east Adriatic coast, only for Khaireddin to seize it back in 1539. In 1543

Doria was faced with a new war on his own doorstep when France allied with Turkey and Khaireddin brought a fleet of 150 galleys west to operate from Marseilles. Doria successfully beat off a Franco-Turkish assault on Nice, but the French soon bought off their increasingly unwelcome allies and Khaireddin returned to Constantinople, where he died two years later.

Doria outlived his great rival by fourteen years, but they were far from idle. He was momentarily ousted from Genoa by a French-inspired *coup* in 1547, but was back in power by the end of the year. One of Khaireddin's captains, Dragut, was a constant source of trouble for Doria and his nephew, Gian Andrea Doria. The old admiral led expeditions against the Turkish corsairs of Algeria in 1550 and the French in Corsica from 1553 to 1555. Exercising his civil and naval powers to the last, Andrea Doria died in 1560 at the ripe age of ninety-four.

Andrea Doria became one of the dominant figures in the troubled Mediterranean in the sixteenth century, remaining actively involved in Genoese maritime campaigns until well beyond his eightieth year.

Lepanto

LAST GREAT CLASH OF THE GALLEYS

The battle of Lepanto at its height, with the galleys closing head-on in order to bring their bow guns to bear on the enemy. Note the proximity of the Greek shoreline.

The battle of Lepanto, fought between the forces of the 'Holy Alliance' of Christian Europe and the Ottoman Empire, was one of the most important naval engagements of all time. It was the last great galley clash fought in that baptismal bowl of sea fighting, the Mediterranean, and it marked the new primacy of the ship-borne gun as a factor in naval tactics. Politically, it meant the end of the Ottoman Empire as a major sea power.

It was Ottoman arrogance which finally welded the forces of such nominally allied but constantly bickering principalities as Spain, Venice, Genoa and the Papal States into a coherent unit, when, in the spring of 1570, Sultan Selim II launched a large expeditionary force against Cyprus, until then a Venetian dominion. Nicosia was sacked by mid-summer, and by autumn the Turks were besieging Famagusta with their land armies, while their battle-fleet raided in the eastern Adriatic; meanwhile a Venetian-Spanish relief fleet broke up in bad weather and political disagreement.

Throughout the winter Pope Pius V worked to promote concord among the Christian nations and by May 1571 the 'Holy Alliance' between Venice, Spain, Genoa and the Papal States was pledged to provide 300 vessels and 50,000 men to counter the

Turkish threat. Their supreme commander was to be Don John of Austria, illegitimate son of the Emperor Charles V and thus half-brother of Philip II of Spain; although only twenty-five Don John had been nominal High Admiral of Spain for some years and had served with distinction against the Moors in Granada.

Under Don John the principal commanders were to be Alvaro de Bazan, made Marquis of Santa Cruz the following year for his gallantry, Marc Antonio Colonna, the Papal admiral, Giovanni Andrea Doria, son of the great Genoan seaman, and two renowned Venetians, Sebastian Veniero and Augustino Barbarigo. Between them they mustered 225 galleys and over seventy sailing ships – including twenty-six large carracks which were, however, left behind by the faster vessels when battle was closed. Most importantly Venice had also provided six galleasses, each fitted with four lateen-sailed masts and mounting among their armament of fifty guns several with a range of over 1km ($\frac{1}{2}$ mile).

These vessels were to provide the principal break with tradition in the coming conflict; their captains had sworn on oath not to engage less than twenty-

five of the enemy at a time. Don John realized that the bow guns of the galleasses, backed up by fire from the Spanish soldiers' arquebuses, could prove decisive.

Against these innovations, however, was to be pitted the Turks' well-known skill with 'saturation' archery, plus their reputation for animal ferocity, and this reputation received a powerful boost from news which reached the Christian fleet at Messina, gathered for the blessing of the Papal Nuncio on 26 September. Famagusta had surrendered to the Turks, but the garrison had received no mercy. Its leaders had been publicly butchered, while its commander had been mutilated and then flayed alive, his skin stuffed with straw and put on public display.

Flaunting this terrible triumph, the Turkish fleet under Ali Pasha anchored off Lepanto, in what is now the Gulf of Corinth, on 27 September to await the coming of Don John. With Ali Pasha was his second-in-command, Mahomet Sirocco, and they were joined by Uluch Ali, an Algerian corsair who had begun life as a Calabrian fisherman, had spurned Christianity, and taken to the cause of Islam with a savage zeal. The Turkish force, comprising a total of 75,000 fighting men, was made up of 210 large or 'royal' galleys, twenty smaller galleys, and forty galliots – light, fast craft with a single lateen sail and between sixteen and twenty oars. Every galliot oarsman was a Turkish soldier, skilled in grappling, boarding and hand-to-hand fighting. The rest of Ali Pasha's fleet was rowed by slaves, including 15,000 Christians. Using a clever psychological tactic, Pasha told these: 'If I win the battle, I promise you liberty; if the day is yours, God has given it you.'

The Turks left harbour on 6 October and were sighted at dawn of 7 October by scouts from Andrea Dorias' Genoese squadron off Cape Scropha near the Gulf of Patras. At 9.30 a.m. the two fleets were in sight of each other, and drew up their battle lines. Half an hour later Don John's galleasses began their artillery barrage, by which time the two sides were close; Don John had specifically ordered that no shot should be fired 'until near enough to be splashed by the blood of an enemy'.

As befitted the last battle fought according to tactics laid down in classical times the two formations were military rather than naval, each with a centre force and two flanks. Ali Pasha commanded his main force with his right led by Mahomet Sirocco and his left by Uluch Ali. Facing Sirocco on Don John's left flank was Barbarigo and his Venetians, with Doria's mixed force of Genoese and Tuscan mercenaries – hired by the Pope – on the right. In the centre were Colonna and Veniero commanding a mixed force of Spanish, Papal and Venetian vessels, backed up by a reserve line of thirty-five Spanish and Venetian galleys under de Bazan, whose orders were to cut in where most needed. The focus of all was Don John's flagship, a

standard showing the crucified Christ flanked by St Peter and St Paul flying at the maintop. Ali Pasha too, flew a proud pennant – a white flag on which the name Allah had been embroidered 29,000 times.

The six gun-carrying galleasses had been towed out in front of Don John's line, two to each squadron, and as they opened fire Don John himself inspected them in a small swift boat, traversing the length of his 5-km (3-mile) front and being cheered by all his troops. Morale on the Christian side was further heightened by the fact that the first barrage sank several Turkish galleys before their archers were within bow-shot. Surprised, the Turks opened their formation, the flanking squadrons seeking independent contact while Ali Pasha drove relentlessly on to meet Don John.

Sirocco, on the left and with a thorough knowledge of the coastline which lay to his starboard side, swept down on Barbarigo and managed to place several galleys behind the Venetian. Sirocco's archers inundated the Christian squadron with close-quarter fire, killing Barbarigo and the two commanders who, in the heat of battle, succeeded him; the Venetian flagship was locked in the thick of hand-to-hand fighting and was twice taken, twice won back. Finally reinforcements from de Bazan's group drove Sirocco's vessels aground in the shallows; Sirocco himself was dragged from the water and beheaded without ceremony.

On the Turk's right, meanwhile, the renegade fisherman Uluch Ali had begun a battle of sheer seamanship with the equally skilled Doria, each trying to outflank the other. Unfortunately they were unevenly matched, numerically. Uluch Ali had ninety-three galleys to Doria's sixty-four, and Doria's efforts to outsail his opponent led him dangerously out to sea. Taking advantage of the gap thus opened, Uluch turned half his force and headed back to hit Don John in the rear.

By now it was early afternoon, and since midday Don John and Ali Pasha had been locked together, the crews of their respective flagships fighting hand-to-hand on the bulwarks. Here, the Christian commander's foresight in stripping his capital ships of their rams paid off, for the guns in his blunted bow pounded round after round into Ali Pasha's water-line, and behind the line of swordsmen Spanish arquebusiers in the rigging calmly picked off Turks. One ball hit Ali Pasha a glancing blow to the head, and as the Spaniards finally broke through onto the poop deck he pleaded for mercy, offering his most valued possession in ransom. It was the right upper canine of Mohammed, enclosed in a crystal and gold case. Unfortunately it meant nothing to the Spanish soldiers, who cut off Ali Pasha's head and carried it triumphantly to Don John. The Christian was horrified and ordered it to be thrown overboard, but before the grisly matter could be settled the galleys of Uluch Ali came up astern.

Guarding Don John's rear was Giustiniani, Prior of the Order of St John of Malta, in his galley the *Capitana*; the Prior was cut down by five arrows and the *Capitana* captured, as were eight Sicilian galleys rowing to his rescue. But de Bazan with his rearguard had stuck to his orders committing him to reserve duties and was able to turn on Uluch Ali and drive him off, winning back the battered *Capitana*. At about the same time, a fortunate act of disobedience occurred. The soldier who had so peremptorily decapitated Ali Pasha had retained the Turk's head, despite Don John's orders. Now he stuck it on a pike and waved it aloft in the midst of a crowd of cheering allies. At the same time the sacred banner bearing Allah's many-times-repeated name was hauled down from the truck of the Turkish flagship, and in despair the Turks still putting up resistance to the centre collapsed and surrendered.

There remained the question of Doria, still fighting out to seawards with part of Uluch Ali's squadron; during the course of an hour and a half, fifteen ships had been captured from Doria's main force but Doria had recaptured thirteen of them. Five had put up such a gallant defence that they were hardly worth saving. The *San Giovanni* and the *Piamontesa* were awash with water and blood, every man aboard them dead. In the *Doncella* a few wounded survived, while in the *Florence* the captain and seventeen men were still fighting, out of a crew of 200. In the *Marquesa* there remained among the wounded officers Don Miguel de Cervantes Saavedra, later to become the author of *Don Quixote*, who had his left arm shattered in the fighting; it is also said that another volunteer with Doria's force was Sir Richard Grenville, although no certain proof has ever been offered.

Of all the Turkish force only sixteen galleys under Uluch Ali remained afloat and serviceable, and they fled for the safety of the port of Lepanto. When Uluch Ali heard of Ali Pasha's death, however, he turned again, late in the afternoon, and fought an unexpected and bloody skirmish with one Don Juan of Cardona, who was outnumbered two to one. Of Don Juan's 500 men only fifty remained unscathed, after which the former Christian Uluch Ali sailed off – the only Ottoman commander to save anything from the rout.

In all, the Christian losses at Lepanto have been estimated at thirteen galleys sunk or captured and 15,000 men killed or badly wounded. The Turks are said to have lost more than 200 galleys – sunk, wrecked, or captured – 30,000 men killed, 8000 captured, and an unknown number drowned. But Ali Pasha's words to his Christian slaves came true – 15,000 of them were freed, one way or another, from the shackles of the rowing benches.

Don John, young though he was, had reached the crest of his career; he had been raised and trained to galley warfare and had brought it to its peak. Six years later he died, ashore, on a mission for Philip II to the Low Countries. But his use of guns in his one great success had determined the course of naval action for the future.

Don John of Austria, whose fleet took on the massed galleys of Turkey in their own waters at Lepanto in 1571 and, after a savage struggle, emerged victorious.

Francis Drake

1542–1596

In his lifetime Francis Drake became a popular hero in England and a notorious devil in Spain. The two views had much in common. They made the man larger than life, invincible, almost inhuman. Lately, in reaction to the Victorian revival of the hero, an anti-Drake school has sprung up. He has been accused of roguery, recklessness, ruthlessness, cowardice, publicity-seeking and pride.

In 1549 when he was about seven years old, Drake's family left Devon and moved to Chatham where the father, Edmund Drake, obtained employment as lay chaplain to ships. The next stage of Drake's boyhood was as an apprentice in a small coaster which also made short sea voyages to France and Zeeland. This was a hard and testing trade in difficult conditions – shallow water, steep seas, lee shores, intricate channels. Drake did well enough for the master to leave the ship to him in his will, so at an early age he had an independent command.

Drake's coastal ventures offered little hope of the large rewards he desired and like other Englishmen he looked to the new trade with the Americas as a means of commercial advancement. These expeditions involved dangers beyond those of seafaring, because of the risk of clashing with the Spaniards and Portuguese. Drake began his apprenticeship in this high-risk business by first serving as lieutenant to Captain Lovell on a voyage to the West Indies in 1566 and then as captain of the 50-ton *Judith*, part of a small fleet under John Hawkins, which in 1567 sailed on a slave-trading enterprise to West Africa and the West Indies. Neither of these voyages was successful and the second ended in disaster when a Spanish fleet trapped the English squadron at San Juan de Ulloa in Mexico. Only two ships escaped, Drake's small 'bark' and a much larger vessel under Hawkins.

Drake was ruined for a time, but by 1572 he was

Sir Francis Drake, whose courage and adventurous spirit typified the swashbuckling attitude of the late Elizabethan 'sea-dogs'.

in business again, in command of two small ships with a total complement of seventy-three men and boys. With this force Drake engaged in a series of privateering raids on Spanish possessions in the Caribbean. The most famous was the capture of the mule train carrying silver along the 'Royal Road' which ran across the Isthmus of Panama. In this daring venture he enlisted the aid of local Indian guerrilla forces and for little loss of life secured for himself and his companions a small fortune.

By the mid-1570s Drake had won a reputation as a successful privateer who could return a large profit on an initial investment. In 1577 a group of investors, led by Queen Elizabeth I, offered Drake command of an expedition against Spanish and Portuguese overseas possessions. This new project was a raiding cruise on the Pacific side of the Isthmus of Panama, into unknown seas, in the

Of Drake's force of five ships and 164 men, only the *Pelican* (renamed the *Golden Hind* during the voyage) made it round the Horn, the other four smaller ships turning back to England after encountering a great storm. It was a magnificent and highly profitable achievement for such a small force.

However, like Magellan before him, Drake had met opposition among his own officers just when the critical, nerve-racking part of the enterprise was before them. He had quelled it by executing one man, Thomas Doughty, and relieving two others of their posts. The sharp social divisions of the time were a major factor in the dispute and were to plague Drake to the end of his life, even after he had been knighted for the success of this voyage.

In many ways Drake was a model commander and by the standards of the day surprisingly

course of which he would circle the globe. As the flow of gold and silver to Spain was as important to the Spanish war effort as oil is to modern states, its disruption would be a strategic gain for England. A careful deception plan worked and Drake arrived in the Pacific with the advantage of complete surprise. Among his captures was a Spanish treasure ship named *Nuestra Señora de la Concepción* (nicknamed *Cacafuego* by Drake's crew) carrying £147,000 in gold. From his circumnavigation of the world, Drake not only brought back booty totalling half a million pounds, but discovered a new route round Cape Horn and claimed California for the queen.

humane, but he had a fierce temper which he kept on a short lead. Ever since the disastrous expedition to San Juan de Ulloa in 1567 Drake nurtured a bitter hatred of the Spanish. During one voyage he hanged two Spanish friars in a fit of rage, hearing of the death of a negro cabin boy at the hands of the Spanish.

His temper blazed out again during the famous fire-raid on Cadiz in 1587, popularly known as 'singeing the King of Spain's beard', which would never have been carried out, let alone brought to triumph, had Drake not first arrested the staid government 'watchdog' naval officer who had been

TOP Sir Francis Drake.

ABOVE A night attack with fireships on the Armada at Calais.

RIGHT A trophy commissioned by Queen Elizabeth I to mark Drake's Caribbean quests.

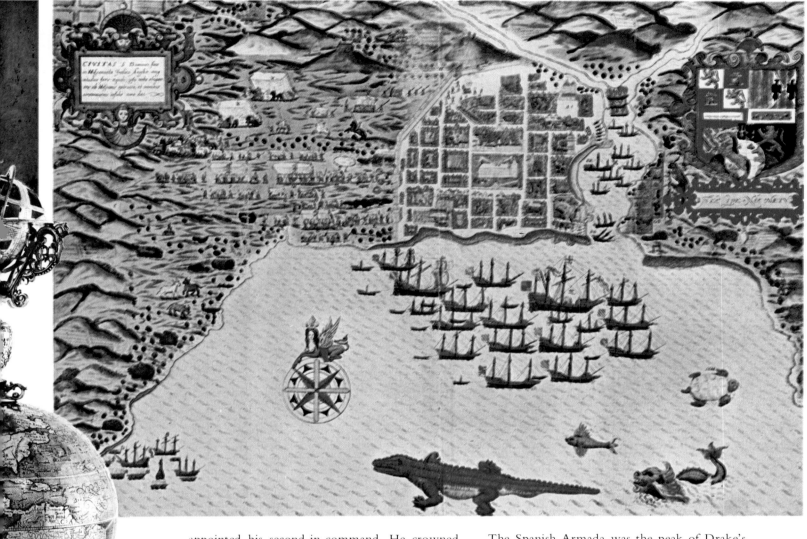

appointed his second-in-command. He crowned this success with the capture of yet another treasure ship, a Portuguese carrack, the *San Felipe*, which more than paid the costs of the daring venture.

In the following year, 1588, when the delayed Armada at last sailed, Drake was appointed vice-admiral under Lord Charles Howard of Effingham. This was not a happy combination and, although the Spanish invasion attempt was utterly thwarted, the English generally felt that a lot more could have been done. There was grumbling about Drake, too, for he had snapped up yet another rich prize, apparently by deserting his post.

His critics also took him to task for lack of nerve because, in the final battle off Gravelines on 29 July, he by-passed a small group of the strongest Spanish ships and carried the attack to a flock of disorganized weaker sisters which, with a little worrying, he hoped to put aground in the shallows. Strategically this was a perfectly correct move. Besides, Drake carried too many scars, received in hand-to-hand fighting, to be convincingly accused of cowardice.

The Spanish Armada was the peak of Drake's career. In 1589 an English 'Armada' attacked Portugal, with inconclusive results. Drake merely commanded the ships, Sir John Norreys led the soldiers. Both were good men, but the political calculations proved to be wrong. Security was bad. The government failed to supply a siege train for Norreys and, as no treasure was taken, the expedition showed a heavy loss. After his previous successes, this was an anticlimax and Drake's reputation suffered as a result.

His final voyage, in partnership with Hawkins, was a tragedy. By 1595 the Spanish defences in the New World were efficient and alert. They had advance warning of the attack and they obtained every detail of the English plan from prisoners. Nor did Drake act with his customary speed. Held back by Hawkins, who was old and dying, he arrived inevitably where and when the Spaniards expected him. He could do little. Then sickness spread in the fleet and struck down Drake himself. He was buried at sea in a lead-lined coffin near Porto Bello on the Spanish Main, the scene of his former triumphs.

John Hawkins

1532–1595

John Hawkins achieved renown not only as an adventurer on the high seas, but also as comptroller and treasurer of the English navy. He also invented the low-charged ship, or galleon, which was the basic warship design for the next 300 years.

In his long and distinguished career Sir John Hawkins demonstrated that he was both a daring seaman and an able naval administrator. Although his reputation was formed by his audacious voyages in the Caribbean, his most important work was in organizing and modernizing the English navy in the years leading up to the battle of the Armada.

Hawkins was born in Plymouth in 1532, the son of William Hawkins, the mayor of Plymouth and a noted naval commander. He was brought up in a nautical family and in his youth he made a number of voyages to the Canary Islands. It was there that he discovered the profitability of the new and growing transatlantic slave trade.

In 1562, at the age of thirty, Hawkins had gained enough experience to set out on his own. Financed by friends and relatives he sailed from Plymouth with three ships in a venture to capture or trade for black slaves in West Africa and then transport them across the Atlantic to sell to the Spanish plantation owners in Mexico and the Caribbean.

A hard and at times a ruthless man, Hawkins soon came up against the Portuguese and Spanish who claimed the monopoly of trade to the New World. On this first voyage he proceeded to Sierra Leone where he acquired 300 slaves and other goods, partly through trade and partly through the plunder of Portuguese trading vessels. Arriving in Hispaniola (Haiti) he traded the slaves with the Spanish colonist for a cargo of hides, spices and pearls. On the return home he sent two of his ships with the less valuable hides to be sold in Spain while he sailed on to London. Hawkins made a great profit from the sale of goods but his two other ships were impounded by the Spanish authorities in Seville. In the Spaniards' eyes Hawkins had broken their stringent trading laws which forbade un-licensed trade to the American colonies and so his crews were imprisoned and his goods seized. Hawkin's strenuous efforts to have the goods and the ships released came to nothing.

Despite the loss of the two ships – which Hawkins estimated at £20,000 – a considerable profit had been made overall and so a second, larger expedition was planned. This second voyage departed from England in October 1564 and soon encountered opposition from the Portuguese and Spanish who had either been warned of or had experienced his rough-shod trading style. Nevertheless, slaves were acquired from Africa and the expedition – which included the queen's ship, the *Jesus of Lubeck* – set sail for the Spanish Main. On instructions from Spain the colonists refused to trade but Hawkins pressed it upon them by force of arms. Having disposed of his merchandise, Hawkins returned to England. His voyage was described as being 'profitable to the ventures, as also to the whole realm, in bringing home both gold, silver, pearls and other jewels [in] great store'.

In some ways the expedition had been too successful as the Spanish ambassador entreated Queen Elizabeth to restrain the piratical activities of her subjects. Although accepting the profits made from these voyages the queen was forced to put on an appearance of prohibiting them and Hawkins was forbidden to sail in Caribbean waters by order of the queen's council.

In 1567 Hawkins planned a third voyage and met no official hindrance, however; the queen's ship, the *Jesus of Lubeck*, again sailed with the expedition. Besides the *Jesus* there was the *Minion* and four other smaller ships including the *Judith*, commanded by Francis Drake, a cousin of Hawkins. As in his previous voyages Hawkins led his small flotilla to Sierra Leone where they found themselves engaged in a native war. Besides gaining 500 black slaves they plundered a number of Portuguese vessels, taking more than 70,000 gold pieces. Once again they sailed to the West Indies and sold their cargo by force, but on the point of returning to England in July 1568 things began to go wrong.

Sailing into the Mexican port of San Juan de Ulloa (near Veracruz) to complete their trade and sell off the remaining slaves, Hawkins was surprised by the arrival of a Spanish squadron of thirteen ships. Although the account is far from clear the English claimed that the Spanish treacherously opened fire on them without warning. Caught at a disadvantage in the confines of the harbour the English were easily overwhelmed and only Hawkins in the *Minion* and Drake's *Judith* managed to escape. The *Jesus* and the remaining ships were either destroyed or captured; the loss of treasure on the *Jesus* alone amounted to around £100,000. The two battered ships arrived in England in January 1569.

Hawkins was under a cloud, not only had he failed to bring back the treasure to repay the investors' handsome profits, he had so enraged the Spanish that they threatened war. Hawkins had hoped to fit out a further expedition to rescue his men and regain the treasure from San Juan de Ulloa but was prevented from doing so.

Deprived of his role as a sea adventurer Hawkins was soon engaged in intelligence work for England under the direction of Lord Burghley. Hawkins was able to help trick the gullible Spanish ambassador in London into a trap which exposed the Duke of Norfolk as a traitor who hoped to free the imprisoned Mary Queen of Scots and set her on the throne. Hawkins and an accomplice, George Fitzwilliam, convinced the Spanish that many people in England were prepared to rise up against Elizabeth in favour of a Catholic monarch. A letter was extracted from Mary outlining her plans and forwarded to the Spanish who took it as proof of Hawkins's and Fitzwilliam's good intentions. The Spanish sent £40,000 to the English conspirators to finance the plot, but which they kept for themselves. Hawkins's work led to the execution of Norfolk in 1572, and indirectly to that of Mary Queen of Scots in 1587.

Hawkins married the daughter of Benjamin Gonson, the treasurer of the navy, and continued his career in administration of the navy. In 1573 he succeeded his father-in-law as treasurer, which he added to his post of comptroller of the navy.

Through his experience as a seaman Hawkins encouraged a number of shipbuilding improvements that gave the English galleon a superiority over all its rivals. It was made more seaworthy by lowering the fore and after castles and faster by increasing the ship's length. Innovatory methods of sheathing the bows to guard against wood-rot and fouling by barnacles were made commonplace, and chain pumps and boarding netting were introduced. A number of new ships were commissioned, some of them at Chapman's shipyard in Deptford in which Hawkins was a partner. This led to charges of corruption but none was sustained. Certainly Haw-kins made considerable sums of money from his two key posts of comptroller and treasurer but what would be called corruption today was accepted practice in Elizabethan England. Hawkins attempted to improve the conditions of the common seaman, and in 1590, with Drake and Lord Howard of Effingham, he helped set up 'The Chest at Chatham', a fund for the relief of destitute sailors.

When the English fleet was mustered to oppose the Spanish Armada in 1588 Hawkins was given command of one of his new 'low-charged' ships, the *Victory*, and made a rear-admiral under Sir Francis Drake. Hawkins took an active part in the several engagements against the Armada from 21 July. He particularly distinguished himself in the fighting off the Isle of Wight and in recognition of his gallantry Hawkins was knighted aboard ship by the Lord High Admiral, Howard of Effingham, on 25 July.

In 1590 Hawkins led a small expedition to raid the Portuguese coast and, if possible, capture the plate-fleet bringing treasure from the colonies. Warned of the English plan, the Portuguese were prepared and Hawkins returned empty-handed.

In 1594 he joined Sir Francis Drake in an expedition fitted out for a raiding cruise in the West Indies. There were many delays and when the expedition sailed in August 1595 the Spanish authorities were well-informed. Too old for the rigours of an ocean voyage, Hawkins sickened and died of dysentery on 12 November off Puerto Rico.

Hawkins, along with Drake, Raleigh, Essex and Frobisher, was one of the greatest of the Elizabethan adventurers: his fine seamanship and navigational skills combined with his daring and brutal temperament made him an enemy to fear. But he was no mere adventurer; his conscientiousness and sustained work as comptroller and treasurer of the navy gave England a battle-fleet when it was most needed and earned him the title of the architect of the Royal Navy.

Queen Elizabeth's ship, the *Jesus of Lubeck*, was lost to the Spaniards during Hawkins's third voyage, when his force was attacked at San Juan de Ulloa.

Spanish Armada

FINEST HOUR OF THE ENGLISH FLEET

In the autumn of 1588 a bronze medallion was struck to commemorate the defeat of the Spanish Armada. Around its rim, in Latin and Hebrew, were the words: 'God blew and they were scattered.'

Although the sentiment smacked of false Protestant modesty in apportioning credit for the total defeat at sea of Catholic Spain, in essence it was true. The Spanish suffered relentless bad luck, the English employed solid, commonsense seamanship, and the result was England's greatest naval triumph prior to Trafalgar.

'I sent my ships to fight the English,' wrote Philip II of Spain disconsolately after the event, 'not the winds and waves.' It was a particularly bitter blow to the monarch who had set himself up as the Catholic Church's leading champion, and convinced himself that God would aid him in crushing Protestantism in the Netherlands and England, returning those countries to the 'true faith'.

Lord Howard of Effingham, whose constant harassment of the Armada led to the final victory. His avowed intention, to deny the Spaniards a landing place, was accomplished.

The Dutch Protestant cause was led by William the Silent, Prince of Orange and Stadholder. The Low Countries, including what is now Holland and Belgium, were Spanish dominions and Prince William served for a time as an adviser to Philip. In 1572, however – the year after Lepanto – William felt that his Protestant followers were strong enough to rise against Spanish domination. His struggle lasted for twelve years, until, in 1584, he was assassinated in Delft. Without William as leader, reasoned Philip, the Dutch resistance forces would break up; to make certain he sent a force of infantry – said to be the finest in Europe – under the Duke of Parma, to mop the Low Countries clean.

But across the North Sea was England, which had officially reverted to Catholicism under Philip's late wife Queen Mary only to turn from Rome again when her step-sister Elizabeth came to the throne in 1558. Philip resented England's apostasy even more than that of Holland and considered that with a bold, two-fisted attack he could conquer both countries and bring them back to the bosom of the Church.

He named his plan 'The Enterprise of England'. To carry it out he would employ Alvaro de Bazan, first Marquis of Santa Cruz, the skilled naval commander who had proved himself at Lepanto. Santa Cruz would take a huge battle-fleet, consisting of 550 ships and 100,000 men, up the Channel to rendezvous with the Duke of Parma's army on the coast of Holland. Together they would then sail into the Thames estuary and take London.

This 'felicissima, invencible' – 'most fortunate, invincible' Armada would be considerably larger in terms of both ships and men than anything England could throw against it. Furthermore, in Philip's eyes Santa Cruz had an edge on his English counterpart, Lord Charles Howard of Effingham, Lord High Admiral. Santa Cruz had a flair for naval command, whereas Lord Howard, although he took meticulous interest in his fleet, was not a natural seaman. Philip also had the impression that Howard would find it hard to control his brilliant but individualist officers; to begin with, Francis Drake and Martin Frobisher were at personal loggerheads, and Philip was advised that the rest – men like Raleigh, Hawkins, and Grenville – were much too idiosyncratic to act in concert. It was a profound misconception.

However it was the freebooting activity of Sir

Francis Drake which drew first blood against the Spanish fleet. In April 1587 Drake led a squadron of about thirty ships in a lightning attack on the port of Cadiz, where part of the Armada was being fitted out. He penetrated to the inner harbour and destroyed several vessels, including Santa Cruz's intended flagship, 'singeing' as he put it, 'the King of Spain's beard'. Then he sailed on to the Azores, and captured the biggest prize of his career, the galleon *San Felipe*. Drake's disruptive activities set the Spanish programme back considerably, which meant that Philip lost a great advantage, for the skilful admiral Santa Cruz died the following February, four months before the Armada was again fit to sail.

In his place Philip appointed his cousin, the Duke of Medina Sidonia. Sidonia was unquestionably brave – throughout the running fight up the North Sea he kept his own ship back to protect his weaker, fleeing vessels – but he had little concept of tactics and the rigidity of his command contributed a good deal to the Armada's defeat.

In May 1588 Philip considered that his forces were ready, though the numbers of both ships and men were lower than in his original estimate – 130 vessels including galleasses and a handful of galleys from his Mediterranean fleet – and 29,000 men, most of them soldiers. Sidonia's orders were to join Parma off the Dutch coast and decide with him on the best plan for the invasion. In the event of bad weather he was to capture the Isle of Wight and set up his headquarters there.

To oppose Spain, Lord Howard had a total of 129 ships large and small and 15,000 men, most of them experienced sailors. The Spaniards would attempt to grapple with and board the English ships, but Howard had no intention of engaging in hand-to-hand fighting; instead he would fight at cannon-shot range, 'playing long bowls' with the enemy. Ship for ship the two sides were fairly evenly matched; Howard's flagship, the fifty-five gun *Ark Royal*, was the same size as Sidonia's *San Martin* while Martin Frobisher's *Triumph* was one of the biggest vessels afloat. Drake in his *Revenge* and Hawkins in the *Victory* were ideally equipped for harassing tactics, and against the Spanish galleys and galleasses – out of their class in the choppy waters of the English Channel – Howard threw his 20-ton pinnaces, fast and handy.

By mid-May the English were disposed for battle. Lord Henry Seymour, with thirty-five ships, was prowling out from Dover, watching Calais for the arrival of Parma's army from the Low Countries. At Plymouth, Lord Howard and Vice-Admiral Drake had a mixed squadron of ninety-four vessels. In Drake's opinion attack was the best policy, if possible hitting the enemy off their own shore, but although he and Howard scouted around as far as the Bay of Biscay no enemy sail was sighted. In fact the Armada had sailed from Lisbon on 28 May, but had run into heavy weather and had put into Corunna for shelter and repairs twenty days later, where it stayed for a month.

Meanwhile the English were not without their troubles; Sir Walter Raleigh and Sir Richard Grenville had been put in charge of shore defences, but were having difficulty in getting sufficient stores and ammunition to the Channel ports in order to supply the fleet as it went along. The situation was still unsatisfactory when, on Friday 19 July, hilltop beacons signalled the sighting of the Armada sailing off the Lizard in a crescent-shaped formation before a strong westerly wind.

Most of Howard's ships were at anchor in Plymouth harbour. Drake, who was almost certainly not playing bowls at the time – the story was first recorded 150 years later – put to sea immediately with about thirty vessels, beating to windward before turning to come up behind the Spaniards to gain the weather gauge.

The defeat of the Spanish Armada, as depicted by a contemporary artist. The tempestuous weather shown here was an important factor in deciding the outcome.

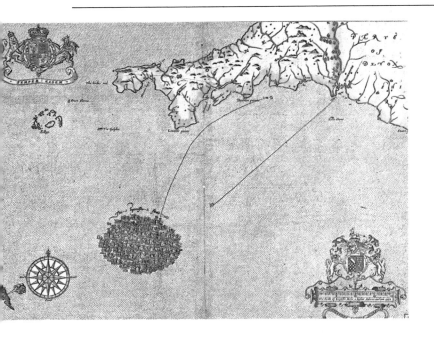

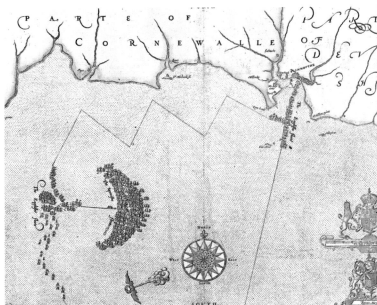

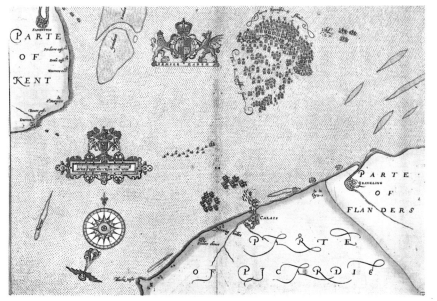

A series of maps showing the progress of the battle of the Armada. The 120 ships of the Spanish fleet gather off the Lizard (top). Howard outflanks the Spanish during the night and a shot from the *Disdain* opens battle (top right). The Armada then sails up-Channel and heads for the North Sea in disarray (above), with the English fleet in pursuit.

The following night Howard led his ships across the enemy front before tacking down to join Drake astern of them. On Sunday morning, 21 July, the English opened fire for the first time off the Eddystone, driving the Spaniards up the Channel before them like a flock of sheep. Sidonia, sticking exactly to instructions, kept his fleet in tight formation while the English divided into four squadrons under Howard, Hawkins, Frobisher and Drake to nip at his flanks and rear. As a result *Nuestra Señora del Rosario*, flagship of the Andalusian squadron under Don Pedro de Valdes, collided with a smaller vessel and lost her foremast and bowsprit. She surrendered to Drake on Sunday evening without a fight and was sent to Dartmouth with a prize crew aboard, while Drake took de Valdes with him aboard the *Revenge*.

For the next few days the exchange of fire between the two fleets was desultory and sporadic, though a lucky shot hit the magazine of the *San Salvadore* and she was captured and towed into Weymouth. On Tuesday the Spaniards, taking advantage of a slight shift in the wind, managed to hit at Frobisher's *Triumph*, but her massive build saved her from crippling damage. By Friday the wind had died almost completely and Howard hove-to off the Isle of Wight to replenish his ships with ammunition and food. He also held a staff conference with his officers, and using his authority knighted Frobisher and Hawkins, leaving the enemy to drift on up-Channel.

On Saturday 27 July, a freshening of the west-south-west wind enabled Sidonia to lay his fleet off Calais, where he anchored to wait anxiously for news of Parma, who was in fact at Bruges.

On the same day Howard's Plymouth-based fleet rendezvoused with the thirty-five vessels under Lord Henry Seymour and his lieutenant Sir William Winter off Dover, and as dusk fell over the Channel the English dropped anchor only 1km ($\frac{1}{2}$ mile) from the enemy, and to windward of them. Sidonia's force was thus caught in the classic trap – hostile ships upwind, and a hostile shore to the lee. Howard on the other hand decided to make the best possible use of his advantage by scattering and panicking the Spaniards before any aid could come from Parma. To this end he used fireships – the most fearsome weapon of the days of sail.

Eight vessels were prepared, their holds packed with gunpowder and their decks covered with pitch and wood-shavings. All their guns were loaded, so that the heat would touch them off. They were lined up to head straight for the enemy and then, with their whipstaff steering lashed steady and mainsails set, torches were tossed into them and their stern mooring lines cut.

Eight blazing hulks bearing down on them in the darkness caused total panic among the Spanish. Anchor cables were cut and they began to claw desperately away from the lee shore. The giant *San Lorenzo* was too unwieldy to handle and grounded herself on Calais Bar while her companions struggled to escape, pounded to seaward by the English and from the coast by a small flotilla of Dutch rebel ships which had belatedly joined the fight. Then came Sidonia's only piece of luck; the wind backed to the south-east and he ran for the North Sea.

Even then he was hard pressed. His victuals and ammunition were running low, and there was now no chance of meeting Parma to seek aid, much less to push ahead with the 'Enterprise of England'. Beating to windward down-Channel was impossible because of Lord Seymour's squadron, which was patrolling off Dover Roads.

His only chance, with Howard and Drake at his back – they had closed their range of fire and were now cheekily sniping at leisure – was to reach, with the wind on his port side, up the North Sea, beat round the Scottish headland and reach again down the west coast of Ireland to home. Drake was jubilant. 'We have them before us,' he wrote, 'and mind with the Grace of God to wrestle a fall with them. There never was anything pleased me better than seeing the enemy flying northwards.'

Howard and Drake pursued the fleeing Spaniards as far as Newcastle. There, confident that the Armada was beaten, most of the English fleet put in to revictual, while a small group followed it, still firing, as far as the Firth of Forth. After that only the small scouting pinnaces remained on the tails of the staggering enemy. When they rounded Cape Wrath the English knew that the elements were against the Armada with a vengeance, and turned away. A screaming, westerly gale was blowing; subsequently it flung the remaining Spanish ships

onto the rocks of the Scottish mainland, the Outer Hebrides, and the Irish coasts of Donegal, Sligo, Connaught and Galway. One ship was driven around again to end up at Bolt Head in Devon. The inhabitants of the Scottish Isles and Ireland were neutral in their disregard for outsiders; they killed the shipwrecked mariners that came ashore and stripped the beached vessels to their bare ribs.

Twenty-five Spanish ships were lost in this way, and altogether sixty-four ships and 10,000 men of the Armada failed to return to Spain. Sidonia wrote an apologetic letter to Philip. 'The troubles and miseries we have suffered cannot be described to your Majesty. They have been greater than have ever been seen in any voyage before.'

The Armada had a profound effect, not only in England but throughout Europe. Suddenly England became a maritime power to be reckoned with, the trade of the world within her grasp. Within twelve years of the Armada she had founded her East India Company, with ships strong enough to take on the Dutch and the Portuguese in the East. She began, slowly, to colonize the west coast of Africa, the West Indies and North America.

Queen Elizabeth I had good reason to compose a 'Songe of Thanksgiving' for England's unexpected victory over the Armada. It includes, again with untypical modesty but a healthy regard for the truth, a tribute to the real hero of the occasion: 'He made the winds and waters rise to scatter all my enemies . . .'.

ABOVE Elizabeth I, who personified the spirit of defiance which enabled the small English force to challenge the might of Spain. This is known as the 'Armada' portrait.

BELOW LEFT Fireships were used by the English against the Armada off Calais Roads. Old vessels were filled with gunpowder, pitch and tar, and all their guns loaded. They were then set alight and released upwind of the enemy.

Flores

BIRTH OF A LEGEND

Sir Richard Grenville, who sailed for the Azores in April 1591 aboard the *Revenge* as vice-admiral to Lord Thomas Howard, in an attempt to intercept the Spanish plate-fleet.

Better known as the last fight of the *Revenge*, the battle of Flores on 31 August 1591 was one of the most one-sided defeats in the history of the English navy. The action formed the last of a chapter of incidents which ruined England's over-ambitious attempt to wage war against Spanish commerce with grossly inadequate means.

There was no question of an all-out English naval offensive against Spain in 1589. The cost of sending the fleet of 1588 to sea had all but ruined the nation, and the exchequer could only bear the cost of limited expeditions. Sir John Hawkins, mastermind of the new navy and its broadside-armed galleons, opposed the resumption of such costly exercises as raids on the Spanish Main or Panama. He favoured stationing a small battle-fleet between Spain and the Azores and periodically relieving it at sea to make it a permanent menace. Its mission should be to intercept the plate-fleets which carried the wealth of the New World across the Atlantic to Spain. The yearly sailing of these plate-fleets was the regular transfusion of wealth which kept Spain's fleets and armies in being; if they could be stopped, the Spanish war effort would collapse.

Hawkins failed to get this plan accepted in 1589 – the year in which Spain, still counting the cost of the Armada's defeat, was unable to send any fleet to sea. Instead Drake headed an abortive expedition aimed at raising the Portuguese against their Spanish masters. The Portuguese expedition was more than a humiliating failure: it cost England about 8000 soldiers. It also allowed the 1589 plate-fleet to get through to Spain, and the rebuilding of the Spanish fleet commenced in earnest.

The plate-fleet of 1589 did not, however, pass unmolested. The Earl of Cumberland, with a solitary Queen's Ship and a handful of privateers, forced it to shelter at Terceira in the Azores until the English crews reached the end of their endurance and were forced to head for home. Cumberland also captured a Spanish plate-ship (subsequently wrecked off the English coast) valued at £100,000. After the fiasco in Portugal, Hawkins's scheme for striking at Spain's economic lifeline was belatedly adopted.

Hopes for success in 1590 were dashed by reports that a Spanish force was preparing to sail for Brittany, which kept Hawkins's squadron in home waters and allowed the first Spanish plate-fleet to pass in safety. By the time Sir Martin Frobisher's squadron arrived off the Azores in June more treasure-ships had got through. Frobisher patrolled the Azores for four months before being relieved by Hawkins, who was recalled in late October because of a revival of the Brittany rumour.

Philip II of Spain reacted to this English activity by ordering a suspension of bullion shipment until the second half of 1591, making the safe arrival of this double convoy vital to Spain's continuation of the war. Lord Thomas Howard sailed for the Azores in April 1591 with six of the best ships in the English navy, with Sir Richard Grenville as vice-admiral in the *Revenge*. Meanwhile, the Earl of Cumberland patrolled the Spanish coast with one ship. The Spanish commander Alonso de Bazan was, however, preparing to guarantee the safe arrival of the plate-fleet with a massive force of twenty large and thirty-five smaller new fighting ships.

Howard and Grenville spent four-and-a-half weary months off the Azores waiting for the plate-fleet to turn up. By the end of August the ships were foul within and without and sickness was mounting, while supplies were nearly exhausted. Howard's squadron was at anchor off the northern end of Flores, changing the filthy ballast in the ships, refilling casks and resting the sick ashore, when a fast pinnace arrived from Cumberland on the Spanish coast. Bazan was at sea in overwhelming strength, while the English squadron was in the worst possible state to counter him.

With only a few hours' warning of his peril, Howard did extraordinarily well to get ready for sea with his weary and undermanned crews. As Bazan came in downwind from the east, the English were hauling off to the north-east, with Grenville, as vice-admiral, duly bringing up the rear in *Revenge*. Almost certainly her sailing qualities had been spoiled by the incomplete replacement of her

ballast, for she was the only English ship that failed to get clear. The leading Spanish ships drove across Grenville's bows, cutting him off and surrounding him. Facing odds of at least four to one, Howard correctly continued his retreat.

Raleigh's well-known poem, 'Report of the Truth of the Fight About the Isles of Azores', which records the *Revenge*'s epic last action, with Grenville finally dying on the Spanish flagship's deck, should be read as patriotic propaganda; no first-hand account of the action has survived. It lasted some fifteen hours, with *Revenge* sinking two of her assailants and crippling many more, only surrendering when she was a defenceless wreck. Tactically, Flores was a superb achievement; strategically it was a clear-cut defeat. Though Howard escaped, the plate-fleet of 1591 reached Spain safely.

An artist's impression of the last fight of the *Revenge*, with Grenville in the foreground. Although immortalized by Raleigh's poem, the precise details of the engagement remain obscure.

PART FOUR

The Ship-of-the-Line

The ship-of-the-line dominated European naval affairs for nearly three centuries, right up to the reign of Queen Victoria. It was a curiously British institution, and was recognized as such by John Ruskin in 1856, when steam and iron were rapidly beginning to replace sail and timber. In his *Harbours of England* he writes:

Take it all in all, a ship of the line is the most honourable thing that man, as a gregarious animal, has ever produced. By himself, unhelped, he can do better things . . . poems and pictures . . . but as a being living in flocks . . . the ship of the line is his first work. Into that he has put . . . as much human patience, common sense, forethought, experimental philosophy, self-control, habits of order and obedience, thoroughly wrought handwork, defiance of brute elements, careless courage, careful patriotism, and calm expectation of the judgment of God, as can well be put into a space of 300 feet long by 80 broad. And I am thankful to

have lived in an age when I could see this thing so done.

Between 1650 and 1850 naval warfare was conditioned by certain technical factors, and by the increasing dominance of the Royal Navy. The technical factors were basically the development of ships firing broadsides with heavy smooth-bore cannon. The largest of these vessels became known as ships-of-the-line, and naval tactics were designed to extract the maximum effect from these broad-sides by fighting in line.

A formalization of tactics took place over a number of years, until, by the mid-eighteenth century, the 'Fighting Instructions' of the Royal Navy, for example, gave commanders very little scope for innovation. Then, towards the end of the century, tactics became rather less rigid, and by the battle of Trafalgar, Nelson was able to encompass the complete destruction of an enemy fleet by sailing across the line and accepting the loss of the conventional formation. By 1850, too, new tech-

This section of a first-rate ship-of-the-line shows its top three decks packed with guns. The orlop deck below was used for general storage, including the anchor cable lockers and powder magazines, as well as for junior officers' cabins.

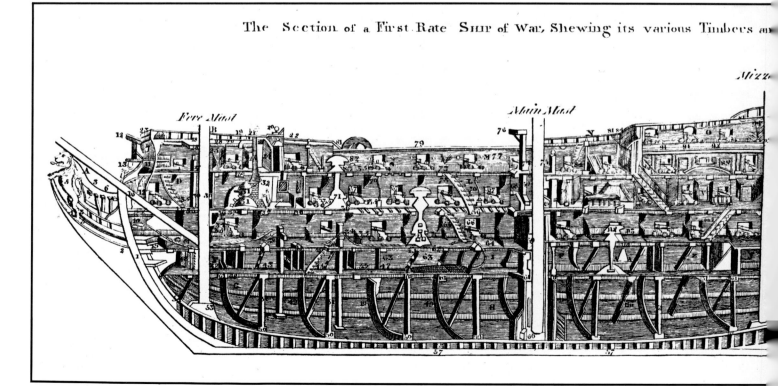

The Section of a First-Rate Ship of War, Shewing its various Timbers a[n]

Fore Mast

Main Mast

Mizz[en]

nical developments were already making the traditional style of warfare outdated. Explosive shells could wreak terrible havoc, and the ironclad was about to appear on the scene.

Apart from the progress of technology, the main feature of naval warfare from 1650 to 1850 was the power of the British navy. From 1649, under Cromwell, the navy was reorganized and a programme of shipbuilding undertaken. Under Robert Blake, the English fleet acquitted itself well in the First Dutch War, then after two more wars with the Dutch and the 'Glorious Revolution' of 1688 began more than a century of close rivalry with France. During the 1690s, England struggled to prevent French invasions of Ireland, but the battle of Barfleur in 1692 was a decisive victory against the French fleet.

During the War of Spanish Succession (1701–14) England extended her naval power, and obtained bases in the Mediterranean (including the priceless asset of Gibraltar) and for the rest of the eighteenth century maintained an ascendancy over the French. Competition was extended from Europe to the Americas and to colonies and trading centres in the Far East. England's supremacy was only really threatened when the fleets of the other continental naval powers – the Dutch or the Spanish, for example – were united with the French fleet. Such an alliance contributed powerfully to England's loss of the American colonies, and during the French conquests of the 1790s and 1800s, the possibility of such an anti-English coalition threatened several

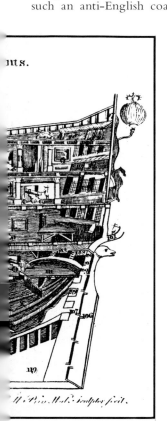

times, and was only dispersed after the battle of Trafalgar. Trafalgar set the seal on the Royal Navy's successes over a century and a half; the aggressive spirit of her captains, the sound training of the men, and the constant expectation of success laid the foundations of a century of unquestioned maritime supremacy from Trafalgar in 1805 to the launching of the *Dreadnought* in 1906.

Naval power was important too in the Baltic Sea, where Swedish dominance was eroded early in the seventeenth century by the Russian victory at the battle of Hangö in a battle fought between fleets of galleys. Complete Russian domination of the eastern Baltic was prevented, however, by the battle of Svenskund, in which the Swedes were triumphant.

During the late seventeenth and early eighteenth centuries, privateering flourished – especially in the West Indies – as trade grew, and small-scale raiders often made contributions to the major wars. The French made particular use of privateers, licensed by letter of marque, to harass English commerce. But the privateer was no longer the potential naval commander he had been in Drake's day; the national navy, not the individual enterprise, now dominated warfare.

The first ship to have gunports cut the whole length of her side was the *Henry Grace à Dieu*, launched in

A model of a seventeenth-century Dutch third-rate warship with two decks holding sixty-four guns. Note the pronounced curve of the upper deck, a feature that was to level out over the next hundred years.

England in 1514, but although she carried heavy guns, she was no more than the first step along the road towards the ship-of-the-line. Her guns had no wheeled carriages to run them out after reloading and so they could be fired only infrequently in battle. The wheeled gun carriage was introduced in about 1580 and by then the guns were 'breeched' to the ship's side with rope and tackle to absorb the recoil and facilitate reloading. Lidded gunports were introduced early in the sixteenth century after the disaster of Henry VIII's 600-ton flagship *Mary Rose*. She was refitted with twenty heavy guns on her lower deck in 1536, but nine years later she sank off Portsmouth when sailing to meet the French fleet. She heeled suddenly in a squall and the sea entered her open gunports. (In 1982 she was raised from the sea-bed and is now preserved in a museum.)

Most warships of this time were still too small to be considered as true ships-of-the-line, which, strictly speaking, only came into being with the invention of the naval tactic of the line-of-battle in the 1660s. However, the basic sixteenth-century warship design was so little changed over the years that a seaman serving in Drake's 500-ton flagship *Revenge* would have easily adapted to performing his duties in, for example, Nelson's 2100-ton *Victory*.

The *Royal Prince*, built in England in 1610, carrying fifty-five guns and with a tonnage of 1330, came closer to the definition. It has been claimed

that she was the first three-decked warship in the world, but she carried most of her guns on only two covered decks, the remainder being mounted on the upper deck. However, when *Sovereign of the Seas* was launched twenty-seven years later, she carried her hundred guns on three covered gun-decks. She was the first true three-decker and the first real ship-of-the-line.

Until the Anglo-Dutch wars of the mid-seventeenth century, battle at sea was a disorganized *mêlée*, with virtually no control by the admirals over their ships. Signalling was still very much in its infancy and individual captains of ships fought their actions as they thought fit. The overriding aim was to get as close to an enemy as possible and engage him in a gun duel, irrespective of the movements of other ships. During these wars, however, fleets of eighty, ninety or a hundred ships were commonplace and so unwieldy a mass called for some sort of organization. So a fleet was divided into squadrons and with this subdivision came the birth of naval tactics. At the Armada, Lord Howard had divided his fleet into four squadrons, but by the early seventeenth century a division into three squadrons, each under an admiral, was considered most efficient. By 1617 the three were denoted by coloured flags – red, white, and blue, in order of seniority – the admiral commanding the Red squadron, the vice-admiral White, and the rear-admiral Blue. A few years later, however, with the

One of the best-known ships-of-the-line was Nelson's *Victory*, which served at sea between 1765 and 1815. She was a first rate of 100 guns and is now preserved at Portsmouth Dockyard, England.

increase in size of the navy, each squadron was again divided into three and flag officers appointed to each division.

The lowest squadron therefore was commanded by an admiral of the Blue, with a vice-admiral of the Blue and rear-admiral of the Blue immediately under him. The rear-admiral of the Blue was the most junior flag officer in the fleet, but on promotion became successively rear-admiral of the White, then rear-admiral of the Red, vice-admiral of the Blue, vice-admiral of the White, and so on through the colours and ranks. The senior admiral of the Red was known as 'admiral of the fleet', flying the Royal Standard (replaced at the end of the seventeenth century by the Union Flag) at the mainmast head to signify his rank.

Generally speaking this chain of command worked extremely well, although in 1798 the detachment of Nelson – then a rear-admiral of the Blue and thus one of the most junior flag officers in the fleet – to command the elite 'roving' squadron which eventually trapped the French at the Nile, caused a great deal of jealousy.

Since all ships carried their guns along the ships' sides to fire out of gunports, and individual guns could not be trained to fire fore or aft, it followed that they could only hit an enemy ship when sailing parallel to her. With the realization that a fleet was a far more powerful weapon of battle, acting in concert, than the total of its individual ships, the line-of-battle formation became the prime factor in naval action. With ships sailing in line, in close formation so that each was able to support her neighbours, and the whole fleet controlled by the squadron admirals, the sailing warship became a formidable weapon indeed.

During the hundred years which followed the launch of *Sovereign of the Seas*, ships were built not only to larger specifications, but to a more uniform design. It needed no great stretch of the imagination to realize that a squadron of ships of the same size and equal sailing qualities was very much easier to control in battle – and particularly in the approach to battle – than a squadron of ships of different sizes. So a system of 'rating' ships was introduced, not strictly according to size but depending on the number of guns they carried, which approximated to much the same thing. Six rates were adopted in Britain. Ships of the first rate carried a hundred guns or more, ships of the second rate eighty to ninety-eight guns, ships of the third rate sixty to seventy-four guns, ships of the fourth rate forty-four to fifty-six guns, ships of the fifth rate thirty to forty guns, and those of the sixth twenty-four to twenty-eight guns. The ratings of all other maritime nations followed the British ratings very closely.

Only ships of the first three ratings were considered powerful enough to take a place in the line-of-battle and it was these that were officially

The British HMS *Cambridge* was dismasted by shore batteries during the attack on Havana in 1762. Solid shot could severely disable a vessel, but rarely sink it.

designated as ships-of-the-line. In the smaller fleets, ships of the fourth rate also fought in the battle line and occasionally did so in the major fleets. For instance in the battle of the Nile in 1798 the British fourth-rate *Leander* anchored herself in a gap in the French line, between the second-rate *Franklin* and the third-rate *Peuple Souverain* and raked them both with her broadsides. Generally ships of the fourth rate were known as cruisers and those of the fifth and sixth rates as frigates. It was a convention of naval warfare in the days of sail, recognized by most countries, that a ship-of-the-line did not engage a frigate unless the frigate opened fire first.

The guns carried by ships of the line ranged from 42-pounders (firing a 19-kg ball), mounted on the lower gun-deck, to 12-pounders (firing a 5.5kg ball), with a few lighter guns, carried on the upper deck and poop. All guns were basically inefficient because of what was known as 'windage', or the difference between the diameter of the ball and the bore of the gun. A loose-fitting ball, on the other hand, did not cause too much wear on the inside of the barrel. The maximum range of a 42-pounder was about 1500m (1600yd) but the hitting range, if the shot was not to bounce harmlessly off the

enemy's side, was no more than half that distance. But almost all admirals and captains preferred to fight at much closer range, and the favourite distance at which British and Dutch captains engaged was what was known as 'half pistol shot' at about 55m (60yd). French and Spanish captains usually tried to engage at greater distances in order to fire at masts and rigging and so disable rather than sink the foe.

A first-rate ship of the line of the eighteenth century had a tonnage of about 2000 and carried a crew of about 850 men. She was about 60m (200ft) long on her gun-deck, with a keel length of about 48m (160ft) and a beam of 17m (55ft). By the nineteenth century she had grown to about 2600 tons, mainly to accommodate larger guns. One of these was the carronade, the invention of the Carron Iron Founding and Shipping Company of Falkirk, which had supplied standard cannon for the British navy for many years. The carronade was a short-barrelled gun with a wide bore, strengthened at the breech so that it could fire a massive ball powerfully over a short range; ideally suited, in fact, for 'yardarm to yardarm' tactics.

Although the 42-pounder was still the largest gun

Isaac Sailmaker's painting shows HMS *Britannia*, built at Chatham in 1682 and rebuilt there eighteen years later. She carried 100 guns.

carried, except for the upper-deck carronades which fired a 68-pound (30-kg) shot (carronades were not counted as guns when a ship was rated), the other batteries were of 32-pounders and 18-pounders instead of the original 24-pounders and 12-pounders. A first rate's sides were of oak 55cm (22in) thick, capable of keeping out all but the heaviest shot fired against her at very close range. She was an immensely powerful engine of war, but she had one weak spot – her unprotected stern with its rows of cabin windows. There was no cross bulkhead to protect the length of the decks, and it was the supreme tactic of naval battle to manoeuvre a ship across the stern of an enemy and pour in broadsides. These, virtually unhindered, thundered down the whole length of the gun-decks, dismounting the guns and decimating the tightly packed gun crews.

Another type of ship that was to have a great impact on naval warfare in the eighteenth century was the frigate, which although a 'rated' ship, was in a class of its own. The term 'frigate' (*frigata, fregatta, frégate*) originated in the Mediterranean, where it described a type of slim, lightly built oared vessel used as a tender to larger craft or for carrying despatches. By the end of the sixteenth century the Spaniards were using the term to describe the light sailing craft employed between the mother country and their American colonies, and by the early seventeenth century the name had spread northwards to describe the swift and handy privateer vessels which sailed from Dunkirk and Ostend to prey on merchant shipping – these were sailing vessels, but they could and did use oars through ports cut in the sides of the hull. What seems to have happened then, although the record is not clear, is that the maritime nations built vessels copied from the lines of the Dunkirkers, and these took the name frigates. They were probably sharper-ended than contemporary warships with a greater length-to-breadth ratio for speed under oars – in any case the term appears to have been associated with swiftness.

The first British men-of-war described as frigates were built in 1646. They were just under 400 tons with a single deck of guns and above this a short forecastle-deck and a quarter-deck for working the rigging, with an open waist in between. They had oarports cut between the gunports. Shortly after mid-century another class of frigates was built with two complete gun-decks mounting nine or ten light carriage guns each side – making a total of forty carriage guns – and retaining a row of oarports between the lower gunports. From this definition the term seems to have spread to embrace any type of sailing warship, however large or small and whether oared or not. The great English naval administrator, Samuel Pepys, described the French *Superbe* of the 1660s as follows: 'she was forty foot broad, carried seventy-four guns and six months' provisions and but two and a half [gun] decks. Our frigates, being narrower, could not stow so much provisions, nor carry their guns so far from the water.' And in the accounts which have come down from the Anglo-Dutch wars of this century even the smallest fighting ships mounting as few as eight guns – none with a larger shot than 1.5kg (3½lb) – are referred to as frigates.

At the same time there were merchant vessels which were also known as frigates. While these

Some nineteenth-century ships-of-the-line were powered by steam as well as sail. Planking had by then supplanted galleries and windows on the stern of many such ships.

A British frigate, the armament of which included 32-pounder carronades on the quarter- and forecastle-decks, in addition to its main 18-pounder cannon.

probably started in the same way as the warships by being a swifter type than the typical broad merchantmen of the period, by the eighteenth century they were a specific build of ship. The term had then become purely technical and referred to a vessel with a single flush deck and short, raised forecastle and quarter-deck above – the same arrangement as the earliest frigates of war – with a particular hull form and type of counter stern beneath the decorated stern gallery.

The more general use of the term frigate in the eighteenth century was to describe a particular class of ship-rigged fighting vessel with a single main gun-deck which was not intended to fight as a part of the battle-fleet. This distinction between frigates and 'battleships' originated during the Anglo-Dutch wars. Before that time naval battles had taken the form of *mêlées* between loose groupings of ships of all sizes and power, which knew no organization save keeping close to their own squadron flagship. During the Second Dutch War 1665–7) this began to give way to what became a highly organized formation known as 'line-of-battle', in which all the squadrons of a fleet formed in one long line of ships, offering their broadside fire to the enemy. At the same time the number of large and powerful ships increased and so the less powerful vessels, which constituted weak links in the chain, were left out of the 'line' and ordered to take station 'on the broadside of the Admiral away from the enemy' (English 'Fighting Instructions', 1665). By this time the rating system had been instituted, so although the term frigate was applied loosely to

most warships at this period, the distinction between the duties of ships-of-the-line and fifth and sixth rates had begun.

By the early eighteenth century fifth rates carried forty to forty-four guns on two main battery decks, and the only single-gun-deck class – and thus the forerunners of what is always regarded as the true frigate – were the twenty-four-gun sixth rates. These vessels of some 500 tons measurement with a keel approaching 30m (100ft) long, had a main battery of ten 9-pounder guns (firing a 4kg ball). Below the main battery deck there was one small gunport each side, about mid-length, where an additional 9-pounder was mounted, and at the level of the lower sill of this port, just above sea level, a row of oarports extended from bow to stern. In addition to the guns these vessels were rated to carry, there were a number of light $\frac{1}{2}$- or 1-pounders mounted as swivels atop stout fire posts rising above the quarter-deck side rails and sometimes light carriage guns were mounted forwards of the two guns which the 'establishment' allotted to the quarter-deck. Consequently the gun rating of a frigate was seldom an absolute guide to her strength – a situation which gave rise to some confusion in the accounts of engagements between frigates, as each side was apt to give the 'establishment' gun rating of their own vessel, but the actual number of guns carried by the enemy. These frigates were ship-rigged in the manner of their time, that is to say with a course and deep topsail and usually a topgallantsail on both fore and mainmasts, a triangular lateen sail – shortly changed to a gaff 'driver' –

on the mizen with a topsail and topgallantsail above. The spritsail below the bowsprit and sprit topsail above it disappeared with the introduction of the jib in 1705, and were completely obsolete even in the largest ships by 1720.

During the course of the century the small sixth rate was built larger, mounted heavier guns and a greater number of them and so moved up into the fifth-rate class, displacing the earlier two-decked fifth rates which were quite obsolete, being far too short, narrow and high to be good sailers or sea-boats. It is this single-deck fifth rate which is the historic frigate of the sailing era.

While this evolution in size can be seen operating gradually from the beginning of the eighteenth century in English sixth rates – with longer quarter-decks which extended farther over the waist to the mainmast and heavier carriage guns in increasing numbers – it was the French with their smaller fleet who continued to build improved designs in the second half of the century. The French pushed up the size of sixth rates in a succession of large steps, for as the English captured each improved ship, they took a draught of her lines and built copies. So it was that while the English entered the Anglo-French war (1793–1815) with almost all their frigates of twenty-four, twenty-eight or thirty-two guns, with main batteries of 12-pounders, they came out of the wars with an overwhelming number of largely French-inspired thirty-six and thirty-eight-gun frigates with main batteries of 18-pounders, and there were scarcely any smaller classes.

A typical thirty-eight gun, 18-pounder fifth rate

in the heyday of the frigate was 45m (150ft) in length on the waterline, 55m (182ft) from bulkhead to stern rail, with a beam of 12m (40ft). This compared with dimensions of 54m (180ft) on the waterline by 15m (49ft) beam for the most numerous class of 'battleship', the seventy-four-gun third rate. The frigate had fifteen gunports on each side of her main deck – the uppermost continuous deck – only fourteen of which actually mounted guns. Above this a long quarter-deck extended to some 1.5m (5ft) forward of the mainmast which was stepped just abaft of the mid-length position. From this quarter-deck two 'gangways' – earlier known as 'gangboards' – extended down each side of the ship to join the forecastle-deck, which had grown to some 14m (45ft) in length. The result was virtually an upper deck for working the ship above the main battery, with a wide hatch over the waist, where spare timbers, spars and the ship's boats were stowed.

In the new frigate, both quarter-deck and forecastle-deck had solid timber bulwarks in place of the open posts and rails on earlier eighteenth-century frigates. Ports were cut in these, usually for seven guns a side on the quarter-deck, four on the forecastle-deck and 'chase' ports faced ahead and astern. Between forecastle and quarter-deck bulwarks, along the sides of the gangways, there were hammock nettings where the men stowed their hammocks by day and, in conjunction with the solid bulwarks topped by hammock rails, these provided a musket-proof parapet all round the ship.

The usual upper battery of these frigates, at least

Fifth-or sixth-rate ships such as the one depicted here were known as frigates and judged too lightly armed to join the line-of-battle. They were used for reconnaissance and fleet communications.

in British service, consisted mainly of 32-pounder carronades, with 9- or 6-pounder cannon as chase guns and a swivel or two. The extreme shortness and lightness of the carronades made it possible for captains to mount many more than 'establishment', and the gun ratings at the end of the eighteenth century, when the carronade was at the height of its popularity, were even more confusing than they had been earlier. For instance a typical thirty-eight-gun frigate might carry twenty-eight long 18-pounders on the main deck, fourteen to sixteen 32-pounder carronades on the quarter-deck and forecastle, together with two long 9-pounder chase cannon and one 12-pounder carronade, making forty-seven sizable weapons without counting any swivels or boat guns.

Frigates were rigged on the same plan as ships-of-the-line and, as they were very nearly as long, it was impossible to tell a frigate from a battleship when hull down over the horizon, as it was not until the battleship's second row of gunports in the hull came into view that the difference became apparent. With a sail area almost as large, and a considerably lighter and slimmer hull, a frigate could outrun any battleship and so the larger classes were very seldom obliged to take on any vessel of superior force.

The complement of a British thirty-eight-gun frigate was some 280 souls – the precise number depended on the renown of the captain and the service on which the ship was engaged. In general French and American frigates carried a larger crew than this, sometimes having a hundred more men. The sailors and boys slung their hammocks at the forward end of the deck below the main battery deck – which was known as the berth deck. Aft of them, around the main hatch and just forward of the mainmast, where the arms rack and pumps were situated, was berthing space for the detachment of marines. Further aft was the 'steerage' where midshipmen, clerks and warrant officers lived. At the extreme stern on this level was the 'gun-room' which was flanked by small cubicles for the lieutenants and marine officer. By comparison with these cramped, dark and musty quarters, the captain had spacious and well-lit accommodation at the after

end of the battery deck, which he shared with four cannon. His great cabin with stern windows, sleeping cabin, and office, all of which occupied about half the area under the quarter-deck, was partitioned off by light bulkheads, which were stored below when preparing for action so that the battery deck was clear from stem to stern.

The main powder magazine and adjoining cartridge-filling room were situated on the lowermost, or orlop, deck, way below the waterline by the foot of the foremast. There was another magazine aft beneath the steerage and nearby was the spirit room. Other store rooms with sufficient stocks to support the crew for a six-month cruise were on the orlop deck and amidships below the main hatch was a great sail room.

The duties of a frigate can be broadly defined as commerce protection, commerce destruction and reconnaissance, the emphasis depending upon the strategy of the power concerned. During the great Anglo-French wars the French emphasis was on commerce destruction and the British on commerce protection. The overall strategy of the British, as overwhelmingly the stronger naval power, was to blockade the French fleets in their harbours with British fleets riding the storms in the offing. This strategy neutralized the heavy enemy ships and left the frigates free to protect trade from enemy frigates, corvettes and privateers. They were helped in this task by many lesser warships like gun brigs and sloops, but it was the frigates' powers of sailing and formidable batteries which provided the stiffening and, in the absence of enemy battleships on the oceans, the frigates themselves became, in effect, the capital ships.

The main ways in which they were used to protect commerce was as convoy escorts – often reinforced by a ship-of-the-line on the way to or from a foreign station – and by patrolling those areas where merchant ships congregated. These patrols were carried out by single ships, pairs or even in important terminal areas by small squadrons. When cruising in this manner, frigates naturally combined trade protection with offensive action against enemy shipping. Indeed the prize

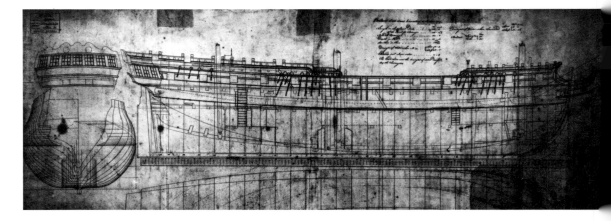

The original plans to which the Royal Navy's frigate *Brilliant* was built in 1757. Frigates could outrun ships-of-the-line due to their lighter and slimmer hulls.

money to be gained from captures often outweighed considerations of commerce protection and many frigate captains made small fortunes for themselves and large fortunes for the admirals commanding their station, who took a percentage of the prize money. The independence and possibilities of a quick fortune which frigate captains enjoyed made them glamorous figures by comparison with captains of battleships who spent a great deal of time sailing or blockading in squadrons and battle-fleets.

However, some frigates were attached to battle-fleets to act as scouts, to keep close watch on a blockaded enemy in order to report any movements to more distant blockaders, to maintain contact between fleets, to carry despatches and in action to tow off damaged ships and rescue survivors. With these and other duties for which fast, handy and powerful warships were needed, it is not surprising that frigates were the most numerous class of rated vessel in the British fleet. In 1812, for instance, the Royal Navy had at sea 126 battleships, the great majority being third rates, and 145 frigates, most of them fifth rates. The French, with little organized commerce to protect by that time and a different battle-fleet strategy, had more battleships than frigates in their naval armoury.

The final development of the frigate during the war period came from the United States. In 1797 the US navy launched three forty-four-gun frigates which were as long and stoutly-built, but not quite so broad as ships-of-the-line. They mounted fifteen 24-pounder cannon each side of their battery deck and above them on each side twelve 32-pounder carronades. These great ships were intended to be so superior to European frigates 'that if assailed by numbers they would always be able to lead ahead; that they could never be obliged to go into action but on their own terms, except in a calm, and that in heavy weather they would be capable of engaging double-decked ships' (US Secretary of War, 1796). When America entered the war against Britain there were three encounters between one of these 'forty-fours' and a British 18-pounder frigate and on each occasion the American frigate's superiority was demonstrated convincingly.

During the whole of the eighteenth century – the heyday of the ship-of-the-line and frigate – remarkably few changes were made to the basic three-masted rig. The principal ones were that a topgallant mast was added to the mizen, with a gaff 'spanker' or 'driver' replacing the lateen mizen sail of the galleon, and the bowsprit was extended by adding a jibboom and flying jibboom so that more headsails could be carried. More fore and aft

staysails were added between the masts, to improve the ships' sailing abilities to windward and while reaching (with the wind on the beam).

For vessels below the rate of frigate and for 'special-duty' vessels alternative rigs were adopted. The brig-of-war – a light fast ship square-rigged on two masts – enjoyed a vogue in both Europe and America during the latter half of the century, and the Americans in particular began to use two-masted topsail schooners for coastal patrols. The French invented the 'bomb' vessel, which was improved by the British and used fairly extensively against shore emplacements – particularly at the battle of Copenhagen. The 'bomb' was usually ketch-rigged, having only a main and mizen mast, and was about 21m (70ft) long and of about 200 tons burden. The wide foredeck, specially strengthened, carried one or two mortars which fired either massive ball, shrapnel, or incendiary devices. Towards the end of the century, the British developed even more devastating ship-rigged 'bombs'.

Among coastal vessels the *chasse-marée*, a three-masted lugger developed from a fishing boat design and carrying a 9-pound 'Long Tom' bow-chaser was used by both the French and the British, but even more efficient was the fore-and-aft rigged cutter, armed similarly to the *chasse-marée* and brought to its finest pitch in the Bristol Channel pilot cutter design.

Carronades were carried on the spar deck of USS *Constitution* in addition to the frigate's usual armament of 24-pounder cannon.

Marten Harpertszoon Tromp

1597–1653

One of the brightest names from the 'heroic age' of the Dutch navy in the seventeenth century, Marten Harpertszoon Tromp belongs to the category of great naval commanders destined from birth for a career at sea. Born at Den Briel near Rotterdam in 1597, Marten Tromp was taken to sea as a boy by his father, a captain in the 'Sea Beggars' – the embryo navy of Dutch resistance fighters which spearheaded the Protestant Dutch in the war of liberation against their Spanish overlords.

Marten Tromp first saw action at the remarkably early age of ten, when his father's ship sailed with Jacob van Heemskerk to destroy a Spanish fleet in Gibraltar Bay. In 1609, however, Tromp's father was killed and his ship taken in an action with an English privateer. Marten Tromp was sold as a slave to the Barbary pirates and spent three years as a captive before he managed to escape. When he did, it was hardly surprising that his next three years of naval service were with the Dutch warships and privateers struggling to put down piracy in the Mediterranean. The early seventeenth century was the golden age of piracy, both in the Mediterranean and Europe's entire western approaches, and the young Dutch republic depended for its life on freedom of trade.

In 1622 Marten Tromp joined the Dutch navy as a lieutenant. Tough and resourceful, he was promoted captain two years later, but his career suffered a ten-year setback when he failed to remain silent about the abuses and incompetence rampant in the Dutch naval administration. Tromp was stripped of his command for his 'undisciplined' outspokenness, but by 1637 it was only too obvious that he had been right all along and he was reinstated with the rank of lieutenant-admiral.

In September and October 1638 Tromp won his first great victory and also precipitated an international crisis of remarkable proportions. Patrolling the Channel with a fleet of about thirty warships, he fell upon a Spanish fleet of seventy-five ships carrying troops to the Netherlands, which fled for shelter into English territorial waters. Heedless of English protests, Tromp blockaded the Spanish ships in the Downs until reinforcements arrived from Holland, then sailed in and annihilated them with fireships and gunfire on 21 October 1639. A small and helpless English squadron had been impotent spectators throughout.

Only when Tromp had finished the destruction of the Spaniards did he acknowledge the English flag by striking his sails and firing a nineteen-gun salute. The ensuing diplomatic furore between England and the Dutch republic was patched up in the following year with a marriage between Charles I's daughter and the son of the Dutch Stadholder. Their son William eventually became King of England, ousting the Stuart James II in 1688.

The first Anglo-Dutch War of 1652–4 began badly for Tromp. On 19 May he lost two ships to an

inferior English squadron under Blake in a fight off Dover, over which Tromp was so incensed that he demanded without success that Blake return the ships. In August Tromp failed to prevent Blake from raiding the Dutch North Sea herring fleet and was temporarily relieved of his command. He was reinstated after yet another victory by Blake, off the Kentish Knock on 28 September, and got his revenge two months later. On 30 November Blake attacked an outward-bound convoy which Tromp was escorting down Channel, and Tromp decisively repulsed the English off Dungeness. It was after this battle that Tromp was said to have hoisted a broom to the masthead of his flagship *Brederode* as an indication that he had swept the Channel clear of the English.

Tromp's triumph was shortlived; on 18 February 1653 he was returning up the Channel with a homeward-bound convoy when he was attacked again by Blake. In a tremendous three-day battle fought across the full width of the Channel from Portland to Gris-Nez, Tromp lost nearly sixty merchantmen and seventeen warships. For all that, he retained his command and held out hopes of tipping the balance again in the next encounter.

This was the battle of the Gabbard on 2 June, when Tromp's fleet of ninety-eight ships was trapped between two English fleets totalling one hundred. At one stage the English boarded the *Brederode* and took the upper deck, but Tromp retreated below and ordered the last of the powder to be used in blowing both deck and boarders clean out of the ship. Despite a splendid resistance, Tromp was beaten by a shortage of ammunition.

After the Gabbard the English carried the war into Dutch waters and blockaded Tromp in the Maas until he skilfully escaped with eighty-four ships. When Admiral de With joined him with twenty-five from the Texel, Tromp finally accepted battle. It was his last fight, for in the action off Scheveningen on 31 July – the last Dutch defeat of the war – Tromp was mortally wounded.

Marten Tromp was too headstrong to make a great naval strategist. He was, however, the most dashing of the Dutch admirals who protected Holland's vital trading routes in the mid-seventeenth century.

Robert Blake

1599–1657

Despite his total lack of seafaring experience, Robert Blake was fully to justify his appointment by Parliament in 1649 to command its fleet against the Royalists.

In the careers of most great seamen, the path to the admiral's cabin began with a teenage introduction to life at sea, followed by a long service career rising through successive promotions. Robert Blake, however, belongs to the handful of prodigies appointed to high naval command without any experience of sea fighting or even serving as a peacetime ship's officer. In his amazingly brief naval career – the last nine years of his life – Blake restored the reputation won by the Elizabethan English navy as one of the most formidable afloat.

Blake was born in 1599, three years after the death of Drake. His father, a prosperous merchant of Bridgwater in Somerset, died when Robert was twenty-five and for the next fifteen years Robert applied himself to running the family business and educating his fourteen brothers and sisters. When the Civil War broke out in 1642 Blake declared for Parliament and over the next four years was prominent in the fighting in the West Country. He made his mark with his tenacity in holding Lyme Regis and Taunton for Parliament and by the end of the war had risen to the rank of colonel.

It was after the execution of King Charles I, in 1649, that a Parliamentary commission appointed 'Colonel Popham, Colonel Blake and Colonel Deane, or any two of them, to be Admirals and Generals of the fleet now at sea'. Apart from his record as a sound Parliamentary commander, one of the reasons why Blake was chosen may have been that the Royalist fleet-in-exile was commanded by Prince Rupert: a cavalry general equally inexperienced in command afloat, against whom Blake had fought in the war.

Throughout the summer of 1649, Blake and Deane blockaded Rupert in the Irish port of Kinsale, but were forced off this dangerous coast by the autumn storms. Blake's tenacity on blockade, as stubborn as his earlier persistence under siege at Taunton, was seen again in the following year. In sole command of a fleet of sixteen ships – Deane being ill and Popham needed in the Channel – Blake pursued Rupert to Portugal and kept him penned in the Tagus for eight months.

Being outnumbered by three ships, Rupert did not risk a battle but applied his singular talents as an inventor to contriving a 'secret weapon' to blow up Blake's ships. This was a cross between a mine and a torpedo, but it failed to deter Blake, who began seizing rich Portuguese merchantmen to dissuade the king of Portugal from extending further hospitality to Rupert. Blake's strategy worked: sixteen lost cargoes were enough to bring about the expulsion of Rupert, which Blake further encouraged by temporarily withdrawing to Spanish waters in order to scrape his ships. Rupert withdrew into the Mediterranean with the last six ships he could man, and Blake followed with seven in November. He found the disheartened Royalists in Cartagena Bay and captured or beached all of them, though without capturing Parliament's archenemy.

This splendid cruise, the like of which had not been seen since Tudor days, was rewarded with the thanks of Parliament and the enormous gratuity of £1000. Blake followed it up in 1651 and 1652 by taking the Scilly Isles and Jersey, the last forlorn outposts of Royalist resistance in the British Isles.

In 1651–2 Blake proved his talents as an administrator in Parliament, serving on the Ordnance and Admiralty Committees; in February 1652, war with the Dutch already being imminent, his command of the fleet was renewed for nine months. The first Anglo-Dutch war opened with a clash between Blake's force of twelve ships and Marten Tromp's fleet of forty-two, off Dover on 19 May 1652, Tromp retiring at nightfall with the loss of two ships.

At the end of June Blake fell on the Dutch North Sea herring fleet, wiping out its escort of frigates, despoiling some hundred fishing boats and sending them home empty. Off the Kentish Knock on 28 September, Blake engaged the Dutch fleet close inshore and, though slightly outnumbered, again obliged it to retire to Dutch waters with the loss of two ships and several others badly damaged. Blake was exonerated from any blame for his ensuing defeat by Tromp off Dungeness on 30 November in which the premature dispersal of the English fleet had obliged him to fight with thirty-seven ships against Tromp's ninety-five.

Badly wounded in the thigh during the three-day battle with Tromp off Portland on 18–21 February 1653, Blake took little part in the victory off the Gabbard on 2–3 June and none at all in the crowning victory over Tromp off Scheveningen on 30 July. His massive contribution to the English republic's naval successes was nevertheless recognized by the Parliamentary award of a gold chain to the value of £300.

Blake's most resounding exploits came after the Dutch War, when Cromwell used the fleets of England to punish the sea powers who had exploited England's internal distractions for the past twelve years. In September 1654 Blake sailed for the Mediterranean with twenty ships to show the flag and punish the Barbary pirates for their raids on English shipping.

In April 1655 Blake sailed into the harbour of Porto Farina near Tunis, bombarded the shore forts into silence and sent boarding parties to burn the entire Tunisian fleet. Having thus thoroughly cowed the raiders of the North African coast, Blake blockaded Cadiz for the next five months, doggedly holding station though atrociously supplied from home. His force returned from its thirteen-month cruise on 9 October.

Blake was a sick man when he sailed with forty ships on his last expedition in March 1656. Resuming the blockade of Cadiz, Blake started by threatening the King of Portugal with the capture of the entire Portuguese merchant fleet if an indemnity of £50,000 were not paid. This was in compensation for the English merchantmen taken by Prince Rupert and sold at Lisbon five years before. The indemnity was duly paid. The biggest

prize of the cruise, however – the Spanish plate-fleet from the Americas, carrying £3 million in bullion – was captured by the guard squadron left on patrol when Blake took the bulk of the fleet to water on the Portuguese coast on 8 September.

Half the fleet returned to England with the booty, but Blake kept up the Cadiz blockade throughout the winter of 1656–7. With the coming of spring he heard that the next Spanish merchant fleet from Mexico had taken shelter at Santa Cruz, Tenerife. Blake sailed at once to attack this new quarry on 20 April 1657, repeating the tactics he had used at Porto Farina two years before. He entered the harbour on the flood tide, silenced the strong shore batteries with gunfire and finally sent in his ships' boats to burn the entire Spanish fleet.

Blake's crowning achievement at Santa Cruz destroyed the last financial transfusion with which Spain might have bought her way to victory. It was not, however, rewarded by recall to England. Blake returned to the Cadiz blockade for another three exhausting months before Cromwell recalled him in July, by which time Blake was a dying man. He set sail for home but died a mere two hours before his flagship anchored in Plymouth on 17 August 1657.

Blake's battles with the Dutch fleet in 1652–3 confirmed his growing stature as a naval commander and tactician of the highest order.

The Dutch Wars

STRUGGLE FOR SUPREMACY IN THE CHANNEL

ABOVE George Monck, Duke of Albemarle, was a notable English sea-commander who served under Charles II during the Second Dutch War.

RIGHT The battle of Solebay on 7 June 1672 marked the commencement of the Third Dutch war. The Earl of Sandwich's flagship, the *Royal James*, was destroyed by a fireship.

The main cause of the First Dutch War (1652–4) was a maritime and trade rivalry which had been developing between England and the United Provinces of the Netherlands since late in the reign of Elizabeth I. This rivalry was aggravated by a series of incidents at home and abroad, such as the Amboyna massacre of English traders in 1623, and it is probable that only the weakness of England under the early Stuarts prevented war coming much sooner than it actually did.

After the English Civil Wars (1642–51) Parliament passed legislation which was aimed directly at Dutch commercial superiority, for example the Navigation Act of 1651. The Dutch, reluctant to go to war, attempted negotiations but their attitude hardened after Parliament authorized privateering against them. On 19 May 1652 Robert Blake and Marten Tromp fought an indecisive action near Dover, and soon afterwards Blake was ordered north to attack the Dutch herring fleet. A large proportion of the Dutch population depended upon

the herring catch and Blake's attack brought a Dutch declaration of war in July 1652. Tromp was sent in pursuit of Blake, but failed, mainly through bad weather, to catch him. On his return to port Tromp was replaced in command of the fleet by Witte Corneliszoon de With.

On 28 September 1652 Blake intercepted the Dutch fleet on its return from a cruise down Channel. The battle of the Kentish Knock was a Dutch defeat and de With was forced to take refuge inside the Dutch coastal sandbanks after having two of his warships captured. The victory was considered decisive by Parliament and Blake was ordered to detach twenty warships to the Mediterranean, where the Dutch had gained complete control and paralysed English trade. Soon afterwards the larger English warships were laid up for the winter. This was the usual procedure in the seventeenth century, but on this occasion the Dutch kept their large warships in commission. During November Tromp, who had replaced de With as

commander-in-chief after the battle of the Kentish Knock, sailed to escort an outward-bound trading fleet through the Channel. Blake, whose fleet was badly outnumbered, was defeated at the battle of Dungeness on 29 November 1652 with the loss of six warships. It was after this victory that Tromp was reputed to have hoisted a broom to his masthead to show that he had swept the English from the seas. Dissatisfied with the performance of his fleet, Blake offered his resignation, but this was refused and measures were put in hand to improve efficiency and discipline in the English naval forces. These measures were to pay off the following year.

On 18 February 1653 Blake intercepted Tromp off Portland as the Dutch were sailing up the Channel escorting the homeward-bound trading fleets. The 'Three Days' Battle' which ensued consisted of a series of rearguard actions fought by Tromp to protect his convoy. However on 20 February several of the Dutch warships ran out of ammunition and the English broke through the weakened escort. Tromp saved his fleet from annihilation by standing close inshore on the French coast and rounding Cape Gris Nez at night to get clean away. Nevertheless he lost nineteen of his warships and fifty-seven merchant vessels.

On 2 June 1653 George Monck (later Duke of Albemarle) and Richard Deane brought Tromp to action at the battle of the Gabbard. Blake arrived with reinforcements on 3 June and the Dutch were decisively defeated with the loss of twenty-five warships. The victorious English fleet now established a close blockade of the Dutch coast. The Dutch attempted to start peace negotiations, but the English terms were so harsh that a final effort was determined upon. Tromp fought the battle of the Scheveningen on 31 July 1653. The result was a decisive Dutch defeat with Tromp killed in action and ten warships lost. The English Parliament now modified its peace terms and the Dutch, who were at the end of their resources, accepted them. The Treaty of Westminster brought the First Dutch War to a close on 5 April 1654 on terms which favoured England.

The Restoration of Charles II in 1660 found the Dutch failing to carry out their obligations under the Treaty of Westminster, whilst their rapidly expanding trade was once again exciting English jealousy. Four years of increasing friction and resentment culminated in a declaration of war upon the United Provinces on 4 March 1665.

Both states had improved and strengthened their battle-fleets since the First Dutch War, but during the next two years the Royal Navy (as it was christened after the Restoration of Charles II in 1660) was to be continually hampered by shortages of stores and victuals resulting from the government's lack of money. During April 1665 the English fleet, commanded by the Duke of York (later James II), cruised on the Dutch coast and after capturing eight Dutch merchantmen was compelled to return to England by shortages of victuals. The Dutch fleet, commanded by van Wassenaer, followed, and on 3 June 1665 it was defeated at the battle of Lowestoft,

Detailed drawings of a typical seventeenth-century man-of-war. The pronounced 'tumble-home' of the vessel's section, giving it a swollen appearance just above the waterline, allowed the large guns of the main and lower gun-decks room to recoil. The upper deck was narrower than the other two gun-decks because the guns mounted there were smaller.

A new Table of all the names of the principal Parts and Rigging of a MAN of WAR Necessary for all sea-faring men and others that desire to be therewith acquainted. Also all the Prospects of a Section of a Ship cut thro' the Keel, both fore & aft with her Boats, Longboats and Sloops.

Stern of the Ship

Sold by Daniel Midwinter at the three Crowns in St Pauls Church yard London.

When George Monck
attacked Admiral de
Ruyter's Dutch fleet on 1
June 1666 he was heavily
outnumbered. In the 'Four
Days' Battle' that ensued,
the English lost about
twenty ships.

losing its commander-in-chief and some thirty-one warships taken or destroyed by the English.

Later in June the English fleet, now commanded by the Earl of Sandwich, went north to intercept the homeward-bound Dutch East Indies trading fleet. This was found to have taken refuge in Bergen, where on 2 August 1665 an English attack was decisively beaten off by the Danes – Norway was then under Danish rule – and Dutch. Soon after the fleet returned to England the Great Plague broke out and this, coupled with the usual shortage of money, made it impossible to fit out more than a small squadron for the remainder of 1665. Michael de Ruyter had been appointed commander-in-chief of the Dutch fleet and, after bringing the East Indies ships from Bergen, he cruised in the Thames estuary during October 1665 before returning to port to lay up his ships for the winter.

Early in 1666 France declared war upon England and the necessity of detaching a fleet to watch the French meant that George Monck, Duke of Albermarle, was badly outnumbered when he engaged de Ruyter on 1 June 1666 at the start of the 'Four Days' Battle'. Although Prince Rupert joined with reinforcements on 3 June and the Dutch finally disengaged on the following day, the battle was a setback for the English, who suffered heavy casualties and lost about twenty warships while the Dutch lost only seven.

Repairs to the English fleet were again hampered by lack of money and stores and meanwhile the Dutch were cruising in the Thames estuary by late June 1666. Albemarle finally got to sea during mid-July and on 25–6 July 1666 defeated de Ruyter in the 'St James's Day Fight' (also known as the battle of the Gunfleet). The English fleet blockaded the Dutch coast, burnt the newly arrived East Indies fleet in the Vlie – an action known as 'Holmes's Bonfire', after Sir Robert Holmes, who led the attack. The English inflicted a vast amount of damage upon Dutch trade before being compelled to return to England by lack of victuals.

In early 1667, following the Great Fire of London, conditions in England were so serious that 'feelers' were put out to the Dutch regarding a possible peace. When the Dutch proved willing to talk, the English government decided not to recommission the larger warships that had been laid up during the winter of 1666–7.

The Dutch, on the other hand, fitted out a strong fleet and whilst talks were in progress at Breda, de Ruyter carried out a devastating raid up the Medway in June 1667, partly to stimulate the English desire for peace and partly in retaliation for the English raids on the Dutch coast in 1666. The Dutch, guided by English deserters, burned many of the warships that had been sunk in shallow waters to prevent their capture. They found *Royal Charles* still afloat and brought her in triumph back to the Netherlands, where part of her stern decoration survives to this day. The war ended with the Treaty of Breda (July 1667) which gave very advantageous terms to the Dutch.

The Second Dutch War had left bitter resentment in England and on 22 May 1670 Charles II signed the Treaty of Dover, by which he agreed to provide a fleet to assist the French in their attack on the United Provinces. The precise terms of the Treaty were kept a secret and the old grievances against the Dutch were resorted to in order to generate enthusiasm for a new war. On 13 March 1672 Sir Robert Holmes attacked the Dutch Smyrna fleet off the Isle of Wight and England declared war on 29 March 1672. France followed

The Sea Gunner
Published
By
John Seller

a Cascable deck
b Base Ring
c Touchole
d The Chamber
e Reinfourd Ring
f Trunions
g Cornish Ring
h Trunion Ring

suit on 6 April 1672 and invaded the United Provinces.

A combined English and French fleet was in Solebay taking on stores before cruising in search of the Dutch homeward-bound trading fleets. This was considered the best method of bringing the Dutch fleet to action as once the enemy fleet had been dealt with the Allies could land an army on the Dutch coast to cooperate with the French. On 7 June 1672 the Dutch fleet, commanded by de Ruyter, suddenly appeared off the combined fleet's anchorage. Although the Dutch broke off the battle of Solebay at nightfall after losing three ships, de Ruyter had succeeded in upsetting the Allied plan to land troops in Holland.

Both fleets were soon at sea again but the Dutch, who had landed a large number of their seamen to serve in the army, remained in coastal waters and only slipped out to bring in the homeward-bound merchant fleets. The Allied fleet cruised on the Dutch coast for a while and then had to return to England, being short of stores and victuals – a constantly recurring problem.

In early 1673 the perennial shortage of money and stores delayed fitting out the English fleet and the resourceful de Ruyter entered the Thames estuary intending to block the Medway by scuttling scores of stone-laden hulks in the Swin Channel. However, his plan was frustrated by fog and the Dutch fell back on their coast when Prince Rupert finally brought out the English fleet.

De Ruyter now executed a brilliant defensive operation. Keeping his fleet in shallow coastal waters and behind the intricate and dangerous sandbanks fringing the Dutch coast, he attacked the superior Allied fleet whenever conditions were in his favour. On 7 June 1673 the Dutch suddenly came out from their anchorage in the Schonveldt and inflicted heavy damage on the Allied fleet in the first battle of the Schonveldt. They repeated the attack on 14 June and this time the Allies were forced to return to England for repairs. They were back off the Dutch coast in late July and on 10 August 1673 de Ruyter fought them to a standstill in the battle of the Texel.

In England some of the more objectionable terms of the Treaty of Dover had been 'leaked' – including that in which Charles II promised to proclaim his conversion to the Roman Catholic faith in return for a large sum of money. A furious outcry swept the country and the king, bowing to the storm, abandoned the French alliance. In February 1674 the Second Treaty of Westminster ended the Third Dutch War for the English, although the United Provinces remained at war with Louis XIV's France, the rising European power which was soon to replace the United Provinces as England's chief rival.

Ships' guns at this time were mounted on wooden carriages with wheels. Their movement backwards under the force of recoil was arrested by rope breeching attached to the side of the vessel.

Michiel Adrienszoon de Ruyter

1607–1676

Michiel de Ruyter succeeded Tromp as commander of the Dutch fleet and proved no less successful. The Medway attack of June 1667 established his reputation.

On the sea-front at Flushing the statue of the greatest of all Dutch admirals still glares defiantly across the North Sea towards England – the statue of Michiel Adrienszoon de Ruyter. Three centuries have passed since the Dutch were England's foremost enemy at sea, but de Ruyter is still remembered as the man who inflicted the biggest humiliation ever suffered by the English in their home waters.

Born at Flushing in 1607, de Ruyter spent his youth at sea in the Dutch merchant service. In 1641 he was given his first independent command and a fleet of fifteen ships to help rebel Portugal against Spain, but returned to the merchant service until the first Anglo-Dutch war in 1652.

Employed by the government of his native province, Zeeland, de Ruyter beat off an English force near the Channel Islands while escorting a convoy down-Channel. He then returned to join de With's fleet and distinguish himself in the Kentish Knock action. De Ruyter went on to fight with Tromp in the battles off Dungeness and Portland, and after the North Foreland defeat strongly supported Tromp in his insistence to fight on. De Ruyter fought in the battle off Scheveningen in which Tromp was killed, his ship *Lam* being so badly battered that she had to be towed back to port.

De Ruyter's reputation for being in the thick of the action did not suffer during the decade of peace between the First and Second Dutch Wars. First came a spell fighting Mediterranean pirates, then, in 1659, command of a Dutch fleet sent to the Baltic to support Denmark in her war with Sweden. De Ruyter's reward for defeating the Swedish fleet was a Danish peerage. This exploit was followed by another two years of anti-piracy operations in the Mediterranean between 1661 and 1663, then cruises to the Guinea Coast of Africa and the West Indies.

De Ruyter was still in the West Indies when the Second Anglo-Dutch war broke out in 1665, and he was perfectly placed to open the conflict with a damaging series of attacks on English shipping. He brought his prizes home safely, evading the English naval forces sent out to intercept him. Once back in home waters de Ruyter set out to succeed where Marten Tromp had failed and win control of the Narrow Seas for the Dutch.

His first action of the war was the epic 'Four Days' Battle' of July 1666, fought off the Thames estuary against George Monck, Duke of Albemarle. This resulted in very heavy English casualties, 7000 men killed, wounded or taken prisoner and twenty warships lost, against Dutch losses of 2000 men and seven ships. It was, however, regarded as a moral victory for the English, whose fleet of fifty-six had stood up to eighty-five Dutch ships for four days and finally driven them off. Seven weeks later the English showed their naval superiority in the 'St James's Day Fight' on 25 July. De Ruyter lost twenty ships to Monck's one, largely due to lack of support from Cornelis Tromp, the son of Marten.

The year 1666 ended with English warships patrolling the Dutch coast, but Charles II's secret treaty with France led to a fatal case of complacency in the English. Charles laid up the bulk of his fleet in the Medway and de Ruyter seized the chance to make his famous attack of June 1667, breaking the flimsy English boom across the Medway and falling on the defenceless fleet as it lay at anchor. The Dutch triumphantly burned or captured sixteen ships, including the splendid flagship *Royal Charles*, which was towed back to Holland as a trophy.

Thanks to their treaty with France the English prospered during the ensuing peace, and in 1672 began a third war with the Dutch in alliance with France. De Ruyter, whose prowess seemed to increase with age, crossed the North Sea and gave the Duke of York's fleet a battering in Solebay, off Southwold. He thus prevented the English from assisting the French in their assault on Holland.

De Ruyter's last fight with the English was the battle of the Texel on 11 August 1673, in which he broke Prince Rupert's attempt to blockade the Dutch coast. Peace with England, made in February 1674, allowed de Ruyter to carry the war against the French into the Mediterranean. On 22 August 1676 he defeated the fleet of the French Admiral Duquesne off Stromboli – but it was to be his last battle. Mortally wounded in the action, de Ruyter died seven days later.

Beachy Head and Barfleur

THE ENGLISH AND DUTCH UNITE

The battle of Barfleur was initiated by the Comte de Tourville, whose force was no match for the combined English and Dutch fleets of more than double its size.

On 10 June 1688 the birth of a son to Mary of Modena, Queen of James II, provided an heir to the throne of England and ruined the hopes of the Protestant party for a peaceful succession by the Dutch Stadholder, William of Orange. It thus brought to a head the long political and religious struggle between James II and his Protestant subjects. The King's opponents invited William to invade England and secure the Protestant succession by force of arms. He landed at Torbay on 5 November 1688 and the English army and navy deserted to him, forcing James II to flee to France. William of Orange became King William III of England and he added the resources of his new realm to the alliance that he had built up to oppose the ambitions of Louis XIV of France. Louis welcomed the exiled James II and promised him French aid in regaining his throne. Thus, from the English viewpoint, the War of the English Succession was fought mainly to prevent the return of James II and the renewal of Roman Catholic dominance.

The first year of war – 1689 – saw a Franco-Irish army, led by James II, achieve considerable success in Ireland, although it was forced to retreat from Derry later in the year. At sea, however, the French navy achieved little. It won the battle of Bantry Bay on 10 May 1689, but did not exploit the success, though a strong fleet was based at Brest.

The following year the English position in Ireland improved slightly. William III landed with a strong army to secure Ulster, although a decisive

battle had yet to be fought. In England, however, party politics were hampering effective government. The army and navy had long been unpaid, the dockyards were neglected and the fitting-out of the fleet was carried out with great difficulty, owing to the lack of money.

On 13 June 1690, seventy-seven ships, commanded by Vice-Admiral the Comte de Tourville, sailed from Brest. De Tourville's orders were to attack Portsmouth and then blockade the Thames estuary and prevent the English and Dutch naval units joining up. However, the Allied fleet, commanded by the Earl of Torrington, was already

TOP The English victory at Barfleur in May 1692 is symbolized on this medal by the lion and unicorn driving away the French cockerel.

RIGHT Louis XIV's triumphant passage over the waves represents the French victory at Beachy Head over the English and Dutch fleets in 1690.

84

at the Nore – though it had been weakened by the despatch of a strong squadron to the Mediterranean and a smaller squadron to the Irish Sea. Reports reaching Torrington indicated that a very large French fleet was at sea. Although he passed this intelligence on to the government, their own sources of information suggested that the French fleet was smaller than that of the Allies. Consequently Torrington's objections were overruled and he sailed on 23 June with thirty-five English and twenty-two Dutch ships.

The Allied and French fleets met off the Isle of Wight on 26 June and for several days manoeuvred for position. During this period, Torrington confirmed his original estimate of the French strength and requested that he be allowed to withdraw to the Thames estuary. The government, however, was still convinced that the French fleet was the smaller. They believed that Torrington was reluctant to fight for reasons other than those he had given. As a result the commander-in-chief received a letter from Queen Mary, who acted as Regent during William's absence in Ireland, ordering him to attack the French with the first favourable wind.

On the morning of 28 June 1690 both fleets were in line-of-battle on a north-westerly course, with the wind from the north-east and the Allies to windward of the French. Torrington decided that the time to fight had come and he ordered his fleet to engage the enemy. The Dutch squadron, which formed the van of the Allied fleet, closed fast with the French van. The Dutch squadron's commander, Lieutenant-Admiral Evertsen, instead of bringing his ships into action along the whole length of the French van, engaged its centre and rear divisions. This manoeuvre forced his rearmost ships to engage the van division of the French centre squadron. This mistake left the leading French ships unengaged and seeing this, their commander, the Marquis de Châteaurenault, ordered them to turn back and attack the unengaged side of the Dutch.

Whilst the Dutch attack and the French counter-move were developing, Torrington was slowly bringing the English centre and rear squadrons down onto the French line. However, by the time that the English squadrons entered the battle, the Dutch had been in action for over two hours. Even then Torrington kept his centre squadron at long range, while the rear squadrons closed and commenced a hard action.

Seeing the hesitancy of the English centre, de Tourville judged that he could risk weakening his centre squadron, in order to reinforce the attack on the Dutch. By early afternoon the Dutch were surrounded and they were receiving heavy damage, but Torrington made no move to assist his allies. It was possible that he did not realize their predicament, but his inertia at this time led to later accusations by the Dutch of incompetence, cowardice and even treachery.

In the middle of the afternoon the wind died and the battle became a confused *mêlée*, with no control being exercised by either commander. Towards evening, however, a strong ebb tide began to run and Torrington took his second positive action of the day, by ordering his fleet to anchor. This command was carried out so quickly that the French were taken by surprise and many of their vessels were carried out of range by the tide, before they could anchor. Torrington, presumably after receiving reports on the state of his fleet, judged it incapable of renewing the action and ordered a withdrawal up-Channel to the Thames estuary.

The arrival of the defeated fleet at the Nore spread alarm throughout southern England, as the landing of French troops was expected hourly. Torrington faced court martial, to satisfy the popular fury in England and the Netherlands. He was acquitted and news of William's victory at the battle of the Boyne changed the mood of the country. Torrington later won fame as the victor at the battle of Cape Passero (1718).

Despite English fears, the French made no real effort to exploit their victory. They landed a small force which burned Teignmouth and destroyed a small English ship. Then the fleet returned to Brest for repairs. When the panic in England was over, efforts were made to repair and fit out the strongest possible fleet. In a surprisingly short time, fifty English and Dutch ships were cruising in the Channel. As the French fleet made no attempt to leave Brest, communications were severed between France and Ireland, where the Franco-Irish forces were in retreat after the battle of the Boyne. The return of James II to France, and the capture of Cork and Kinsale by the English towards the end of the year, promised success for the Allies in 1691.

The naval events of 1691 did not, however, come up to expectations. The Allied fleet, now commanded by Edward Russell, simply could not catch de Tourville's ships. The French achieved some success against Allied convoys and prevented any serious raids on the French coast by keeping Russell's fleet chasing after them. De Tourville, now outnumbered by ninety ships to his seventy, sensibly avoided a general action with the Allied fleet, which was more ably commanded than it had been in 1690. However, his circumspection raised doubts about his loyalty and courage, which were to produce a disastrous result in 1692.

The remnants of the French and Irish forces were finally evacuated from Ireland towards the end of 1691. The French now determined upon invasion of England. A powerful fleet was collected at Brest and it was to have sailed early in 1692, before the English and Dutch had finished fitting out their vessels. The Allies, however, learned of the French plans at an early date and ninety-eight English and Dutch ships were despatched to patrol the Channel.

The French finally sailed from Brest on 2 May 1692 with forty-four ships, under de Tourville. Another twenty ships were left behind to complete

As the former William of Orange, King William III of England was able to combine English and Dutch forces in opposition to Louis XIV of France.

TOP Admiral the Earl of Torrington, whose defeat at Beachy Head resulted in his facing court martial.

ABOVE The Comte de Tourville, Torrington's victorious opponent.

their manning. De Tourville had received orders to fight, whatever the risk, with the object of inflicting so much damage on the Allied fleet that it would be unable to stop the invasion force. Later orders to avoid action until reinforcements arrived failed to reach him. The fleets came into contact off Cape Barfleur on the morning of 19 May 1692. Both were on a southerly course, with the wind from the south-west, and the French were to windward. De Tourville, still smarting from accusations of cowardice, led his ships into action against an Allied fleet more than twice the size of his own.

A general action, known as the battle of Barfleur, developed. At two o'clock in the afternoon the wind shifted to the north-west. Taking advantage of this, the Dutch squadron in the van of the Allied fleet attempted to encircle the French van – a similar manoeuvre to that used by the French at the battle of Beachy Head. However, the French followed the Dutch ships around and managed to hold them off, although the head of their line was now almost at right-angles to the main body of the fleet.

At the same time the English rear squadron pushed through a gap which had appeared towards the end of the French line. Here also the French managed to hold their attackers off, but as evening approached the English rear squadron tried to attack the French centre, which had been holding its own against superior English forces throughout the day. However, the wind died before the attack had any effect. As the fleets drifted, de Tourville was reminded of Torrington's tactics at Beachy Head and he ordered his ships to anchor. Many of the Allied vessels were carried by currents out of range of the French and the action died away as a thick mist came down. It cleared at eight o'clock that evening and the day's fighting ended with an abortive attempt by the Allies to use fireships.

De Tourville then ordered his fleet to withdraw to Brest. Hampered by damaged ships, which slowed the fleet, de Tourville finally ordered it to disperse. Twenty-two ships got safely to St Malo, five reached Brest, two Le Havre, three Cherbourg and twelve the La Hogue Roads. On 21 May the ships at Cherbourg were attacked and burned by the Allies, and two days later the twelve vessels in La Hogue Roads suffered the same fate at the hands of a squadron commanded by Vice-Admiral George Rooke.

After their defeat at Beachy Head, the Allies reacted strongly and quickly regained control of the Channel. Although the French replaced their losses after Barfleur and La Hogue, they made no attempts to regain control at sea. However, it would not be true to say that the battle crushed the fighting spirit of the French navy. It was a political decision that finally laid up its larger ships and switched the smaller vessels to commerce raiding – a policy which had the attraction of largely paying for itself at a time when resources had to be diverted to the French army.

René Duguay-Trouin

1673–1736

René Duguay-Trouin made his reputation as a swashbuckling privateer. His capture of twelve British merchant ships in 1707 and his expedition to Rio de Janeiro in 1710 were the highlights of his career.

In the 1820s the French government decided to erect twelve statues, carved in Carrera marble, of Frenchmen who, in their time, had helped to make their country illustrious. One of them stands today in the Place de Duguay-Trouin in St Malo, a monument to the achievements of the greatest of St Malo corsairs in the square named after him.

René Duguay-Trouin was born into a seafaring family in 1673. Sent to a Jesuit college to train for holy orders, then transferred to the University of Caen, he at last persuaded his family to place him on one of the family ships as a corsair. The year was 1689. The War of the League of Augsburg had just broken out. On his second voyage Duguay-Trouin experienced his first hand-to-hand fighting and took part in his first capture of an enemy ship. In 1692 came a turning-point in his career. Thanks to his sharp observation that the guns on three of the biggest ships of an English fleet in Bantry Bay were wooden fakes, the captain of the *Grenaden*, on which Duguay-Trouin was serving, decided to attack. Three ships, carrying valuable cargoes of sugar and tobacco, were captured and taken to St Malo. Duguay-Trouin's part in that successful cruise raised him in the esteem of his St Malo colleagues and in April 1692, at the age of eighteen, he set sail as captain of the small, fourteen-gun frigate, the *Danycan*. After a barren cruise, Duguay-Trouin complained that the *Danycan* was too small and too slow to capture prizes. He was given command of a larger ship, the *Coetquen*.

Then began a year, aided by the French government's decision to lend ships of the French navy to corsairs, of relentless privateering. On one occasion the capture of two heavily armed English ships by Duguay-Trouin yielded a prize of sugar, indigo, silver and gold which sold for 330,660 livres. The year 1693 was one of record prizes for the St Malo corsairs and at the end of it Duguay-Trouin stood at their head, a position of leadership which had not lightly been won, for he had been wounded and captured by the English, imprisoned at Plymouth, and avoided answering accusations that he had fired on enemy ships while flying the English flag only by an adroitly executed escape. Despite knowing that to be captured again would almost certainly cost him his life, he set out to sea almost immediately upon his return to St Malo. By defeating two enemy warships he achieved a lifelong ambition. He was invited to join the French navy.

Three years passed before Duguay-Trouin was asked, in March, 1697, to take command of a squadron to sail towards Spain and intercept a convoy of Dutch ships from Bilbao. The battle which ensued was one of the fiercest in his career. The French suffered heavy losses, but three Dutch warships and twelve merchantmen surrendered. In recognition of Duguay-Trouin's gallantry, Louis XIV appointed him to the rank of 'Captain of a Light Frigate'. At the age of twenty-four he was a captain in the French navy.

There followed four years of peace until the outbreak of the War of the Spanish Succession, when the government decided that Duguay-Trouin could best serve France by leaving the navy and returning to privateering. He lavishly repaid that trust and in 1705 he received a letter from Louis, who, 'knowing your zeal and loyalty of which you have given so many proofs', promoted him to full captain. A year later he was made a Chevalier of the Order of St Louis.

Two episodes stand out in the latter part of Duguay-Trouin's career. In 1707 he captured twelve British merchantmen in a battle off the Lizard, and although his chief rival, the Comte de Forbin, claimed the credit, Louis XIV was not deceived. He awarded Duguay-Trouin a pension of 1000 livres from the royal treasury. In 1710 Duguay-Trouin led the expedition which bombarded Rio de Janeiro and, against a threat to burn the Portuguese colonial capital to the ground, exacted an enormous ransom from the Portuguese governor.

The Treaty of Utrecht, signed in 1713, brought Duguay-Trouin's career to a close. He was already suffering from gout, failing eyesight, severe headaches and bouts of fever. Although he was appointed commander of the navy in Brest, he only once more went to sea. Ill-health was his constant companion for the last twenty years of his life. He died in 1736, at the age of sixty-three, an honoured patriot and a national hero.

Velez Malaga

AND THE CAPTURE OF GIBRALTAR

For over 270 years a British flag has flown from the rocky promontory of Gibraltar, and a British naval presence has nestled in the harbour at the foot of the great granite mound; the whole place has a 'little Britain' atmosphere, and as recently as the late 1970s, 95 per cent of its population voted to remain under the jurisdiction of the Crown. Yet, in 1704, it became a British colony almost as an afterthought, on what was virtually the whim of a martinet admiral engaged in fighting a 'foreign' war.

'The Rock' takes its name from the Arabic phrase *Jabal Tariq* – mountain of Tariq – commemorating the Moorish conqueror Tariq ibn Ziad who first realized its potential as a natural fortress and captured it in the early eighth century. 'In form resembling a lion couchant, connected tailward to the mainland by a narrow strip of sand' as one seventeenth-century chronicler put it, it was given a coat of arms by its first Christian king, Henry IV of Castile, which featured a golden key, for Henry quite rightly thought it the 'key to the Mediterranean'. Indeed, long before the advent of the Moors, Gibraltar had been one of the 'pillars of Hercules' which effectively defined the western bounds of Mediterranean navigation. From the time of Henry until 1700, the rocky fortress was Spanish.

In that year the childless Charles II died, and willed that the Duc d'Anjou, grandson of Louis XIV of France, become Philip V of Spain. Austria had a rival to the throne in the person of the Archduke Charles, and for her own part Britain disliked the idea of a Bourbon king ruling Spain alongside his French grandfather. Accordingly, in 1701 Britain, Austria, and their ally Holland declared against the French and Spanish in what was to become known as the War of Spanish Succession.

Although Britain controlled the Channel and western Atlantic seaboards of both France and Spain, she needed to keep a route open to the Mediterranean and her Italian and Neapolitan allies. In command of the Anglo-Dutch fleet was Admiral Sir George Rooke, flying his flag in the *Royal Catherine*. His attempts against the Spanish started badly, with a mistimed and disastrous attempt to take Cadiz, but a swift and shrewdly planned attack on Vigo resulted in the destruction of a great deal of Spanish shipping and the fortuitous capture of bullion from vessels arriving from the Spanish West Indies.

Early in January 1704, Rooke sailed at the head of a fleet from Spithead, carrying the Archduke Charles of Austria to Lisbon, and from there on to a scouting expedition off the coast of North Africa. Shortly after his arrival the British court heard that the French had mustered a large fleet at Brest, and a secondary British naval force, under the command of the ill-fated Sir Cloudesley Shovel, Admiral of the White, was sent to rendezvous with Rooke. Under Shovel were Vice-Admiral Sir Stafford Fairborne and Vice-Admiral George Byng, whose son Admiral John Byng was to be shot fifty years later for failing to defend the island of Minorca and, as Voltaire put it, '*pour encourager les autres*'. With Shovel sailed three battalions of marines, numbering 1300 men in all, under the command of the Austrian Prince George of Hesse-Darmstadt.

Shovel's force rendezvoused with that of Rooke on 17 July in Tetuan Roads, off Fez, and the joint commanders conferred aboard the *Royal Catherine*. Both fleets had been at sea for nearly six months, and in the absence of direct Admiralty orders, had to decide on a course of action, but they were uncertain on what lines to proceed. Information had been received, however, that Gibraltar's defences were weak, and on impulse Rooke decided to attack the rock-bound fortress.

On the morning of 21 July the combined fleets of Rooke and Shovel put into Gibraltar Bay, and immediately landed Hesse-Darmstadt and his force of marines on the sandy isthmus to the north of the rock with orders to cut off all communication with the mainland of Spain. The prince sent an order to surrender to the governor, the Marquis de Salines, who refused, although he had only 150 regular soldiers and a number of armed civilians. Rooke lost two days because of a flat calm which forced him to warp his fleet into position, but on the morning of 23 July twelve British and six Dutch ships-of-the-line opened a six-hour bombardment, unleashing an estimated 15,000 cannonballs into the Spanish batteries and driving the gunners from their weapons. To consolidate the position a shore party landed, captured an eight-gun battery intact and turned it on the town. De Salines realized that his position was completely hopeless, and surrendered on honourable terms to Rooke, being allowed to march out with three cannon and provisions for six days' march. Prince Hesse-Darmstadt was installed as governor in his stead.

For almost a year the French and Spanish repeatedly mounted expeditions against the rock and its new defenders, but after three major defeats, they gave up the task as hopeless. Meanwhile, Rooke took his ships to Ceuta for revictualling, and then put to sea again. On 9 August, sailing eastward of Gibraltar, he sighted a French fleet.

Under cover of darkness, however, the French gave Rooke the slip, and he spent two laborious days beating to windward, following them only by the distant sound of their signal guns. On 12 August the reason for their flight became apparent; they were joining up with a larger force off Velez Malaga and the following day they turned south, to the leeward of the Anglo-Dutch fleet, and prepared to fight. The French commander was Admiral the Comte de Toulouse, and his fleet numbered fifty-one ships carrying a total of 3596 guns. Rooke's fleet was almost exactly equal in strength, comprising fifty-one ships and a total of 3636 guns. Rooke, with Rear-Admirals Byng and Dilkes, led the centre, Shovel and Sir John Leake led the van, and the Dutchmen Calembourg and Vanderdussen the rear.

Rooke's career, though brilliant at times, was erratic. He was capable of grave misjudgments and at least two major errors stood against him at Velez Malaga. He had had time, during his months of inaction off Fez, to careen his ships for cleaning, but had neglected to do so. As a result their hulls were foul, making them far less handy than their French counterparts. In addition – and more seriously – he had neglected to rearm properly after his massive bombardment of Gibraltar. As a result his guns had only twenty-five balls apiece, and at the height of the subsequent battle his gunners had to break off action to fill canvas cartridges with powder – a dangerous and time-wasting practice.

Nevertheless he was now committed to fight or run, and as the French looked likely to weather him if he wasted further time, at ten o'clock in the morning he ordered close action, and opened fire. From then until dusk both sides battered each other at half-cannon-shot range. By two in the afternoon, the French van gave way under Shovel's fire and broke off the action, followed shortly by the rear;

Admiral Calembourg had re-equipped his squadron independently after Gibraltar, and was able to make better headway in the fighting than his allies. By late afternoon, however, the centre squadron under Rooke himself was desperately low on ammunition and their only hope seemed to be to grapple and board the enemy; but the French managed to evade such close grips.

Nightfall came as a relief to both fleets. The French and Spanish galleys were employed in towing away the crippled line-of-battle ships, and though the wind veered around in the night to westward, giving the French the weather gauge, de Toulouse made no effort to re-engage. Instead, the two fleets lay within 10km (6 miles) of each other, making hasty repairs and burying their dead.

In terms of dead, wounded, and damage both sides came out more or less equal; surprisingly, no ships were lost or captured on either side, but Shovel later recounted that in the whole Allied fleet 'there were not three spare topmasts left'. De Toulouse retired two days later for Toulon, where repairs took several months to carry out; even when he was fit to put to sea again, Sir Cloudesley Shovel's squadron pinned him in harbour for many more months. Rooke took his ships back to Gibraltar for refit and by September was able to report in person to Queen Anne at Windsor.

The War of Spanish Succession went on until 1713, and from the point of view of the Anglo-Dutch allies was in vain. Philip V remained on the throne of Spain despite their efforts. From Britain's standpoint, however, Rooke's hasty decision had brought her the most valuable naval prize she was ever to win – Gibraltar. Over half a century later the Spanish made a determined effort to win it back, besieging the governor-general, George Augustus Elliot, for three years between 1781 and 1783. But by that time British engineers had improved the old fortifications of Tariq until they were totally impregnable. As one artillery colonel wrote afterwards: 'No power whatever can take that place, unless a plague, pestilence, famine, or the want of ordnance, musketry and ammunition, or some unforeseen stroke of Providence should happen.'

A reconstruction of the bombardment and capture of Gibraltar by Admiral Sir George Rooke in 1704. The 'Rock' became one of the foundations of British maritime power during the eighteenth century.

Quiberon Bay

THE FOILING OF THE FRENCH INVASION

Augustus Keppel, captain of HMS *Torbay* at the Quiberon Bay engagement in November 1759.

A succession of British victories in 1759 led to the year being named the *annus mirabilis* (wonderful year) or the Year of Victories. The Seven Years' War had begun badly for Britain with the loss of Minorca and the occupation of George II's electorate of Hanover by the French. However, by 1759 Britain had regained the initiative both at sea and in the struggle on land.

An Anglo-Hanoverian force defeated a superior French army at Minden on 1 August 1759 and this success opened the way for the reoccupation of Hanover. Unfortunately Britain's ally, Frederick the Great of Prussia, fared less well and his defeat by the Russians and Austrians at Kunersdorf prevented the advantage won at Minden from being fully exploited. Britain's campaigns overseas met with no such setbacks. Clive conquered large parts of India, Guadeloupe in the West Indies was captured and in Canada Wolfe's amphibious assault took Quebec. Wolfe's army was carried up the St Lawrence river by a British fleet under Admiral Saunders.

The key to Britain's conquest of French colonies was her command of the sea. The strategy of blockade which was adopted by the Royal Navy prevented France from reinforcing her territories overseas. It also served to guard against Louis XV's projected invasion of England, by bottling up the ships that Louis needed to carry his invading army. In July 1759 Sir George Rodney destroyed a fleet of flat-bottomed boats which had been collected at Le Havre. The following month Edward Boscawen defeated the Toulon fleet off Lagos in Portugal, capturing three ships and driving two others aground.

Most of France's warships were concentrated at Brest, France's principal naval base, under the command of the Comte de Conflans. There they were closely blockaded by the British Channel Fleet, which was led by Admiral Sir Edward Hawke. Hawke was an experienced officer, who had won his knighthood in a spirited action against a French squadron in 1747. It was he who devised the tactics for the blockade. In addition to the main fleet which lay off Ushant, an inshore squadron watched the approaches to Brest in order to warn Hawke immediately if the French fleet set sail.

In fine weather, the ships of the British fleet were constantly at sea, their stores being replenished by victuallers from Plymouth. However, when a westerly gale blew up, they were forced to run for shelter in Torbay, 320km (200 miles) from Brest. In November 1759, de Conflans took advantage of the interval between the ending of a storm and Hawke's fleet regaining its station to slip out of the harbour at Brest with twenty-one ships-of-the-line.

Hawke had detached a number of his frigates, which rode out the storm in Douarnenez Bay, to guard against a French escape. Nevertheless, de Conflans eluded them and sailed south to Quiberon Bay where he was to embark the French army of invasion. His escape had not gone unnoticed, however, for two British supply ships had sighted the French fleet and they alerted Hawke when he regained Ushant on 19 November.

On the afternoon of the following day, in wild

squally weather, de Conflans was approaching Quiberon Bay. There he sighted the detached English frigates and gave chase. Soon afterwards his masthead lookout reported Hawke's fleet to the west and de Conflans altered course for the safety of Quiberon Bay. He believed that Hawke would not dare to follow him, as darkness was falling and the wind was blowing straight on to the rocks and shoals which surrounded the anchorage off Vannes.

The English admiral confounded his opponent by signalling the 'general chase'. This order freed the individual commanders from the rigid line-of-battle formation and enabled each to attack the first ship encountered. Hawke's fleet, with *Magnanime*, *Torbay*, *Dorsetshire*, *Resolution* and *Warspite* in the van, came up with the French at the entrance to Quiberon Bay. The first casualty was the French *Thésée*, which was laid on her beam ends by a squall and quickly sank. *Héros* was forced to strike her colours to *Magnanime* (a British ship which had been captured from the French eleven years before), but before the British could board her she was blown aground.

Hawke's flagship *Royal George*, in pursuit of de Conflans's *Soleil Royal*, came upon the battered *Superbe* and sank her with two broadsides. The eighty-gun *Formidable* was taken as a prize by the British and as night was falling Hawke ordered his fleet to anchor. The wind continued to blow hard onto a lee-shore and during the hours of darkness two British ships, *Essex* and *Resolution*, went aground. They could not be refloated and so they were burned and their crews taken off.

At daybreak Hawke's *Royal George* lay within gunshot of *Soleil Royal*. The French admiral had no wish to resume the battle, but in his haste to escape he ran his ship aground. She was burned by her crew and all Hawke's men could salvage from the inferno was her carved figurehead. Most of the surviving French ships slipped away during 21 November. However, to complete Hawke's triumph, *Juste* foundered off the Loire estuary and *Inflexible* broke her back while attempting to cross the shallow bar of the River Vilaine.

In all the French had lost seven ships and their defeat forced Louis XV to abandon his invasion plans. Hawke's bold attack under difficult and dangerous conditions was widely acclaimed in Britain. When, shortly afterward, David Garrick composed the song 'Hearts of Oak', the triumph of Hawke and the men under his command at the battle of Quiberon Bay was fresh in his mind.

ABOVE Sir Edward Hawke, whose boldness in ordering a 'general chase' resulted in a notable British victory.

LEFT A contemporary painting of the battle of Quiberon Bay, in which the French lost seven ships.

George Anson

1697–1762

Popularly known as 'father of the navy', Admiral Lord Anson followed a notable plundering expedition with a career as one of the Admiralty's most far-sighted administrators.

The career of Admiral Lord Anson heralded one of the most glorious epochs in the history of the British navy. His pioneering work at the Admiralty, which earned him the nickname of 'father of the navy', revitalized naval organization and reinforced Britain's standing as a seapower. And yet, today, he is remembered best for his circumnavigation of the world in 1740–44. This hazardous voyage saw the capture of the most valuable booty ever brought home in a British vessel. But ironically Anson's historic expedition was to be the last of its kind and marked a turning point in naval strategy.

Born in Stafford in 1697, George Anson soon developed a passion for the sea and entered the navy at the tender age of fifteen as a volunteer. In 1718 he saw action at the battle of Cape Pessaro and four years later he was given command of the sloop *Weasel*. However, his real opportunity came when, as a seasoned commander in his early forties, he was placed in command of a fleet to be sent to disrupt Spanish trade in the Pacific.

In 1739 war had broken out with Spain. This was the so-called War of Jenkins's Ear which later developed into the War of Austrian Succession. It was Anson's task to sail around Cape Horn and inflict as much damage on the enemy in the Pacific as he could. Such an expedition was little better than licensed piracy, but had long been standard naval practice and was sometimes highly successful in terms of the treasure captured.

Anson's fleet consisted of six ships – his flagship *Centurion, Gloucester, Severn, Pearle, Wager* and *Tryall*, together with two small supply vessels. Of these only *Centurion* was to complete the voyage. In terms of human life the expedition was to prove a catastrophe. Even before setting sail there were problems over finding a crew suitable to endure the hardships that lay ahead. There was such a shortage of sailors that press-gangs had to cudgel 'volunteers' into signing on. When this procedure failed to produce sufficient numbers, Anson was sent 500 pensioners from Greenwich Hospital, out of whom 300 were taken on. These men were totally unfit for service at sea. They had already served their country once, and now, bearing the scars of former battles, they were forced to do so again.

Anson's crews, unfit as they were and undernourished, began to fall victim to illness soon after setting sail in September 1740. Scurvy, caused by the lack of fresh fruit and vegetables, became rampant and by the time the fleet reached the island of St Catherine's off the Brazilian coast the sickness had claimed a heavy toll. Although the fresh food supplies obtained on the island brought some relief, scurvy was to remain a major problem throughout the voyage.

After leaving St Catherine's, having narrowly avoided being attacked by a superior Spanish fleet, Anson continued towards Cape Horn. Rounding the Horn was always a hazardous undertaking, but for Anson it proved exceptionally dangerous. For three months the fleet was met by storms, snow and adverse currents. In addition, ever-increasing sickness was decimating the crews. Anson wrote 'My men are falling down every day with scurvy . . . I have not men able to keep the decks, or sufficient to take in a top-sail, and every day some six or eight are buried'.

In the face of such adverse conditions *Severn* and *Pearle* were forced to turn back, and *Wager* was shipwrecked off the coast of Chile. Only *Centurion, Gloucester* and *Tryall* managed to limp to a safe anchorage off the island of Juan Fernandez. This was the island where the original Robinson Crusoe, Alexander Selkirk, had spent five years, and its abundant supplies of fresh food and water brought relief to Anson's stricken men.

The cost of the voyage so far had been heavy. The three surviving ships had had crews totalling some 900. Of these 626 had already died. Yet Anson was undeterred by these losses and remained determined to carry out his orders to the letter.

After transferring men and supplies, *Tryall* was abandoned while *Centurion* and *Gloucester* went on to capture Payta, the chief seaport of Peru. It was now hoped to attack the Spanish treasure-ship which sailed from the Philippines to Acapulco in Mexico. But by this time the Spanish were alerted to Anson's presence and the galleon managed to avoid his ships.

Thwarted in his intention, Anson set sail for China. Again scurvy broke out among the crew and *Gloucester* had finally to be abandoned. *Centurion* herself was almost lost in a storm off the island of Tinian: while most of the crew were ashore, the ship was swept out to sea and it was only after several days and with the utmost difficulty that the small crew managed to return her safely to the island.

After refitting at the Portuguese settlement of Macao on the China coast, Anson again set out in pursuit of the treasure-ship that had evaded him the previous year. On 20 June 1743 the galleon *Nuestra*

Señora de Cobadonga was sighted off Cape Espíritu Santo in the Philippines. She was fully manned, unlike *Centurion* which had only a fraction of her full crew, but Anson decided on the apparently suicidal plan of direct attack.

The battle lasted less than an hour and a half with Anson's determination overcoming the superior power of the Spanish. The value of the treasure captured amounted to some £50 million in present-day terms. It was a prize that would make Anson rich for life.

On his return to England Anson was the popular hero of the day. In recognition of his achievement he was promoted to a seat on the Admiralty where he remained, with only a short break, for seventeen years, eventually becoming First Lord.

After commanding the victorious British fleet in the first battle of Finisterre in 1747, Anson devoted the rest of his life to work at the Admiralty. Here he was instrumental in modernizing naval organization and ship construction, and it was in this role that Anson made his most enduring contribution to naval history – albeit a less celebrated one than his more lucrative circumnavigation of the globe.

HMS *Centurion* engages the Spanish treasure-galleon *Nuestra Señora de Cobadonga* off Cape Espíritu Santo. Despite being undercrewed, Anson's vessel emerged victorious.

Chesapeake Bay

THE BATTLE THAT LOST AMERICA

The outcome of the American War of Independence was largely decided by the battle of Chesapeake Bay – known in the United States as the battle of the Virginian Capes. It was fought on 5 September 1781, between a French fleet under the Comte de Grasse and a British force under Admiral Thomas Graves, near what was to be the scene of the famous battle of Hampton Roads in 1862, during the American Civil War.

In 1781, Washington's army was besieging the British, under General Cornwallis, at Yorktown, but both commanders had insufficient forces to deal with their opponent and were anxiously awaiting seaborne reinforcements. The French despatched de Grasse from the West Indies, with twenty-eight ships and 3500 troops, to augment Washington's militiamen. They arrived in Chesapeake Bay on 30 August 1781, where they were joined by eight more ships-of-the-line.

Meanwhile, the British were assembling a fleet to relieve Cornwallis. Sir Samuel Hood sailed from the West Indies to a rendezvous with Admiral

ABOVE   Comte François de Grasse, whose arrival from the West Indies precipitated the battle of Chesapeake Bay.

RIGHT   British tactics permitted de Grasse's numerically superior force to reach the open sea.

LEFT   Sir Thomas Graves, whose insistence on the rigid line-of-battle was to prove his undoing and result in the defeat of the British both on land and sea.

When battle was finally joined in Chesapeake Bay, it soon became apparent that Graves's fleet could achieve little without the element of surprise he had thrown away. His rear division, in rigid line-of-battle, was unable to close with the enemy.

Graves at New York and the combined force of nineteen ships hastened south to Yorktown. Neither admiral knew of the other's movements and both were surprised when Graves came upon de Grasse's ships struggling out of Chesapeake, on 5 September.

Although the French fleet was the larger, de Grasse was caught at a disadvantage. Only the van of his force had reached the open sea and so his fleet would have been attacked before it deployed into line-of-battle. Had Graves been a leader of dash or originality, he would have fallen upon part of the enemy with his entire force, with a good chance of gaining a decisive victory and aiding Cornwallis's army. However, Graves missed this golden opportunity. He hoisted the signal for line-of-battle and, while his ships were sorting themselves into this rigid formation, de Grasse was able to prepare his fleet for battle.

The action that followed was little more than an inconclusive cannonade. Samuel Drake led the British van alongside the leading Frenchman and a number of ships in Graves's centre division came within range of the enemy. However, the remaining ships, including all of Hood's rear division, took no active part in the fighting, as they would have been forced to disregard the admiral's signal for 'line-of-battle' in order to close with the enemy.

Graves's conduct, which was defensible according to principles then accepted, was nevertheless criticized by his second-in-command, Sir Samuel Hood. Hood did not, however, have the courage to take the independent action with his rear ships which might have rendered the engagement less unsatisfactory. He allowed a sense of discipline to inhibit him and contented himself with acid comment on Graves's dispositions. It is fair to say that, had the system of signals then in use by the Royal Navy been more flexible, it is possible that Graves and Hood between them might have made something of their opportunity. As it was, the honours of the engagement were entirely with de Grasse.

The British and French fleets remained in sight of each other for two days and Hood urged his admiral to renew the action. Cautious counsels prevailed however, and Graves decided to withdraw his ships to New York. This decision sealed the fate of the British army at Yorktown and, within a month of the battle of Chesapeake Bay, Cornwallis was forced to capitulate.

The British revenged themselves on the French at the battle of the Saints, which was fought in the West Indies in 1782. On this occasion Admiral Rodney decisively defeated de Grasse's smaller fleet, by breaking the sacrosanct line-of-battle. This victory restored Britain's prestige, but her American colonies could not be regained. The success of the rebel colonists was ensured as much by the fleet of Admiral de Grasse as by George Washington and his army.

George Brydges Rodney

1719–1792

Although criticized by many for his extravagant lifestyle and avaricious nature, George Rodney was nevertheless one of Britain's most talented naval commanders.

The eighteenth century was the golden age of patronage in England, and the career of George Brydges Rodney stands as one of the rare successes of a basically unjust and inefficient system. A professional sailor in the unpleasant sense of the phrase – an avaricious man who extracted the last shilling out of his navy career – Rodney was nevertheless a gifted tactician and commander.

Born in 1719, Rodney began his career in the Royal Navy as the archetypal place-seeker, playing his influential contacts for all they were worth. Entering the service at thirteen, he was a lieutenant at nineteen and a post-captain, with the certainty of admiral's rank before him if he lived long enough, at twenty-three. In 1747 he commanded the *Eagle* under Hawke in the victory over the French off Cape Finisterre, coming ashore in the following year for four years as governor of Newfoundland.

It took until 1759 – the year of Minden, Quebec and Quiberon Bay – before Rodney hoisted his flag as rear-admiral. He at once earned renown for his close blockade and bombardment of Le Havre, ending all French hopes of an invasion of England from that port. Rodney ended the Seven Years' War (1756–63) as commander-in-chief of the Leeward Islands station, despoiling the battered French of their West Indian possessions of Martinique, St Lucia, Grenada and St Vincent.

Rodney's wartime achievements were rewarded by his appointment to the lucrative post of gover-

nor of Greenwich Hospital in 1765, but he soon fell into official disfavour. When he was given the Jamaica command he tried to employ a deputy in order to continue drawing payments as governor of Greenwich Hospital, but such cupidity was considered excessive even by the standards of the eighteenth century. It led Rodney into a fierce quarrel with the First Lord of the Admiralty, Lord Sandwich, as his luxurious life-style led him deep into debt. For nearly five years, from 1775 to 1779, Rodney lived in Paris to escape his creditors.

While Rodney languished in financial exile, France declared war on England in support of the rebel American colonists. The French Marshal Biron chivalrously furnished Rodney with a loan which enabled him to return home in the midst of a war which was going disastrously wrong for Britain. The Royal Navy was starved of able commanders, and the old quarrel with Lord Sandwich was soon patched up. Rodney returned to sea in 1780, his first assignment being an attempt to raise the siege of Gibraltar. In so doing he fought the famous 'Moonlight Battle' of 16 January 1780 against a squadron of nine Spanish ships, sinking one and capturing six. The prize money they brought him was no less welcome than his ensuing knighthood of the Bath.

Rodney's last command took him back to the West Indies, where he had an excellent second-in-command in Samuel Hood but a formidable enemy in the Comte de Grasse. Greedy as ever, Rodney shelved the problem of de Grasse for a prior assault on the Dutch island of St Eustatius and its treasure. This duly fell, but Rodney's claims were challenged in the courts by British merchants; the ensuing lawsuits were lengthy. Meanwhile Rodney's health was breaking down and he came home in 1781. He returned to the West Indies station in early 1782 but the Admiralty had already decided to replace him.

Before official notice of his replacement had reached the West Indies, Rodney had temporarily silenced his critics by his decisive victory over de Grasse at the battle of the Saints on 12 April 1782. This erased the temporary French naval supremacy west of the Atlantic, established by the French victory in Chesapeake Bay, and enabled the British to emerge from an otherwise disastrous war with much better terms than had seemed possible before the battle. The Saints also brought Rodney a peerage, which he enjoyed until his death in 1792.

The Saints

A TRIUMPH FOR REVOLUTIONARY TACTICS

The British naval victory on 12 April 1782 known as the battle of the Saints was instrumental in saving Britain from defeat at the hands of a most powerful enemy coalition comprising France, Spain and the American colonies; it also ended a seven-month period of French naval supremacy in the western Atlantic and marked the beginning of a new era in naval tactics.

By 1781, the British forces had clearly failed in their bid to crush the rebellion of the thirteen American colonies. The naval defeat of Chesapeake Bay (5 September 1781) and the subsequent surrender of Cornwallis's army at Yorktown (19 October) left the Americans with independence assured, and the French thirsting for future conquests to avenge their losses during the Seven Years' War. The obvious targets were the British possessions in the Caribbean, and the French prepared to send massive reinforcements out to Martinique. With the Comte de Grasse and his fleet still masters of the southern American seaboard and the Caribbean, these reinforcements could well have resulted in Britain losing her colonies in the Caribbean as well as the American colonies.

Britain's recovery from this peril began on 12 December 1781 when Rear-Admiral Kempenfelt, with a small fleet of twelve ships-of-the-line, intercepted the French convoy on the first stage of its Atlantic crossing, 240 km (150 miles) south-west of Ushant. The French Admiral de Guichen was escorting the convoy with nineteen ships-of-the-line, and Kempenfelt refused to court certain disaster in a fleet action. In a splendid demonstration of combined nerve and seamanship he ducked round the rear of de Guichen's line, worked up to windward and got in among the merchantmen. Twenty ships of the convoy were captured and the rest were sunk or scattered. It was a decisive blow at France's long-term strategy, for the chronically ailing French economy could not meet the cost of assembling another convoy. Kempenfelt's victory, however, only meant that de Grasse would not be getting the substantial reinforcements for which he had hoped. As de Grasse still had over thirty ships-of-the-line against the nineteen of Rear-Admiral Hood, the chances of further French successes in the Caribbean were still high.

To counter this the British Admiralty sent out another seventeen ships to reinforce Hood under Admiral Sir George Rodney, who resumed his command in the West Indies in February 1782 after a year's sick leave in England. Sixty-three years old, tired and still far from well, Rodney was nevertheless determined to bring de Grasse to action and add a third victory to his relief of Gibraltar and the 'Monlight Battle' against the Spaniards back in 1780.

Instead of waiting for de Grasse to show his hand, Rodney and Hood headed south-east to the French Antilles to seek him out. As a result they collided with the French fleet in the Saints Passage, between Guadeloupe and Dominica, as de Grasse came north to attack Jamaica. The British had a slight numerical advantage: thirty-six line-of-battle ships to the thirty-four of de Grasse. The latter, however, was escorting a French convoy and had been planning to rendezvous with a Spanish battle-squadron; the sudden appearance of the British fleet was a decidedly unwelcome surprise.

De Grasse reacted with great courage and tactical skill. His first concern was naturally for the convoy, and he contrived to bring about three days of sparring with Rodney and Hood which enabled the convoy to get clear. On 9 April Hood, leading the British van, came up with the rear of the French fleet, and de Grasse rounded on him in full strength. Hood fell back as Rodney came up with the British main body, whereupon de Grasse drew off in turn. On the night of 10 April, however, two of the French ships were damaged in a collision; rather than abandon them to the British, de Grasse made the decision to accept a fleet action.

The rival fleets formed the traditional lines-of-battle at first light on 12 April. The French and British lines approached each other on opposite tacks, de Grasse having won the advantage of the weather gauge. The action began at 7 a.m. as the leading ships crossed, and the result of the first clash between the fleets would probably have been an inconclusive bombardment with honours roughly even. At 9.15 a.m., however, the wind suddenly veered four points, no easy problem for first rates reduced to 'fighting sail', with their handling qualities reduced in consequence. The British fleet managed to hold formation but two French ships were taken aback by this shift in the wind; as a result, two yawning gaps opened in the French line.

There is still considerable debate over who deserves the credit for what happened next. Various sources aver that Rodney reacted instinctively in

ordering his fleet to drive through the gaps; it is more likely, however, that Rodney's captain of the fleet, Sir Charles Douglas, was responsible for the tactic. In any event, Rodney's flagship *Formidable* led the British centre division through one gap while Hood's rear division, headed by Captain Affleck in the *Bedford*, penetrated the other. One ship from the British van also broke through.

Thus for the first time in naval history a fleet in formal line-of-battle had its formation pierced and its ships engaged from the other side to the enemy's original position. This move by the British, being unrehearsed, failed to bring about the destruction of the French fleet, partly because Rodney ruled his captains with an iron hand and never made the remotest effort to take his subordinates into his confidence. Twenty-three years later, at Trafalgar, Nelson knew that he could rely on his captains to carry out his overall intentions, but that was not Rodney's way. As a result, the breaking of the French line at the Saints caused almost as much confusion on the British side as on the French, far too many of whose disengaged ships were allowed to fall off to leeward, re-form and escape.

De Grasse was not among them. His flagship, the *Ville de Paris*, was trapped by Hood's division. For over eight hours the 112-gun *Ville de Paris* heroically beat off attack after attack, until she finally struck her colours to Hood's *Barfleur* at 6.29 p.m. after suffering appalling casualties. Only four other French ships were captured, one of them being the former British *Ardent*. Rodney was quite content to have captured the French admiral and sent the enemy fleet running for its life. He overruled Hood's urgent pleas for an all-out pursuit through the night of 12–13 April and the British fleet remained hove-to until the following day.

Rodney's caution lasted for six days after the action in the Saints Passage, when he finally let the furious Hood off the leash and sent him off with ten line-of-battle ships and a couple of frigates to find out what the French were up to. Hood set off at once for the Mona Passage – the strait between Puerto Rico and Santa Domingo – and made such good time that he overtook the rear French ships on 19 April, falling on them with a 'general chase'. Hood's subsequent capture of two French line-of-battle ships, a frigate and an ex-British sloop, completed the discomfiture of the French, who attempted no further fleet operations in this theatre until peace was signed in the following year.

The great contribution of the Saints action was its liberating effect on British naval tactics, encouraging later admirals such as Howe, Jervis, Duncan and Nelson to bring their full strength to bear against weak spots in the enemy line instead of relying on inconclusive gunnery duels in which victory would go to the side with the highest firepower. Writing the year after Trafalgar, Lord St Vincent stressed that 'the great talent is to take prompt advantage of disorder in the fleet of the enemy, by shifts of wind, accidents, and their deficiency in practical seamanship, to the superior knowledge of which much of our success is to be attributed'. For all its flaws, Rodney's victory at the Saints blazed the way to later triumphs.

The French and British fleets clash at the battle of the Saints, where Rodney succeeded in piercing his opponents' line-of-battle and putting them to flight.

Pierre-André de Suffren Saint Tropez

1729–1788

Honoured by the bestowal of the special rank of vice-admiral, Pierre-André de Suffren St Tropez ended his career in the service of France without having suffered an outright defeat in battle.

Many French historians consider Pierre-André de Suffren St Tropez to be the finest admiral in their country's history. He was born into the minor nobility of Provence and, like many younger sons, took up the navy as a career at the age of thirteen, when he enlisted as a *garde de la marine* (midshipman) and became a member of the Order of Malta. The middle years of the eighteenth century presented splendid opportunities for young Frenchmen seeking naval action, and while he was still a *garde* Suffren fought in a battle off Toulon, at Fort Louisburg and at Monarque, where, during the brave attack which l'Etanduère led against Hawke, he was taken prisoner by the British. Promoted to lieutenant, Suffren continued to serve in France's long struggle for mastery against Great Britain, and in 1759 he was again captured, when the *Océan* was taken by Admiral Boscawen off Lagos. Promoted to commander in the Order of Malta, he joined Chaffault's somewhat unsuccessful expedition to Morocco in 1765.

When the American revolution began in 1776, Suffren was forty-seven years old. He was short, unbecomingly fat, but self-assured and knowledgeable. In 1778 he was given command of the *Fantasque* and despatched to the American coast, where he served under the Comte d'Estaing, distinguishing himself especially in the battle of Grenada. But it was the entry of Holland into the war which provided the circumstances in which Suffren made his lasting reputation. By coming in on the side of France and America, Holland exposed her colonies to British attack. Suffren was ordered, in 1781, to carry troops to reinforce the Dutch colony at the Cape of Good Hope. Commodore Johnstone and five ships (three of them fifty-gunners) were already sailing towards the tip of Africa to capture the colony.

En route to the Cape, Suffren made for Porto Bravo on Santiago Island, one of the Cape Verde group of islands, to pick up water. One of his ships, which was sailing ahead in a scouting mission, reported that Johnstone's squadron was already anchored in the roadstead there. Customary French tactics called for Suffren to sail at full speed in order to beat the enemy to the Cape. That was the cautious course. Suffren chose the other option, preferring to attack the British where they lay in the hope of preventing their reaching the Cape at all. For years Suffren had been critical of French naval operations and he seized the opportunity to demonstrate what *élan* and initiative could achieve. Sailing ships, lacking high speed and very long-range guns, were scarcely ever able to surprise the enemy. But Suffren did, at least, catch Johnstone off guard, and although his attack was somewhat hasty and therefore ill-coordinated (the French suffered heavier losses than the British), it succeeded in saving the Dutch colony. By the time that Johnstone reached the Cape Suffren had landed his troops and organized his squadron into a powerful position which the British dared not attack. Unorthodox though his action had been, Suffren was rewarded by promotion from commander to the high rank of *bailli* in the Order of Malta.

In the years 1782–3 Suffren engaged the British admiral, Sir Edward Hughes, on five occasions in the Indian Ocean. The odds were greatly in the enemy's favour. The British fleet out-gunned the French and it had a base at which to refit its ships. There is, too, little dispute about the inferior capacity of Suffren's captains. Nevertheless, in each action Suffren met the enemy at close range and fought it to a standstill. By his determination and tactical resource he managed to land troops in India and save French and Dutch possessions in the East.

Suffren's patriotism, courage, daring and skill were acclaimed in France. On his return home Louis XVI created the special post of vice-admiral for him (the rank did not survive Suffren's death). In 1788 he was appointed commander of the Brest fleet. But Suffren did not again put out to sea. In the autumn of 1788 he died, whether from gout or wounds received in a duel remains unclear. By then his place in history was secure. It is true that he never commanded more than fifteen ships in the line and that he never won an outright victory. More to the point, for a French admiral opposing the might of the Royal Navy in the second half of the eighteenth century, he never suffered an outright defeat.

Hangö and Svenskund

RUSSIA AND SWEDEN BATTLE FOR THE BALTIC

During the course of the sixteenth and seventeenth centuries, Sweden gradually replaced Denmark and the declining medieval Hanseatic League as the dominant power in the Baltic Sea. With this increase in naval power Sweden acquired control of the lucrative Sound tolls between Sweden and Denmark and became involved in the affairs of Germany, Poland and the Baltic States. Swedish power was dependent less on Swedish strength than on the weaknesses of her neighbours. If these powers combined then the days of the Swedish Empire were numbered. By the end of the seventeenth century such a combination was organized by the ambitious Tsar of Russia, Peter the Great, and at Poltava in 1709, he inflicted on the Swedes a crushing defeat, capturing the bulk of the Swedish army. The following year the Swedish Baltic provinces of Karelia, Ingria, Livonia and Estonia fell to Peter's advancing armies, and he gained control of the Baltic coast. The emergence of Russia as an important naval power was about to begin.

Swedish difficulties were exacerbated by the

An engraving of Peter the Great, dating from 1707. He took little part in naval battles, leaving the command of his fleet to mercenary officers who served the Russian cause.

naval tactics that Peter introduced into naval warfare in the Baltic. Although he relied on British master shipbuilders to design his ships-of-the-line, he also imported Greek and Italian shipbuilders into Russia to design and build galleys along Mediterranean lines for use along the heavily indented Finnish coastline. Peter had great difficulty finding crews for these ships. He had to impress soldiers and reluctant peasants, and eventually convicted criminals, whose conduct was considered barbarous even by the standards of the eighteenth century. Officers were usually foreign mercenaries, for efforts to acquire a cadre of Russian officers by sending out young nobles to observe foreign navies failed; when they returned it was found that these young men, 'instead of attaining the rudiments of a seaman . . . acquired only the insignificant accomplishments of a fine gentleman'.

It is difficult to compare Russian vessels with their Western counterparts. Ships-of-the-line were similar, though frigates were much smaller with only one deck and thirty guns. Large galleys were 45m (150ft) long, with crews of 260 and large guns fore and aft – though most galleys were much smaller. Russian vessels were weak in armament, with poor cannon, powder and shot. There were about 200 galleys in the Russian fleet though this number often varied. A social division was also marked: a distinction between the professional Russian navy serving in the larger vessels and the uncouth convicts labouring below decks in the galleys.

The naval actions of the Great Northern War (1700–1721) were largely confined to the western Baltic, but the battle of Hangö (1714) took place in the Gulf of Finland. The Finnish coast is jagged, fringed with rocks and islands – ideal waters for the shallow draught of the Russian galleys. Russian victory was due both to this and to their superior speed. A hundred Russian galleys had successfully outmanoeuvred a squadron of seven Swedish ships-of-the-line, moved between it and the coast, and forced the Swedes to take refuge near Hangö. They drew up in battle formation to await the inevitable Russian attack. There followed a long and bloody battle during which forty galleys were sunk before the Swedes were overwhelmed.

Despite the general expansion of Russian power in the eighteenth century, the Baltic never became a Russian lake, for the Swedes maintained their naval

ПЕТРЬ ВЕЛИКIЙ

A Russian galley of the eighteenth century. The galley remained an important element in the Baltic fleets of both Sweden and Russia until the beginning of the nineteenth century.

presence. Indeed, later in the century they inflicted a decisive defeat on the burgeoning empire of Catherine the Great at the second battle of Svenskund – the largest naval battle ever fought in the waters of the Baltic.

Gustavus III of Sweden had attacked Russia in 1788, but his land forces were halted and his navy suffered a defeat at Viborg in July 1790. While the Swedish fleet was reorganizing at Svenskund, the Russians regrouped. The Russian commander, Nassau-Siegen, a mercenary adventurer, was confident that the attack could be successfully renewed on 9 July and the Swedish fleet annihilated.

The Swedish fleet at Svenskund consisted of six sailing vessels, eighteen galleys, eight bombs, one yacht and 153 gunboats, a total of 186 ships and 1200 guns. Nassau-Siegen had thirty sailing ships, twenty-three galleys, three batteries, eight bombs, and seventy-seven gunboats, a total of 141 ships and 1500 guns. These figures reveal a twenty per cent margin of superiority in favour of the Russians, and this should have guaranteed victory. But the command factor is usually crucial in war, and on this score the odds were stacked heavily in favour of the Swedes. The Swedish commander, Gustavus III, arranged his forces in a curved line with his most powerful vessels, the gunboats, on the wings; his

centre was therefore comparatively vulnerable and liable to be driven back, exposing the attackers to the devastating enfilading fire of his gunboats. The Russians played into the hands of the crafty Swedish king. They mounted a strong, frontal attack on the Swedish right, and a combination of Swedish fire and high winds drove them back.

Nassau-Siegen thereupon ordered his ships to move forward on the Swedish centre and as they did so they became enveloped on both flanks – a manoeuvre reminiscent of Hannibal's defeat of the Romans at Cannae. They were raked by fire from both sides, and by 7 p.m. in the evening Nassau-Siegen ordered the retreat. The Russians, however, could not disengage so easily and firing continued for another three hours.

The second battle of Svenskund was a great Swedish victory. It allowed Sweden to make peace with Russia without territorial loss even though she lost all the battles except the last. It was also the last time galleys were used in naval warfare. The Swedish fleet only lost four vessels and 300 men. The Russian fleet sustained losses of sixty-four vessels sunk or captured, and 7369 casualties. The main strategic significance of the battle was that during the Napoleonic Wars Sweden managed to keep control of the eastern Baltic.

Richard Howe

1726–1799

Richard, Earl Howe, Admiral of the Fleet, was a fighting admiral whose stature as a model for any British naval officer was only exceeded by Nelson. Hawke, the victor of Quiberon Bay, once said of him: 'I have tried my Lord Howe on most important occasions. He never asked me how he was to execute any service entrusted to his charge, but always went straight ahead and performed it.'

Howe's family had profited greatly from the Protestant succession in England and his father had married a daughter of George I's mistress, Richard being born in 1726. Influence helped him to a place in one of Anson's ships, the *Severn*, at the outset of the famous world voyage in 1740. Though Captain Legge of the *Severn* had to turn back in the South Atlantic, Howe learnt much from him.

Howe's insistence on discipline combined with efficiency earned him rapid promotion: he was a captain at the age of twenty and distinguished himself in the War of Austrian Succession and Seven Years' War. At Quiberon Bay in 1759, Howe's *Magnanime* led Hawke's line in the tempestuous destruction of the French fleet. Howe later served as commodore in charge of combined operations off the coast of France.

In the 1760s Howe served on the Board of Admiralty and became treasurer of the navy before hoisting his flag as rear-admiral in 1770. At the outset of the American War of Independence he did his best to support his brother, General Sir William Howe, in the defence of the colonies. In 1778, however, Howe resigned in disagreement with Lord North's government in London and saw no further service for four years. He was recalled on the urgent request of King George III to take command of the Channel Fleet in 1782. Howe's prime task was to run a supply fleet through to besieged Gibraltar, which had been holding out against the Spanish since 1780. This was the third relief attempt, and Howe always considered its accomplishment the greatest achievement of his career.

From 1783 to 1788 Howe served as First Lord of the Admiralty, normally the crowning glory of any British sailor's career, especially an officer of Howe's age and distinction. Howe left the Admiralty with the grant of a peerage, but in 1790 George III once more recalled 'his Earl Richard' to command the Channel Fleet.

The result was the first great naval victory of the Revolutionary and Napoleonic Wars with France:

the 'Glorious First of June' (1794). Ironically, considering that most of Howe's fame still rests on this action, it was in fact a strategic defeat. The vital French grain ships which their battle-fleet had been escorting reached France in safety.

Even after the First of June, Howe's services to the Royal Navy and his country were not over. It took 'Black Dick', as his sailors called him, to defuse the crisis caused by the great Spithead Mutiny of 1797, when the sailors of the Channel Fleet finally agreed to return to duty in return for no victimization and an inquiry into their many grievances. Before the crisis was resolved Howe insisted on visiting every mutinous ship in the fleet, though the effort nearly killed him. While the mutiny lasted, the sailors themselves chose to maintain the discipline of the Channel Fleet which Howe had made a watchword.

Only one distinction remained to Howe after quelling the Spithead Mutiny: his reception into the Order of the Garter, becoming the first knight to be created for purely naval services. He died in 1799.

RIGHT Admiral of the Fleet Richard Howe was recalled after a distinguished career to gain the victory most often associated with him: the 'Glorious First of June'.

The Glorious First of June

A TRIUMPH FOR BRITISH TACTICS

ABOVE The French commander on 1 June 1794 was Admiral Villaret-Joyeuse, who claimed a moral victory.

RIGHT The British *Brunswick* comes under attack on both sides from the French vessels *Achille* and *Vengeur*. The latter was one of seven ships lost by the French that day.

The battle fought on 1 June 1794 far out in the Atlantic was the first major naval engagement in the wars between Britain and France which lasted from 1793 until 1815 and which left the Royal Navy as undisputed master of the seas. The 'Glorious First of June' came at a period of transition during which the rigid formalism that had atrophied naval tactics for much of the eighteenth century gave way to the flexible system under which Nelson and his 'band of brothers' fought.

France had made a clean break with her past by the Revolution of 1789. The navy which had helped Britain's American colonies to gain their independence was transformed by the revolutionary ideas of liberty, equality and fraternity. The practical effect of these doctrines was seen in the fleet which gave battle to the Royal Navy in 1794. Its commander, Admiral Villaret-Joyeuse, had been a lieutenant three years before and his meteoric advancement was by no means untypical. He was assisted by Jean Bon Saint André, a political officer of great ability but no previous naval experience. However, the revolutionary fervour of all ranks went far to offset the lack of experience of the French commanders.

The commander of the Royal Navy's Channel Fleet was certainly not lacking in experience. Richard Howe, then approaching his seventieth year, had served under Anson and in 1759 he had led Hawke's line at Quiberon Bay, earning the praise of his admiral. In 1782 he led a fleet to the relief of Gibraltar and there followed a five-year period as First Lord of the Admiralty. By 1788 Howe was over sixty and intended to retire to his country estate. However, his services could not be spared and in 1790 George III recalled him to command the Channel Fleet – a post he was to hold for the remaining nine years of his life.

Although Howe came from the class of aristocratic naval officers which the Revolution had swept away in France, he was far from being a reactionary. He was instrumental in introducing a new system of signals and first used it during his relief of Gibraltar in 1782. This system was modified in the early 1790s and then remained almost unchanged for the next forty years. As well as being a thoughtful student of naval tactics, he was genuinely concerned for the welfare of the men under his command. The lower-deck nicknamed him 'Black Dick' – a reference to his swarthy

complexion and saturnine temperament – yet they had sufficient confidence in him to accept his mediation during the Spithead Mutiny in 1797.

The serious famine which swept France in 1794 was the immediate cause of the first naval battle of the Revolutionary Wars. More than a hundred ships carrying American grain were assembled in Chesapeake Bay and the French fleet was to sail from Brest to bring the convoy into port. In May 1794 Howe put to sea with the Channel Fleet to intercept the grain convoy and bring the French fleet to action. On 5 May he reached Ushant and, learning that the French had not yet sailed, he turned to the west in search of the convoy. The British fleet returned to Brest on 19 May to find that Villaret-Joyeuse had sailed three days before. Howe set off in pursuit and on 28 May the lookout at the masthead of his flagship, *Queen Charlotte*, sighted the French 16km (10 miles) to windward.

The Admiral hoisted the signal for a 'general chase' and four of his ships managed to close with the French rear. The powerful French three-decker *Révolutionnaire* was put out of action in this skirmish, at the cost of one British ship damaged. The

following day Howe succeeded in still further shortening the odds in his favour. He led three of his ships through the enemy line, thus gaining the weather gauge, which enabled him to attack the enemy at any time he chose. In the process more French ships were put out of action and Villaret-Joyeuse now had twenty-two vessels to Howe's twenty-five. However, on the following day, during which no fighting took place, the French fleet was joined by four more ships, thus making good their losses to the British fleet.

On the morning of 1 June the British admiral was seen to smile – evidently a rare occurrence – and the crew of *Queen Charlotte* rightly took this as an omen that action was imminent. Howe's plan of attack was a daring departure from conventional practice. He proposed that his ships pass through the French line at all points along its length, enabling them to engage the enemy from leeward, thus cutting off their retreat. Such a complex manoeuvre was only possible because the new system of signals enabled it to be properly synchronized.

However, no one was more aware than the British admiral that a well-conceived plan of attack

The scene on board the *Queen Charlotte*, Howe's flagship, during the battle. He stands to the left of the picture, while a mortally wounded soldier, Captain Neville of the Queen's Regiment, receives attention.

was worthless unless it was carried out with panache. As the opposing fleets came together, he closed the signal book which he habitually carried and, turning to his officers, said:

And now, gentlemen, no more books, no more signals. I look to you to do the duty of the *Queen Charlotte* in engaging the French admiral. I do not wish the ships to be bilge and bilge, but if you can lock the yard arms so much the better, the battle will be the sooner decided.

Howe's plan resulted in a *mêlée* such as had not been seen at sea since the Dutch Wars of a hundred years before. HMS *Brunswick* took Howe's injunction to close with the enemy so literally that she was unable to raise the covers of her gunports as they fouled the side of her opponent. They were blown away by the first broadside in her celebrated duel with *Le Vengeur du Peuple*. After receiving a tremendous battering, the French ship struck her colours, but she was so badly damaged that she sank shortly afterwards. The political officer, Jean Bon Saint André, who prudently remained below decks throughout the action, later invented the story that *Vengeur* sank with her colours flying.

None of the British ships was lost, although HMS *Queen* had a narrow escape. When dismasted and to leeward of the British, she was set upon by eleven French ships. She returned their fire to such good effect that none of them closed with the disabled *Queen* and she was able to rig jury masts and return to port without any help from the rest of the fleet.

In addition to *Vengeur*, the French lost two eighty-gun ships-of-the-line, *Juste* and *Sans Pareil*, and the 'seventy-fours' *America*, *Achille*, *Northumberland* and *Impétueux*, all of which were captured.

The surviving French ships were very battered, their decks crowded with wounded, and Howe has been criticized for failing to pursue them after his overwhelming tactical success on 1 June.

There are several factors which account for the British failure to follow up their victory. The sixty-nine-year-old admiral was exhausted by his exertions at the end of the action. Indeed he was so weak that a roll of his ship would have tumbled him into the waist had not one of his officers caught him. Sir Roger Curtis, the fussy and over-anxious captain of the fleet, was against pursuing the defeated enemy and his view prevailed. Furthermore, although no British ship had been lost, the battle had been a fierce one and many ships had suffered damage and heavy casualties.

Not all of Howe's ships were present at the Glorious First of June. A force of eight warships had been detached under Admiral Montagu before the battle to escort a British convoy. These ships were off Brest when they sighted the battered remnants of Villaret-Joyeuse's fleet returning to port. However, Montagu let slip this opportunity of cutting off the French ships from their base and sailed back to port without giving battle. Montagu's action not only allowed the French warships to escape without further punishment, but also enabled the vital grain convoy to make Brest unscathed. This gave the French the strategic advantage, for although they had been soundly trounced by the British, they had gained a safe passage for their convoy. As Villaret-Joyeuse later said, 'while your admiral amused himself refitting his prizes, I saved my convoy and I saved my head'.

There were few in Britain, however, who were disposed to deny Howe the credit for a remarkable feat of arms. When his ships and their prizes lay at anchor at Spithead, George III came down to dine aboard the flagship and to present the admiral with a diamond-encrusted sword. Howe was also offered a marquisate, but this he declined. Of all the tributes and rewards that he received, probably that which moved him most was the congratulations of his seamen. When a deputation from the lower deck came to him after the battle, he replied to them with tears in his eyes, 'No, no, I thank you – it is you, my brave lads – it is you, not I, that have conquered.' That these were not the empty phrases usual on such occasions is shown by Howe's donation of his prize money from the battle for the succour of the wounded seamen.

Not everybody was satisfied by the distribution of awards after the Glorious First of June. George III ordered a gold medal to be struck to commemorate the action, but not all the captains involved received one and this naturally caused resentment. When the Naval General Service medal was introduced in the following century, clasps were authorized to be added to it for all major actions of the Revolutionary and Napoleonic Wars, including the Glorious First of June.

The sorry state of HMS *Defence* at the close of action on 1 June 1794. She had been one of the six British vessels to take the battle to the French line.

John Jervis

1735–1823

To the casual student of naval affairs John Jervis, first Earl St Vincent, is famous for one thing above all others: as supreme commander of the Mediterranean campaign against Napoleon he sponsored a young post-captain named Horatio Nelson. For that piece of judgment alone, St Vincent deserves his niche. 'Without you', observed Nelson with uncharacteristic modesty, 'I am nothing.'

But his patronage of England's greatest admiral was only a by-product of Jervis's true genius; as seaman, tactician, administrator, reformer, and student of humanity he stands out as one of the first and certainly one of the finest all-round naval men that any nation has ever produced. Until his day, high command had lain in the hands of men of birth and preferment, who had little contact with the lower deck. After Jervis, the 'common touch' had become important. Ironically the man responsible for all this was Jervis's father, the mean-minded and inefficient solicitor and treasurer of Greenwich Hospital for seamen.

John Jervis was born inland, at Meaford, Staffordshire, but when his father Swynfen Jervis was appointed solicitor to the board of governors at Greenwich Hospital the family moved to the Thames-side town. The movement of ships on the river fascinated the boy, and eventually he stowed away and hid for three days on a ship moored in Greenwich Reach. He threatened to run away to sea again unless he was allowed a naval career and finally, when he was thirteen, his father gained him a place as midshipman.

In the early eighteenth century – and for many years afterwards – a young midshipman had to meet many expenses. There were uniforms and equipment to be bought as well as luxuries such as wine and extra victuals to improve the quality of life in the gunroom – the midshipmen's mess. In 1751, when he was sixteen, Midshipman Jervis drew what he thought was a perfectly legitimate draught of £20 on his father's account to pay these bills, and his father, short of cash at the time, refused to honour it.

To a youth in Jervis's position such an event should have been disastrous. The least of his worries was the scorn of his colleagues, for without money to pay his bills he had literally no fixed place in the ship to sleep. Discipline prohibited him from slinging a hammock from the beams of gun-decks with ordinary seamen, and pride prevented him from borrowing money to re-establish himself. His answer was to mess with the warrant officers – sailing master, bosun, master gunner, purser, carpenter, cook and surgeon's mate – meanwhile paying off his debt with such petty cash as came his way. On occasion he slept beneath tarpaulin on the upper deck and made himself a pair of trousers from hammock canvas.

The three uncomfortable years he spent in this fashion gave him a view of the navy which was probably unique for his class and time. Not only did he gain first-hand insight into the bad diet, harsh discipline, and indifferent medical treatment of lower-deck men, but he developed an almost telepathic gift for spotting hidden talent; his own peculiar position also developed in him a special kind of gift for leadership, wielded without reference to his rank.

At the end of that time he also had a consummate knowledge of the day-to-day running and navigation of a fighting ship and its crew, with the result that he was quickly promoted to the rank of captain of an unrated ship – its equivalent today would be commander – and then given 'post' rank or command of a ship-of-the-line at the age of twenty-five. In 1759 he sailed with Sir Charles Saunders up the difficult reaches of the St Lawrence River to assist

Wolfe in the taking of Quebec, but after that his career suffered a period in the doldrums; for fourteen years – much of them spent on half pay as an officially 'beached' post-captain – he busied himself learning the science of hydrography, re-drawing Admiralty charts and taking accurate soundings of the waters off Sweden and Russia.

The outbreak of the American War of Independence sent him back to sea in fighting earnest, and in the last year of that war he laid his eighty-eight-gun *Foudroyant* alongside the newly launched French first rate *Pégase* and captured her without death or serious injury to any of his crew – he personally suffered two black eyes in the action. In England the fight caught the public imagination, and Jervis was made a baronet, the first step on a long ladder of promotion and ennoblement. By the opening of the Revolutionary War with France in 1793 he was a vice-admiral, and he was sent with a small squadron to capture the West Indian islands of Guadeloupe, St Lucia and Martinique. Two years later, at the age of sixty and as commander-in-chief, he began the Mediterranean campaign during which he was to engineer two spectacular victories – St Vincent and the Nile – though the success of both was popularly accredited to Nelson.

However, one of Jervis's decisions in the Mediterranean had further-reaching effects than any of his tactical actions. He met an elderly naval surgeon, Dr Andrew Baird, who had been quietly interesting himself for some time in the problems of scurvy and typhoid in the fleet. Scurvy – caused through lack of vitamin C – became rife among crews who were at sea for more than a few weeks and forced to exist on a diet of dried and pickled meat and ship's biscuit. It caused teeth to fall out and skin to become blotchy and eventually led to weakness and lethargy which often ended in death. Since 1753 it had been known that orange, lemon or lime juice was effective against scurvy, but little had been done to supply the fleet with this remedy. Jervis listened to Dr Baird's views on the subject and then gave him *carte blanche* to order sufficient lime juice for the whole Mediterranean fleet, later making a regular supply compulsory throughout the navy. Limes were the citrus fruit chosen because they were freely available from British possessions in the West Indies. (Incidentally, the practice of issuing lime juice on board British ships led US sailors to call British seamen 'limeys', a nickname that later came to be used of all Britons.) Under Jervis's instructions Dr Baird also attacked the problem of typhoid, instituting rigorous cleansing procedures in order to rid the cramped lower decks of the typhus-carrying louse.

It was on 14 January 1795 that Captain Horatio Nelson first reported to Jervis and the two men struck up an immediate but curious rapport. Temperamentally they were totally dissimilar, and in later years Jervis was to criticize Nelson harshly for his private conduct, particularly over his affair with Lady Hamilton and his tactless boasting. On one occasion he wrote: 'He is a partisan devoured with vanity . . . his sole merit animal courage, his private character most disgraceful.' But Jervis's ability to see to the heart of a character was unfailing and he instantly recognized Nelson's abilities as a naval tactician and leader of men. Nelson complained that he felt that he was being passed over; Jervis's reply was to promote him to commodore, with command of the seventy-four gun *Captain*. Seventeen months later Nelson gave resounding proof of his worth at the battle of Cape St Vincent. During the battle the apparently telepathic contact between the two men came into play, for at the very minute Nelson wore his ship out of line to attack the Spaniards independently, Jervis was making a general signal from his flagship *Victory* for all vessels to do just that.

For their parts in the battle, Nelson was created Knight of the Bath and promoted to rear-admiral, while Jervis became Baron Meaford, Earl and Viscount St Vincent, a title suggested by George III himself. Later that year Nelson lost his right arm at Santa Cruz, but after a period of recuperation he was back on the active list and St Vincent sent for him, Nelson flying his flag in the *Vanguard*. At that time St Vincent was blockading Cadiz with his fleet, his immediate underlings being Rear-Admiral Sir William Parker, his number two at Cape St Vincent, and Sir John Orde.

News had reached St Vincent that Napoleon himself was manoeuvring in the Mediterranean, and he conceived the idea of sending a detached British squadron to hunt him down while the main body of ships kept to the Cadiz station. As soon as Nelson reached Cadiz, St Vincent appointed him commander of the 'roving' squadron. It was another snap decision, though based soundly on his psychological judgment, for after the Cape St Vincent battle Nelson's name had become a rallying cry in the fleet. Unfortunately it cut clean across Admiralty rules and general practice; either Parker, fifteen years Nelson's senior, or Orde, with seven years' seniority, should have had the plum job of leading a hand-picked squadron to almost certain glory and prize money.

Both of them were furious, confronted St Vincent and demanded that he cancel the order, but St Vincent, having made up his mind, was obdurate, even at the risk of offending the two admirals. Orde, when he persisted, was sent home and remained 'beached' – without command – for six years. Parker was a different proposition. He had become a minor public hero while commanding the *Audacious* at the 'Glorious First of June' battle under Howe, and at Cape St Vincent his ninety-eight-gun command *Prince George* had pounded the 112-gun Spaniard *San Josef* into helplessness, leaving Nelson to board and capture her. Refusing to accept St Vincent's decision he and Orde tried to go over their chief's head by sending letters of complaint to the Board of the Admiralty. Unfortunately for themselves,

Parker and Orde were still writing these missives when Nelson scored his resounding victory at the battle of the Nile in August 1798. St Vincent's judgment was again remarkably vindicated and in fact he had been laying his own head on the block, not only in choosing Nelson above the two senior officers, but also by splitting his fleet on what was little more than a calculated gamble. Tactically – and although he was not present at the battle – the Nile victory was as much St Vincent's as it was Nelson's.

After the Nile, Nelson went first to Naples, where he recovered from a slight head wound, and then travelled overland back to England with Sir William and Lady Emma Hamilton. The affair between Emma and Nelson was flagrantly blooming, and news of it was widespread in London by the time the party reached home four months later. St Vincent sided with Nelson's wife, Frances, and denounced his protégé in what appear to be unnecessarily vicious terms, although there were strong reasons for this. He was suffering a bad health breakdown which was a direct result of his own tireless devotion to the Royal Navy, and he felt that a man in Nelson's position should not act in a way that might reflect badly on the service. But his concern was for his country, not directed against Nelson as an individual; shortly before the little admiral put to sea for the last time in the campaign which was to result in Trafalgar, St Vincent, to

whom Nelson alluded affectionately as 'My dear Lord' wrote to him: 'God bless you, no man loves and esteems you more truley.'

In 1800 St Vincent was recovered from his illness, but at sixty-five was too old for sea service. He was made First Lord of the Admiralty, however, and spent almost the whole of the last twenty-three years of his life in the House of Lords battling for better conditions in the navy; he was a gregarious man and kept excellent cellars at his London house in Margaret Street and at Rochetts, his country retreat in Essex, having a pension of £2000 a year from the Cape St Vincent victory and a great deal of invested prize money. Much of the entertaining was used to influence prominent figures. He managed, for instance, to abolish almost single-handedly the corruption rife in naval dockyards and other shore establishments, and whose practitioners were, in a way, exemplified by his father, who had cut him off at sea without a penny. In 1821, on the coronation of George IV, he received his ultimate accolade and was made admiral of the fleet, remaining in naval harness to aid old seamen and their wives both from his own pocket and from Admiralty coffers. His generosity was well known; 'I never yet have forsaken any man who served well under me,' he said. His kindness extended beyond the ranks of mankind: he even composed an epitaph for his pet cat. St Vincent died in 1823, only two years after his appointment as admiral of the fleet.

Jervis's tactics at the battle of St Vincent yielded a fine harvest of Spanish ships; depicted here is the surrender of two enemy vessels to Nelson's seventy-four-gun *Captain*.

Cape St Vincent

A VICTORY AGAINST THE ODDS

Cape St Vincent, or the 'St Valentine's Day Battle' of 14 February 1797 was one of the most dramatic British sea victories in the decade before Trafalgar. It was an interesting anticipation of Trafalgar, being fought in the same waters, shattering the Spanish battle-fleet and preventing Spain from helping France to launch an invasion of England. On the tactical level Cape St Vincent has always been famous for an inspired act of disobedience on the part of Commodore Horatio Nelson, without which the British fleet would probably have scored only a limited success.

By the New Year of 1797 the future was looking grim for Britain in her struggle with Revolutionary France. French land victories over the past four years had largely cancelled out Britain's supremacy at sea, forcing the British to pull their fleet out of the Mediterranean and operate from Portuguese waters. When Spain declared war on Britain in 1796, the latter faced the prospect of the Spanish fleet breaking out from the Mediterranean, joining forces with the French fleet in Brest and so creating an overwhelming enemy naval concentration for a cross-Channel invasion. The French republican government put heavy diplomatic pressure on Spain to carry out this move. The circumstances which brought the Spanish and British fleets into collision off Cape St Vincent were, however,

accidental rather than the deliberate workings of grand strategy.

Admiral Juan de Cordova sailed from Cartagena in the Mediterranean on 1 February 1797, his fleet consisting of twenty-seven ships-of-the-line. These included the biggest, most heavily armed warships in the world. Cordova's flagship was the *Santissima Trinidad* of 136 guns, and he had six ships of 112 guns. In contrast, there were only two 100-gun ships, *Victory* and *Britannia*, in the fifteen-strong British fleet off Lisbon commanded by Admiral Sir John Jervis. The Spaniards therefore had a crushing advantage in firepower, but their ships were wretchedly equipped and manned, with insufficient trained seamen and gunners. Jervis had twelve fewer line-of-battle ships, but their discipline, training, seamanship and gunnery were superb. The toughest of disciplinarians to his officers as well as his men, Jervis was a ruthless foe of incompetent commanders. The captains of his ships were a highly gifted team, all capable of thinking for themselves and carrying out the admiral's intentions in the confusion of close action. They included several of the great names from Nelson's later 'band of brothers': Collingwood, Troubridge, Foley and Saumarez, with Nelson himself flying his commodore's broad pennant from the seventy-four-gun *Captain*.

Disregarding odds of nearly two to one in the enemy's favour, Admiral Jervis split the Spanish fleet and joined battle at close quarters.

PLAN of the ACTION between the BRITISH AND SPANISH FLEETS, off CAPE St VINCENT, the 14.th of February, 1797.

Cordova's immediate mission, however, was not a set-piece battle with Jervis's fleet. His ships were escorting four priceless merchantmen laden with mercury, essential for amalgamating the silver to finance the Spanish and French war efforts. The Spanish fleet had sailed to bring these mercury ships safely from Malaga to Cadiz, but strong easterlies carried the Spanish ships much further out into the Atlantic than Cordova had intended, and he was still trying to re-form his fleet when the British were sighted on the morning of 14 February.

The night of 13–14 February was foggy, and the British had heard the Spanish signal guns in the night as Cordova struggled to keep in contact with his straggling fleet. Jervis's scouts had told him that the Spanish fleet was out; his only uncertainty was the enemy strength. For his part Cordova had heard, from an American neutral, that the British had only nine line-of-battle ships. This had made him ready to fight if need be – but his intelligence was out of date. Winter storm damage had indeed cut the strength of the British fleet down to nine, but on 6 February Jervis had been joined by six more ships-of-the-line from England, bringing the total British strength up to fifteen.

Daylight on the 14th revealed the Spanish fleet still in considerable disarray, with a large gap separating the Spanish main body (two-thirds of the fleet in all) from the van warships and the mercury ships. This more than cancelled out the Spaniards' tenure of the weather gauge and their apparently crushing numerical superiority. Growling 'If there are fifty sail I will go through them,' Jervis ordered his fleet into line at 11 a.m. and sailed close-hauled straight for the gap. Half an hour later the leading British ship, *Culloden*, passed through the gap to the

accompaniment of a devastating broadside which received only a feeble reply. Instead of forming line and giving full scope to their own massive broadsides, Cordova's magnificent gun-platforms huddled together like sheep, unnerved by the precision of the British approach.

By 12.08 p.m. half the British line was through the gap and the Spanish van had been decisively split from the main body. Jervis now ordered his line to tack in succession, swinging to starboard to hook into the Spanish main body and tear it to pieces. Cordova replied by heading downwind in the opposite direction, bidding fair to pass clean astern of the rearmost British ships. This move caught Jervis, already committed to his ship-by-ship reversal, completely on the wrong foot, for by 1 p.m. the British line had only half completed its turn. Victory was kept in the British admiral's grasp, however, by a daring move on Nelson's part.

From his vantage-point in the *Captain*, third from the end of the British line, Nelson saw the danger that the Spaniards would escape and promptly abandoned one of naval warfare's most sacred principles: that the line-of-battle, once formed, was sacrosanct. He wore the *Captain* out of the line and flung her across the bows of the leading Spanish ships, his intention being to slow them down until the full weight of the British line could be brought to bear. It was not a reckless charge, but was based on the proven ineffectiveness of Spanish gunnery and the fact that help would not be long in coming from the leading British ships. These had already completed their turn and indeed had been in close action for the past half-hour. As it happened, Nelson's friend Collingwood was swift to follow the *Captain* in *Excellent*, the rearmost British ship,

ABOVE A diagram representing the disposition of the fleets off the Cape prior to the battle.

BELOW Rear-Admiral Collingwood, whose timely support of Nelson when the line-of-battle was broken was a major factor in the British victory.

Nelson accepts the surrender of the *San Josef*. The Spanish admiral lies mortally wounded on deck after losing both legs to a cannonball.

and was soon joined by *Culloden* and *Blenheim*.

Without this prompt support, Nelson's dash across the bows of the Spanish leaders must have ended in ruin. As sheer luck would have it, Collingwood's intervention was perfectly timed. He hammered the 112-gun *Salvador del Mundo* until she pretended to strike her colours, forged on and repeated the process with the seventy-four-gun *San Ysidro*. 'I had been deceived once,' wrote Collingwood, 'and obliged this fellow to hoist English colours before I left him.' He then came up with the *San Nicolas* (eighty guns) and the *San Josef* (112 guns), both of which were engaged in cutting Nelson's *Captain* to pieces. 'I came happily to his relief,' admitted Collingwood, 'for he was dreadfully mauled.' *Excellent*'s arrival on the scene caused *San Nicolas* and *San Josef* to collide, thus enabling Nelson to perform one of the most famous exploits in Royal Navy history. As Nelson himself put it:

At this time the *Captain*, having lost her foretopmast, not a sail shroud or rope left, her wheel shot away, and incapable of further service in the line, or in chase, I ordered Captain Miller to put the helm a-starboard (steering by the ship's tiller) and calling for boarders, ordered them to board.

Captain's seamen and marines swarmed into the *San Nicolas* and rapidly cleared the upper deck, taking the poop and hauling down the Spanish colours. But the surviving officers of *San Nicolas* had not formally surrendered when the British boarders came under fire from the *San Josef*, still locked alongside. Nelson immediately called for more men from *Captain* to make sure of *San Nicolas* and led a second boarding attack into *San Josef*. This knocked the heart out of *San Josef*'s officers, whose admiral was expiring below decks after having had both legs shot off. By means of what Nelson later described as his 'patent bridge for boarding first rates' – taking the second over the decks of the first – a crippled British seventy-four had captured two Spanish first rates in less than a quarter of an hour.

The battle petered out as darkness closed in around 5 p.m., Jervis contenting himself with making sure of the four captured ships (*San Nicolas, San Josef, San Ysidro* and *Salvador del Mundo*). British expenditure in powder and shot had been prodigious and Jervis was no more willing to risk another fight on the 15th than was Cordova. Had Jervis known about the Spanish mercury ships – all of which arrived safely – it might have been different; as it was, he was justly content with a brilliant and timely victory against odds of nearly two to one.

Camperdown

THE FINAL ANGLO-DUTCH ENCOUNTER

One of the bloodiest and most hard-fought naval battles of the Napoleonic Wars, Camperdown was fought on 12 October 1797, between the British fleet under Admiral Duncan and the Dutch republican fleet under Admiral De Winter. It was the third in a trio of British victories at sea, following Admiral Howe's success on the 'Glorious First of June' in 1794 against the French and Admiral Jervis's victory over the Spanish fleet on St Valentine's Day 1797.

The year 1797, however, was a year of disaster for the British war effort against Revolutionary France. The Dutch, who were the most recent and dangerous recruits to the revolutionary cause, had a most formidable navy and for several months there was a danger of invasion from Holland. Everything went wrong with the fortunes of Britain's allies on the Continent. Admiral Duncan, charged with the blockade of the Dutch coast, was forced to watch ship after ship in his command sail home to join the British fleet, which had mutinied at anchor off the Nore. He ended up with two ships, which main-

The cutter *Active* speeds to bring news to Admiral Duncan that the Dutch fleet has put to sea. Sixteen British men-of-war were promptly despatched from Great Yarmouth to do battle.

tained the blockade by the ingenious device of signalling to imaginary reinforcements over the horizon.

By October the dangers had receded. The mutinies were over and the French had abandoned the idea of launching an invasion of England from Holland. Nevertheless, the Dutch fleet was still as formidable as ever. Duncan, with his fleet back to full strength and its seamen anxious to prove their loyalty to King and Country, was eager for a decision at sea.

Admiral Adam Duncan, a Scot of impressive physique – he was nearly 2m (6ft 4in) tall – was aged sixty-six in 1797. He had joined the navy in 1746 and reached captain's rank in 1761. In the following year he commanded HMS *Valiant* in the action which led to the capture of Havana and in 1780 he served as vice-admiral under Rodney at the relief of Gibraltar. In 1795 Duncan was appointed as admiral commanding the North Sea station, which was responsible for blockading the Dutch coast. The post was not an enviable one, as Duncan's ships were the oldest on the Navy List and his flagship – the aptly named HMS *Venerable* – of seventy-four guns – leaked so much that she was unable to stay at sea for long periods.

Jan Willem De Winter, the Dutch commander, was nearly twenty years younger than Duncan. At the age of twelve he had joined the Dutch navy, but, as he was a confirmed republican, he transferred to the French Revolutionary army in 1789 and rose to the rank of brigadier-general. Thus, although he was a capable soldier, he lacked experience in naval warfare.

Against his better judgment, De Winter was ordered to sea on 7 October 1797 at the head of a force of eighteen ships-of-the-line, accompanied by five frigates. The Dutch fleet's sortie from Texel was quickly reported to Duncan at Great Yarmouth and he put to sea at once with sixteen men-of-war. When De Winter heard that the British fleet was on his track, he decided to return to port. His ships were of shallower draught than the British vessels and consequently he decided to sail close in to the coast, hoping that he could lure Duncan's force onto a lee-shore, where there was every chance of manoeuvring the British fleet aground.

The two fleets were evenly matched in several respects. The Nore Mutiny had had no lasting effect on the morale of the British seamen and the Dutch

the weather division of the British fleet into the Dutch rear. Onslow's nine ships engaged five Dutchmen and battered four of them into submission within an hour.

Duncan, at the head of the lee division, put HMS *Venerable* alongside De Winter's flagship *Vrijheid*. The ships following him engaged the Dutch van and a confused *mêlée* developed around the admiral's ships. Only seven Dutch ships regained Texel, under Rear-Admiral Storij. De Winter's ship was in the thick of action and lost fifty-eight men killed and ninety-eight wounded. HMS *Director*, captained by William Bligh of *Bounty* fame, delivered the *coup de grâce* to *Vrijheid* and the action ended when she surrendered to Duncan at 3.55 p.m.

The battle was a vicious pounding-match and casualties on both sides were frightful. Unlike their Latin allies, who favoured aiming high to cripple enemy rigging, the Dutch preferred to smash their broadsides into the enemy hulls. Sound as their gunnery was, however, that of the British was better.

Camperdown was the last naval battle to be fought between the Dutch and the English. Duncan wrote of De Winter's reactions to his defeat: 'He says nothing hurts him, but that he is the first Dutch admiral ever surrendered. So much more credit to me.' The two admirals became firm friends during De Winter's imprisonment in England. Duncan continued in command of the North Sea fleet until 1800, when he retired to his estate in Scotland where he died four years later. De Winter was repatriated to Holland, on giving his parole that he would never again fight the British. After the Peace of Amiens in 1802, he commanded an expedition against the Barbary corsairs. He died in 1812 and was buried in the Pantheon in Paris.

ABOVE Admiral De Winter surrenders on the deck of Duncan's *Venerable*, thereby becoming the first Dutch admiral to yield to the enemy.

RIGHT HMS *Director*, under the command of Captain William Bligh, delivers a final broadside to De Winter's *Vrijheid*.

sailors upheld the fine naval tradition established by De Ruyter and Tromp. Although the British ships were older and less seaworthy than those of the Dutch, the Royal Navy crews were more practised in seamanship and gunnery than their opponents. The British ships also mounted carronades, a more effective weapon at close range than cannon.

On the morning of 12 October Duncan sighted the Dutch fleet 8km (5 miles) from the shore, between the villages of Camperdown and Egmont. Ignoring the danger of running aground, Duncan ordered his pilot 'Go on at your peril, for I am determined to fight the ships on land if I cannot by sea.' As there was no time for the British fleet to deploy into line-of-battle, if the Dutch were to be prevented from escaping, they went into action in two loosely formed groups. Admiral De Winter later told Duncan that had the British waited to form into line, the Dutch would have been able to get nearer the coast and meet them in battle on their own terms.

The action began at 12.30 p.m., when HMS *Monarch*, the flagship of Vice-Admiral Onslow, led

The Nile

A SEA–BATTLE OF ANNIHILATION

Since the mid-eighteenth century, France had shown a strong interest in the colonial possibilities of the eastern Mediterranean, and in 1798, encouraged by Napoleon Bonaparte, the revolutionary French government made preparations for an expedition to Egypt. On 19 May 1798 the French set sail; the expedition comprising 400 troopships escorted by a number of Venetian ships plus thirteen French ships-of-the-line and eight frigates.

Reports of the French preparations had reached England, though the final destination of the flotilla remained a matter of conjecture: Portugal, Naples and Ireland were all seriously considered. Nevertheless orders were sent to Lord St Vincent, commander-in-chief of the British fleet off Cadiz, to send a squadron into the Mediterranean to intercept the French. Sir Horatio Nelson, a junior rear-admiral, was chosen to lead this force; an appointment which caused considerable resentment amongst his more senior colleagues who had been passed over.

On his arrival in the Mediterranean Nelson met with near disaster: his seventy-four-gun ship *Vanguard* was dismasted and badly damaged in a gale off Sardinia and in the confusion his two accompany-

ing frigates returned to Gibraltar thinking he had done the same. The absence of frigates for reconnaissance purposes was to prove a major problem for Nelson in his search for the elusive French fleet. On 7 June Nelson was joined by ten other ships, all of seventy-four-guns, bringing his total up to thirteen ships-of-the-line.

The British fleet sailed eastwards and discovered that the French had taken Malta and, after a brief stay, had departed from the island. In consultation with his captains Nelson reckoned that the French might be making for Egypt and he set after them with all haste. The British fleet sailed into the eastern Mediterranean, just missing the French by hours on two separate occasions. Nelson arrived off Alexandria on 29 June but no enemy ships were to be seen. Despondently he turned westwards towards Sicily, without realizing that his inspired guess was correct, and he had, in fact, anticipated Bonaparte's own arrival by a day.

Having replenished his fleet's supply of water Nelson continued his search and on 28 July he learnt that the French had landed in Egypt. On this information he returned to Alexandria and on 1 August he sighted the masts of the French fleet several kilometres east of Alexandria in Aboukir

RIGHT The British fleet sails in to engage the French lying at anchor as the light fades on 1 August 1798. By dawn of the following day, only three French vessels remained afloat.

115

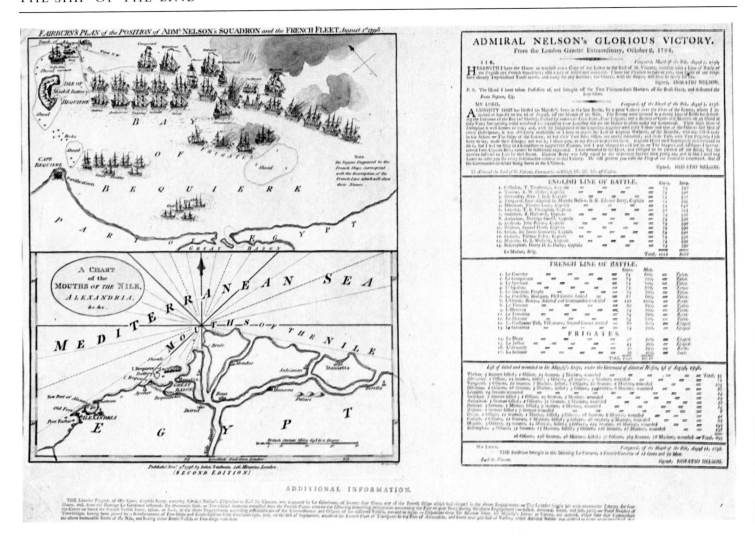

The *London Gazette* of 2 October 1798 published this plan of the battle of the Nile to illustrate the despatches in which Nelson outlined the magnitude of his victory.

Bay. Almost without pause, Nelson bore down on the French.

The French commander, Admiral Brueys, had been at anchor for three weeks but had done little to secure his fleet, adopting a weak defensive position on Aboukir Bay. His ships were moored on single anchors at a distance of over 135m (150yd) apart, which in effect meant that the ships were too spread out to provide themselves with mutual support, and allowed any enemy ship to cut in between them and consequently to break the French line-of-battle. More alarming was the tactical error made by Brueys in anchoring his fleet at such a distance from the shore as to allow the skilfully piloted English ships to range inside the French line and attack them from the landward as well as the seaward side. Despite this, Brueys felt confident enough to dispense with strong shore batteries. When he sighted the British fleet, Brueys did not expect them to attack as the day was drawing to a close, but at 5.30 p.m. he ordered the decks to be cleared for action.

As the British ships sailed into Aboukir Bay, Nelson flew a signal to his captains to concentrate on the French van and centre. At about 6.30 p.m., with the light fading, the *Goliath* led the British assault, followed by *Zealous*, *Orion*, *Theseus* and *Audacious*, all of whom cut inside the French line. Nelson in the *Vanguard*, supported by *Minotaur* and *Defence*, engaged the French line from the seaward side. The five oldest and weakest French ships were surrounded by eight opponents. The French commanders were caught by surprise, several not having run-out their guns on the landward side, and took a heavy battering from the English guns.

Further down the French line the seventy-four-gun *Bellerophon* set upon the flagship *L'Orient*, a massive ship of 120 guns and a complement of 1000 men. Shattered by a massive double-shotted broadside from the French ship the dismasted *Bellerophon* was forced to retire out of the line. *Bellerophon*'s place was taken by the *Alexander* and *Swiftsure* who concentrated their fire on *L'Orient*. At this time Nelson suffered a minor head wound and was carried below, but recovered sufficiently to take command of the latter part of the engagement.

A fire had broken out on *L'Orient* at 9 p.m. which continued to grow in intensity as the battle progressed. Brueys was badly wounded, losing both legs, but continued to direct the battle, seated on an armchair with tourniquets on the stumps. Towards 10 p.m. the ships around *L'Orient* began to withdraw, fearing an explosion when the fire reached the ship's magazine. A few minutes later the French flagship was blown out of the water in a tremendous explosion that could be heard in Alexandria, 30km (18 miles) away. As if by mutual consent firing ceased for ten minutes as the wreckage of *L'Orient* settled in the water. Incidentally, the young son of the captain, Casabianca, was present on *L'Orient*, and it was he who was immortalized in the famous poem 'The Boy Stood on the Burning Deck'.

The French ship *Le Franklin* resumed firing but was battered into submission around midnight. The British ships moved down the French line silencing any remaining opposition: the *Tonnant* was dismasted at 3 a.m., and *Heureux* and *Mercure* struck their colours an hour later. The *Guillaume Tell*, commanded by Rear-Admiral Villeneuve, with the *Généreux* and two frigates managed to escape; of the remaining ships-of-the-line, one had been sunk, nine had surrendered and two were wrecks. On the British side, although casualties had been heavy, not a single ship was irreparably damaged, repairs being effected from the captured French ships. The battle at Aboukir Bay was a decisive victory for the British, and of his achievement Nelson wrote, with a characteristic lack of modesty: 'Victory is not a name strong enough for such a scene.'

The battle of the Nile can be termed a battle of annihilation: not content with the technical victories of his eighteenth-century predecessors Nelson had succeeded in destroying Brueys's fleet. The Nile was part of a new style of warfare which had its parallels in the 'Napoleonic' battles of land warfare.

The immediate result of the battle was that it marooned General Bonaparte and his army in Egypt and denied them the use of the Mediterranean. Although Bonaparte managed to escape to France in a French frigate his army was forced to surrender following the British invasion of Egypt. The victory at the Nile was a great boost to Allied morale which had suffered from the spate of French triumphs in the preceding years. Britain gained access to the court of Naples where support for Britain had been wavering before the battle. The Mediterranean was opened up to British shipping and new ventures were planned to increase British influence: Malta was seized from the French and Minorca was regained from the Spanish.

Nelson returned home to a hero's welcome, receiving honours from home and abroad, and becoming Lord Nelson of the Nile.

The scene aboard the French vessel *Tonnant* after being dismasted at 3 a.m. The British fleet took only one further hour to complete the rout.

Trafalgar

THE ROYAL NAVY'S FINEST HOUR

Trafalgar is the sea battle of superlatives. It ensured the survival of the United Kingdom to carry on the struggle against Napoleon's empire, with or without allies on the Continent; it was the last and greatest of Nelson's three classic victories (the first two being the Nile and Copenhagen); and it was the last fleet action of the age of sail to be fought on the open sea. But Trafalgar was in fact the tailpiece to an extraordinary six-months' campaign, the like of which has never been seen since. In that campaign Napoleon had sought in vain to block the separate fleets and squadrons of the Royal Navy, using the western Mediterranean and north Atlantic as a gigantic gaming-board; his object being to assemble a superior naval force in the English Channel for the French invasion of England.

Napoleon issued the orders for his naval master-plan at the end of February 1805. The three decisive elements in the plan were Villeneuve's Toulon fleet (blockaded by Nelson), the Spanish fleet of Gravina in Cadiz (blockaded by Orde), and Ganteaume's Brest fleet (blockaded by Cornwallis). Villeneuve was to escape from Toulon, head for Cadiz and join forces with Gravina. The combined fleet thus formed would then cross the Atlantic to the West Indies and collect all available French warships there. Ganteaume was also to escape from Brest and join forces with the combined fleet in the West Indies. The resultant Franco-Spanish massed fleet would then re-cross the Atlantic to sweep the Channel clear for Napoleon's invasion. Nothing if not grandiose, Napoleon's scheme made no provision for counter-measures by the British, and failed to grasp the interdependence of the separate British blockading fleets. For all that, the plan got off to a deceptively promising start.

Villeneuve escaped from Toulon with eleven ships-of-the-line and eight frigates on 30 March, aided by good intelligence of Nelson's whereabouts and the fact that Nelson himself wanted to meet the French at sea rather than keep them penned in harbour. Nelson did not at first understand that Villeneuve was bound for the West Indies, but when he did he set off at once in hot pursuit. Villeneuve had arrived off Cadiz on 9 April and sailed at once with the only six ships-of-the-line which Gravina had ready for sea.

The combined fleet reached Martinique in the middle of May, and joined in an assault on the daring British garrison holding the nearby Dia-

mond Rock in defiance of France. By the time the Diamond Rock fell (6 June) Nelson had arrived at Barbados on the heels of the combined fleet. Though the precise strength of the latter was still unknown to him, Nelson looked forward eagerly to a fleet action. 'Powerful as their force may be,' he commented, 'mine is compact, theirs must be unwieldy; and although a very pretty fiddle I don't believe that neither Gravina or Villeneuve know how to play upon it.'

When Villeneuve accepted that Ganteaume was still in Brest, he cut his losses and decided to head back to France, but Nelson had narrowed the lead to a mere three or four days. He continued the pursuit on the long haul home, sending ahead the brig *Curieux* which overhauled the combined fleet, noted its strength and course, and arrived at Plymouth on 7 July. The news brought by *Curieux* enabled Lord Barham, the British First Lord, to issue the orders which ruined Napoleon's master-plan.

Cornwallis maintained the vital blockade of Brest, while powerfully reinforcing Calder's squadron off Ferrol. This gave Calder the strength to intercept the combined fleet off Cape Finisterre. But the resultant action (22–3 July) was a bitter disappointment for the British. It was drawn out over two days of desultory clashes in thick weather, and all Calder managed to do was capture a couple of Spanish ships. The combined fleet was still intact and might yet strike north for Brest and the Channel. Villeneuve meanwhile headed first for Vigo and then for Ferrol, where more Spanish reinforcements raised his strength to thirty of the line.

The crisis did not pass until the week of 13–20 August, when Villeneuve sailed from Ferrol but was baulked of a clear run to Brest by a strong north-easterly wind. He fell back to Cadiz to avoid another untimely fleet action, and it was this move which ruined the last vestige of Napoleon's hopes for an invasion in 1805. Now all the British had to do was build up a powerful blockading fleet off Cadiz, strong enough to finish Villeneuve when he came out and headed for the Mediterranean, the only destination now left to the combined fleet as autumn drew on.

Nelson had reached England via Gibraltar on 18 August, before the combined fleet had arrived at Cadiz. Most of his guesses about Villeneuve's plans

Admiral Villeneuve, commander of the Toulon fleet which comprised the greater part of the combined Franco-Spanish massed force at the battle of Trafalgar.

over the past three months had been wrong, but as soon as Lord Barham read Nelson's log and journal he realized that Nelson's conduct had been sound enough in the circumstances. Flying his flag in the *Victory*, Nelson resumed command of the fleet off Cadiz on 28 September, with his old friend Vice-Admiral Collingwood as second-in-command in the *Royal Sovereign*.

The plan of attack which Nelson revealed to his delighted captains aimed at the swift and decisive destruction of two-thirds of the combined Franco-Spanish fleet when it emerged from harbour. It involved forming the British fleet into three columns (amended to two columns, as Nelson was left with fewer ships than he had originally hoped for) which would approach the Franco-Spanish line at right angles and plunge through, severing the enemy van from the centre and rear. Ship-to-ship fighting would then destroy the centre and rear of the combined fleet before its van could reverse its course to intervene.

Nelson's plan was not original: it was a masterly distillation of experience gained in fleet actions ever since Rodney had first broken a French line at the Saints. At Cape St Vincent, the British thrust through the Spanish fleet had been left on the wrong foot by the Spanish riposte until Nelson's own breach of the sacred line had redressed the balance. At the Nile, Nelson had proved the potency of the dictum 'that the order of sailing is to be the order of battle' – but the year before, Duncan had fallen on the Dutch line at Camperdown with a broadside attack in two divisions which was a striking anticipation of the Trafalgar attack plan. Nelson's genius and confidence drew all these

strands of experience together in an attack plan which was received enthusiastically by every captain in his fleet. The traditional insistence of the line-of-battle and the capturing of prizes went out of the window. 'It is', Nelson insisted, 'annihilation that the country wants, and not merely a splendid victory.'

By the beginning of October 1805, Villeneuve was under orders from Napoleon to sail for the Mediterranean, land troops at Naples and return to Toulon. Two factors prompted him to sail on 19 October. He knew that Admiral Rosily was on his way to replace him; and an attempt to capture the vigilant frigates of Captain Blackwood had misfired, leaving Rear-Admiral Magon out at sea with seven of the line and a frigate. Villeneuve thereupon decided to sail the whole fleet.

The 20th was spent in manoeuvring, with Villeneuve puzzled by the apparent lack of order in the British fleet while Nelson was fed with all the information he needed from Blackwood's frigates. By first light on the 21st Nelson was 15 km (9 miles) to windward of the combined fleet and Villeneuve knew that his chances of getting clear unmolested had disappeared. He signalled his ships to reverse their ungainly line and make for Cadiz, but it was too late. Nelson and Collingwood were already at the heads of the two British columns, driving like two slow-motion lances at the heart of the combined fleet – twenty-seven British ships-of-the-line against thirty-three (eighteen French and fifteen Spanish).

Nelson's famous signal 'England expects that every man will do his duty' was made at 11.45 a.m., when less than 2km (1 mile) separated the fleets.

The British ships break the combined fleet's lines and profit from the resulting confusion. Nelson allowed his captains the freedom to engage in any way possible.

might adopt whatever they thought best, provided it led them quickly and closely alongside an Enemy'. Here was the true virtue of the 'Nelson touch': no rigid adherence to a formal line-of-battle, but flexibility: the swift and natural progression to the all-out 'pell-mell battle . . . to surprise and confound the enemy'. Nelson added to the confusion by feinting towards the combined fleet's van, then, after enduring the enemy's fire for nearly fifteen minutes, swinging to starboard, opening fire, and crashing into the Allied line between *Redoutable* and Villeneuve's flagship *Bucentaure*.

As it happened, Nelson never did achieve his intention of breaking through the combined fleet: *Victory* was grappled and fought magnificently by the *Redoubtable* of Captain Jean Lucas, one of whose mizentop sharpshooters, at short range, picked off Nelson as he paced *Victory*'s quarter-deck. The British commander was mortally wounded at about 1.15 p.m., when the fight with *Redoubtable* had been raging for half an hour. *Redoubtable* crippled *Victory* before herself being beaten into a wreck by the *Temeraire*, and Lucas did not strike his colours until he was certain that his ship was sinking. By this time Villeneuve, trapped aboard the battered *Bucentaure* by the destruction of all ship's boats and therefore unable to shift his flag to one of the undamaged ships in the van, had been obliged to surrender to a boarding party from the *Conqueror*, fifth ship of Nelson's division to engage after *Victory*.

By the time Nelson died at 4.30 p.m., the British victory was complete. A half-hearted attempt by Rear-Admiral Dumanoir, commanding the Allied van, to come to the assistance of the centre had been headed off by the last ships in Nelson's division to get into action: *Minotaur* and *Spartiate*. Though twenty French and Spanish ships were captured, only four were eventually brought into Gibraltar. This was due to the four-day gale which followed the battle and which threatened victors and vanquished alike with destruction on the shoals off Cape Trafalgar. While Gravina limped back into Cadiz with eleven battered ships, Dumanoir made for Rochefort with four French ships from the van. These were intercepted and captured by Sir Richard Strachan in a brilliant tailpiece to the main Trafalgar action, on 4 November.

The smashing of the combined fleet at Trafalgar meant that Napoleon, for all his supremacy over England's continental allies, was never again able to revive his grand design for a possible conquest of England. In the words of the late Oliver Warner, that great historian of Nelson and his era:

Trafalgar marked the end of the career of the most illustrious admiral in his country's history, fulfilled his wish for the annihilation of his opponents as a coherent force, and secured for the Royal Navy a supremacy which was unchallenged for more than a century.

That was enough for one autumn day.

TOP The French vessels taken as prizes of war by the British are burned on 28 October 1805.

ABOVE HMS *Victory* is portrayed at the close of the battle. The ship had been badly damaged by the *Redoubtable*, one of whose sharpshooters had fatally wounded Nelson.

(Collingwood's reaction, in *Royal Sovereign*, was to mutter 'I wish Nelson would stop signalling: we know well enough what we have to do!') As the signal was repeated through the fleet, Collingwood was coming under increasingly deadly fire from the Spanish *Santa Ana* and the French *Fougueux*. *Royal Sovereign* passed between the two ships at about noon and remained locked with the giant Spaniard for the next two and a half hours. The French *Neptune* turned and came to *Santa Ana*'s assistance and kept *Santa Ana* from striking her colours until 2.30 p.m., but by this time *Belleisle* and *Mars* had already followed *Royal Sovereign* through the Franco-Spanish line, and the rearmost ships of Collingwood's division had encompassed the ruin of the combined fleet's rear.

Nelson kept Blackwood and the frigate captains aboard *Victory* until he was certain that the approach and 'break-in' phase of his plan would succeed. He then released the frigate captains to speed down the following columns and signal all captains 'that if, by the mode of attack prescribed, they found it impracticable to get into Action immediately, they

Horatio Nelson

1758–1805

Towards the end of a life of arduous sea service, Nelson's friend Collingwood wrote: 'Fame's trumpet makes a great noise, but the notes do not dwell long on the ear.' Collingwood was thinking of himself, and for him the remark was true. It was, however, otherwise with Nelson. The fame of this admiral has remained undiminished from the time it first came to him in 1797, after the battle of Cape St Vincent, until the present day, when the literature concerned with him has reached vast proportions and seems unlikely to diminish.

Horatio Nelson, son of a Norfolk parson, was born at what must have seemed a propitious time for anyone aspiring to make a profession of the navy. In September 1758 Great Britain was on the eve of a succession of victories which would establish her predominance at sea and give her the nucleus of a world-wide empire. During the course of his comparatively brief life, Nelson would play an outstanding part in the defence of what had been won.

He possessed initiative, merit, influence, and a sufficient measure of luck, though he also had his full share of adversity and defeat. The uncle who first took him to sea, Captain Maurice Suckling, later became comptroller of the navy and could ensure that Horatio was given good appointments. Hence, by the time he went to the West Indies, during the American War of Independence, he had already visited the area once before aboard a merchantman. He had also served both in the Arctic and in the East Indies, besides having a wide experience of home waters.

By the age of twenty-one Nelson was a post-captain with the certainty that one day, if only he lived long enough, he would achieve his flag – since promotion to the highest ranks was then by strict seniority. He had already been on active service against the Spaniards, who, like the French, were helping the American colonists against the mother country. The campaign in Nicaragua in which he was involved was at once romantic and futile. It was also costly in life, not from the hand of the enemy but from disease.

Nelson was invalided home, but the war dragged on long enough to give him a further chance of operational command. He was again sent to the West Indies, this time in the frigate *Albemarle*, but he had no chance of distinction. One exploit into which he entered entirely on his own responsibility

was an attempt to take Turks Island from the French. He was repulsed, and at the end of the conflict could reflect ruefully that he had missed all the principal naval engagements. He had, however, made three contacts which would be renewed: one was with Lord Hood, an admiral he greatly admired; another was with Prince William Henry, the fourth son of George III and one day to reign as William IV, who even as a young captain was already remarkable for his irksome discipline; the best and most lasting of all was with Collingwood, an officer with a very different outlook from his own, but as fine a seaman as he was ever to know.

During the uneasy peace between the war with America and that with Revolutionary France, which broke out in 1793, Nelson, somewhat surprisingly considering the reduction in the fleet, was

The exploits of Admiral Horatio Nelson established Britain as the undisputed world maritime power for more than a century. His death in action was a fittingly heroic end.

given the Hull-built frigate *Boreas* by Lord Howe. Once more he found himself in the Caribbean, at one time or another in company with both Collingwood and Prince William Henry. Nelson made himself highly unpopular in his efforts to suppress the island trade with North America, which had become illegal. He also married, the prince being his best man. His wife, Fanny Nisbet, was a widow with one child, who Nelson later took with him to sea.

Before that time, greatly to his chagrin, he was to suffer five years on the beach. However, once war became certain, the prospects for active-minded officers brightened. Nelson was given command of HMS *Agamemnon*, a sixty-four-gun ship-of-the-line. For four arduous years he served ashore or at sea in the Mediterranean theatre of war, at first under Lord Hood and later under William Hotham. He lost the sight of his right eye at a siege in Corsica in 1794, and was engaged in many actions with the French, though never in a major fleet action.

The great change in Nelson's fortunes came when he was serving as a commodore in the fleet of Sir John Jervis, a leader after his own heart. The British had been forced by continuous French successes ashore to leave the Mediterranean. Nelson, after withdrawing garrisons and stores, had orders to join Jervis off Cape St Vincent, on the Atlantic coast of Portugal. He did so early in February 1797, flying his broad pennant in HMS *Captain*, and played a brilliant part in Jervis's victory over a much superior force of Spaniards on 14 February. It was an occasion which brought Jervis the Earldom of St Vincent, and Nelson a Knighthood of the Bath and a gold medal from the king. Promotion to rear-admiral came his way by seniority within a week or two of the battle, a happy conjunction.

Nelson's part was paramount. Jervis's idea was to split the Spaniards into two separate bodies, and to attack the larger, which was to windward. Nelson perceived the plan, and deliberately turned out of the line to anticipate it, an action for which he could well have been court-martialled. His success was phenomenal. He took two first-rate enemy ships by boarding and, ably supported by Collingwood in *Excellent* and other zealous captains, he had a hand in an attack on *Santissima Trinidad* – the largest ship of war then afloat. This vessel is believed

Nelson's victory at the Nile was final and complete, Brueys's fleet having been destroyed. Nelson received a peerage as a reward for his leadership.

to have struck her colours, but escaped before a party could take possession. Jervis's fleet had taken four prizes without loss to itself; the news cheered the country at a very gloomy time.

If Nelson had returned home after the February battle, he would have been spared another unfortunate experience such as occasionally attended him. His early attack on Turks Island had failed; Corsica had cost him the sight of an eye; Santa Cruz in Tenerife – yet another island – where he went on an expedition in the hope of capturing a Spanish treasure ship, was a disaster. His force was driven off and his right arm was shattered. He was saved from bleeding to death only by the prompt action of his stepson, Josiah Nisbet, who managed to get him back to his flagship, where the limb was amputated. Nelson bore his misfortunes with great fortitude, but the wound cost him much suffering. When he returned home to his anxious wife, she had to nerve herself to attend an invalid. She did so with success, and the months which Nelson spent in England brought him some of the happiest moments of his married life.

Nelson thought his active career was over, but

the Admiralty had other views. Lord St Vincent chafed at his absence from the fleet, and when he returned to sea with his flag in HMS *Vanguard* he was at once sent off into the Mediterranean with a small squadron on observation. His duty was to discover the purpose of a huge armada preparing at Toulon for a sortie under Bonaparte. Although *Vanguard* was damaged in a storm which dispersed Nelson's frigates, Lord St Vincent soon reinforced him.

Lacking frigates, the admiral had a weary and frustrating search. However the time involved was not wasted, for it enabled Nelson to train his ships and their captains, so that when the enemy was eventually tracked down, everyone would have complete confidence in his leadership and would realize the full scope of his ideas. He was the least conventional of tacticians, his aim being to allow his subordinates as much scope for initiative as possible. This attitude was revolutionary, and it had a magnificent reward. On 1 August 1798 the French fleet was found at anchor in Aboukir Bay, the army having already been landed.

The peace of the Egyptian dusk was shattered by the roar of cannon as Nelson's ships sailed in to the attack. Some of his captains went boldly inshore of the French, and after a struggle lasting until the early hours of the morning, Bonaparte's naval force was totally defeated. Only two ships-of-the-line out of thirteen escaped under Rear-Admiral Villeneuve, who was later to meet his fate at Nelson's hands at Trafalgar. The great French flagship *L'Orient* blew up, taking treasure plundered from the Knights of Malta to the sea-bed. Eleven ships were captured or sunk. As Nelson said when morning came, 'victory' was not a strong enough term for such a feat. There had been nothing like it in naval history.

Although no British ships were sunk, some were badly damaged, while both Nelson and Saumarez, his second-in-command, received wounds. Saumarez was not seriously wounded, but Nelson suffered concussion from a shot which struck him just above his sightless eye. He was more shaken than he appeared to be, or than he himself realized.

Sending Saumarez to Gibraltar with the prizes, Nelson himself proceeded to Naples. He was received with frenzied joy, and there came under the spell of Emma Hamilton, the wife of the British minister. The attachment was to endure for the rest of his life, and was eventually to ruin his marriage.

Nelson urged the King of Naples to act against the French, but this led to nothing but misfortune. The admiral felt obliged to support a regime whose military effort had failed ignominiously. He took the Neapolitan royal family to Sicily, leaving the mainland capital to the French. For two years Nelson was at the service of the Bourbon court, a fact which did nothing but harm to his reputation. It led to his approval of summary justice for 'collaborators' when, in a brief re-appearance at

Naples in the summer of 1799, Nelson showed the British flag.

When Nelson returned to England with the Hamiltons the following year, although by then a peer of the realm and a Sicilian duke, he found himself very much out of favour with the authorities. However, they could not afford to keep so able an officer unemployed, so Nelson was made second-in-command of a fleet under Sir Hyde Parker which was ordered to the Baltic. This was the very last area Nelson would have chosen after his sunny years in Italy.

Parker was to face an Armed Neutrality of the northern powers, actuated by Russia, whose activities threatened British supplies drawn from the Scandinavian countries and the eastern Baltic — from which nations she derived some of her most essential naval stores and supplies.

The Danish fleet resisted an attack at Copenhagen, brilliantly conducted by Nelson. At the height of the action Parker signalled to order a ceasefire, an appalling decision, and one to which Nelson, as the signal flags were seen by his officers, turned his blind eye. Resistance soon slackened, and Nelson then began negotiations for an armistice with the Danish Prince Royal. Parker had left everything to his subordinate, and it was no surprise that he was replaced by Nelson when the news from Denmark reached the Admiralty.

With danger from the north eliminated, Nelson was soon allowed to return home. He was charged with the coastal defences against Bonaparte's army encamped across the Channel, ready to invade. He ordered an attack on the flotillas at Boulogne, but did not lead it in person and suffered the last reverse he was ever to know.

In 1803, during an interlude in the war, Nelson lived at Merton in Surrey, on an estate which he shared with the Hamiltons. Early in the following year Sir William Hamilton died, and Nelson returned to sea as commander-in-chief in the Mediterranean. There, for many months, with his flag in *Victory*, his duty was to blockade the French fleet at Toulon. In the words of the great American naval historian, Alfred Mahan, 'those far distant, storm beaten ships, upon which the Grand Army never looked, stood between it and the dominion of the world'.

Nelson's last service to his country was the defeat, at Trafalgar, of the combined Franco-Spanish fleet under Admiral Villeneuve, an event which took place on 21 October 1805. Nelson died in the hour of triumph, after writing the famous prayer which includes the words – 'May the great God whom I worship grant to my Country and for the benefit of Europe in general a great and Glorious Victory.' By the time he had died of his wound in the cockpit of his flagship, his wish had been fulfilled.

The nation he loved has cherished the memory of Nelson for his tactical brilliance, his personal magnetism, his powers of expression, and his complete dedication to duty. He had long been the pride of the navy to which he belonged. Even so, his successors did not always perceive or remember the great secrets of his success – his faith in his subordinates, his openness in taking them fully into his confidence, his single-minded determination to exploit to the utmost whatever advantage he gained over his opponents. He learned the hard way, step by step, his experience of war being etched into him like the wounds on his body. His personal story is as remarkable as that of his feats in battle.

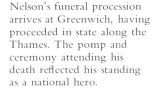

Nelson's funeral procession arrives at Greenwich, having proceeded in state along the Thames. The pomp and ceremony attending his death reflected his standing as a national hero.

John Paul Jones

1747–1792

From the Caribbean to Gibraltar, British interests lay exposed and threatened in 1779 as the American rebellion continued to occupy the time and energy of George III's Royal Navy. It was a thirty-three-year-old Scot in command of a converted French East Indiaman who brought the war home to British shores. His engagement off Flamborough Head placed John Paul Jones among the ranks of history's fighting seamen.

Born John Paul, in 1747, the son of a gardener in Kirkcudbrightshire on the Solway Firth, he sailed at the age of thirteen from Whitehaven to Virginia where an older brother had settled. Seven years later, in 1768, he had worked his way to the captaincy of a West India merchantman. But if ability sped his career, misfortune clearly dogged him as well. Paul was difficult to get along with. His ambition and arrogance brooked little disagreement, with the result that his career was punctuated with histories of petty quarrels. Paul's enemies never forgot that he had once been accused, albeit falsely, of having a sailor flogged to death, and that, only three years later, he had fled to America from the Caribbean island of Tobago after having driven a sword through the chest of the ringleader of a mutinous crew.

The reasons that made John Paul run to America remain a mystery. Although he would have been acquitted in a trial, he fled, abandoning wealth and great promises in the West Indies, apparently on the advice of the gentry of Tobago who feared for his safety.

Paul spent the next two years living incognito in America before re-emerging in Philadelphia in 1775 as Naval Lieutenant John Paul Jones. His experience at sea and the competence with which he harried the enemy from small ships brought him recognition in the nascent Continental Navy. He was given acting command of a thirty-gun frigate, then command of the sloop *Providence*. Then in 1777 he was appointed to a newly built frigate, the eighteen-gun *Ranger*. Yet his enemies frustrated plans to make him fleet commander and ensured that he was kept in smaller craft. In November of 1777, he was despatched to France to deliver the news of General Burgoyne's capitulation at Saratoga and to accept command of a new frigate.

The frigate he hoped for never materialized and a severely disappointed Jones eventually sailed from Brest on 10 April 1778 to harass shipping in his

former home waters in the Irish Sea. During the expedition, Jones temporarily took the port of Whitehaven and, on the same day, attempted to kidnap the Earl of Selkirk for ransom. Finding that Selkirk was away from home, he was persuaded to allow his crew to take the Selkirk silver as loot. Wild stories and even ballads circulated which told of 'pirate' Paul Jones and his ragged crew. But once back in France, acclaimed a hero for having captured *Drake*, a British sloop of war, Jones purchased the silver from his crew and returned it to Lady

John Paul Jones was not destined for high command, and was never to receive in his lifetime the credit due to him for his audacious and unconventional captaincy.

HMS *Serapis* (left) engages Jones's *Bonhomme Richard* off Flamborough Head on 23 September 1779. The American frigate *Alliance* (on the right) unaccountably fired several broadsides into both ships.

Selkirk with a quixotic note of apology.

Jones was asked to remain in France to head a future naval expedition and so turned command of *Ranger* over to a mutinous crew who returned home. As a result Jones was forced to sit on shore for six months, furious with frustration, before a ship could be found for him. When he finally did sail from Lorient in August in 1779 he had no more than a small squadron – his own *Bonhomme Richard*, *Alliance* and a handful of smaller vessels including *Pallas*, a French frigate. They sailed through the Irish Sea, around the north of Scotland and attempted a landing at Leith, near Edinburgh. However, ill winds forced Jones to abandon the scheme and head down the east coast towards his squadron's last rendezvous point off Scarborough.

It was there that Jones sighted the forty-four sail of the Baltic merchant fleet, under the escort of two British ships, in the early afternoon of 23 September 1779. By seven o'clock, the convoy's principal escort – Captain Richard Pearson in the fifty-gun HMS *Serapis* – intercepted the attacking Jones under the cliffs of Flamborough, while the twenty-gun HMS *Countess of Scarborough* engaged *Pallas*. Unaccountably, Captain Landais of *Alliance* seemed content to stand off and watch. Without Landais and heavily outgunned, Jones had no choice but to grapple and board *Serapis*. Jones's and Pearson's batteries opened fire almost simultaneously, but two of *Bonhomme Richard*'s six ancient 18-pounders – *Serapis* had twenty – burst, killing their gunners and wrecking the gun-deck. After one abortive boarding attempt, the ships separated and with volley after volley of British broadsides ripping into *Bonhomme Richard*, Jones's situation seemed hopeless. It was at this stage that Pearson called out to Jones, 'Has your ship struck? Back came the immortal reply: 'I have not yet begun to fight!'

Nor had he. Somehow – and the manoeuvring remains unclear – Jones managed to bring the two ships together through the barrage of cannon fire. A yardarm of *Bonhomme Richard* caught in the rigging of *Serapis*. Jones himself lashed the rigging to *Bonhomme Richard*, binding the ships together. They swung alongside one another, bow to stern. Virtually muzzle to muzzle, the destruction continued unabated. *Bonhomme Richard* held onto *Serapis* in a death grip and returned her fire with fewer and lighter cannon. Cries rang out from below decks as *Bonhomme Richard*'s old, dry timbers collapsed under the intense cannonade. The ship shuddered with each British broadside and her holds filled with water. A panicked gunner rushed topside screaming across to Pearson 'Quarter, quarter, our ship is asinkin'. . .' At this, an enraged Jones jumped from the 9-pounder that he himself had been firing, and hurled his empty pistols at the man, knocking him unconscious. He bellowed out, 'No! I will sink. I will never strike!'

Captain Pearson was one of the few to survive the hail of musket-fire from marksmen in the rigging of *Bonhomme Richard* that otherwise slowly cleared the British decks. The hopes of the men on *Bonhomme Richard* were further raised when *Alliance* appeared, but the treacherous Landais sent a series of broadsides into both ships. Jones reported that his crew called to Landais that he was firing into the wrong ship, but it was to no avail. All seemed lost once again until one of the American marksmen managed to crawl out on a yardarm and drop a grenade into a powder store of *Serapis*. Fire and explosions tore through the length of the ship.

By 10.30 p.m. Captain Pearson had had enough and struck his colours. One-third of the 300 men on each ship were dead and many more injured. The British frigate had lost her spars, sails, and rigging, and dead and injured lay everywhere. But *Bonhomme Richard* was beyond description. Jones wrote 'No action was ever before, in all respects, so bloody, so severe and so lasting.' Having transferred his crew to *Serapis*, Jones sailed for the Texel and preferred charges against Landais. Captain Pearson was later knighted for having saved the convoy, but he had done so at the expense of *Serapis*, a superior ship that was taken by Jones's tenacity as an American prize. When Jones heard of Pearson's knighthood, he offered to meet the English captain again and 'make him a lord'.

The rest of Jones's career was an anticlimax. He was lionized in France for a short time and showered with honours, but he never received the first ship-of-the-line that he wished for. His enemies at home and abroad never forgave his early arrogance. Even his victories counted against him, as the stories popularized by the ballads of 'pirate' Paul Jones, which were largely imaginary, were as well known as the true story of the valiant battle of Flamborough Head.

Years later in 1788 when Jones, still a captain, accepted Catherine the Great's offer to command the Russian navy against the Turks, he was to be disillusioned again. His victories in the Black Sea

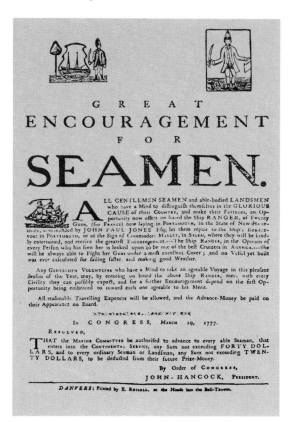

A recruiting poster intended to attract crew members for *Ranger*, the frigate which Jones took to France in November 1777. A mutiny ended his command the following year.

were credited to others, and, when Jones went to St Petersburg to protest, he suffered the greatest indignity of his life. He was arrested on dubious charges of having criminally assaulted a young girl. Catherine granted him leave of absence and so he retired to France where he died a frustrated, broken man on 18 July 1792.

It was over a hundred years later that America finally remembered the courageous Scot and sent a fleet of cruisers and gunboats to bring his body back to be buried in the land of his adoption.

The War of 1812

EMERGENCE OF THE US NAVY

The War of 1812 between Great Britain and the United States had two main causes: the ambitions of certain American politicians to take over Canada; and general American indignation over British demands that neutral vessels should be searched as part of Britain's blockade of Napoleon's French Empire. Tension grew until war was declared in June 1812.

The US was fighting ostensibly for 'freedom of the seas' and naval operations, therefore, were clearly going to have great importance. Given the enormous size of the Royal Navy in 1812 (191 ships-of-the-line and 245 frigates and ships of 50 guns), the prospects for the US were none too good on paper. But the American war imposed a tremendous strain on the Royal Navy, which was already committed to blockading Napoleon's ships in every European port from Lübeck to Venice. Although the diminutive US navy had no battle-fleet, it boasted some of the newest, toughest and hardest-hitting warships in the world — ships whose hulls and rigging were not foul and strained with years of non-stop cruising, or manned with scratch crews.

As a result, within the first six months of hostilities these American warships chalked up an impressive string of victories. The naval actions of the war showed how a small, well-constructed navy could tie down and embarrass a much larger force – a situation which foreshadowed the achievements of the German surface fleet during World War II.

The trumps of the US navy were the six splendid frigates authorized by Congress in March 1794 and built over the next three years: *United States, Constitution, Constellation, President, Congress,* and *Chesapeake.* They were the work of the brilliant naval constructor Joshua Humphreys and they were conceived as super-frigates of forty-four guns apiece, solidly built and able to give even a small ship-of-the-line a run for its money. Their roomy living conditions and storage space enabled them to keep the seas for long periods.

The US declared war on 18 June 1812 and the first American success came within a month. *Constitution,* captained by Isaac Hull, sailed from the Chesapeake on 12 July and was intercepted within days by a British squadron of five frigates com-

The victory of the American frigate *Constitution* over the British *Java* south of Bahia on 29 December 1812 was the crowning achievement of a successful year for the US navy.

manded by Captain Philip Broke in HMS *Shannon*. After a dramatic three-day chase in alternating flat calm and light airs with the ships being towed by their boats, *Constitution* got clean away from her pursuers and a month later encountered one of them on her own, far beyond the aid of her consorts. This was the thirty-six-gun frigate HMS *Guerrière* commanded by Captain Dacres, detached by Broke to go into Halifax for a much-needed refit.

Guerrière was undermanned – she even had aboard ten Americans, whom Dacres allowed to stay out of the fight – her masts were strained and, worst of all, her gunnery drill was sadly jaded. In a spirited two-hour fight on 19 August *Constitution* dismasted her outmatched British opponent and raked her twice from bow to stern with broadsides of roundshot and grape, killing and wounding seventy-eight out of the crew of 272. With *Guerrière* defenceless, rolling wickedly and leaking like a sieve, Dacres had no choice but surrender. *Guerrière* was in fact so badly damaged that she had to be fired and sunk, Hull embarking the British survivors as prisoners-of-war. Hull, whose losses and ship damage had been minimal, returned in triumph to Boston on 30 August, a national hero.

Eight days later a second American warship returned to port with triumphant news. The forty-gun frigate *Essex* under the command of Captain David Porter had sailed from New York on 3 July, heading for Bermuda to prey on British shipping from the West Indies. She fell in with a troop convoy to Halifax and captured a transport with 200 soldiers, hammered the tiny sloop HMS *Alert* into surrender on 13 August, and took nine other

prizes before returning to New York on 7 September. The following month Porter sailed again, this time taking *Essex* into the Pacific for a seventeen-month commerce-rading cruise which caused considerable nuisance to the British.

October 1812 saw the Americans in action again. On the 18th of that month the brig HMS *Frolic*, escorting a Bermuda convoy, fought gallantly but in vain against the American sloop *Wasp*, finally being out-gunned at point-blank range and boarded. The American captain, Jacob Jones, barely had time to put a prize crew aboard *Frolic* and start to repair her battle damage, however, when a sail appeared on the horizon. This was the British ship-of-the-line *Poictiers*, which had no trouble in turning the tables, taking the *Wasp* and recapturing *Frolic*. But Jones and his crew were soon back on American soil after an exchange of prisoners.

Not quite so fortunate was the frigate HMS *Macedonian* (Captain John Carden), unlike *Guerrière* a comparatively new ship and newly refitted, which sailed from England to reinforce the West Indies station. On 22 October, near Madeira, she encountered the *United States* under Captain Stephen Decatur, who had made his name in the Tripolitan wars in 1803–4. Unaware of the fate of *Guerrière*, Carden automatically sought to close the range and engage; but Decatur gave a model demonstration of how to exploit, with superior firepower, the normally disadvantageous lee gauge. He lay a little off the wind as *Macedonian* gamely struggled towards him, losing her mizen mast, fore- and main-topmasts to *United States*'s 24-pounders and suffering terrible losses on deck: 100 British casualties compared with

HMS *Guerrière* loses her masts to fire from the *Constitution* on 19 August 1812 in the first conclusive naval engagement of the war. The *Guerrière* was so badly damaged that the Americans fired and sank her.

General Ross and Rear-Admiral Cockburn advanced from Chesapeake Bay in August 1814 to attack Washington. This feat of arms was achieved, however, against a background of American victories.

only twelve Americans. *Macedonian* was a wreck before she had got anywhere near close enough to hurt *United States* with her 18-pounders; all Decatur had to do was to take up position for raking, and Carden wisely surrendered to avoid further useless butchery. *Macedonian* was brought into New York, the Stars and Stripes flying over the British colours, for refit as an American warship.

The year closed with another American *coup*, a second victory for the *Constitution*, now commanded by Captain William Bainbridge. On 29 December she encountered the British frigate *Java* of forty-four guns south of Bahia, the British crew having been weakened by sending a prize crew into a captured American merchantman. The ships met south of Bahia, the *Java* plunging in to fight, only to be out-sailed and out-gunned by her massive opponent. *Java* shot away *Constitution*'s wheel as the range closed, but the American gunners shot away *Java*'s headsails, main-topmast and mizzen-mast. Lambert, the *Java*'s commander, made an abortive attempt to board *Constitution*, only to be shot down at close range by an American marksman. Lieutenant Chads took command and gamely tried to carry on the fight, but when the mainmast went and *Constitution* took up position for the kill he surrendered. *Java*'s survivors were taken aboard *Constitution* and the beaten frigate, which had been damaged beyond all hope of salvage, was fired and sunk.

The year 1813 began with another American

success: a totally one-sided fight between brigs (the American *Wasp* and the British *Peacock*), fought off the coast of British Guiana on 24 February. Abysmally poor British gunnery left *Wasp* free to batter *Peacock*'s hull wide open, sinking her with her masts still standing. Lawrence, the American commander, was promoted and given command of the heavy frigate *Chesapeake*.

Fortune began to smile on the British in the summer of 1813, when Broke's *Shannon* outgunned and captured *Chesapeake* off Boston, Lawrence being killed. British reaction was hysterical in its relief, for the ships had met on completely equal terms; Broke and his officers were showered with honours and promotions rivalling those dealt out after such great fleet actions as Cape St Vincent or Camperdown. Significantly, the defeat only added to American naval tradition, particularly Lawrence's famous dying plea: 'Don't give up the ship!'

On the long Canadian frontier, American interests were secured by two spirited victories on the Great Lakes: Lake Erie (10 September 1813) and Lake Champlain (11 September 1814), won by Commodores Perry and Macdonough respectively. These successes by the American lake flotillas secured the US from invasion from Canada, but the strengthening British stranglehold on the Atlantic coast intensified through the latter half of 1813 and 1814 as victory over Napoleon in Europe left the British free to send massive reinforcements across the Atlantic. In August 1814 General Ross and Rear-Admiral Cockburn landed in Chesapeake Bay, advanced overland and burned Washington, although the propaganda value of this victory was more than offset on 8 January 1815 when Andrew Jackson's forces repelled General Pakenham's clumsy assault on New Orleans.

The shadows started to lengthen for the US navy on 28 March 1814 when the splendid career of Porter and the *Essex* was cut short in the Pacific. She was intercepted and captured off Valparaiso by the British frigate *Phoebe* and the sloop *Cherub*, having taken fifteen prizes in her seventeen-month cruise. By this stage of the war British self-esteem had so far recovered that the *Naval Chronicle* called it 'an event of comparative insignificance', of which 'owing to our superiority of force we have nothing to boast'. This was in marked contrast to the hysteria over the capture of the *Chesapeake* the year before.

The last months of the war saw the American warships on the Atlantic seaboard increasingly penned in harbour by the British blockade. Though peace was signed at Ghent on 24 December 1814 it took several weeks before the news crossed the Atlantic, in which time Decatur, trying to break out of New York in the *President*, was captured off Long Island by the frigates *Pomone*, *Tenedos* and *Endymion*. Not even this last setback, however, could erase the memory of the heady days of 1812: the first bright chapter in the US navy's history.

Navarino

LAST BATTLE OF THE SAILING MAN-OF-WAR

The War of Greek Independence started in 1821 and lasted for some eight years. Popular feeling in western Europe, particularly in England, favoured the insurgents. Volunteers such as Lord Cochrane unsuccessfully attempted to develop Greek resistance but in 1827 Athens fell to the Turks. Piracy developed over much of the Levant and the Royal Navy became involved in its suppression, suffering numerous casualties amongst the fleet in the process.

In July 1827, by the Treaty of London, Great Britain, France and Russia agreed to make a concerted effort to suppress the piracy and enforce an armistice between the Greeks and Turks to allow negotiations to take place. Meanwhile a Turkish and Egyptian fleet had sailed from Alexandria for the Bay of Navarino, in the south-west of the Morea. It was commanded by Ibrahim Pasha, who also commanded the Egyptian troops in the Morea. Having received instructions to maintain an armistice by sea, if possible without fighting, and to intercept Turkish supplies, the British fleet under the command of Vice-Admiral Sir Edward Codrington sailed for Navarino and there waited for his allies. By 25 September the French contingent under Rear-Admiral Henri de Rigny had arrived and a conference was held with Ibrahim Pasha in a tent outside Navarino.

When Ibrahim Pasha heard that Lord Cochrane, who was serving with the Greek patriots, had landed a force at Patras, he insisted that he be

ABOVE The Turkish and Egyptian ships lie at anchor in a horseshoe formation as the Allied fleet enters Navarino Bay.

RIGHT The battle at its height. Extensive losses were incurred by the Turkish–Egyptian fleet during the four-hour engagement.

allowed to send a force sufficient to oppose him. His demand was refused, and so he sent couriers to Constantinople for further instructions from his government. Assuming that the Turks would cease hostilities until these instructions were received, the Allied fleet left Navarino. As soon as they had sailed Ibrahim put to sea, but Codrington returned swiftly to drive the Turkish fleet back into Navarino. This move persuaded the Allied admirals that Ibrahim Pasha could not be trusted to fulfil the agreement of 25 September – an impression strengthened when the troops which had been embarked perpetrated atrocities on the local inhabitants as soon as they were put ashore.

On 13 October the Russian fleet under Count Heiden joined the British fleet and by 17 October, with the return of the French fleet, the Allies were united. As a close blockade of Navarino would have been difficult to maintain through the winter, it was decided to take the Allied fleet into the bay and

moor in such a position that they could overawe the Turks. Ibrahim's fleet – three ships-of-the-line, four (double-banked) sixty-four-gun frigates, fifteen forty-eight-gun frigates, twenty-six corvettes, twelve brigs and five fireships – was anchored in the almost land-locked bay in a semicircle facing the narrow entrance. The only available anchorage remaining, therefore, was inside the semicircle and, if the Allies' approach were opposed, their situation would be extremely dangerous, exposed to the crossfire of the enemy.

The Allied fleet had a considerable superiority in ships-of-the-line with three British, four French and four Russian, but had only sixteen smaller vessels. On the morning of 20 October 1827 Codrington, in fine weather and a light following wind, gave the order to advance in two columns – British and French to starboard, Russians to port. His orders were for his flagship, HMS *Asia*, eight-four guns, to be moored abreast of the Turkish flagship, which lay near the middle of the semicircle, with his other ships-of-the-line abreast of the two Turkish ships immediately ahead of her. The French were to cover the ships forming the south-easterly horn of the semicircle, while the Russians would moor abreast of the ships forming the other horn. His seven corvettes and brigs, under the control of the frigate *Dartmouth*, were to remove the fireships to an anchorage where they could no longer be a threat.

No gun was to be fired by any Allied ship unless ordered by signal, or in reply to fire from a Turkish ship – in the latter case, the Turkish ships opening fire were to be destroyed. In the light wind prevailing it took more than two hours for the rearmost ships to take up their allotted berths and in the meantime battle had broken out. The opening rifle shots came from a Turkish fireship, killing several of the crew of a boat from *Dartmouth* approaching to request them to shift berth. *Dartmouth* and the French flagship *Sirène* replied with small-arms fire and when the latter came under cannon-fire the action became general throughout the opposing fleets.

The battle lasted for four hours. The Turkish-Egyptian fleet lost one ship-of-the-line, three sixty-four-gun frigates, nine smaller frigates, twenty-two corvettes, ten brigs, a schooner and five fireships as well as some 4000 men killed. Damage and casualties amongst the Allies were slight in comparison.

The battle of Navarino was the last to be fought between sailing men-of-war, and was an overwhelming victory for the Allies. Though honours were showered on the victorious participants, there was a body of public opinion in England which condemned Codrington's behaviour as rash and unnecessarily provocative, criticisms which cannot be entirely refuted. However, the destruction of the Ottoman fleet at Navarino secured the eventual liberation of Greece, although the final treaty was not signed for another two years.

PART FIVE

The Age of Steam and Shell

From the mid-nineteenth century, a series of revolutions took place in naval warfare which profoundly altered its nature. These changes were basically brought about by the industrial revolution in western society: steam-powered ships, protected by iron plates and firing high-explosive shells from rifled, breech-loading guns, made the old ship-of-the-line totally outmoded. This basic change – which led directly to the development of battleships, battle-cruisers, cruisers and other large surface vessels – was only the first step, however. The industrial revolution unleashed a process of technical development which engendered constant change. New ideas were applied to naval warfare. Some of these, such as the revolving turret, were capable of slotting into the existing framework of war; others, such as the torpedo and the submarine, opened up totally new possibilities which were not always fully comprehended at first but which were of profound significance.

In the 1850s, when ironclad warships first began to appear, Great Britain was incontestably the leading naval power, but the first battles involving ironclads took place in North America (the encounter between the *Merrimack* and the *Monitor* in 1862) and in the Mediterranean (the battle of Lissa in 1866) and did not involve British ships. The century closed without there having been any more major

encounters between fleets of new warships, but the rapid development of new weapons had brought with it a diversification of battle-fleets; torpedo-boats, destroyers and submarines were all being introduced into the world's navies.

The year 1904 did see an encounter between two modern fleets, when the Russian Pacific Squadron was forced back to Port Arthur by the Japanese during the Russo-Japanese war. In the following year, the Russian Baltic Squadron, which had sailed halfway round the world, was destroyed by Togo's fleet at Tsushima. The crushing power of well-directed capital ships had been amply demonstrated. The importance of these capital ships seemed confirmed in 1906 when the *Dreadnought* – a battleship clearly superior to any other afloat – was launched by Great Britain. Amid mounting international tension, the major nations began building fleets based around this new style of vessel.

When war broke out, the British navy was still supreme in the world, with twenty-eight dreadnoughts and battle-cruisers to Germany's eighteen, and its superiority was confirmed during the next four years as German bases around the globe were swiftly and efficiently taken over, and the German battle-fleet confined to harbour, only daring to venture forth for the battle of Jutland. Jutland was inconclusive as an encounter, but a decisive strategic victory for the British.

Yet Germany did possess an effective weapon in its submarine arm, which almost brought Great Britain to its knees by commerce raiding. And a new element – air power – was just beginning to attract the attention of naval theorists as the war ended.

The battleship, which long remained the principal or capital class of man-of-war in all navies, evolved as an armoured and heavily gunned vessel, possessing adequate speed for fleet actions. It was a symbol of maritime power and indeed of national prestige, a high proportion of defence budgets being given to battleship construction and maintenance. Its performance in war was, in general, limited and uncertain, and it proved vulnerable to a variety of weapons. It is now obsolete, and was last used mainly for secondary duties such as heavy bombardments of targets ashore.

During the whole era of sail, the ship-of-the-line was modified only in detail. Wooden ships could, if

HMS *Devastation*, the first British warship to rely solely on steam power. Her mast served only as a point of observation and as a staff for signal flags.

they had sound timbers, be extremely long-lived. There is a well-documented instance of a ship, *Royal William*, originally launched in 1670, which was not broken up until 1813. She served in three wars, with nearly a century between the first and the last. No steel battleship has lasted nearly as long, though a very successful class, the British 'Queen Elizabeths', was in commission for upwards of thirty years and was actively engaged in the two World Wars.

The first designation of what developed into the latter-day battleship was the 'ironclad'. This was an appropriate description for a man-of-war with a wooden hull, but with a protective sheath of metal. The vulnerability of wood to shellfire was effectively demonstrated by the battle of Sinope in 1853, in which the shells from six Russian ships set on fire a total of thirteen Turkish ships in a matter of minutes. The invention of the explosive shell meant that it was not long before wooden construction was abandoned altogether in favour of iron and later steel.

Wooden ships-of-the-line were being built as late as 1858, but the following year marked the beginning of what was to develop into a confusing series of experiments in naval shipbuilding. This was due to the launch, by the French, of *Gloire*, which was designed by Dupuy de Lôme. *Gloire*, ancestor of so many fine French vessels, was considered to represent the equivalent power of the most heavily armed ship-of-the-line, though she had only sixty guns compared with the 130 carried by the highest rate of wooden ship, and she was deceptively classified as an 'armoured frigate'. She was built of wood, but along her waterline and in vital places elsewhere she was protected by armour plating 12.5cm (5in) thick. She carried sail, but her engines, of a nominal horsepower of 4200, could propel her at about 13 knots.

Britain, which was at that time the paramount naval power, reacted quickly to what was seen as a challenge. She produced *Warrior*, which was built mainly of iron, though backed by teak amidships. She was 115m (380ft) long, as against the 77m (252ft) of *Gloire*, but she was less thoroughly protected. She also carried sail, and her engines gave her a nominal speed of nearly 15 knots. Neither the French nor the British ship ever saw action.

Ironclad designers were given food for thought by two events which occurred in the 1860s. The first was the inconclusive duel during the American Civil War between the improvised ironclad *Merrimack* and the specially built *Monitor*, the creation of a Swede, John Ericsson. The other was the power of the ram, as shown by the sinking of *Re d'Italia* by the Austrian ship *Ferdinand Max* at the battle of Lissa, which was fought in 1866.

The designers' problems resolved themselves into the inevitable compromise between armour and

Developed from the floating batteries of the Crimean War, *Gloire* was the world's first sea-going ironclad, and was launched in 1859.

TOP The ironclad frigate
HMS *Warrior* was intended
as the British response to the
French *Gloire*, but was faster
and featured a completely
iron hull.

ABOVE HMS *Royal
Sovereign* represented an
important step towards the
modern battleship, being
fitted with gun turrets.

ordnance, and into providing such mobility as to
make ramming unlikely. Over the years improvements to the explosive shell made it capable of
penetrating almost all types of armour practical for
sea-going purposes, while improvements in marine
engineering, added to the ever-increasing range of
broadsides, made it improbable that the ram would
prove a useful weapon in future fleet actions. Even
so, it took several decades before naval architects
could decide on the most effective design for the
capital ship of the future, and the antiquated ram
remained a common feature of the warship long
after it had become little more than a curiosity.

It took a long time for conservative-minded
naval officers to realize that sail was as anachronistic
as the ram. In 1869 *Captain* was launched, designed
by Captain Cooper Coles of the Royal Navy and
one of the last of the sailing warships. Her principal
features were turret guns, tripod masts, and a spar-
deck over the turrets to facilitate working the sails.
Professional constructors believed the ship would

prove unseaworthy due to its lack of freeboard and
they were right, for *Captain* foundered in 1870
with heavy loss of life.

The immediate result was the construction of
Devastation, designed by Sir E.J. Reed. She was
armed with four 12-inch muzzle-loaders, with
protective plating 25–35cm (10–14in) thick. She
had a single mast and twin screws, but there was no
provision for sail. She proved to be as successful as
Reed had hoped.

The continuance of muzzle-loading guns so far
into the nineteenth century was due to the practical
difficulties in making a strong enough breech. The
principal of breech loading had long been known,
but it had been neglected, owing to unsatisfactory
materials and frequent accidents.

It was an Italian constructor, Benedetto Brin,
who conceived the idea of really big-gun ships. His
theories were embodied in the *Duilio* and *Dandolo*,
which were launched in 1876. They were of striking
appearance, having a single, central mast; two tall

funnels, widely spaced; a strong boat deck, and two heavily armoured gun turrets, which gave a wide field of fire for 18-inch guns. They were large ships, of over 11,000 tons displacement, and although far from elegant, they looked thoroughly fit for the purpose for which they were built. They had the then high speed of 15 knots.

The British answer to Brin's challenge was the slightly larger *Inflexible*. This ship mounted four 16-inch guns, two forward and two aft, and she was given secondary armament protected within casements. Her two funnels were abreast. She had waterline armour 55cm (22in) thick, and her speed was comparable with that of Brin's creations.

first time, to take a leading place at sea. Earlier German battleships such as *Kaiser Barbarossa* of 1900 were nearer to French than to British or Italian design. They had a mixed gun armament, five torpedo tubes, and good protection. Three propellers gave them a speed of 18 knots. Though a late arrival, Germany very soon showed that it meant business.

As if the German challenge was not enough in itself, an event took place on 27 May 1905 in Far Eastern waters which provided matter for thought in admiralties all over the world. This was the only fleet engagement in history where battleships proved decisive at sea. Lissa had been little more

Improvements in steel soon enabled hulls to be made lighter and stronger than before, and the armour in *Royal Sovereign*, next to come from British yards, was 35−45cm (14−18in) thick, and was considered to be the best yet provided. But the development of the torpedo, credited to the Austrian Johann Luppis and the British engineer Robert Whitehead, working originally at Fiume, meant that by the 1880s battleships would have to protect themselves from attack by fast torpedo-boats equipped with the new weapon. Secondary quick-firing armament was added as appropriate, and the battleship, particularly the French type as exemplified by *Charles Martel* of 1893 continued to resemble a rather bizarre mobile fortress, its primary purpose still being to fight its own kind.

During the 1890s Admiral von Tirpitz became the leading spirit at the German Admiralty. With the wholehearted encouragement of the Kaiser, Tirpitz became responsible for a building programme such as would enable his country, for the

than an ill-conducted *mêlée*; Jutland, which was eleven years in the future, was to prove unsatisfactory in a tactical sense; but at Tsushima, where the Japanese Admiral Togo defeated a Russian fleet commanded by Admiral Rozhdestvensky, the big gun with a 12-inch shell showed its power as a destructive force. The 'cult of the big bang' found factual justification, and, moreover, as guns proved effective at what was then considered the astonishing range of over 9000m (10,000yd) the pattern of the immediate future became apparent − big guns to fire in salvoes, adequate speed, strong armour.

The result was *Dreadnought* of 1906, which under Lord Fisher's direction was built in just over a year. She rendered all earlier battleships obsolete, and gave a new word to the nautical vocabulary. Henceforward there were dreadnoughts and predreadnoughts in the navy lists of the world: no other distinction mattered so much.

Dreadnought had ten 12-inch guns mounted in

Launched in 1876, the Italian ironclad *Duilio* was singularly advanced in design. Its turrets housed heavy-calibre guns and were quickly imitated by other nations.

five turrets, and twenty-seven quick-firers to repel torpedo attacks. She had five torpedo tubes and armour plating 28cm (11in) thick over vital parts, including the barbettes for her big guns. Her displacement was 17,900 tons and she had four propellers, driven by turbines which were the creation of Sir Charles Parsons. Her engines gave her a speed of 21 knots.

The turbine, which transformed marine engineering, just as it was later to affect aviation, arrived when the steam reciprocating engine, for all its various improvements, was rapidly becoming archaic. In earlier battleships, the noise and mess of an engine-room was appalling; in *Dreadnought* it was necessary only to look at a dial to realize the immense power that was being applied almost in silence.

First to follow Fisher's lead were the Germans. In the same year that *Dreadnought* was launched, they began work on *Nassau* and *Westfallen*, and the differences were significant. The German ships were slightly heavier, well subdivided to minimize battle-damage, and had thicker armour. The French continued for some time with a mixed big-gun

armament (12-inch and 9.5-inch in *Danton* of 1909), but the Italians and Russians built ships on dreadnought lines – *Dante Alighieri* of 19,500 tons, the creation of Vittorio Cuniburi, being capable of high speed – and the ships of both these nations favoured 12-inch guns mounted in triple turrets.

The Americans soon decided on a programme of very big ships, which included *Texas* and *New York* built in 1912. These were over 27,000 tons. They carried ten 14-inch and twenty-one 5-inch guns, and had a speed equivalent to that of *Dreadnought*. One of their most notable characteristics were steel lattice masts, which made their profile unmistakable.

What was perhaps the most remarkable of all classes of battleship appeared in 1915 and 1916 – comprising *Queen Elizabeth, Barham, Malaya, Valiant* and *Warspite*. These could steam at 24 knots, were armed with eight 15-inch guns and were well protected. They displaced 33,000 tons, and were designed to burn oil, which from the point of view of engineering convenience was nearly as great a boon as the turbine. Only one of these fine ships was lost in war, after a quarter of a century's service, and she had not been fully modernized. *Barham* was sunk by a German U-boat in the same year, 1941, that *Hood* succumbed to the fire of the brand new German battleship *Bismarck*.

The battleship in World War I was used chiefly to form the core of 'fleets in being', for there was only a single general engagement of any consquence. Off Jutland, on 31 May 1916, the British Grand Fleet and German High Seas Fleet came within sight of each other for the first and last time in the war. The German admiral, Scheer, manoeuvred to withdraw, thus avoiding destruction by greatly superior forces under Jellicoe. Losses were mainly among battle-cruisers, cruisers and destroyers, the British losing three of the former during earlier phases of the action.

After Jutland the Germans, strategically confined as they were to the North Sea and the Baltic as regards surface forces, turned to unrestricted submarine warfare and came close to success through attrition. Even before the war was over, exponents of air power were predicting that the battleship was doomed. The class took a long time to die, but it was becoming increasingly expensive in materials and manpower, and on its war record had too little to show in relation to its cost.

The modern naval gun was first introduced in the middle of the nineteenth century. Up to that time naval guns were smooth bored and fired solid shot, chain or grape shot. Around 1850, however, the ironclad warship started to make its appearance. Solid shot was of little use against iron armour, so the shaped shell was evolved. In addition, to give the shell a better trajectory and to prevent it turning over in flight, the rifled barrel was introduced. Rifling – spiral grooves in the gun barrel – caused the shell to spin rapidly in flight and greatly improved both its trajectory and penetration power.

Up to that time, guns had been loaded by ramming the shot and the charge down the barrel, but with rifling this became impossible. Consequently breech loading, which had been tried somewhat unsuccessfully before, was reintroduced. This was a slow process, however, and the first large breech-loading gun in the Royal Navy did not arrive until *Colossus*, launched in 1886. A further improvement was suggested in the 1850s, the idea of guns being mounted in the centre line of the ship and being able to train to either side. In Britain Commander Cowper Coles designed a rotating gun housing and offered to design a complete turreted vessel which he claimed would put *Warrior*, then the largest armoured ship in the Royal Navy, out of action in less than half an hour. He

ABOVE   The launch of the British *Dreadnought* at Portsmouth in February 1906 heralded a new era in battleship design.

OPPOSITE PAGE
ABOVE   Designed in 1855 by Captain Cowper Coles, this primitive gun-raft was the inspiration for the revolving turret.

BELOW   The gun-deck of HMS *Monarch*, the Royal Navy's first sea-going turret ship.

stated that his vessel would be smaller than *Warrior*, cheaper and would require only half the crew of the larger warship.

Encouraged by the Prince Consort, Coles eventually got the Admiralty's permission to proceed and his ship, named appropriately enough *Prince Albert*, was completed in 1866. She was not a great success as the shrouds and rigging made it difficult for the turrets to find clear arcs of fire. Undaunted, Coles then designed *Captain* with a flying deck above the turrets to which the shrouds and rigging were attached. To accommodate this extra deck, the weather deck had to be placed very low in the water and in rough weather the waves used to wash right over it. The ship was barely seaworthy and eventually in September 1870 she ran into a gale and was sunk. Commander Coles went down with the ship of which he had such high hopes.

The Royal Navy was not the only navy to experiment with turret guns. Sweden too was working on the problem and the Swedish designer, John Ericsson, designed a turreted ship for the Union navy in the American Civil War. Built in 1862, she was called *Monitor* and mounted 11-inch guns. Despite achieving fame in the battle of Hampton Roads against the *Virginia*, she was basically unseaworthy and foundered off Cape Hatteras before the end of the year.

In parallel with the development of turrets and guns, shells were being greatly improved. They were divided into three main types. Armour-piercing shells penetrated the ship's armour and exploded inside the hull; common shells burst against the ship's side and were used against unarmoured ships; and shrapnel shells were filled with small steel balls which were intended to cause the maximum casualties among enemy seamen in exposed positions.

By the end of the nineteenth century, sail had all but disappeared and so there was no longer a problem of the rigging obstructing the ship's guns. At the same time ranges were increasing and it was necessary to introduce aiming devices to enable the gunners to see the targets. The first of these, a telescopic sight, is attributed to an American naval officer named Bradley Fiske. Shortly afterwards Captain Percy Scott of the Royal Navy, who did more for gunnery in its early days than any other naval officer, introduced a system of aiming using a .303 rifle. He was in command of a 4.7-inch gun cruiser, HMS *Scylla*, and spent much of his time evolving new systems to improve the ship's gunnery. Another device introduced by Scott which greatly increased the rate of fire was a method of 'hunting' the roll. Up to that time the procedure had been for the gunners to wait until the roll of the ship brought their sights onto the target and then fire the guns. Scott's device was a sight which could be moved up and down with the roll of the ship, enabling the guns to be aimed and fired at any time. By the time Scott left *Scylla*, his innovations had made her the crack gunnery ship of the entire navy.

As ranges increased, so a system for working out the relative velocity problem became essential. As both the firing ship and the target ship were moving, it was necessary to aim off the target to take account of both ships' movements, rather in the same way that the sportsman with his shotgun aims ahead of a bird in flight. The problem can be appreciated if one realizes that at modern long ranges of 27,000m (30,000yd) or so, a shell may take as long as one minute to reach its target. In this time a ship steaming at 30 knots would travel half a nautical mile. Thus the firing ship, if stationary, would have to aim at a point some 900m (1000yd) ahead of the target. However, the firing ship is unlikely to be stationary. She may be on a parallel course or on a converging course, or even on a reverse course. Similarly the target ship need not necessarily be proceeding on a course exactly at

Breech-loading cannon with rifled barrels replaced muzzle-loading weapons from the middle of the nineteenth century, greatly increasing accuracy and range.

ABOVE This view of the Brazilian battleship *Minas Gereas* shows the director gunner's position at the top of the tripod mast.

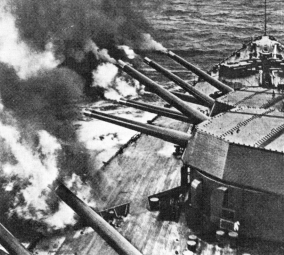

TOP RIGHT A plan
view of a ship's gun
turret of 1871 with two
25-ton rifled guns.

CENTRE RIGHT The
12-inch turret of the
Invincible, launched in
1907, showing the hoist
used to feed shells and
charges.

RIGHT The 16-inch
guns of HMS *Rodney* in
action.

TOP The superimposition of turrets pioneered by the US on the battleships *Michigan* and *South Carolina* (shown here) enabled hull length to be minimized.

ABOVE *Viribus Unitis*, one of the battleships which formed part of the Austro-Hungarian navy before the collapse of the empire in 1918.

right angles to the line of sight. So it is obvious that calculating the distance to aim off – or deflection – is a complicated mathematical problem, which is nowadays easily solved by an electronic computer, but in the 1900s it was largely a matter of guesswork.

The first requirement to solve the fire-control problem is to find the enemy's range and this was done by optical rangefinders. In Britain the first rangefinders were small devices made by Barr and Stroud, which were not very accurate. The first actual fire-control system was produced in 1905 by Arthur Pollen, the managing director of a linotype firm whose only connection with the sea was that his brother was in the navy. His apparatus plotted the bearing and range of the target and thus its relative position, but unfortunately the method of taking bearings and ranges was inaccurate if there was any motion on the ship.

Pollen continued to improve his system and before long he produced a second one which was more accurate and made use of a simple mechanical computer. Other aids to gunnery followed. Lieutenant Dumaresq invented a device, to which his name was given, on which was set the firing ship's course and speed and the enemy's bearing. The estimated course and speed of the target were also fed into it. The device then gave a read-out of the rate of change of both range and bearing. It was complemented by a range clock, which was initially set with the enemy's range as found by the range-finder and the rate of change of range as found by the Dumaresq. In principle the clock should then show the range of the target at all times. If it was obviously not doing so, it would mean that the enemy had altered either course or speed, or both, or that the original Dumaresq estimation was wrong.

In 1911 Lieutenant Dreyer (later Admiral Sir Frederic Dreyer) started work on a fire-control system and he succeeded in producing an apparatus which was the forefather of all fire-control systems up to the advent of radar. Although Lieutenant Dreyer gave his name to it, Pollen, who in fact had contributed many of the ideas, received a £30,000 award for this invention. In the meantime, the development of turret armament was making progress and culminated in 1906 in the revolutionary battleship HMS *Dreadnought*, with ten 12-inch guns in five gun turrets. She could fire four-gun salvoes twice a minute and was soon acknowledged by all naval authorities to be the very last word in gunnery.

The time-honoured method of firing guns was for the gunlayer to fire as soon as his sights came onto the target, after the order to open fire had been given. Captain Scott, however, pointed out the advantages of firing all guns together on the order of the director gunner stationed with his fire-control instruments in a position aloft; clear of the cordite fumes and in the best possible position to see the target. Scott installed a director gunner in his own ship around 1899, but the system was not officially approved by the navy until 1912.

When World War I broke out, director firing had just been introduced to the capital ships of the Royal Navy. At the battle of Jutland in May 1916 the main armament of all ships of the Grand Fleet save two was director controlled, whereas the Germans had not yet introduced the system. At Jutland the British mustered 324 guns against the Germans' 196. The British main armament consisted of 13.5-inch, 14-inch and 15-inch guns, whilst the Germans mostly had 12-inch weapons. The British guns could outrange those of their opponents. However, the German ships did have one big advantage – their rangefinders were far superior, largely because the British ones tended to over-read at long ranges.

By 1916 the method of spotting the fall of shot had been standardized. Ships fired in salvoes – that is to say a number of guns fired at once. Spotting was carried out by the bracketing method. This meant applying range corrections, usually in 366-m (400-yd) steps, until the splashes from the fall of shot were seen to have crossed the target. Once the target had been crossed, the next range correction would be half the original ones – for instance up or down 183m (200yd). The next salvo should then straddle the target with some of the shots falling short and others over, or even hitting. Rapid fire was then opened. Range corrections were never applied if the shots fell out of line with the target due to the difficulty of seeing whether the splashes were over or short. If the initial salvoes were out of line, the applied deflection had to be corrected until they fell exactly in line with the target.

The system was slow in the opening stages and depended a great deal on the rangefinder giving an accurate initial reading. With rangefinders over-reading as the British ones did at Jutland, it was often necessary to apply two or more corrections before the target was crossed. The Germans, on the other hand, with far more accurate rangefinders, were able to find the range more quickly.

On the face of it, purely from the gunnery point of view, the British should have won the battle of Jutland easily. However, apart from the inaccurate rangefinders, the British shells tended to disintegrate on the outside of the German armour instead of penetrating and exploding inside. In the event, neither side gained a decisive victory. British losses

were the heavier, but the German fleet thereafter avoided battle.

Independent patrolling by solitary warships for the purpose of protecting merchant ships against privateers and hostile warships was termed 'cruizing' in the seventeenth and eighteenth centuries. Thus in the days of sail a 'cruizer' was usually a smaller man-of-war operating on her own. The name indicated a function and not any particular degree of firepower or size.

This was changed, however, by the introduction of steam and armour plating in the mid-nineteenth century. The battleship needed armour plating to protect her from the shellfire of enemy battleships and the weight of this protection meant that she

View of the stern of the *Dreadnought*, a vessel which provoked a storm of controversy due to its standardized armament of 12-inch guns and the cost of its construction.

RIGHT The 'Queen Elizabeth' class of battleship was the first to mount 15-inch guns, to be completely oil-fired and to attain a speed of 25 knots.

BELOW HMS *Inflexible*, one of the first of the battle-cruiser class.

could only be driven at moderate speed. On the other hand the old task of 'cruizing' required higher speed and a good radius of action. As this meant that armour plate had to be omitted, it was inevitable that the steam-powered 'cruiser' would evolve as a specialized type of warship, distinct from the ironclad battleship.

The 1880s saw the first appearance of the modern cruiser. It was a decade of many innovations in ship-design – breech-loading guns, better machinery and, most important of all, steel construction. Steel was important for two reasons – it saved weight without sacrificing strength and speed could thus be increased. It also allowed the use of armour in cruisers for the first time. HMS *Shannon* had introduced an armoured deck carried below the waterline in 1875 and steel-armoured decks became a standard feature in the British corvettes built in the 1880s. The next step was a hull built entirely of steel and in 1879 the British unarmoured 'despatch vessels' *Iris* and *Mercury* astounded the world by steaming at 18 knots. The term 'cruiser' was firmly established in this decade, for in 1887 the Royal Navy regraded all its old frigates, cruising ironclads, corvettes, etc. as cruisers and the change was soon introduced by other navies.

The cruiser with a steel-armoured deck under-went rapid development in the 1880s. The British firm Armstrong of Elswick, Newcastle-upon-Tyne, soon established a reputation as the world's leading cruiser builders. In 1885 they completed the famous *Esmeralda* for Chile, which was armed with a single 10-inch gun forward and aft, and a battery of 6-inch guns on the broadside amidships. Not only did she steam at 18 knots, but she had a complete steel armoured deck 2.5cm (1in) thick.

Cruisers of the new Elswick design were built for Italy, Japan, Argentina, Austria, Germany and China and the French and Russians were spurred on to build their own fast steel cruisers. The French, and to a lesser extent the Russians, believed that the best opportunity for defeating Britain was by raiding her enormous seaborne trade. In France the theorists of the *Jeune Ecole* – the 'younger school' of naval officers – believed in building warships solely to attack merchant shipping and for many years their doctrines went unquestioned. Throughout the decade cruisers were built in Europe for the purpose of attacking or protecting seaborne commerce. Similarly the United States relied mainly on commerce-destroying cruisers for her offensive strength.

The French and Russians began to build a number of larger cruisers to act as 'corsairs' on the trade-routes, with large coal-capacity and enough heavy guns to make them a match for anything less than a battleship. This concept was later to be developed by Germany as the 'pocket battleship'. The British answer was to build a class of large cruisers protected not only by an armoured deck

but also by a 'belt' of vertical side armour 25cm (10in) thick. The 'Orlando' class of 1885 were similar to the contemporary 'Admiral'-class battleships in layout, and proved quite successful, but unfortunately the only heavy armour available was the compound type, a double layer of iron and steel. The weight was so great that the *Orlandos* could only have a shallow strip of armour at the waterline, which became submerged with a full load of coal aboard.

In an attempt to avoid this problem, large commerce-protection cruisers reverted to the horizontal armoured deck. The British *Blake* and *Edgar* were examples of the new type of larger cruiser and the threat of a new powerful Russian corsair – *Rurik* – led the British to design the largest cruisers with protected decks that the world had ever seen. *Powerful* and *Terrible* were bigger than contemporary battleships – over 14,000 tons – and they

The Royal Navy's battle-cruiser HMS *Indomitable* shown at full speed. Heavy losses of the class in battle proved that it could not fully replace the battleship.

The German battle-cruiser *Goeben*, armed with ten 11-inch guns, which escaped through the Mediterranean to reinforce Turkey in 1914. She remained bottled-up at Constantinople until January 1918.

were armed with single 9.2-inch guns fore and aft. To counter the menace of large armed liners preying on British shipping, *Powerful* and *Terrible* were capable of a speed of 22.25 knots and had a high forecastle to allow speed to be maintained in rough weather. Their huge coal capacity enabled them to pursue any cruiser or passenger liner afloat.

The French, in their ceaseless quest for more powerful cruisers to harass their potential enemy's trade, replied by reintroducing the armoured cruiser. *Dupuy de Lôme* of 1890 displaced 6300 tons and was protected by a 10-cm (4-inch) steel belt covering the whole hull from below the waterline to the level of the upper deck. The cruiser was the first in a spate of armoured cruiser construction, with Britain, France and Italy leading the way. The biggest were similar to *Powerful* and *Terrible*, but with 15-cm (6-in) armour belts instead of their arched armour decks. The Italian design proved very popular with other navies, and four vessels named *Giuseppe Garibaldi* were built in quick succession, as the first three were snapped up by foreign buyers before they were finished for the Italian navy.

By the end of the century the navies of Europe had reached a state of confusion over cruiser design. On the one hand there were the large 'armoured' and 'protected' cruisers, which were distinguished by having either vertical or horizontal armour protection. These costly ships were in some cases virtually battleships and the Japanese did in fact use their armoured cruisers in the battle line at Tsushima in 1904. Below these ranked the second-class and third-class cruisers, all with some degree of protective deck armour. The second-class vessels had guns of 6-inch calibre, while the smaller and slower third class had lighter guns. A fourth type, the torpedo-cruiser, had appeared briefly in the

1880s, but it proved to be too small for cruiser-duties and too slow to make proper use of the Whitehead torpedo.

The main problem for the British – as the principal naval power with enormous seaborne trade and an empire to protect – was to design a cruiser which met their basic needs for a wide radius of action, adequate protection with only a modest armament. British designs constantly emphasized cheapness and large numbers, but these criteria were frequently overridden by the need to match the latest foreign designs, such as *Dupuy de Lôme*, *Rurik* or the American *Columbia*. Commerce-protection was to be achieved by cruisers patrolling the trade routes, since convoys were not seriously considered. Cruiser actions were envisaged as being a matter of high-speed chases, with the superior cruiser running down and annihilating its weaker opponents one by one. With the invention of the powerful, rugged and reliable triple expansion engine it became possible, for the first time, to maintain high speed for long periods.

Cruiser development was thrown into even greater confusion by the building of the battleship *Dreadnought* in 1906. Her Parsons steam turbines drove her at a speed of 21 knots, 3 knots faster than existing battleships. Scouting cruisers needed to be about 4 knots faster than the battle-fleet and, when all battleships followed the pattern of *Dreadnought*, it became necessary to build scouting cruisers capable of 25 knots. Steam turbines were the only answer and the British *Amethyst* of 1904 was the prototype of the new cruisers. Steam turbines not only made higher speeds possible but also reduced the likelihood of machinery breaking down. The large cruiser with reciprocating machinery rapidly became obsolete and the fast scouting cruiser of medium size emerged as the principal type.

The old subdivision into classes also disappeared with a new division into cruisers (comprising the obsolescent armoured and deck-protected cruisers armed with guns from 6-inch up to 10-inch calibre, or even 12-inch guns in a few cases) and light cruisers (comprising the smaller cruisers, 5000 tons and under, armed with guns of 6-inch calibre or less). The scouting function of the armoured cruiser was taken over by the battle-cruiser, but this did not prevent the British from using both types at the battle of Jutland in May 1916, where they suffered disastrously.

At about the same time the Germans and the British concentrated on developing a cruiser for fleet work – a type which justified itself over and over again during World War I. German practice differed from that of the British on one major point. They clung to the 4.1-inch gun in the belief that high muzzle-velocity and rate of fire were more important than weight of shell. The British pinned their faith on the well-tried 6-inch gun, while retaining the 4-inch for a few scouting cruisers. Although the 6-inch was at first outranged by the German gun, later developments gave it an overwhelming advantage in destructive power. Belatedly the Germans realized their mistake and rearmed many of their cruisers with 5.9-inch guns in 1916–17.

In 1912 the British introduced oil fuel for cruisers and, as a result of the weight thus saved, they were able to give an armour belt to a cruiser displacing under 4000 tons. This was a great step forward, as the 8-cm (3-in) belt of the 'Arethusa' class was thick enough to keep out 4.1-inch shells, and this gave them a decided advantage in battle. The 'Arethusa' type was developed throughout World War I as the standard light cruiser and it proved to be an outstanding success. Capable of 28–9 knots, these cruisers also operated with destroyers and proved ideal for North Sea conditions. The original 'Arethusa' class was followed by the 'C' groups and the 'D' class.

When World War I began in August 1914 a number of German cruisers were stationed in the Pacific and they immediately dispersed to begin their task of harassing British commerce. The British and their French and Japanese allies immediately began a widespread search for the German cruisers, but for some time they were unsuccessful. *Emden* soon made her mark, with deadly raids on British bases and shipping over a wide area, but she was caught at Cocos Island by the Australian cruiser *Sydney* while trying to cut the submarine cable. *Sydney's* 6-inch guns enabled her to destroy *Emden* without suffering any serious damage.

Graf von Spee commanded the most powerful German force at large – the armoured cruisers *Scharnhorst* and *Gneisenau*, and three light cruisers. At the battle of Coronel, von Spee destroyed a

The German armoured cruiser *Blücher* was lost during the Dogger Bank action between British and German squadrons on 24 January 1915.

British squadron under Rear-Admiral Cradock composed of two elderly armoured cruisers, a light cruiser and an armed liner. The two smaller ships were the only British survivors. Retribution followed swiftly, for Spee lingered near the scene of his triumph too long and tried to raid the British colony in the Falkland Islands. There he found two battle-cruisers, *Invincible* and *Inflexible*, and a large force of cruisers. In the ensuing action Spee's squadron was destroyed and Cradock was avenged.

The medium-sized liner could and did prove a welcome addition to naval strength, when armed with 4.7-inch and 6-inch guns as an 'armed merchant cruiser', but she proved extremely vulnerable in action. The giant liner, on the other hand, proved quite useless on account of her enormous consumption of coal, and the larger British transatlantic liners were used as troopships or hospital ships. The only German liner converted to an armed merchant cruiser was the *Kaiser Wilhelm der Grosse*, and she spent her short wartime career hiding in a remote west African anchorage waiting for fresh coal supplies before she could move.

The armed merchant cruisers proved most suitable for manning the Northern Blockade, a patrol line established to prevent contraband goods reaching Germany from neutral countries. As there was little likelihood of their meeting regular warships, it proved an economical way of using them and it released proper cruisers for more urgent duties. In World War II this was again done and fifty liners were taken up as armed merchant cruisers. However, they again proved too vulnerable against any type of warship, however valiantly they fought, and they were relegated to transport duties.

When *Dreadnought* was launched in 1906, the era of the all-big-gun battleship had dawned. The British First Sea Lord, Admiral Sir John Fisher, had already decided to extend the same concept to the armoured cruiser. As he correctly judged, contemporary armoured cruisers would be unable to fulfil their function of scouting for the battle-fleet of the new epoch, owing to their limited speed. As he had said when discussing the role of these ships on foreign stations, they were too weak to fight and too slow to run away.

The two essential characteristics for the new ships had to be – as with *Dreadnought* – the elimination of all intermediate-sized guns and the concentration on armament of as many large guns as possible, with the incorporation of reliable machinery to give a high top speed. The cruisers' speed had to be higher than that of the battle-fleet for which they were to scout, so armour protection had to be sacrificed to achieve it. This was in accordance with Fisher's idea that speed and firepower were the best defence.

For the first of these essentials the 12-inch guns mounted in twin turrets as on pre-dreadnoughts and on *Dreadnought* herself, were available. For the

second requirement, the marine turbine, invented and developed by the Honourable Charles Parsons and driven by steam produced in coal-fired, water-tube boilers, proved to be a suitable system. The British light-cruiser *Amethyst* and the German *Lübeck* laid down in 1903 had incorporated the new machinery.

In February 1906 the keel was laid of *Inflexible*, of 17,250 tons displacement, mounting eight 12-inch guns in twin turrets and a secondary (anti-torpedo-boat) armament of sixteen 4-inch quick-firers. Her armoured belt was 15cm (6in) thick amidships tapering to 10cm (4in), but not extending aft beyond the after turret. This was the same thickness of armour as that used by the armoured cruisers of the 'Minotaur' class and, at first, *Inflexible* was also classed as an armoured cruiser. But the speed of 25 knots achieved by she and her sisters, *Indomitable* and *Invincible*, led to their being reclassed as battle-cruisers.

The Germans soon followed Britain's lead with the *Von der Tann*, which mounted eight guns of only 11-inch calibre, although she was larger than *Inflexible*. Thus it was possible to give her a complete armour belt 25cm (10in) thick amidships, tapering to 10cm (4in) at bow and stern. She was driven by Parsons turbines at speeds up to 25 knots.

In the armaments race developing between Britain and Germany, the same pattern was followed in the comparative design of battle-cruisers: while the Royal Navy preferred large-calibre guns at the expense of armour, the Germans sacrificed heavy armament for greater armour protection. The British ships *Indefatigable* and *New Zealand*, launched in 1911 and 1912, were of similar size and armament to their predecessors. Their German contemporaries *Goeben*, *Moltke* and *Seydlitz*, of between 22,635 and 24,600 tons with ten 11-inch guns, had armour belts of a maximun thickness of 30cm (12in). So too had the *Derfflinger* and *Lützow*, completed in 1914 and 1915. Although they had increased their armament to eight 12-inch-guns, the nearly contemporary British ships *Lion*, *Princess Royal*, *Queen Mary* and *Tiger* mounted eight 13.5-inch guns but had only 23-cm (9-in) belts of armour.

Japan's was the only other navy which adopted the battle-cruiser design before World War I. Their first was the 27,500-ton *Kongo*, designed by Sir George Thurston of the British firm of Vickers. Her main armament comprised eight 14-inch guns and her maximum speed was 28 knots with her Parsons turbines. She was launched in 1912 and was followed by the *Hiyei*, *Kirishima* and *Haruna*, which were built in Japan. All these ships were modernized in 1930 and 1936 and became fast battleships.

When World War I broke out, the battle-cruisers on both sides were soon in the forefront of the action. In the Mediterranean *Goeben* bombarded Philippeville and Algeria and, in company with the light cruiser *Breslau*, headed for the Dardanelles and

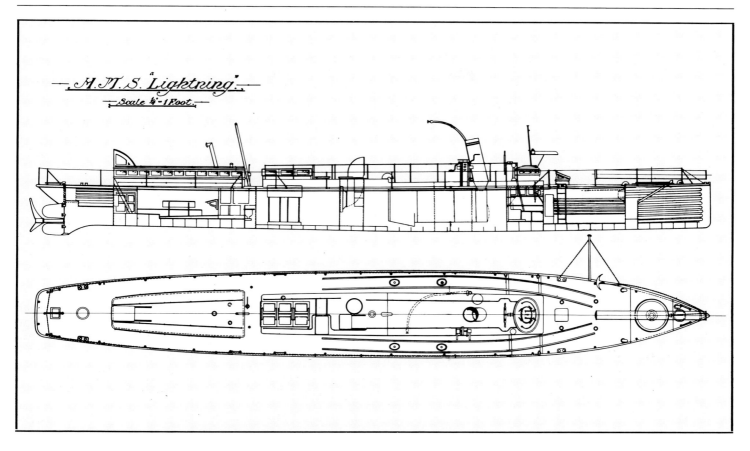

H.M.S. Lightning.
Scale ¼"–1 Foot.

Constantinople to join the Turks, who were expected to declare themselves allies of Germany. The failure of the British Mediterranean Fleet, which included the battle-cruisers *Inflexible*, *Indomitable* and *Indefatigable*, to intercept the German ships and bring them to action, ruined the professional reputation of the admirals concerned.

Four months later the *Invincible* and *Inflexible* intercepted a German squadron under Vice-Admiral Graf von Spee, centred on the armoured cruisers *Scharnhorst* and *Gneisenau*, off the Falkland Islands. The latter, fresh from their triumph in the battle of Coronel, where they had destroyed the armoured cruisers *Good Hope* and *Monmouth*, were in their turn overwhelmed and sunk – a striking demonstration of the superiority of the battle-cruiser.

In the North Sea, the British Grand Fleet was so superior to the German High Seas Fleet that naval encounters were at first confined to skirmishes between scouting squadrons. During the first of these, on 28 August 1914, the squadron of five battle-cruisers under Vice-Admiral Sir David Beatty intervened in an engagement in the Heligoland Bight. Their arrival turned impending disaster to Commodore Tyrwhitt's Harwich Force, which consisted of destroyers and light cruisers, into a victory in which three German light cruisers and a torpedo-boat were sunk.

The Germans then decided to mount 'hit-and-run' operations with their First Scouting Group. This force was commanded by Rear-Admiral Hipper and its main strength comprised the battle-cruisers *Seydlitz*, *Moltke*, *Derfflinger* and *Von der Tann*. The armoured cruiser *Blücher* was attached to the group on account of her top speed of 25 knots, though her 8.2-inch guns made her a weak member of the team.

The first of these sorties, a bombardment of Yarmouth on 3 November 1914, achieved surprise and was completed without interference from the British. But in December when a bombardment of Scarborough and Whitby by Hipper's battle-cruisers, supported by the whole of the High Seas Fleet, was attempted, the British were forewarned through their ability to decipher German wireless signals. They were thus able to deploy forces to intercept the Germans and, but for confusion in the mists of a North Sea winter dawn and mistakes on both sides, a major battle might have taken place. In the event Hipper had a narrow escape.

In spite of this, a fresh sortie by Hipper's battle-cruisers *Seydlitz* (flag), *Moltke* and *Derfflinger* with *Blücher* was made against the Dogger Bank fishing fleet in January 1915. Early on 24 January, they were intercepted by Beatty's *Lion*, *Tiger*, *Princess Royal*, *New Zealand* and *Indomitable*. As Hipper fled, a running fight developed during which *Blücher* was sunk. *Seydlitz* was hit by a 13.5-inch shell which pierced the barbette of her after turret, where the

Builders' plans for HMS *Lightning*, the first torpedo-boat. The craft was developed from the design of a fast steam launch.

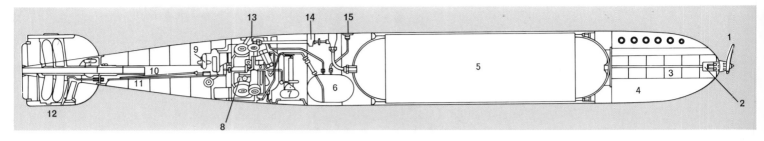

Diagram showing the parts of a 'hot' compressed-air- and steam-driven torpedo: 1 pistol; 2 primer; 3 charge; 4 warhead; 5 air flask; 6 fuel or water tank; 7 depth gear; 8 engine; 9 gyro-servometer; 10 propeller shafts; 11 afterbody; 12 tail section; 13 air regulator; 14 air-charging valve; 15 fuel- or water-charging valve.

flash of the explosion set fire to ammunition both in the gunhouse and the magazine and she was only saved from destruction by a prompt flooding of the magazine. *Lion*, hit by three 12-inch shells from *Derfflinger*, was heavily damaged and her speed reduced. A misunderstood signal then concentrated the remainder of Beatty's force on the already doomed *Blücher* and allowed the German battle-cruisers to escape.

The Germans profited from the harrowing experience in *Seydlitz* by taking steps to avoid a recurrence of the danger from flash. The British, though they had observed instances of the danger, from which they might have learned a lesson, failed to take any remedial steps. The consequences were to be disastrous when the battle-cruisers next met, at the battle of Jutland on 31 May 1916. On that date the German High Seas Fleet put to sea with Hipper's battle-cruisers – now brought up to five in number by the commissioning of *Derfflinger*'s sister ship *Lützow* – some 100km (62 miles) in advance of the battle-fleet. They hoped to lure out and bring to action a portion of the British fleet, before support from the Grand Fleet could arrive. Aided by their radio intelligence, however, the British were again forewarned. Both Beatty's battle-cruiser fleet from Rosyth and the main body of the Grand Fleet from Scapa Flow and Cromarty had already sailed.

Beatty's force was composed of the battle-cruisers *Lion*, *Princess Royal*, *Queen Mary* and *Tiger*, each mounting eight 13.5-inch guns; *New Zealand* and *Indefatigable*, with eight 12-inch guns; and a squadron of four fast battleships, *Barham*, *Valiant*, *Warspite* and *Malaya*, carrying eight 15-inch guns each. These last had been exchanged with the battle-cruisers *Invincible*, *Inflexible* and *Indomitable*, which had joined the Grand Fleet to gain the gunnery practice which all Beatty's ships lacked. The two British forces were due to meet off the entrance to the Skagerrak at about three o'clock on 31 May.

However, before they reached the rendezvous, Beatty and Hipper encountered one another at the Jutland Bank at 2.30 p.m. The German manoeuvred to lead Beatty south towards the advancing German battle-fleet. Beatty, over-confident of the superiority of his six battle-cruisers to the enemy's five, pursued without waiting for his battleships. In the ensuing gunnery duel, which lasted for about fifteen minutes before the battleships could intervene, the German ships proved themselves superior in several ways.

Firstly, the German ships were more stoutly armoured than the British. However, this was of less importance than it seemed, as the ships of each side were about equally protected against the plunging impact of shells at the range at which the duel was fought. More significant was the quality of the German shell, which had a better delayed-action fuse than the British and a less sensitive explosive charge, so that when it hit, it penetrated before exploding, whereas the British shell tended to explode before penetrating. Furthermore the British ships suffered more extensive damage, owing to their having fewer internal bulkheads than the German ships. As their ships were designed for North Sea operations, the Germans did not need to pay so much attention to living conditions for their crews, who generally lived ashore in harbour. German damage-control measures also were more thorough than those of their opponents.

However, the most important differences between the opposing warships were the methods employed to protect ammunition in the 'pipeline' between magazine and breech. Should it catch fire as the result of a hit and project the fatal flash to gunhouse and magazine, the ship would be destroyed or severely damaged by the resulting explosion. In the German ships, besides anti-flash doors at all points at which cartridges for the guns passed into or out of the hoists, the cartridges were transported in metal covers and the final section of the propellent charge went into the gun in a metal cartridge case. The British cordite was transported unprotected, in a silk covering with bare igniters at each end of the cartridge.

As a result of this weakness, during the gun duel between Beatty's and Hipper's ships, first *Indefatigable* and then *Queen Mary* blew up and sank, when their turrets were penetrated. *Lion* was saved from a similar fate by the heroic devotion to duty of the Royal Marine crew of one of her turrets. They flooded the magazines at the cost of their own lives, when a German shell penetrated their turret. None of the German ships was forced out of the line, though they were repeatedly hit and suffered particularly heavily from the 15-inch guns of the fast battleships. All survived to follow Beatty, who had discovered the German battle-fleet approaching from the south and turned to lead them into the trap prepared by the Grand Fleet.

At a later stage in the battle, when Hipper's battle-cruisers came briefly into action against the

three battle-cruisers leading the Grand Fleet, *Invincible* suffered the same fate as her sister ships. On the German side, by the end of the day *Lützow* had suffered so heavily that she had to be scuttled, while *Derfflinger*, *Von der Tann* and *Seydlitz* were all out of action with damage that would have sunk the British battle-cruisers, which had fewer watertight compartments. Indeed *Seydlitz* sank in shallow water before she reached harbour.

The comparatively poor showing of the faster, more powerful, but less well protected, British battle-cruisers against the Germans at Jutland was taken by many to demonstrate the fallacy of Admiral Fisher's theory that speed and firepower were the best protection. Even though the battle-cruiser concept lost favour, the British were committed to acquiring more of them through the laying down of *Repulse* and *Renown* in 1914. By 1920, however, the battle-cruiser concept had been abandoned in favour of that of the fast battleship and no more were laid down before World War II.

The advent of the torpedo in the second half of the nineteenth century had a profound effect on naval

tactics. It enabled a small high-speed craft to attack a powerful battleship with a good chance of sending her to the bottom. The offensive capabilities of the torpedo were further enhanced by the development of the sea-going submarine in the early years of the twentieth century and during World War I a torpedo was developed which could be launched from an aeroplane.

Originally the name 'torpedo' was applied to what would today be called a naval mine. The mine developed by the American inventor Robert Fulton during the Napoleonic Wars was named a torpedo, perhaps after the ray of that name. The spar torpedo, which was introduced later in the nineteenth century, consisted of an explosive charge attached to the end of a spar carried by a warship. It was intended to detonate the charge against the hull of an enemy ship, but the device met with little success and it was not widely used.

The self-propelled, or locomotive torpedo, was developed by an English marine engineer named Robert Whitehead. The idea for the device derived from the work of Giovanni Luppis, an officer in the Austrian navy. Luppis devised an explosive-

Sown by such vessels as the minelayer pictured here, mines have long been potent weapons of naval warfare. In both world wars the British laid mine barriers across the North Sea to discourage U-boats etc. Their military use to inhibit access to canals and harbours continues to this day.

carrying boat which could be remotely guided to its target by means of long yoke lines. Whitehead, who was working at Fiume (in modern Yugoslavia, but then part of the Austrian Empire), took up the basic idea. By 1866 he had produced the prototype of the modern torpedo and in 1872 he bought the Stabilimento Tecnico Fiumano, which he converted for the manufacture of torpedoes.

The early Whitehead torpedo was 4.25m (14ft) in length with a diameter of 35cm (14in), and it weighed some 135kg (300lb). An explosive charge, weighing 8kg (18lb), was carried in the nose of the 'tin fish'. Early torpedoes were powered by compressed-air engines and the depth at which they ran was regulated by a hydrostatic valve connected to rudders on the horizontal tail surfaces. A speed of

these was the introduction of the torpedo-boat. They first came on the scene in 1876 as small, fast steamboats of some 20 tons and a speed of 18 knots, mounting a single 14-inch torpedo tube. Ten years later they had doubled in size and had added several knots to their speed.

Although the British shipbuilders Yarrow and Thornycroft were the pioneers of these craft, it was the French navy – inspired by the 'Jeune Ecole' under Admiral Aube to believe that the age of the large man-of-war was over – which required the greatest number of them. The British, still looking on the French as the 'traditional enemy' and disturbed by this threat to their battle-fleets, decided that they must develop a countermeasure to the torpedo-boat. In 1886, therefore, they built Grasshopper, the

The Japanese cruiser Asama, which was among the fleet led by Admiral Togo against Russia at Tsushima in May 1905. Commanded by Admiral Uriu, it sank the Variag.

6 knots was achieved and the range of the Whitehead torpedo was estimated as 180–640m (200–700yd).

The chief shortcoming of Whitehead's design was his torpedo's lack of directional control. This problem was not overcome until 1895, when the Austrian Ludwig Obry devised a system which made use of the gyroscope. Any deviation from a pre-set course was registered by the gyroscope, which signalled the necessary corrective movements to vertical rudders in the torpedo's tail. In Britain the Whitehead torpedo was further improved by the development of a 'hot' torpedo engine (powered by compressed air, light oil and steam) and contrarotating propellers, which eliminated the torque effect of a single propeller.

The first recorded use of the torpedo in anger was during the engagement between HMS Shah and the Peruvian ironclad Huascar in 1877. Huascar was in the hands of Peruvian rebels when she was engaged by the British frigate on 29 May. The encounter was inconclusive and the single torpedo that Shah launched at her retreating opponent was easily avoided.

In spite of this undramatic beginning, the torpedo had swift repercussions. The most immediate of

first of a class known as 'torpedo gunboats' or 'torpedo catchers'. They were followed three years later by the 'Spanker' class and in 1892 by the 'Jason' class. All were primarily armed with quick-firing guns.

Their design was ill-conceived for their role. Bulky ships of 700–800 tons with a top speed of 20 knots were too conspicuous, too slow and too unmanoeuvrable to oppose fast torpedo-boats making their sneak night attacks. Similar, contemporary ships built for the French navy, such as the 'Bombe' and 'Lévrier' classes, also proved unsatisfactory. However, the prototype of a more suitable craft had been built in 1884 at the Clydebank yard of Thompson's – later world-famous as John Brown's – for the Spanish navy, following suggestions made by Captain Villamil. Justifiably enough, her name Destructor ('Destroyer') was to be given to the type of small warship known at first to the British as the torpedo-boat destroyer (TBD).

Destructor was the first warship to be driven by twin triple-expansion reciprocating engines and she had a speed of 22.5 knots. However, this was not enough to prevent her rapid obsolescence as the speed of torpedo-boats rose with each successive class. It was the two pioneers of the torpedo-boat –

Yarrow and Thornycroft – who built the first 'torpedo-boat destroyers' in 1893, *Havock* and *Hornet* by the former, *Daring* and *Decoy* by the latter. Although basically simply larger torpedo-boats, their displacement of 240 tons permitted the installation of twin reciprocating engines which gave them a speed of 27 knots, and the mounting of one 3-inch, 12-pounder gun and three 6-pounders as well as three torpedo tubes. They thus combined the offensive capability of the torpedo-boat with the defensive gun armament of the destroyer. The Admiralty was so satisfied with their performance that thirty-six more boats of similar design were ordered.

By the time they were commissioned, however, they had already been surpassed – in speed at least. *Forban*, a torpedo-boat built by the French yard of Normand's and *Sokol*, a TBD built by Yarrow for the Russian navy, each achieved 31 knots on trials. The next class of boats for the British navy, therefore, was larger (300–400 tons) and, from their nominal speed, were designated '30-knotters'. In fact, few of them actually reached that speed in loaded condition, although two, *Viper* and *Cobra*, powered by the marine steam turbine developed by Charles Parsons, achieved 36 knots.

Twelve boats of the '30-knotter' type, supplied to the Japanese from British yards, began the Russo-Japanese War on 9 February 1904 by delivering a night torpedo attack on the Russian Far Eastern Fleet, which was lying in the roads outside Port Arthur. Although no declaration of war had been made and the Russians were taken completely by surprise, the attack achieved surprisingly little. Only three hits were scored, one each on the battleships *Retvizan* and *Tsarevitch* and the cruiser *Pallada*.

Subsequent torpedo attacks by the Japanese destroyers on several occasions were unsuccessful. It was not until the closing stages of the battle of Tsushima in the following year, between the Japanese fleet and the far from battle-worthy Russian Baltic Squadron, that destroyer attacks again penetrated the Russian fleet's defences.

Daylight attacks on the crippled Russian flagship *Suvorov* possibly achieved a few hits but evidence is conflicting. As darkness fell the real opportunity for the Japanese flotillas came and through the night twenty-one TBDs and thirty-seven TBs harried the damaged and fleeing Russian ships, pressing in close to fire more than a hundred torpedoes. The seven hits achieved resulted in the loss of the battleships

Photographed at Toulon in 1903, the battleship *Czarevitch* had been launched some two years earlier. The Russian squadron at Tsushima included five such modern ships.

An Italian battleship of the 'Duilio' class is pictured with a torpedo-boat in the foreground. Unlike the destroyer, the torpedo-boat was not destined to play a large part in fleet actions.

Navarin and *Sissoi Veliki* and the armoured cruisers *Nakhimoff* and *Vladimir Monomakh*, which were scuttled to avoid capture.

The British 30-knotters were constructed with very light scantlings and side-plating of high tensile steel only 6mm (0.25in) thick. The loss of *Cobra*, which broke her back in heavy weather and foundered on passage from her building yard to receive her armament, led to a reaction against such a design and against high speeds and turbine drive. The next class, built for the Royal Navy between 1903 and 1905 and named after rivers, were therefore larger at 550 tons. Their high, flared forecastles, which replaced the low turtle-back decks of their predecessors, made them more seaworthy. However, the 7000 horse-power reciprocating engines gave them a top speed of only 25.5 knots, except in *Eden*, which was powered by Parsons turbines. At the same time their armament was increased to four 3-inch guns as compared to the single 3-inch and five 6-pounders of the 30-knotters.

The French navy, which up to 1899 had contented itself with large numbers of torpedo-boats of no more than 190 tons displacement, had meanwhile received its first *contre-torpilleur*. *Durandal*, of 300 tons, although powered by reciprocating engines, achieved a reliable top speed of 27.5 knots. She and the large number of French *contre-torpilleurs* for which she was the model retained the low turtle-back forecastle, but a fore-and-aft superimposed 'flying-deck' permitted better serving of her gun and torpedo armament in a seaway, even at the 31 knots which later boats of the type achieved.

In the meantime the imperial Germany navy had been growing out of its infancy and developing similar craft of between 300 and 600 tons. These were designated torpedo-boats as they mounted three 18-inch torpedo tubes, as compared to the two in contemporary British boats, and a gun armament of only a few 4-pounder guns. The demand for high speed returned with the advent of *Dreadnought* and led to a return to turbine drive and the development of oil-fired destroyers.

Thus the British navy acquired the 'Tribal' class with a speed of 33–5 knots and an armament of two 18-inch torpedo tubes and either five 3-inch or two 4-inch guns. French destroyers, now called *torpilleurs d'escadre*, of the 700-ton 'Casque' class, achieved speeds of more than 35 knots and mounted two 3.9-inch and four 9-pounder guns and four 18-inch torpedo tubes. Torpedo boats of the German navy, which had replaced the French as the Royal

Navy's main rival, were boats of some 600 tons, mounting one 3.5-inch and three 9-pounders with three 18-inch torpedo tubes and a speed of over 33 knots.

By the outbreak of World War I, the typical British destroyer had become a ship of 1200 tons with a speed of 27–9 knots, mounting three 4-inch guns and four 21-inch torpedo tubes. The contemporary German 'high seas torpedo-boat' was of some 700 tons displacement and mounted two or three 3.5-inch guns and four or six 19.7-inch torpedo tubes. Most of the very large number of destroyers on both sides were organized in flotillas of up to a score of boats and they were deployed as part of the main fleets. Their duty was the dual one of moving out to attack the enemy battle line with torpedoes when ordered by the fleet commander and repelling the attacks of the enemy's torpedo craft with gunfire.

Other destroyers were allocated to naval ports as local defence flotillas and became the maids-of-all-work in their area. On the British side, also, a force of some thirty destroyers and a few light cruisers was based at Harwich to protect the east coast shipping and North Sea fishing fleets. Another force, the Dover Patrol, was stationed at that port to

patrol the anti-submarine barrier across the Straits and to oppose German flotillas which were based at Zeebrugge and Ostend.

The Harwich force expected to be, and usually was, the first to make contact with units of the German High Seas Fleet making 'tip-and-run' raids on the British coast. A series of such operations culminated in the battle of the Dogger Bank in January 1915 after which they ceased for a year. However the Harwich Force took no part in the fleet movements which resulted in the battle of Jutland on 31 May 1916, in spite of the appeals of its commander, Commodore Tyrwhitt. It was therefore the fleet flotillas which were tested in the role envisaged for destroyers ever since *Havock* was built in 1893.

In the opening stages of the battle, which was fought out between Admiral Beatty's six battle-cruisers and the five ships commanded by Admiral Hipper, the British got the worst of it. When Beatty ordered his destroyers into the attack, to gain respite, they met their German opposite numbers moving out to attack the battle-cruisers. In a wild, confused fight at high speed the German boats were forced to fire their torpedoes ineffectively at long range and two of the German ships were sunk.

The Royal Navy's torpedo-boat destroyer *Tipperary*, which was sunk at Jutland. The destroyer was developed from the torpedo-boat in the 1890s to become a significant fighting vessel in its own right.

The British destroyers then pressed on and some penetrated to within 3200m (3500yd) of the enemy battle-cruisers to fire their torpedoes. Met by a storm of gunfire from the light cruiser flotilla leader *Regensburg* and the secondary armament of the capital ships, they lost two of their number. One torpedo scored a hit on the battle-cruiser *Seydlitz*, but, though it tore a huge hole in her side, her inner torpedo bulkhead and stout construction enabled her to maintain her station in the line. While this was going on, the German battle-fleet had come on the scene and Beatty turned away to lure the High Seas Fleet northwards to where Admiral Jellicoe was bringing the full strength of the Grand Fleet to take the Germans in a perfectly prepared tactical trap. This encounter opened the next phase of the battle and destroyers were again in action.

When a squadron of four German light cruisers of Hipper's force encountered a division of three battle-cruisers in the van of the Grand Fleet, Commodore Heinrich in *Regensburg* launched all of his torpedo flotillas to relieve Hipper. At the same moment four British destroyers moved out to attack the light cruisers and they were met not only by the cruisers' gunfire but also by that of the greatly superior force of torpedo-boats. The destroyer *Shark*, under Commander Loftus Jones, was set ablaze and brought to a halt. Refusing the proffered aid of the also damaged *Acasta*, Loftus Jones, whose leg had been shot off, continued to direct the fire of his last remaining gun until his ship went down.

The German boats, broken up into small groups in the wild confusion of this fight, got only a few torpedoes away and these at such a long range that they were easily avoided by the British battle-cruisers. The British boats had thus not suffered in vain.

The torpedo craft attached to the battle-squadrons on either side had not yet been in action. Those with the Grand Fleet were, indeed, not to do so before nightfall. However when the German Admiral Scheer extricated himself from Jellicoe's trap by an emergency reversal of course, he ordered all available torpedo-boats out to the attack. Eighteen answered the call and, in the face of a storm of fire from light cruisers and battleships, succeeded in launching twenty-eight torpedoes. Not one of them found a target, but the attack had, in effect, decided the outcome of the battle. Jellicoe ordered a 45-degree-turn of his battle line to avoid them, thereby losing contact with the fleeing enemy. When night fell, Jellicoe, unwilling to accept the chances of a night action which favoured the smaller fleet, contented himself with holding a position which he believed would cut Scheer off from his line of retreat.

Scheer, for his part, decided that his only hope of avoiding a renewal of action on the following day was to hold a direct course for the entrance to the swept channel through his defensive minefield at the Horns Reef Light Vessel. In following this course he passed across the rear of the Grand Fleet where Jellicoe had massed his destroyers – more than sixty of them in their several flotillas with two light cruiser flotilla leaders. In theory it was a situation that was tailor-made for effective employment of torpedo craft, but the British flotillas were revealed as lacking in equipment, training and practice for night action. One after the other throughout the night they encountered the German battle line. They attacked gallantly enough but, at the cost of six of their number destroyed and many more severely damaged, they succeeded in torpedoing and sinking only the pre-dreadnought battleship *Pommern* and the light cruiser *Rostock*. They also caused the loss through collision of the light cruiser *Elbing*. These skirmishes failed to divert the

BELOW A beached David submersible, with its propeller, rudder and hydroplanes all clearly visible.

BOTTOM A submarine built by John P. Holland, whose craft served both the British and US navies. They employed electric motors underwater.

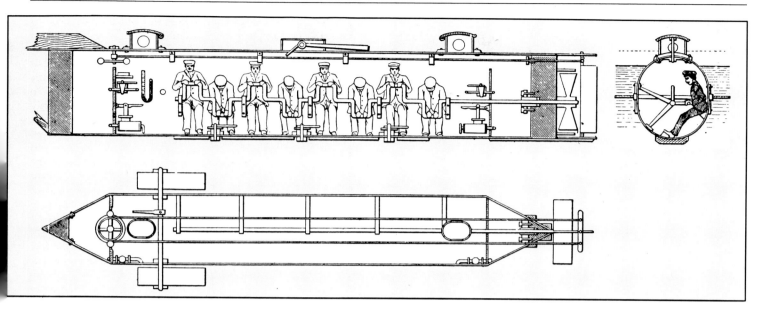

German fleet which escaped behind its minefields.

Torpedo craft, as such, had been proved to be far less effective than expected. They had come, however, to assume other vital roles, not least that of anti-submarine escort for major warships and merchant convoys, and they continued to be built in large numbers for all navies.

William Bourne, writing in 1578 in his book *The Treasure for Travellers*, described 'how it is possible to make a ship or boat that may goe under the water unto the bottome, and so come up again at your pleasure . . .'. There is no record that his boat was ever built, but his description is precise enough to show that he was one of the first men to appreciate the principles by which a submarine dives or surfaces at will.

The dream of a vessel that could make herself invisible by diving under the water was one which fired a host of inventors through the centuries. Most of them ignored Bourne's principle of creating temporary negative buoyancy by admitting water to internal tanks. They concentrated instead on trying to construct a watertight hull, ballast it externally with stones or iron weights until it was awash, and then force it under water with oars or similar means. One of the first of these was a Dutch physician named Cornelius van Drebbel. He built two wooden boats in 1620 and covered them with tightly stretched leather soaked in grease to keep the water out when submerged. Rowers sat inside, their oars passing through leather-lined holes cut in the sides. The boats were then ballasted until they were awash and forced just below the surface by the oars. It is recorded that James I watched a trial of one of Drebbel's boats on the Thames when, occasionally awash and occasionally just submerged, it travelled from Westminster to Greenwich.

The problem of maintaining a supply of fresh air

for the rowers to breathe when submerged needed in those days a magical faith. Drebbel had a:

chymicall liquor which he accounted the chief secret of his submarine navigation. For when, from time to time, he perceived that the finer and purer part of the air was consumed or even clogged by the respiration and steames of those that went in his ship, he would, by unstopping a vessel full of this liquor, speedily restore to the troubled air such a proportion of vitall parts as would make it again for a good while fit for respiration.

If the 'chymicall liquor' perchance did not work, Drebbel thought that another miracle might produce the answer. 'He seems inclined to think that long use and custom (which in other things doth produce such strange, incredible effects) will produce a race of men to whom it will not, perhaps, be so necessary to have the air for breathing so pure and desiccated as is required for breathing.'

The next inventor on the scene was a Frenchman named de Son who constructed a 'submarine' at

Rotterdam in 1653. To overcome the difficulty of providing fresh air, his boat required no rowers but was propelled with a paddlewheel turned by clockwork. He made some startling claims for his invention. 'He doeth undertake in one day to destroy a hondered ships, can goe from Rotterdam to London and back againe in one day, and in six weeks to go to the East Indiens, and to run as swift as a bird can flye, no fire, no storme, no bullets, can hinder her, unlesse it please God.' Possibly God was not pleased, for when the 'submarine' was launched, the clockwork was not powerful enough to turn the paddlewheel and she was unable to move.

A submarine was built on the Thames in 1747 by a man named Symons. She was an interesting boat as the designer returned to the principles which Bourne had set out in 1578. The boat was dived by admitting water to internal tanks (in this case leather bottles) with their openings in the bottom of the

boat, and brought back to the surface by squeezing the water out of the bottles and tying their necks with string. Propulsion was by eight rowers, four each side. It was an ingenious idea, but was unsatisfactory as the leather bottles took up too much space in the boat for the rowers to operate.

Another submarine was built in 1773 by a ship's carpenter named Day. It was constructed on the old principle of being ballasted down by attaching large rocks to the keel of the boat. The weight took her down, and when the rocks were released by an internal mechanism, she rose to the surface again. He succeeded in diving his boat to a depth of 9m (30ft) in the Thames, but this success was to prove his undoing. In 1774 he took her to Plymouth Sound to try her in deeper water and he chose a spot where the depth was 40m (132ft). Unhappily he did not realize that water exerts a pressure which increases as the depth increases. On 20 June he made

Germany was probably the most feared exponent of undersea warfare. Here, U-boats are pictured at Kiel in October 1918, shortly before the end of World War I.

his dive and undoubtedly his boat, with him inside it, was crushed by the pressure of water. He was probably the first of many to give their lives attempting to prove that the submarine was a viable weapon.

Two Americans were the next to turn their talents to designing a submarine, and they are usually regarded as the true fathers of the modern submarine. They were David Bushnell and Robert Fulton and in both cases their boats were designed to sink ships in war. Bushnell graduated from Yale University in 1775, the year before the start of the American War of Independence, and he was quick to see in the submarine a chance to strike a blow against the British navy. He realized that gunpowder, exploded under water, had a much greater destructive force than when exploded in the air. He constructed an egg-shaped hull of iron, with a brass conning tower, which was just large enough for one man to operate. It had a 320-kg (700-lb) lead keel to make it float upright and two small internal tanks into which water could be admitted through a valve to make the vessel submerge. The water could be expelled from the tanks by a hand pump to bring it to the surface again. Externally it carried a charge of 68kg (150lb) of gunpowder which could be attached by a screw to the wooden bottom of a ship. Movement was by two hand-operated propellers, one mounted vertically to adjust the depth of the vessel, the other mounted horizontally for lateral movement.

Bushnell's submarine went into action in 1776 when the British fleet, under the command of Lord Howe, was at anchor off New York. An American sergeant named Ezra Lee took the small vessel to sea and managed to get her alongside HMS *Eagle*, Howe's flagship. He submerged her there and attempted to screw home the charge. Bushnell, however, did not know that at this time British ships had their bottoms sheathed with copper as a protection against the teredo worm. Consequently

his screw was not strong enough to penetrate the copper and the operation failed.

Robert Fulton, born in 1765, moved to France in 1797 after spending three years in England. He was a fervent prophet of universal disarmament and, believing that sea power was the most powerful weapon in the world, thought that if he could destroy it, he would eventually achieve his main objective. So he invented a submarine and attempted to sell it to Napoleon for use against the British navy. Named *Nautilus*, the initial trials on the Seine in 1801 were completely successful, and the submarine was taken to Brest for trials at sea. An old schooner was moored in the bay and *Nautilus*, approaching her under water, blew her up with a charge of gunpowder. Unhappily for Fulton, the French Minister of Marine, Admiral Pléville le Pelly, was not prepared to become associated with so terrible a weapon and decided against the project. Fulton immediately crossed the Channel and offered *Nautilus* to Britain for use against France. Once again the trial arranged to demonstrate its powers was completely successful, but again the project was turned down, in spite of the Prime Minister, William Pitt, being in favour of it. 'Pitt', said Lord St Vincent, the great British admiral, 'was the greatest fool that ever existed to encourage a mode of warfare which those who commanded the seas did not want and which, if successful, would at once deprive them of it.'

The next inventor was a Bavarian non-commissioned officer named Wilhelm Bauer, who built *Le Plongeur-Marin* in 1850. The boat was constructed of iron plates and had internal tanks which, when filled with water, gave her negative buoyancy. A sliding weight was then pushed into the bows of the boat to give her an inclination downwards, and so she slid under the waves. Bauer tested her at Kiel on 1 February 1851 but unfortunately the weight was slid too far forward and *Le Plongeur-Marin* hit the bottom at 18m (60ft) and

A sea-going submarine of World War I, the first conflict in which specialist sub-hunting ships were commissioned to combat this new menace.

stuck there. Bauer and his two companions managed to escape by admitting water to the hull to compress the air inside the boat until it equalled the pressure of water outside. When the hatch was opened, all three of them came up safely in the air bubble. Thirty-six years later, a Kiel dredger got her bucket caught in a large object on the bottom and when divers went down to fit lifting wires, it was discovered to be the wreck of Bauer's boat. It was brought to the surface and placed in the courtyard of the Naval School, remaining there until 1906 when it was removed to the Oceanographical Museum in Berlin.

Bauer was not yet finished, however. He persuaded the Russian government to finance the building of a new submarine, 16m (52ft) long, named *Le Diable-Marin*. She was launched at the Leuchternberg works at St Petersburg, now Leningrad, in 1855. Bauer created a sensation with her at the coronation of Alexander II in September 1856, when he embarked an orchestra on board at Kronstadt and played the Russian national anthem when submerged at 6m (20ft). The anthem was clearly heard in all the ships in harbour. It is recorded that *Le Diable-Marin* made 134 successful dives, but she was lost on the 135th.

The next submarines were those famous little boats named Davids, which were built by the Confederate States during the American Civil War. They were of two main kinds. One was driven by a hand-operated propeller through a series of cranks worked by a crew of eight men. The other was driven by a small steam engine with a crew of four men. The Davids were made of boiler iron shaped into a long, slim hull and they carried a spar torpedo with 60kg (134lb) of gunpowder on a 9-m (30-ft) spar. The first David, a steam one, attacked the armoured monitor *Ironsides* on 5 October 1863, but was challenged before she could get alongside. Nevertheless she managed to explode her spar torpedo against the monitor's side, though without sinking her. The David was swamped in the waves caused by the explosion and her crew was drowned. The next attack was by a hand-operated David against the Federal ship *Housatonic*, which was blockading Charleston. She was sighted when 90m (100yd) off and the *Housatonic* slipped her cable, but it was too late. Urged on by their officer, the eight men on the cranks redoubled their efforts and drove the David into the *Housatonic's* side, where the torpedo exploded and blew a hole large enough to sink her. This David never returned and some years later her hull was found alongside the ship she had sunk, with the eight dead rowers still in it.

The exploits of the David proved to the navies of the world that here indeed was a new weapon of sea power. Enough was known from all the experiences of the past 200 years to produce a submarine that could dive and proceed under water. All that was needed was a viable underwater weapon. Two years after the sinking of the *Housat-*

onic, an Austrian captain named Luppis invented a floating torpedo and took his plans to the British engineer named Robert Whitehead. From this was developed the Whitehead locomotive torpedo and the submarine at last had her weapon.

By the end of the nineteenth century the submarine had been developed into the form in which it was to remain for the next sixty years. It achieved negative buoyancy by the admission of sea water into tanks. High-pressure air was used to blow this water out of the tanks when positive buoyancy was required to bring the submarine to the surface again. Underwater propulsion was by electric motors fed from batteries. Petrol engines, later replaced by diesels, were fitted for surface propulsion and for driving the motors as dynamos when the batteries required recharging. Hydroplanes, fitted fore and aft, controlled the angles of dive and ascent. Internal trimming tanks enabled small adjustments to be

made to the trim when submerged, so that the boat was stable in the water with neither positive nor negative buoyancy. Her weapon was the locomotive torpedo, fired through torpedo tubes, and periscopes gave visibility when submerged.

The final shape of the submarine was mainly evolved through the work of four designers – Holland and Lake of the US, Goubet of France, and Nordenfelt of Sweden. They were all working along similar basic lines and by 1900 several of the world's navies included submarines in their fleets. Britain was the last of the great navies to adopt the new weapon, but in 1901 she too introduced them with, initially, an order of five Holland boats from the US.

It was with developments of these submarine boats that the two world wars were fought. They were, of course, larger, with stronger hulls for deeper diving. Their torpedoes increased in size and speed and carried more lethal warheads. Their endurance at sea increased from a few days to weeks and, in some cases during World War II, to months at a time. Although, in both world wars, they proved themselves to be the dominant weapon at sea, they still had one built-in weakness. Every so often – normally every night – they had to come to the surface to recharge their batteries, which were exhausted by running submerged during the day. They then lost the invisibility which was their most precious attribute.

The cruiser *Pennsylvania* provided the launching platform for Eugene Ely to fly-off his Curtiss biplane in 1911. It was to be some years, however, before the aircraft-carrier became a viable proposition.

Hampton Roads

THE CLASH OF THE IRONCLADS

A new chapter in the history of naval warfare was proclaimed on 8 and 9 March 1862 in an extraordinary sequence of engagements in Hampton Roads, the estuary through which the James and Elizabethan Rivers enter Chesapeake Bay. On the first day a steam-driven ironclad warship destroyed two conventional wooden sailing warships and proved beyond doubt their total obsolescence; on the second day, also for the first time, ironclad fought ironclad.

Though sail augmented steam until the 1870s and 1880s, steam power had come into its own on the introduction of the screw propeller in the 1840s in place of the battle-vulnerable paddlewheel. So had the use of explosive shells instead of traditional solid shot, and the technique of armouring warships to withstand the formidable blast of the new projectiles. French ironclad floating batteries, powered by feeble steam engines, had proved their worth in the Crimean War. In 1859 the French produced the ironclad warship *Gloire*, and the British riposted the following year by building the greatly superior *Warrior* (still in existence 122 years later, and happily now scheduled for restoration).

When the Southern American states seceded from the Union and formed their own Confederacy in 1861, the biggest problem facing the South was the lack of a navy with which to fight off the blockade imposed by the Federal navy. But the inexperienced civilian appointed as Secretary of the Confederate States' navy, Stephen Mallory, saw at once that ironclads were the only real answer to the wooden steamships imposing the Federal blockade. Though all the leading ironworks and shipyards lay in the North, materials for a rapid conversion job were available at Norfolk, Virginia. These were the hull and engines of the big steam frigate *Merrimack*, which the panicky Northerners had burned to the waterline and scuttled when Virginia seceded and the US navy evacuated Norfolk in April 1861.

Merrimack's hull was pumped out, raised and placed in dry dock, and her conversion began in July 1861. An angled penthouse was built on her deck, covering eight guns mounted four per broadside plus one each in the bow and stern, the latter able to pivot and fire through a choice of three ports. The penthouse was covered with plates hammered from rails – the South possessed no ironworks capable of delivering custom-forged plates quickly, and the iron for *Merrimack*'s armour caused the biggest delay. A modest iron beak was bolted to her bow to serve as a ram. As the deck was virtually level with the water surface, *Merrimack* (proudly rechristened CSS *Virginia*) strongly resembled a derelict barn torn loose by a flood. Her wheezy engines had not been improved by several weeks at the bottom of the James and could not deliver more than about 5 knots. As she was never intended to operate on the high seas – she would certainly have sunk in anything more than a flat calm – this did not matter. A bigger problem was her prodigious draught of 6.7m (22ft) – about the depth of the deep-water channel in Hampton Roads, where the blockading Federal warships rode at anchor.

Had the South been able to complete *Merrimack*/*Virginia* in total secrecy, she would have placed every warship in the US navy in deadly peril. As it was, rumours about what was afoot at Norfolk began to alarm naval circles in the North in September 1861. Orders for the US navy's first two ironclads, *Galena* and *New Ironsides*, had been placed the month before, but the news of *Merrimack*'s conversion made it clear that neither of these new ships would be ready in time to meet the Southern monster. In desperation, US navy Secretary Gideon Welles snatched at the design for a revolutionary

The two ironclads *Monitor* (foreground) and *Virginia* do battle in the Hampton Roads. Although neither could claim victory, their encounter on 9 March 1862 revolutionized the future course of naval warfare.

ironclad offered by the brilliant but controversial inventor John Ericsson.

Ericsson's *Monitor* looked like no other warship ever conceived outside the realms of science fiction: a steam-powered, shallow-draught hull topped by an armoured raft, carrying a cylindrical turret armed with two 11-inch guns. What made her revolutionary was the fact that this turret was designed to rotate in order to bring the guns to bear, irrespective of the ship's course. She would be able to fire on any bearing except dead ahead, where a stubby pilot-house jutted above the deck to enable the ship to be steered in action.

Ericsson got the contract to build *Monitor* at New York because he promised that she could be completed in 100 days. Work on her started in October 1861 and she was launched on 30 January 1862. The Southern builders had been soundly beaten, thanks to the North's industrial wherewithal, but it took Ericsson the whole of February to overcome teething troubles in *Monitor*'s steering gear. She did not leave New York to join the Union squadron blockading Hampton Roads until 6 March, and even then was under tow and just as unseaworthy as her future opponent.

By chance, 6 March was the day that Captain Franklin Buchanan, commander of the *Virginia* (as she now was), announced to his officers that he would attack the Union warships on the following day. This proved impossible, for a storm blew up and made the estuary too rough for *Virginia* to sail in safety. Out at sea to the north, the same storm all but sank *Monitor* as she proceeded slowly down the coast under tow. This delay meant that *Virginia* was given one day in which to show what would happen when an ironclad attacked conventional wooden warships, before *Monitor* arrived to show what would happen when ironclad met ironclad.

The morning of 8 March 1862 was still and sunny, with conditions near perfect for *Virginia*'s first sortie. The Union and Confederate troops confronting each other across the 8-km (5-mile) expanse of Hampton Roads had a grandstand view of the ensuing action. Taking advantage of the calm sunshine to dry their sails and laundry, the Union flotilla rode easily at anchor under the shelter of its army's shore batteries. The vessels comprised the sail sloop *Cumberland* and sail frigate *Congress* furthest to the west, opposite the mouth of the Elizabeth River, and the powerful steam frigates *Minnesota* and *Roanoke* – the latter with a broken propeller shaft – about 5 km (3 miles) to the east.

Shortly after noon the lookouts on *Cumberland* and *Congress* stiffened: a slowly-moving dense column of black smoke was observed to be coming from the direction of Norfolk. The long-awaited crisis was at hand: the Southern monster was coming out, heading straight for *Cumberland* and *Congress*. Along the coast, *Roanoke* signalled frantically for steam tugs to tow her into action; *Minnesota* raised steam and slipped her cable, only to run ignominiously aground. *Cumberland* and *Congress* were on their own, unable to manoeuvre in the flat calm.

Aboard *Virginia*, Buchanan chose to attack *Cumberland* first. With his ship's sloping armour –

The crew of the US navy's *Monitor* relax on the ironclad's deck, with the 11-inch gun turret behind. The latter shows evidence of damage from the *Virginia*'s fire.

An eyewitness view of the Confederate and US navy fleets at Hampton Roads. The larger *Virginia* is bringing its beam guns to bear, while the *Monitor*'s fire is augmented by that of *Minnesota*.

greased with pork fat to help deter boarders and deflect enemy shot – shrugging off the fire of the Northern shore batteries, he opened a destructive fire on *Cumberland* with *Virginia*'s 7-inch bow gun. Buchanan was not relying solely on shellfire, deadly though this was against the completely unarmoured hull of *Cumberland*. He brought *Virginia* in fine on *Cumberland*'s starboard bow and rammed her deep below the waterline, *Virginia*'s ram breaking off and remaining in her victim. *Cumberland* at once began to heel and sink, but with great gallantry her gunners stayed at their posts and fired a broadside as soon as *Cumberland*'s increasing list allowed her main battery to bear. It was wasted effort: the Union shells smashed against *Virginia*'s armour at point-blank range and ricocheted into thin air.

Leaving *Cumberland* to sink with most of her wounded, Buchanan took *Virginia* further up the James in order to turn round, then came back to close with *Congress*. She was so close inshore that she was covered not only by the Union artillery but by infantry rifle fire, and Buchanan was wounded by a rifle bullet from the shore as he ventured on deck for a better view. Lieutenant Catesby Jones took command and directed a pitiless bombardment which set *Congress* ablaze. She struck her flag in surrender and the rickety wooden Confederate gunboats dashed in to take possession, only to be driven off by gunfire from the shore.

Minnesota and *Roanoke* now lay at *Virginia*'s mercy – but the Southern ironclad could do no more that afternoon. With the tide ebbing she would have certainly run aground if she had tried to attack the Union frigates, and Jones took her back to Norfolk to anchor for the night. Night drew on and *Congress* blazed furiously, finally blowing up and sinking at midnight. *Monitor*, however, had arrived at last, steaming into the Roads under her own power to anchor near *Minnesota*. As another still dawn on 9 March revealed *Virginia*'s tell-tale column of funnel smoke approaching, Lieutenant John Worden took *Monitor* out to intercept.

Though dwarfed by *Virginia*'s bulk, *Monitor* had several advantages. She drew 3.6m (12ft) less water, had a tighter turning circle, presented a smaller target than her opponent and, above all, her rotating turret allowed her to attack without presenting a broadside. *Monitor*'s pair of 11-inch guns were also bigger than *Virginia*'s heaviest (9-inch) guns.

From 8 a.m. to noon on 9 March, the two ironclads hammered at each other at point-blank range, neither able to hurt the other. Several attempts by both ships to ram each other were unsuccessful. The closest *Virginia* came to success was when one of her shells damaged *Monitor*'s pilot-house and wounded Lieutenant Worden. Before Lieutenant Greene could take command, *Virginia* had turned on *Minnesota* and set her on fire, but by desperate efforts the Northerners managed to save their ship. *Monitor* returned to the action and the stalemate continued, *Virginia* momentarily running aground and refloating only when her stokers tied down the safety-valves and stuffed the furnace with oil-soaked rags. By noon, however, Lieutenant Jones was worried that *Virginia*'s bow, now riding higher out of the water, might be pierced by a lucky Northern shot, and decided to withdraw. *Monitor* in turn pulled back to shield *Minnesota*.

Monitor's eleventh-hour intervention had restored the *status quo* in Hampton Roads, though the ironclads never fought again. Her presence enabled the planned Union offensive to proceed on the Yorktown peninsula, and in May 1862 it was the South's turn to evacuate Norfolk. *Virginia*'s crew fired their ship to save her from capture, and subsequent explosions wrecked her. *Monitor* survived until the last day of the year when she sank off Cape Hatteras in heavy seas.

By the end of the Civil War the North had commissioned thirty-one armoured successors to *Monitor*; the duel in Hampton Roads on 9 March 1862 had changed the course of naval history for ever.

David Glasgow Farragut

1801–1870

David Glasgow Farragut was the first officer in the history of the United States navy to be given the substantive rank of admiral. He won fame as a Union commander during the Civil War and ranks among the great American leaders.

David Farragut was born in 1801 near Knoxville, Tennessee, a southern state of America. His father was Spanish and had emigrated from Minorca at the time of the French Revolution. Farragut entered the navy in 1810 at the early age of nine and went to sea the following year on board the USS *Essex*. He was twelve years old when the *Essex*, in which he was serving as a midshipman, was engaged in a desperate fight with an English frigate, HMS *Phoebe*, during the war of 1812–14.

Farragut did not take part in another battle, except against Caribbean pirates in 1823, until he was over sixty. This is unique in the career of an outstanding naval commander. He rose steadily, though slowly in his profession – lieutenant in 1825, commander in 1841, captain in 1855 and rear-admiral in 1862, by which time the Civil War had begun. Despite his southern birthplace, Farragut remained loyal to the Unionists and he was assigned to command the naval units enforcing the blockade of Confederate ports.

The Confederate armies received supplies from countries sympathetic to their cause through these southern ports, and through them they exported their cotton to pay for the supplies. Farragut dealt a blow to this import and export traffic when he captured the city of New Orleans, which he attacked early in 1862. He sailed up the estuary of the Mississippi, running past the enemy forts in the dark, and reached the defences of the city on 24 April 1862. The Confederates towed fire-rafts

Admiral David Farragut, pictured here on board the USS *Franklin* during a European cruise, established a reputation for courageous leadership during the Civil War.

down the river and the flames drove some of the men from their guns. 'Don't flinch from the fire, boys,' said Farragut, 'there's a hotter fire than that waiting for those who don't do their duty. Give that rascally tug a shot!' Cut off from its forts, the city of New Orleans soon surrendered.

Even more spectacular was Farragut's victory at Mobile, the southern stronghold on the Alabama River, east of New Orleans. Farragut made a preliminary reconnaissance of the forts in January 1864, but the attack was not finally mounted until the summer. Then ironclad monitors, the precursors of the battleship, began to arrive. Two of them, the *Tecumseh* and the *Manhattan*, had two 15-inch guns, the most powerful ordnance afloat.

Apart from the powerful line of forts defending Mobile Bay, the bay was mined and the Confederates had an armoured ship, the *Tennessee*, which was commanded by Franklin Buchanan. Farragut's determination in the face of difficulties and hazards, rather than Confederate weakness, brought him victory at Mobile.

By 4 August, the day of the assault, Farragut had the help of a number of troops ashore who were to attack the forts from the landward side. That day the wind came from the south and Farragut decided that this would blow the smoke of battle into the eyes of the defenders and confuse their aim.

The run-in was led by the steam sloop *Brooklyn* which Farragut had once commanded, and the monitors were place in a column nearest the enemy batteries. Disaster struck swiftly, when the monitor *Tecumseh*, leading the ironclad line, struck a mine and sank almost at once. Captain Drayton, leading the line, hesitated on seeing the disaster and reported that he could see mines and torpedoes ahead. 'Damn the torpedoes,' shouted Farragut who was following in the *Hartford*. 'Captain Drayton, go ahead!' As so often in history, the bold course was justified. Mines scraped along the bottoms of the ships, including the *Hartford*, but none of them exploded. After a battle lasting three hours even Captain Buchanan was prepared to surrender.

Farragut's health now forbade further active service. The following six years, until his death in 1870, were full of honour. His scope as an admiral had been limited by the brief time he spent in command, but he never failed in any task he set himself and was renowned for his coolness and courage in action.

Lissa

THE BATTLE OF THE RAM

The island of Lissa, known today as Vis, dominates the central Adriatic Sea, and for that reason has been the focus of two decisive sea battles in modern history. The first of these took place on 13 March 1811, when a Franco-Venetian fleet tried to dislodge the British from the island and was roundly defeated by a British frigate squadron. The second battle was the first engagement between rival fleets of iron-clads and was fought less than five years after the historic duel between *Virginia* and *Monitor* in the American Civil War. This second battle of Lissa occurred on 20 July 1866, during the war in which Italy attacked Austria to exploit Austria's humiliating 'Seven-Week War' with Prussia.

Italy's war aim was the recovery of Venetia and the Trentino, the last Italian provinces still under Austrian occupation after the unification of Italy in 1859–60. The Italians planned to use their navy to sweep northwards up the Adriatic and second the efforts of the Italian army north of the River Po. The Austrians, in striking contrast to the dismal performance of their armies north of the Alps,

The fleets of Austria and Italy met at Lissa on 20 July 1866. The loss of the Italian flagship *Re d'Italia* proved a decisive blow, despite that fleet's superior strength.

mounted a spirited resistance on the Italian front. They held the Dalmatian coast, where their small but efficient Adriatic fleet was based under the forceful leadership of Rear-Admiral Wilhelm von Tegetthoff. They had also garrisoned Lissa, which the Italians would have to take if the Austrians were not to use it as a base against Italian naval operations in the northern Adriatic.

The Italian commander-in-chief in the Adriatic was Admiral Count Carlo di Persano, an officer poles apart in temperament from the aggressive Tegetthoff. Pleading that his force was insufficient, Persano had virtually to be bullied into attacking Lissa by the Italian Minister of Marine. On 17 July 1866, however, the Italian admiral began a tentative bombardment of the island with a fleet of twelve ironclads, fourteen wooden steamships, five scouting vessels and three transports. As soon as news of the Italian attack reached Tegetthoff, he headed south to intercept and attack. On the morning of the 20th the Austrian fleet, numbering only seven ironclads, seven wooden ships and four scouts,

sighted the outliers of the Italian fleet off Lissa.

Heavily outnumbered as he was, Tegetthoff was determined to seize the initiative and hold it. His objective was to break up the Italian assault on Lissa and he planned to do it by scattering the Italian fleet in an all-out assault. Standing off and trading shellfire would be suicide against the Italians' superiority in strength: he therefore signalled his captains to close at full speed and ram. As if to simplify recognition the Austrian ships were painted black, while the Italians favoured grey; and Tegetthoff's standing order of attack was 'Ram everything grey!'

So it was that this action, for all the steam power, armour plate and explosive shell used by both sides, was more like a throwback to the clash of the Christian and Turkish galleys at Lepanto in 1571 than the first fleet action in modern naval history. Tegetthoff's fleet steamed clean through the scattering Italian warships, in wedge formation, black smoke belching from the funnels. Tegetthoff himself, flying his flag in the *Erzherzog Ferdinand Maximilian*, made straight for Persano's flagship *Re d'Italia*, pouncing on his stationary victim when her steering gear had broken down. These were still the days when armoured protection stopped short at the waterline, and the ram of the *Ferdinand Max* punched an enormous hole in *Re d'Italia*'s hull below the surface. The stricken Italian flagship heeled and sank so quickly that Persano barely had time to shift his flag.

It took Tegetthoff under two hours to win his battle. By noon he had re-formed his fleet between the Italian warships and the island of Lissa. The sight of the Austrian fleet apparently willing to renew the action was too much for the shaken Persano, who signalled his fleet to withdraw after making only the sketchiest attempt to reform. The Italians had only lost two ships – *Re d'Italia* and the aptly named *Affondatore* ('sinker') – but their casualties were appallingly high: 612 officers and men. Tegetthoff only had one of his wooden ships severely damaged, and human casualties amounting to no more than thirty-eight officers and men.

Not surprisingly, the humiliation of Lissa spelled ruin for Persano. His pusillanimous tactics and refusal to renew the action were bad enough, but he sealed his own fate by sending back a despatch so mendaciously worded as to suggest that he had won some sort of victory. Persano was tried for cowardice and incompetence, found guilty on the latter charge, and dismissed from the Italian navy.

Lissa was the only naval action of the war of 1866. Prussia made a separate peace with Austria six days after Lissa was fought, releasing massive Austrian forces for the Italian front and leaving Italy with no choice but to cease hostilities as well. As if to complete Italy's humiliation, Bismarck's Prussia obliged Austria to yield Venetia but not the Trentino – a consolation prize of some importance to Austria.

Tsushima

THE FIRST BIG-GUN BATTLE OF THE MODERN ERA

A contemporary painting of the battle of Tsushima, in which the Russian fleet was overwhelmed by the faster Japanese ships.

Soon after the start of the Russo-Japanese War in 1904, the Japanese army besieged Port Arthur. This port, in southern Manchuria, was leased by the Russians from China and transformed into their main naval base in the East. Their other Pacific base, Vladivostok, was far from the theatre of war. However, by the summer of 1904 it seemed that Russia's Pacific Squadron had the choice of being sunk or captured in Port Arthur by the advancing Japanese army, or of facing the superior Japanese fleet in an attempt to escape to the safer waters of Vladivostok. In August an attempt was made to escape, but the Japanese commander, Admiral Togo, soon forced the Russians back after a lucky shot had disabled their flagship.

After this defeat, the Russians decided to send their Baltic Squadron to combine with the Port Arthur ships and defeat an outnumbered Japanese navy. This plan had been long discussed, but it had been postponed because Russia possessed no bases between the Baltic and the Pacific. International conventions made it impossible to use the neutral coaling ports normally visited along this route. However, Kaiser Wilhelm of Germany, eager at this time to do a good turn for his cousin Tsar Nicholas II, helped the Russians charter a fleet of German colliers. On its way to the East the Baltic Squadron took coal from these ships, in secluded anchorages or the open sea.

The unprecedented passage of the Russian squad-

ron halfway round the world, without benefit of bases, took seven months. *En route* the Russians sank a British trawler in the North Sea, having mistaken the Hull fishing fleet for Japanese torpedo-boats. The Russians dallied two months off Madagascar while St Petersburg decided what to do in the light of the news that Port Arthur had fallen and its squadron been sunk in harbour. It was eventually decided to push on in the hope of a miracle, even though the Russian commander, Admiral Rozhestvensky, realized that his Baltic Squadron with its half-trained crews and weed-fouled hulls would be no match for the Japanese.

The Russians' one hope lay in reaching Vladivostock without encountering Togo, after which the squadron could work up to fighting efficiency. This was almost achieved. Rozhestvensky entered the narrow Tsushima Strait (between Japan and Korea) at night and for several hours escaped observation. While the Russian warships proceeded with dimmed lights, the squadron's hospital ship, some way astern, was fully illuminated in accordance with wartime convention. The Japanese spotted this vessel and this enabled them to locate the Russians.

The following day, 14 May 1905, the Russian squadron (five modern and three old battleships, one old armoured cruiser, three coast defence ships and a few cruisers and destroyers) was confronted with Togo's war-hardened fleet (four modern battleships, eight modern armoured cruisers and numerous cruisers and destroyers). The gun battle opened with the Japanese battleships and armoured cruisers concentrating their fire on the leading Russian battleships. With the advantage of the light

and the wind, with better gunners and better ammunition, the Japanese shattered the Russian upperworks with a rain of high-explosive shells. One hour after the first shot, a Russian battleship – her armour belt displaced by the shock of repeated detonations – had a hole blown in her unprotected side and capsized. After this the battle resolved itself into the successive devastation of the Russian battleships by the faster Japanese armoured ships. By nightfall four Russian battleships had been sunk and the wounded Rozhestvensky had been carried from the scene of battle in a fugitive destroyer.

During the night three Russian cruisers escaped to Manila, where they were interned by the Americans. The remaining ships plodded on, enduring attacks by myriads of torpedo craft. The next morning the surviving Russian ships were confronted once more by Togo's heavy ships, which were relatively unscathed after the previous day's fighting. With only two long-range guns still operable, and unable because of inferior speed to get closer, the Russian squadron was in a hopeless situation and its commander soon ordered white flags to be hoisted. The surviving Russian ships were taken triumphantly to Japanese ports.

Of the Russian battleships, two had been captured and the others destroyed. Only a light cruiser and two destroyers managed to slip through to Vladivostok. The battle of Tsushima was the most crushing naval victory of the twentieth century and it was not long before the Russians decided to start peace negotiations. The battle was also the first occasion on which the theories of the steam and steel era were fully tested in practice.

TOP The battleship *Asahi*, one of the powerful modern vessels with which the Japanese fleet was equipped at the time of Tsushima.

ABOVE Russia's Admiral Rozhestvensky.

Heihachiro Togo

1847–1934

Pictured here in ceremonial uniform, Admiral Heihachiro Togo became a national hero after leading the Japanese fleet to victory at Tsushima.

Japan's greatest naval hero, Heihachiro Togo, embodied the fierce and deadly spirit of the samurai warrior. His long career was also seen in his own lifetime as a symbol of his country's amazing transformation from feudal isolation to the status of a leading world power.

Togo was born in 1847 to a samurai family of the Satsuma clan on Kyushu, and he first saw action at the age of sixteen. Armed in traditional style with a brace of samurai swords and an antique matchlock musket, he helped his father and two brothers fire stone cannonballs from a Satsuma coastal fort at British warships in Kagoshima Bay.

The young Togo first went to sea as a volunteer in the coast-defence flotilla of the Satsuma: the first naval force organized after the visits of Commodore Perry's US squadron in 1853–4 which began the opening-up of Japan to foreign trade. In February 1867 the young Emperor Mutsuhito ascended the throne and the 'Meiji Restoration' of imperial power began. Firmly believing that Japan should learn all that the 'foreign barbarians' had to teach, Togo took service with the government and was one of the first officers of the imperial Japanese navy. Having attended school and a foreign language academy to learn English, Togo was selected to go to England in 1871 to study at the naval training college HMS *Worcester*.

Togo's next assignment was to join the team of Japanese officers attending the building of two iron-hulled cruisers, *Fuseo* and *Hiei*, ordered from the British. This second spell in England was most fortunate for Togo: it saved him from involvement in the ill-fated revolt of the Satsuma in 1877 in which, honour-bound by traditional loyalty, the rest of his family had served with the rebels. As it was, Togo returned to Japan in *Hiei* in 1878 untainted by treason and in the following year was promoted lieutenant-commander, commanding the wooden warship *Jingei*.

It was as captain of the British-built cruiser *Naniwa* from 1892 to 1895 that Togo proved his fitness for flag rank, helped by the timely war with China. The Sino-Japanese War of 1894–5 saw the first use of a ploy which was to become almost standard with Japan in the twentieth century: a preemptive strike by the fleet before war was declared. *Naniwa* and three other cruisers formed Rear-Admiral Tsuboi's flying squadron, which sailed to intercept Chinese transports heading for Korea.

Togo not only sank the Chinese sloop *Kwang-yi* and damaged the protected cruiser *Tui-Yuen*: he also sank the *Kowshing*, a British ship chartered by the Chinese as a troop transport, and much wrangling by international lawyers resulted. Togo emerged fully exonerated when the British government decided that he had not exceeded his rights. He went on to distinguish himself in the defeat of the Chinese fleet in the Yalu River, the capture of Port Arthur and the occupation of Formosa, and came out of the war with the rank of rear-admiral.

In 1900, now a vice-admiral, Togo added to his laurels by commanding the Japanese squadron in the international operations against China which followed the Boxer Rising. Tension with Russia, however, had continued to grow since combined German, Russian and French pressure had obliged Japan to give up Port Arthur in 1895. Russia subsequently obtained the lease of Port Arthur, which became the main bone of contention in the Russo-Japanese war of 1904–5.

This war brought Togo the supreme command of the Japanese Grand Fleet, flying his flag in the battleship *Mikasa* – still preserved in Japan with all the pride lavished on Nelson's *Victory* in England. Again the war opened with a surprise attack, this time on Port Arthur. This was beaten off on 9 February, but the blockade of the Russian squadron by Togo gave Japan complete control of the Korean and southern Manchurian coasts. On 24 August the Russian Admiral Vitjeft broke out of Port Arthur, but was defeated by Togo's outnumbered force in a hard-fought action in the Yellow Sea.

This was Togo's hardest battle. Vitjeft's force was a much more formidable opponent than the ill-assorted and untrained Russian Baltic Fleet which was intercepted and destroyed by Togo at Tsushima on 27–8 May 1905.

Tsushima not only ensured and accelerated Russia's acceptance of defeat: it made Togo a national hero, giving Japan both a Nelson and a Trafalgar for posterity. Incidentally, the comparison with Nelson is one that Togo would have appreciated, as he modelled himself on the great English admiral, a portrait of whom used to hang in his cabin on board ship. Togo's last memorable appointment was as supervisor of the education of Crown Prince Hirohito. Fêted and honoured at home and abroad, Togo remained Japan's most respected elder statesman until his death in 1934.

Maximilian von Spee

1861–1914

Admiral Maximilian von Spee who, at the outbreak of World War I, commanded the peerless East Asiatic Squadron of the German navy. His qualities of leadership were legendary.

Maximilian von Spee, one of the most successful German cruiser commanders in history and the admiral most respected by the British, was born in Copenhagen into one of the oldest and most respected Prussian Catholic families, one that traced its ancestry back to the twelfth century. At the age of sixteen, fair-haired, fair-skinned and blue-eyed, he entered the imperial German navy as a cadet. He passed out as a sub-lieutenant two years later and at the age of twenty-two, by which time he had been promoted to the rank of lieutenant, he was given his first opportunity to demonstrate his talents. He was ordered to serve in the mission led by Gustav Nachtigal to establish a German empire in west Africa. The party left for Africa in April, 1884, and did not return until more than a year later. During the voyage von Spee suffered an attack of rheumatic fever so severe that his constitution was weakened for the rest of his life.

In 1887 von Spee returned to Africa to serve in the chiefly administrative role of port commander at Cameroon. Ill-health compelled him to return to Germany and for the next few years he served in home waters on the training ship, *Moltke*. It was in these years that his honesty, fair-mindedness, devotion and sociability won him the respect and affection of officers and ratings, respect and affection which he was never to forfeit. His career advanced slowly but steadily, and in 1897 he was given the command of the first-class cruiser, the *Deutschland*, on its mission to impress parts of Germany's empire in the Far East with a show of strength. Von Spee returned to Germany in the summer of 1899, but was back in China during the Boxer Rebellion in the following year.

Von Spee was raised to the rank of captain in 1905 and given the command of a new battleship, the *Wittelsbach*. But ever since his years in the Far East he had set his sights on the command of the crack East Asiatic Squadron based at Tsingtau. It was the most sought-after command in the whole of the German navy, because, although the squadron was remote, its standards were unmatched and its responsibilities were wide. In November 1912, his ambition was realized. He was appointed to the command of the East Asiatic Squadron and raised to the rank of rear-admiral. He was then fifty-one years

old and had reached the summit of his professional career.

Until this time von Spee had been involved in scarcely any naval action on the high seas. But he had matured into a disciplined commander whose stern sense of loyalty and extensive knowledge of naval warfare were proof against any test. He arrived at Tsingtau to take up his new duties just before Christmas 1912. When war broke out twenty months later, he commanded the most redoubtable squadron of ships of their class in the world: his own flagship, the *Scharnhorst*, her sister ship, the *Gneisenau*, and the three light cruisers, *Emden*, *Leipzig* and *Nürnberg*.

After the initial action at Heligoland Bight, the focus of naval warfare shifted to the Far East, where the British were eager to protect their trading routes and where von Spee's squadron constantly menaced Allied merchant shipping. At the battle of Coronel, where British and German squadrons met on the evening of 1 November 1914, he enjoyed the signal success of his career. The Germans sank two British cruisers, the *Good Hope* and the *Monmouth*, while escaping unscathed themselves. But von Spee's hour of triumph was scarcely more than that. Shocked by the defeat at Coronel, the British sent the two dreadnoughts, the *Invincible* and the *Inflexible*, under Vice-Admiral Sturdee's command, to reinforce the squadron at Port Stanley in the Falkland Islands. They arrived on 7 December. The next morning, von Spee, ignorant of the strength now opposed to him, led his squadron towards Port Stanley to engage the British. Discovering his error, or rather that of the German intelligence services, he tried to make good his escape. His cruisers were no match for the British dreadnoughts. The battle of the Falkland Islands was the one decisive British naval victory of the war. Throughout the long summer day the exchanges were furious. Neither von Spee's courage nor the skill of the German gunners were found wanting. They were simply helpless victims of the dreadnoughts' superior strength. Of the German cruisers, only the *Dresden* survived the onslaught. Von Spee himself went down with the *Scharnhorst* shortly after four o'clock in the afternoon, dying, as he had lived, in the unstinting service of the German nation.

Coronel and the Falklands

VON SPEE'S LAST STAND

When the British Empire went to war on 4 August 1914 the Royal Navy was the strongest fleet in the world – but nearly all of its newest and most powerful warships were concentrated in Scapa Flow, hoping for a decisive showdown with the imperial German High Seas Fleet in the North Sea. The remote British naval stations dotted around the world to safeguard the empire's long sea-routes were necessarily entrusted to squadrons of old slow warships, many manned by untrained reservists, whose task it was to hunt down and destroy the German squadrons and individual surface raiders known to be at large.

On 1 November 1914 one of these *ad hoc* and aging British squadrons was destroyed in an engagement known as the battle of Coronel. And the powerful, hard-hitting German East Asiatic Squadron, which had crossed the Pacific from China to fight this battle off the coast of Chile, was only brought to bay off the Falkland Islands in the South Atlantic by the most prodigious efforts on the part of the British Admiralty.

On the outbreak of war the biggest problem facing Rear-Admiral Sir Christopher Cradock, commanding the North American and West Indies station, was the threat posed to British and French commerce by the new and fast German light cruisers *Karlsruhe* and *Dresden*. In the first week of the war *Karlsruhe* ran clean away from Cradock's pursuing cruisers and escaped, continuing to operate in the southern Caribbean until her destruction by an internal cordite explosion on 4 November. *Dresden* vanished down the South American coast to prey on Allied shipping in the South Atlantic. Cradock moved south in pursuit and on 3 September was ordered by the Admiralty to stay in the South Atlantic and take command of the South-East Coast of America station. His widely dispersed cruisers nevertheless failed to prevent *Dresden* from escaping into the Pacific on 18 September.

Only thirteen years after the first weak wireless signal had been painfully transmitted across the Atlantic, the British and German Admiralties were beginning to appreciate the immense difficulty of coordinating the movements of warships on both sides of the world, acting on wireless and telegraph data which might either be out of date or simply wrong. The British, however, were labouring under self-created problems from which the Germans were largely free. The recently-formed Admiralty War Staff was a cumbrous body with a chief-of-staff, Vice-Admiral Sir Doveton Sturdee, who insisted on handling every important matter himself. Higher up, the British Admiralty was beset with the wide-ranging enthusiasms of the First Lord, Winston Churchill, and a First Sea Lord, Prince Louis of Battenberg, who was forced to resign on 28 October after a vicious press campaign objecting to his German birth.

As a result of all these inhibitions, the Admiralty was fatally slow in guessing the intentions of Vice-Admiral Maximilian von Spee of the German East Asiatic Squadron, who had sailed from the German treaty port of Tsingtau before the outbreak of war and vanished into the Pacific. Though Spee detached one of his light cruisers, *Emden*, to embark on a brilliant lone commerce-raiding cruise in the Indian Ocean and Bay of Bengal, his own long-term plan was to fight his way home to Germany via Cape Horn after inflicting maximum damage to Allied trade in the Pacific and Atlantic, and forcing maximum inconvenience on the Allied navies.

In total contrast to the ill-assorted scrapings which were to be sent against him by the British Admiralty, Spee commanded one of the elite gunnery squadrons of the German navy (his flagship, the armoured cruiser *Scharnhorst*, had won the

ABOVE RIGHT Rear-Admiral Sir Christopher Cradock, whose attempted pursuit of Germany's raiders was hampered by poor communications.

OPPOSITE PAGE
ABOVE HMS *Good Hope*, Cradock's own flagship, whose two 9.2-inch guns were no match for the *Scharnhorst*'s firepower.

BELOW HMS *Canopus*, the venerable battleship sent to reinforce Cradock and later detailed to protect Port Stanley in the Falkland Islands.

Kaiser's special prize for gunnery two years running). In addition to *Scharnhorst* Spee had her sistership *Gneisenau* and the light cruiser *Nürnberg*. Another of his light cruisers, *Leipzig*, had been showing the flag off the North American coast before war broke out and was still on the far side of the Pacific. She eventually rejoined the rest of Spee's squadron at Eastern Islands – as did *Dresden*, which compensated for the earlier detachment of *Emden*.

Spee's voyage across the Pacific was guided by the need to ship coal at regular intervals, either by prearranged rendezvous with colliers or at shore coaling stations. His squadron steered from one German-controlled group of islands to the next. Spee moved from Pagan Island in the Marianas (11–13 August) to Eniwetok in the Marshalls (19–22 August), south-east to Christmas Island (7 September), south-west to Samoa (14 September), then east for an abortive attack on French Tahiti (22 September). From Tahiti the squadron headed north-east to the Marquesas group (26 September–3 October) and finally south-east to Easter Island (12–18 October) where Spee was joined by *Leipzig* and *Dresden*.

On the British side it was a sad story of confused and misleading signals between the Admiralty and Cradock: the Admiralty assuming that Cradock

Full steam ahead, as British battle-cruisers pursue the retreating German cruiser squadron in the inhospitable coastal waters of South America.

would not attack with an inferior force, Cradock assuming that the Admiralty had more information than he did. As early as 14 September Cradock heard from the Admiralty that there was a 'strong possibility' of *Scharnhorst* and *Gneisenau* appearing off the South American coast, that he was being sent the old battleship *Canopus* and the new cruiser *Defence*, the latter from the Mediterranean. Two days later, however, Cradock was told that Spee had been sighted steaming away from Samoa to the north-*west*, and that on the basis of this (erroneous) report, 'two cruisers and an armed liner would appear sufficient for Magellan Straits and west coast'.

Cradock never did hear that *Defence* would *not* be joining him from the Mediterranean. What he did hear, from Captain Grant of the *Canopus*, was a mistaken report that the old battleship was unable to steam faster than 12 knots. He therefore decided to leave her behind and patrol the southern Chilean coast with the light cruiser *Glasgow*, armed liner *Otranto*, and the ageing armoured cruisers *Good Hope* (Cradock's flagship) and *Monmouth*.

This, then, was the British force at sea off Coronel in the late afternoon of 1 November 1914, when at 4.40 p.m. *Glasgow* sighted the one German warship which Cradock expected to find off the American coast: *Leipzig*. Within minutes, however, Cradock learned that *Leipzig* was not alone: Spee and his entire squadron were with her.

When Spee's cruisers hove in sight, Cradock could have retired to the south to rejoin *Canopus*, 400km (250 miles) away; but he seems to have decided to force a close battle and do Spee's ships as much damage as possible, knowing that they could find no friendly port in which to effect repairs to battle damage. In a strong wind and high sea, he turned to the south and formed line-of-battle, steering a course to converge with the line of Spee's approach. He tried to get between Spee's line and the coast but Spee turned away, leaving the British

ships silhouetted starkly against the setting sun and 'afterglow' while the German ships blended in with the deepening gloom of evening to the east. This was a severe disadvantage for the British gunners, but it was the disparity in firepower which proved disastrous for the British. When *Scharnhorst* opened fire, shortly after sunset (7.00 p.m.) Cradock's line was within range of twelve German 8.2-inch guns, to which only *Good Hope*'s two 9.2-inch guns could answer.

Shooting superbly from their opening salvoes, the German ships plastered Cradock's frail line with hits in the first ten minutes. *Scharnhorst* and *Gneisenau* hammered at *Good Hope* and *Monmouth*; *Leipzig*, less effectively, began to engage *Glasgow*; and *Dresden* bracketed *Otranto*, causing the latter to edge prudently out of the line and follow Cradock out of range of further shells. By 7.15 p.m. *Scharnhorst*, with her third salvo, had knocked out *Good Hope*'s forward 9.2-inch turret and *Gneisenau* had inflicted similar damage on *Monmouth*.

As the range continued to narrow the British ships tried to hit back, but it was virtually impossible to see their fall of shot. By 7.35 p.m. the range was down to 5000m (5500yd) and the Germans were scoring so many hits on *Good Hope* and *Monmouth* that *Scharnhorst*'s spotting officer found it impossible to note them in sequence. Both the British armoured cruisers were blazing furiously; at 7.45 p.m. *Monmouth* yawed out of the line, and five minutes later *Good Hope* was blasted by a terrible explosion between her mainmast and after funnel. She went down at about 8.00 p.m., taking Cradock and all his crew with her.

Captain Luce of the *Glasgow* realized that the battle was lost. *Otranto* had prudently vanished into the darkness half an hour before, *Monmouth* was virtually dead in the water, and the German cruisers were free to overwhelm him with their combined fire. Hard though it was to leave *Monmouth*, Luce therefore disengaged and ran south, losing sight of his pursuers at 8.50 p.m. About thirty-five minutes later, Captain Luce sadly counted the flashes of seventy-five shots as *Nürnberg*, Spee's rearmost ship, completed the German victory by sinking *Monmouth*.

The British Admiralty, now with Lord Fisher as First Sea Lord, reacted to the appalling news of Coronel with an outburst of furious energy which had been totally lacking in the weeks before the battle. With the aid of the French and Japanese navies, the Pacific was sealed tight to make it suicide for Spee to remain there. Nearly thirty British warships, twenty-one of them armoured, were set in motion to hunt down Spee's five cruisers. Above all, two 12-inch-gun battle-cruisers, *Invincible* and *Inflexible*, were taken from the Home Fleet and sent to the South Atlantic under Sturdee to make Spee's destruction inevitable.

Spee's movements after Coronel were unaccountably leisurely, given that his best chance of survival was a swift break into the South Atlantic before British reinforcements could reach the scene. He lingered off Valparaiso until 14 November and did not pass Cape Horn until the night of 1 December. The German ships coaled from their colliers on the 6th, and Spee made the fateful decision to commence operations in the Atlantic by attacking Port Stanley in the Falkland Islands. What he did not know was that *Canopus* had been anchored to protect the harbour with her 12-inch guns, and that Sturdee had just arrived with his two battle-cruisers and five cruisers (including *Glasgow*, the only British ship to serve in both actions).

When Spee was sighted approaching Port Stanley at 8.00 a.m. on 8 December, the British fleet was coaling – but a spirited 12-inch broadside from *Canopus* caused Spee to turn and run. It took Sturdee's force nearly two hours to raise steam and weigh, but by 10.00 a.m. he was hard on Spee's trail with both battle-cruisers and the cruisers *Kent*, *Glasgow*, *Carnarvon* and *Cornwall*. (The cruiser *Bristol* and the *Macedonia*, a converted liner, spent the day in rounding up and sinking Spee's colliers, *Baden* and *Santa Isabel*.)

By 12.47 p.m. Sturdee, flying his flag in *Invincible*, was close enough to open fire, echoed by *Inflexible* and *Glasgow*. Spee realized that his force was totally out-gunned, and about 1.20 p.m. bravely signalled to *Nürnberg*, *Leipzig* and *Dresden* to try to escape while he fought the British with *Scharnhorst* and *Gneisenau*. The German gunnery was as excellent as it had been at Coronel, and the British were hampered by the obstruction of their own smoke; but the sheer weight of shell thrown by the British battle-cruisers meant that the issue was never in doubt. Fighting bravely to the last, both *Scharnhorst* and *Gneisenau* had been battered to wrecks by the time they sank, *Scharnhorst* at 4.17 p.m. and *Gneisenau* at 6.00 p.m. Only 190 survivors were rescued from *Gneisenau* out of her complement of about 800.

Meanwhile the British cruisers *Kent* and *Cornwall* raced on in pursuit of the fleeing German light cruisers. *Dresden* sheered off to the south-west and escaped, but *Nürnberg* was overhauled and sunk by *Kent* at 7.27 p.m. and *Leipzig* followed at 8.35 p.m. *Dresden* was finally trapped by *Kent* and *Glasgow* off the Chilean coast at Mas a Tierra and was scuttled to avoid capture on 14 March 1915. The British revenge for Coronel was complete.

BELOW Admiral Sturdee, whose battle-cruiser squadron was to punish von Spee's failure to make good his escape after his victory at Coronel.

BOTTOM The British cruiser *Kent*, which led the pursuit of the German light cruisers fleeing from the Falklands battle.

John Arbuthnot Fisher

1841–1920

Entering the Royal Navy at the age of thirteen, 'Jacky' Fisher rose through the ranks to become First Sea Lord in 1904, subsequently instituting many timely reforms and improvements.

In July 1914 the massed warships of the Royal Navy lay at anchor off Spithead for the Royal Review: the most powerful battle-fleet in the world. Surveying the awesome assemblage of sea power, which stretched from horizon to horizon, Rear-Admiral Sir Robert Arbuthnot was moved to comment: 'All that is best and most modern here is the creation of Lord Fisher.' It was a just tribute to this remarkable man, the turbulent genius who had created the world's first dreadnought battle-fleet – one of the strongest tools of Allied victory in World War I.

Fisher was a prodigy; he knew it and he delighted in it. 'I have had to fight like hell,' he once said, 'and fighting like hell has made me what I am.' Fisher's greatest enemy was red tape in all its manifestations; anything and anyone which, in his eyes, obstructed the advancement of efficiency in the Royal Navy. In his self-declared crusade he made enemies by the hundred. 'Parasites in the shape of non-fighting ships', he wrote in 1907, 'non-combatant personnel, and unproductive shore expenditure must be extirpated like cancer – cut clean out.' He would support to the hilt any officer, no matter how many black marks might be against him, who thought the same way: 'I don't care if he drinks, gambles, and womanizes: *he hits the target.*'

Gunnery was the key to Fisher's early career. Born in 1841 and joining the Royal Navy at the age of thirteen – 'penniless, friendless and forlorn', as he put it – Fisher's immense physical and mental stamina and energy helped establish him as a highly competent officer. Right from the start, he realized the full extent of the technological revolution through which the Royal Navy must pass if it were to remain the world's strongest. His own specialist field, however, was gunnery and the improvement of the fleet's marksmanship in an age when many captains discouraged gunnery drill because it made the paintwork dirty.

As captain of the battleship *Inflexible*, Fisher took part in the bombardment of the Alexandria forts in 1882 and went on to a long series of shore appointments. He was captain of the gunnery school, *Excellent* from 1883 to 1885, Director of Naval Ordnance and Torpedoes (1886–91), Admiral Superintendent at Portsmouth Dockyard (1891–2) and Third Sea Lord and Controller from 1892 to 1897. In the latter post he was responsible for the Royal Navy's adoption of the water-tube boiler and the destroyer.

Promoted rear-admiral in 1890 and vice-admiral in 1894, Fisher commanded the North America and West Indies station from 1897 to 1899 before serving as the British naval delegate at the Hague Peace Conference of 1899. Here he won notoriety for his contempt for wishful thinking about war and peace. He rejected the notion of 'humanizing' war as hypocritical nonsense: 'You might as well talk of humanizing Hell', he claimed; 'as if war could be civilized.'

Fisher's last sea-going command was that of the Mediterranean Fleet from 1899 to 1902. His greatest enemy, Admiral Beresford, admitted that 'From a 12-knot Fleet with numerous breakdowns, he made a 15-knot Fleet without breakdowns.' Above all Fisher encouraged the improvement of gunnery through constant practice, particularly at long range.

As Second Sea Lord from 1902 to 1903, Fisher and the First Lord, Selborne, introduced the 'Selborne Scheme' to improve and standardize officer training. This consisted of common entrance to the new naval colleges at Dartmouth and Osborne, followed by a basic naval education suited to an era of mechanization. Four or five years at sea were then to precede specialization. A strong believer in 'the career open to talents', Fisher always believed that 'we are drawing our Nelsons from too narrow a class', but this battle against class prejudice in the Royal Navy was too tough a struggle for him to win during his career.

After a year as commander-in-chief, Portsmouth, Fisher went to the Admiralty on 20 October 1904 as First Sea Lord. Thus commenced five of the most astonishing and constructive years in the history of the Royal Navy.

Fisher had come to realize that the new German navy was the biggest menace to Britain's naval supremacy. He threw himself into the task of remodelling the navy and its deployment in order to ensure the biggest possible concentration of the strongest possible battleships in home waters. A ruthless scrapping programme weeded out scores of 'warships' which could 'neither fight nor run away'. This not only saved the navy an annual bill of £845,000 on repairs alone: it released much-needed officers and men to man the new ships, whose construction he rushed ahead.

These were the dreadnought battleships and battle-cruisers, armed with large-calibre guns and

all capable of speeds over 20 knots. They made every other type of capital ship in the world obsolete as soon as they appeared. This fact, together with the marked reduction in the ability to 'show the flag' caused by the scrapping programme, added to the ranks of Fisher's enemies. He aroused further antagonism through his enthusiastic use of the popular press to ensure widespread support for his policies. This earned him the reputation of a demagogue and publicity-hound, but it did the job and got the British people 'navy-minded'.

Fisher also put through much-needed personnel reforms to make life more tolerable on the lower deck – reforms which earned him the respect of the sailors, who nicknamed him 'Jacky'. Not the least important of his reforms was the overhaul of the naval reserve, keeping old but still serviceable warships in service, manned by 'nucleus crews'. They were to be given full complements in order to raise the overall strength of the fleet in the event of war. This paid full dividends in the summer crisis of 1914.

Fisher's departure from the Admiralty in 1910 was timely, for his ruthless methods and notorious public feud with Lord Charles Beresford had caused deep dissension within the navy and was threatening to bring the service into disrepute. His most important work, however, was done: the creation of a modern fleet, stronger than that of its most dangerous rival, and its deployment at the point of greatest potential danger in home waters.

When Winston Churchill became First Lord in 1911 he relied heavily on Fisher's advice to adopt oil fuel and the 15-inch gun for the newest 'Queen Elizabeth' class of battleship. In October 1914 Churchill recalled Fisher to the Admiralty as First Sea Lord, and for a time their dynamic partnership prospered. Fisher sponsored anti-submarine patrol airships and a wide range of anti-submarine vessels, realizing the menace submarines would prove to fleets of orthodox surface warships. He also took the bold decision to detach two battle-cruisers from the Grand Fleet in order to avenge Coronel and destroy Spee's cruiser squadron.

The partnership ended in May 1915, Fisher deciding that Churchill's refusal to admit defeat at the Dardanelles spelled potential ruin for the Grand Fleet's vital superiority in home waters. Fisher resigned, perhaps precipitately, never again to fill an Admiralty post. However, he lived to see the total victory of all he had worked for in the surrender of the German battle-fleet.

It was fitting that Fisher had been raised to the peerage as Baron Fisher of Kilverstone; this was in 1909, when he became one of the very few naval officers to be ennobled for services performed in peacetime. It was just recognition for the immensity of his achievement. He died in 1920.

HMS *Inflexible*, launched in 1907, was one of the early battle-cruisers built for the Royal Navy. Battle-cruisers were the brainchild of Admiral Fisher, who intended them to be used as advance scouts for the battleship fleet.

Dogger Bank

BEATTY LETS HIPPER OFF THE HOOK

The running fight over the Dogger Bank in the North Sea between British and German battle-cruisers, on 24 January 1915, was a colossal disappointment for the British. With all the advantages of surprise and superior strength, their own errors caused them to waste a unique opportunity to destroy the German force and stretch the numerical lead of the British Grand Fleet over the German High Seas Fleet to an unbeatable margin.

By December 1914, that lead had shrunk to an alarming degree. Two of the Grand Fleet's eight battle-cruisers had not yet returned from hunting down Spee's cruiser squadron at the Falkland Islands. In the rest of the Grand Fleet, so many capital ships and cruisers were constantly 'reporting sick' with major and minor defects that Admiral Sir John Jellicoe, the British commander-in-chief, believed that he no longer had sufficient superiority to fight a fleet action with the High Seas Fleet.

Jellicoe's opposite number, Admiral Friedrich von Ingenohl, appreciated that now was the time to try to cut off part of the Grand Fleet, particularly its battle-cruisers, by launching German battle-cruiser sorties which the British could not afford to ignore. What he did not know was that the British Admiralty's 'Room 40', intercepting and decoding German radio signals as units of the High Seas Fleet came to readiness for sailing, gave the British ample warning and time to mobilize intercepting forces of their own.

This happened on 16 December 1914, when von Ingenohl's battle-cruisers bombarded the Yorkshire

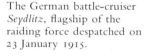

The German battle-cruiser *Seydlitz*, flagship of the raiding force despatched on 23 January 1915.

towns of Scarborough, Whitby and Hartlepool. Duly alerted by 'Room 40', Vice-Admiral Sir David Beatty came south with the Grand Fleet's battle-cruisers to intercept. However, although Beatty's screening cruisers actually sighted the German force as it retired, an error in signalling allowed the Germans to escape.

It was all very well for Beatty and Lord Fisher, First Lord of the Admiralty, to complain that the cruiser captains should have disregarded their orders and raced in to locate the German main body; the calculated insubordination of the 'Nelson touch' had not been encouraged among the officers of the late Victorian and Edwardian navy. And this tendency to follow orders to the letter was the root cause of the great British disappointment on the Dogger Bank in January 1915.

Encouraged by the success of the Scarborough 'hit and run' raid, von Ingenohl ordered another for the following month. Four light cruisers and a torpedo-boat flotilla, backed up by the battle-cruisers *Moltke*, *Seydlitz*, *Derfflinger* and the armoured cruiser *Blücher* headed into the North Sea late in the afternoon of 23 January under the command of Rear-Admiral Franz von Hipper. Their objective was to surprise and destroy British scouting forces and possibly to raid the British Dogger Bank fishing fleet.

Forewarned by 'Room 40', the British Admiralty laid a perfect trap for the German sortie: Beatty's battle-cruisers and Goodenough's 1st Light Cruiser Squadron from Rosyth, and Tyrwhitt's

Harwich Force of three light cruisers and thirty-five destroyers, made their rendezvous according to plan on the north-east part of the Dogger Bank at dawn on the 24th.

As the sun rose on a sparkling clear day perfect for gunnery, Beatty and Goodenough sighted gun flashes to the south-south-east at about 7.20 a.m. It was the light cruiser *Aurora* of Tyrwhitt's force, already in action with the *Kolberg* of Hipper's light-cruiser screen. Goodenough's light cruisers raced in to join the fray and at 7.30 a.m. reported that Hipper's battle-cruisers were heading off to the south-east, presumably until the German admiral could judge the situation more clearly. When, at 8.40 a.m., he realized that his pursuers included battle-cruisers, Hipper cracked on speed and headed for home.

The German battle-cruisers could not make full speed as they were held back by *Blücher*, which could make no more than 23 knots. Rather than abandon *Blücher*, Hipper kept to her speed, with the result that soon after 9.00 a.m. Beatty's battle-cruisers were within extreme range and opening fire. Beatty was leading the line in his flagship *Lion*, followed by *Tiger*, *Princess Royal*, *New Zealand*, and *Indomitable*. Ahead and to port lay an inferior and surprised German squadron: Hipper in the *Seydlitz*, followed by *Moltke*, *Derfflinger*, and the labouring *Blücher*. As the range continued to close, Beatty had what seemed to be the makings of a crushing victory in his hands.

At 9.35 a.m. the range was down to about 16,000m (17,500yd) and Beatty signalled his ships to engage their opposite numbers in the German line. There now occurred the first of several errors of judgment on the British side which robbed the Royal Navy of the total victory it should have won. Captain Pelly of the *Tiger* misunderstood the order and began to engage Hipper's *Seydlitz*. As a result *Moltke* was left free to join *Seydlitz* and *Derfflinger* in showering Beatty's *Lion* with damaging hits, knocking out two of her dynamos, contaminating her port feed tank with seawater, and finally (about

10.45 a.m.) forcing her to shut down her port engine.

As *Lion* dropped astern of her undamaged consorts, Beatty signalled his second-in-command, Rear-Admiral Moore in *Indomitable*, to concentrate on the destruction of the already-crippled *Blücher* at the rear of the German line. By now Beatty was reduced to signalling by flag hoist, as *Lion*'s last dynamo failed at 10.54 a.m. Thinking that he had sighted a submarine's periscope to starboard he ordered his line to make a sharp turn to port, sending them careering off across the wake of Hipper's line on a course north by east.

It was at this point that a fatal misunderstanding arose in signalling Beatty's orders. Beatty, realizing that his force was veering too far away from the prey, ordered 'Course N.E.' and then 'Attack the rear of the enemy.' What he was trying to do was to urge Moore to keep up the pursuit and engagement of Hipper's squadron. However, Beatty's lieutenant signalled the two orders together and Moore read them as one: 'Attack the rear of the enemy, course N.E.' As luck would have it this was the bearing of *Blücher*, which had now fallen far behind Hipper's battle-cruisers. Moore never saw Beatty's last frantic signal from *Lion*, 'Keep nearer the enemy.'

As a result of these confused signals and his own lack of imagination, Moore turned on the hapless *Blücher* with all four of the undamaged British battle-cruisers and battered her until she eventually rolled over and sank. The fuming Beatty came pelting up in a destroyer and shifted his flag to *Princess Royal* at 12.20 p.m. by which time Hipper had made good his escape.

The British claimed a victory – *Blücher* sunk and Hipper chased back to port – but because none of their gun turrets was hit they failed to adopt anti-flash precautions for the magazines of their heavy ships after the battle. Not so the Germans, who had come within an ace of losing the flagship *Seydlitz* to a cordite explosion. Eighteen months later, at the battle of Jutland, the British were to regret not having learned this lesson earlier.

An action photograph of the sinking of the *Blücher*. The three German battle-cruisers, a more important target for Beatty's squadron, were allowed to escape because of a signalling error.

The German Rear-Admiral Franz von Hipper.

The Dardanelles

SHORE-BATTERIES VERSUS BATTLESHIPS

Vice-Admiral Sir John de Robeck (right) converses with Vice-Admiral Boué de Lapeyrère, commander-in-chief of the French navy in the Mediterranean. Between them stands a French flag lieutenant.

The Allied attempt to penetrate the Dardanelles and seize the Turkish capital of Constantinople in the spring of 1915 will surely remain one of the most controversial, not to say notorious, episodes of World War I. Conceived as a strategic masterstroke with which to break the tactical deadlock in the trenches of the Western Front, the Dardanelles gamble only resulted in another eight months of trench warfare and the loss of 120,000 troops, the net gain, tactical or strategic, being nil.

The long ordeal of the ANZACs (Australian and New Zealand corps) on the beaches and in the trenches of the Gallipoli peninsula has tended to eclipse the fact that, to start with, no troops at all were landed. The Dardanelles venture was originally an attempt to exploit the surplus sea power of Britain and France.

As conceived by the fertile brain of Winston Churchill, Britain's First Lord of the Admiralty, the Dardanelles plan was the grandest of grand strategy, replete with awe-inspiring images. An Allied battle-fleet would, he was certain, be able to steam

majestically through the Narrows of the Dardanelles and debouch into the Sea of Marmara. It would then appear before Constantinople, joining hands with the Russians in the Black Sea, cutting the Turkish army in half and compelling the country's instant surrender. Inspired by this *coup*, all the wavering Balkan states would promptly embrace the Allied cause and range themselves against Germany and Austria-Hungary. So exciting were these prospects that they were never seriously challenged by Churchill's political colleagues in the British War Cabinet, and Churchill's enthusiasm for the plan swept all before it.

Churchill admitted that it would not be easy: the Turks had forts and guns on both sides of the Dardanelles, and the Narrows were ideal waters for mining. The assault fleet could not be expected to get through without losses. But Churchill was convinced that the massive firepower of a fleet of even pre-dreadnought battleships would easily silence the fire of the Turkish shore guns while minesweepers cleared the way for the advance of the capital ships. In fact, what the Dardanelles campaign proved once and for all was that a battleship's main armament is not ideal for destroying gun emplacements sited on high ground, and is virtually useless against mobile batteries.

The problem that some Admiralty gunnery experts foresaw was that until all their guns were silenced ashore, the Turks would be able to prevent the minesweepers from clearing a lane through the Narrows and the fleet would not be able to advance. Even if the fleet did get through, the Turks would still be able to bring up guns and shell every ship feeding the fleet's sole line of communications with the Mediterranean. The only real solution to this vicious circle was to land troops and clear the Turks off the Gallipoli peninsula – but in January 1915 British War Minister Lord Kitchener was adamant that there were no troops to spare.

Before he revealed his scheme to the War Council on 13 January, Churchill consulted Vice-Admiral Sackville Carden, blockading the Dardanelles, as to whether or not the Dardanelles could be forced by ships alone. Carden cautiously replied that the Dardanelles could not be rushed, but might be passed by a four-stage extended operation using far more ships than he had at the moment. On 11 January Carden submitted his vague outline plan for accomplishing this: first, knock out the entrance

forts at Seddülbahir and Kumkale; second, knock out the forts as far as Kephez; third, knock out the forts in the Narrows; fourth, sweep the minefields between Kephez and the Narrows and steam through into the Sea of Marmara. Carden thought that a month would suffice·for the job.

Churchill therefore revealed his plan to the War Council on the 13th, citing Carden's 'expert opinion' as evidence in favour of the scheme. (What he did not tell the Council was that he had offered command of the Dardanelles fleet to the navy's foremost gunnery expert, Admiral Sir Percy Scott, and that Scott had refused the command as an impossible task.) Though the politicians were enthralled by the prospects offered, it took until the 28th to overcome the objections of the First Sea Lord, Lord Fisher. The latter was unhappy about sending new battleships out to the Mediterranean when they were needed with the Grand Fleet, and felt that such a large force of older battleships (ten British and four French) was a dangerous drain of reserve warships from home waters. Fisher sensed from the first that troops would be needed to supplement the efforts of the fleet, but was finally persuaded not to resign in protest against an all-naval effort as proposed by Carden.

The first three weeks of February 1915 saw a steady flow of naval reinforcements joining Carden's command in the Mediterranean. In addition to the fourteen old French and British battleships, he was sent the battle-cruiser *Inflexible* and the newest British pre-dreadnought battleships, *Lord Nelson* and *Agamemnon*. But the most important reinforcement was the brand new super-dreadnought battleship *Queen Elizabeth*, sent out to calibrate her 15-inch guns against the Dardanelles

forts instead of in sterile target practice.

While these preparations were in hand Lord Kitchener decided that he could, after all, spare troops for the Dardanelles venture (16 February). The troops in question were the 29th Division from England and the ANZAC (Australian and New Zealand) corps. This revelation changed the whole operation: it offered certain victory if the troops were used in conjunction with the warships. The fleet could land the troops on the Gallipoli peninsula; the troops could clear the western shore of the Straits; thus relieved of enfilade fire from both shores, the fleet could finish the job at point-blank range. But no such combined operation was decided upon. Instead it was decided to let the fleet show what it could do first – and then, if the warships admitted failure, send in the troops as a second string.

So it was that the naval assault went ahead, giving the Turkish army and its able German military adviser, General Liman von Sanders, over two months' advance notice that a major Allied offensive was being prepared against the Dardanelles.

Carden began his bombardment of the outer forts on 19 February, conducted in leisurely fashion from 10.00 a.m. until dusk. Not one gun position was destroyed, but Carden believed that he had blown up all the Turkish magazines and wrecked their fire-control communications. An immediate resumption of the bombardment at close range might have yielded more positive results, but six days of gales and bad visibility postponed further operations until the 25th. This time the outer forts were silenced, but landing parties were driven off before all the guns could be destroyed. Carden was nevertheless encouraged to send in his mine-

The French cruiser *Edgar Quinet* pictured at Port Said in 1915. Anglo-French domination of the Mediterranean was to prove of no avail in the Dardanelles action.

sweepers and small numbers of battleships to tackle the gun positions as far as Kephez. The results of this phase (25 February–5 March) were indecisive. The guns below Kephez were not all silenced, let alone destroyed; but Carden moved on to his planned 'phase three': the assault on the minefields and guns at Kephez.

Not surprisingly, *Queen Elizabeth* failed to knock out the Kephez guns by firing 'blind' across the Gallipoli peninsula with her 15-inch main armament. On the following days (6–8 March) she joined the French and British battleships sent in to hammer ineffectively at the intermediate gun positions below Kephez. But the decisive failure was on the part of the minesweepers: hapless North Sea trawlermen, recruited by the navy with their fishing boats, equipped with unfamiliar gear and told to sweep mines by night in the full glare of Turkish searchlights under a withering fire. No wonder the job was too much for them, and they scarcely deserved the scathing rebukes they received from Commodore Roger Keyes, Carden's fire-eating chief of staff.

By the 15th, after ten days of sustained failure, the Kephez defences were still intact and Carden, on the point of a nervous breakdown, accepted that he could do no more. He resigned and was replaced by his second-in-command, Vice-Admiral Sir John de Robeck, who wasted no time in grasping the nettle and ordering an all-out assault on the Narrows for 18 March.

On the morning of the 18th, eighteen British and French battleships entered the Dardanelles, and promptly came under spirited fire from the elusive and virtually invisible batteries of Turkish howitzers. These scored several hits on the warships' superstructures but failed to stop the leading British battleships (*Queen Elizabeth*, *Inflexible*, *Lord Nelson* and *Agamemnon*) from causing severe damage to the Turkish guns at Canakkale in the Narrows. Aided by Admiral Guépratte and the four French battleships, the bombardment force had caused the Turkish fire to slacken by 2 p.m., and de Robeck ordered up the minesweepers. But just as it seemed that the Allies had victory in their grasp, disaster struck the retiring battleships. At 1.54 p.m. the French battleship *Bouvet* blew up and sank; the minesweepers were driven back yet again by furious fire from the Turkish howitzers; both *Inflexible* and *Irresistible* were badly damaged by mines, and de Robeck, shaken, ordered his fleet to retire. As it did so the battleship *Ocean* was also mined and, like *Irresistible*, sank during the night.

Not until long afterwards did the Allies discover that the savaging of the fleet was due to a row of twenty mines laid ten days before, *parallel* to the shore instead of at right-angles to it. Though the ammunition and morale of the Turkish gunners had run dangerously low on 18 March, it was the still-intact minefield defences which forced de Robeck to report, four days later, that he saw no future for a renewal of the naval offensive. Though delayed for over a month by incompetent planning and loading of stores, the ordeal of the soldiers of Gallipoli was at hand. On 25 April the landings began in earnest.

The British fleet's bombardment of the Dardanelles as seen by a contemporary artist. The disastrous outcome of the naval offensive was mirrored in the subsequent land action.

David Beatty

1871–1936

Pictured here in the uniform of an admiral, David Beatty was to be appointed First Sea Lord in 1919 at the zenith of his distinguished Royal Naval career.

Few commanders have more distinguished themselves by their courage, knowledge and foresight, and their readiness in battle than Earl Beatty, the British admiral of the fleet. He was born, of Irish descent, at Howbeck Lodge, a modest estate near Nantwich, in Cheshire. At the age of thirteen he joined the Royal Navy and passed into the training ship *Britannia*.

In 1892 he was promoted to lieutenant, but his first taste of real action did not come until 1896. When gunboats were sent to the Nile to assist Kitchener in his campaign in the Sudan, Sir Stanley Colville invited Beatty to be his second-in-command. Colville was injured by artillery fire from the Dervishes and Beatty took command of the flotilla. He showed exceptional spirit and tactical acumen in leading the gunboats past the Arab position and on to Dongola. Kitchener praised him and he was awarded the DSO. In 1897 he saw further action on the Nile, in the advance to Omdurman, and eyebrows were raised when, at the age of only twenty-seven, he was given a special promotion to commander over the heads of 395 senior officers on the lieutenants list. After action on the battleship *Barfleur* during the Boxer Rebellion, in which he showed great bravery and perseverance when wounded, he again caused a stir, when he was promoted to captain, in November 1900, at the age of twenty-nine.

During the following decade as captain, Beatty commanded four cruisers and one battleship. Although for much of that time he was on half-pay, he was promoted to rear-admiral at the age of thirty-nine, just a few years older than Nelson had been and younger than anyone since then. Shortly afterwards Beatty's preference for questions of fleet deployment during battle over technical aspects of naval administration disclosed itself to Churchill, then First Lord of the Admiralty, who chose him as his naval/secretary in 1912. A year later, when the prospects of peace were receding, Churchill signified his great confidence in Beatty by giving him the command of the battle-cruiser squadron.

When war broke out, it owed much to the insistence of Beatty, who believed Scapa Flow to be too distant from the enemy, that Cromarty and Rosyth were outfitted as operational bases for the fleet. They were not ready until December and a major reason for the Germans' failure to exploit the unpreparedness of the British navy was Beatty's bold offensive at Heligoland Bight at the end of August. Despite evident perils, his battle-cruiser squadron inflicted severe damage on the German naval force (which lost four cruisers and one destroyer in the battle) without the loss of a British ship, and turned what might have been a disaster into a striking success which noticeably shook the German command.

In January, 1915, he was not so successful in the action off Dogger Bank against German cruisers commanded by Admiral Hipper. A combination of signals errors and damage to his own ship, the *Lion*, which fell behind, rather than misjudgment on Beatty's part, accounts for the German cruisers' escape. The episode did not injure Beatty's reputation, for in December 1915 he was appointed vice-admiral, commanding ten battle-cruisers.

Six of those battle-cruisers, supported by a battle-squadron, Beatty led out from Rosyth on the evening of 30 May 1916, for the decisive naval engagement of the war. Beatty has been criticized for leading his cruisers into action at Jutland before the battleships had manoeuvred themselves into position. But it is well to remember that the sighting of the enemy came unexpectedly and that Beatty did no more than carry out Admiralty instructions to locate the enemy and, if his forces were superior, to attack it. Beatty had six cruisers to Hipper's five. He lost two ships, mainly due to faulty design and anti-flash preparations, but he acted as a decoy to draw the German fleet towards the main British battle-fleet under Jellicoe, thus laying the foundations for what should have been an overwhelming British victory.

In December, 1916, Beatty succeeded Jellicoe as commander-in-chief of the fleet and chose the *Queen Elizabeth* as his flagship. His chief contribution in the remaining years of the war was his decision, inspired by his impatience with the Admiralty's slowness to combat the U-boat campaign, personally to organize the convoys to Norway.

Honours fell upon Beatty in 1919. He was awarded the Order of Merit, voted an address of thanks by both Houses of Parliament, presented with a gift of £100,000 by the nation and raised to the peerage. In April he became admiral of the fleet and in November, First Sea Lord. He remained in that office until 1927, a longer period than any of his predecessors had spent there. He died in 1935.

Jutland

THE DECISIVE SEA-BATTLE OF WORLD WAR I

The only major naval action of World War I took place off the coast of Jutland on 31 May 1916. On 30 May the German fleet put to sea with the object of attacking British shipping in the Skagerrak. It comprised a battle-cruiser force under Vice-Admiral Franz von Hipper, which consisted of five battle-cruisers, four light cruisers and thirty destroyers, supported by the battle-fleet under Admiral Reinhard Scheer, which comprised twenty-two battleships – six of which were pre-dreadnought types – five light cruisers and thirty-one destroyers. From radio intelligence, the British Admiralty deduced that a sortie by the German fleet was imminent, so on the same day the British Grand Fleet sailed from its bases at Scapa and Rosyth to take up a position to intercept the enemy fleet. It comprised the battle-cruiser fleet under Vice-Admiral Sir David Beatty, which contained six battle-cruisers, four fast battleships, fourteen light cruisers and twenty-seven destroyers. Beatty's force was to rendezvous with the three battle-cruisers, twenty-four battleships, eight armoured cruisers, twelve light cruisers and fifty-four destroyers of Sir John Jellicoe's battle-fleet. Both British fleets had the advantage of their opponents in the calibre of their guns and the four 'Queen Elizabeth'-class battleships were superior to any in the German fleet.

It had been agreed that if Beatty's fleet, in position some 105km (65 miles) ahead and to the south-east of Jellicoe's fleet, had sighted nothing by 2 p.m. on 31 May it should turn about. It had just done so when the cruiser HMS *Galatea*, on the eastern wing of the screen, made contact with the German cruiser *Elbing* on the western wing of Hipper's force. Beatty at once turned back to the south-east and at 3.20 p.m. he sighted the enemy's battle-cruisers. Unfortunately delay by the fast battleships in following Beatty's movements opened a gap of 16km (10 miles) between them and the battle-cruisers. At 3.45 p.m. battle was joined and Hipper turned to the south-east to fall back on his battle-fleet. Twelve minutes later the British battle-cruiser *Indefatigable*, in action with *Von der Tann*, blew up. The range between the two squadrons was now about 12,800m (14,500yd) and within a short time the remaining British ships had all suffered serious damage. At this critical moment the four fast battleships joined in the action, but at 4.26 p.m. *Queen Mary*, engaged by *Derfflinger* and *Seydlitz*, also exploded. But now the German ships were suffering from the 15-inch broadsides of the *Queen Elizabeth* and Hipper turned away.

At 4.38 p.m. the cruiser *Southampton*, scouting ahead, sighted the German battle-fleet hastening northward to the support of its battle-cruisers. Hipper now resumed a northerly course and Beatty, having verified the cruiser's report, followed suit. It was now his turn to try and lead the German ships into the trap from which he had fortuitously escaped. Neither Hipper nor Scheer suspected that the main British battle-fleet, which they believed to be in harbour, was just over the horizon.

Meanwhile Jellicoe – to whom the presence of the German battle-fleet was also a surprise, the Admiralty having led him to believe that it was still in harbour – was anxiously awaiting information as to its position, course, and speed. He was steaming south-eastward at 20 knots through curtains of mist, with his fleet formed in six columns, each comprising four battleships in line-ahead, with leading ships disposed abeam. Ahead and to port were three battle-cruisers under Rear-Admiral Hood, spread across the centre were the light cruisers, and on the starboard wing the armoured cruisers. At 5.30 p.m., as Beatty led his fleet round to the north-north-eastward to head Hipper off, visual contact was made between the two British fleets. Twenty minutes elapsed before their positions were coordinated and Jellicoe discovered that the enemy battle-

Battleships of the German High Seas Fleet in line-ahead. Although suffering fewer casualties than the British at Jutland, the German navy failed to challenge Britain's overall maritime superiority in World War I.

fleet was 18km (11 miles) nearer than he had supposed. This meant that a decision on deployment into battle formation could not long be delayed. Jellicoe was however still without accurate information as to the bearing of the enemy fleet. While he was waiting for this vital intelligence, Hood's three battle-cruisers sighted and engaged three light cruisers of Hipper's force. They soon were themselves observed by the enemy battle-cruisers, who reported them as four battleships. This led Scheer to believe that he was faced with only a small detachment of the Grand Fleet so he pressed on northward.

At 6.15 p.m. Jellicoe obtained from Beatty the information he so badly needed and ordered his battle-fleet to deploy on the port-wing column. While this manoeuvre was in progress, the armoured cruisers *Defence* and *Warrior* came under fire from the German battle-cruisers. *Defence* blew up and *Warrior* was so badly damaged that she had to be towed away and later sank. Scheer, however, was still unaware that he was heading towards the entire British battle-fleet. As a result of Jellicoe's deployment, the British battle-fleet was in a position of great tactical advantage at right angles to the German line of advance, as well as being between Scheer and his base. By now the smoke of 250 ships, combined with the mist, was seriously affecting visibility in the battle area. Beatty, leading his four surviving battle-cruisers to take up a position in the van of the Grand Fleet and join forces with Hood's three ships, again came within range of Hipper's battle-cruisers and the duel between them was renewed. At 6.29 p.m. a salvo from *Derfflinger* struck Hood's flagship, *Invincible*, and she broke in half and sank.

As the German battle-cruisers, followed by their battleships, emerged from the mist into the view of the waiting British battle-fleet, they were greeted by a devastating hail of fire, the brunt of which was borne by the leading ships. Quickly realizing that he had been caught at a grave disadvantage, Scheer extricated his fleet by a 'battle turn', all ships turning 180 degrees starting with the rear ship. A quarter of an hour later, his fleet had disappeared into the mist steering west. The bad visibility had prevented Jellicoe from observing this unexpected move on the enemy's part and those who did so failed to report it.

Somewhat half-hearted attacks by two German destroyer flotillas now took place and the battleship *Marlborough* was struck by a torpedo which reduced her speed to 17 knots. At 6.55 p.m. Scheer decided to reverse the course of his fleet and executed another battle turn onto a course towards the British fleet. This move was reported to Jellicoe by the cruiser *Southampton* and five minutes later the action recommenced. The range dropped to 3000m (3300yd) before Scheer, at 7.15 p.m., executed another battle turn. But during this brief engagement his battle-cruisers and leading battleships had

HMS *New Zealand* pictured at full steam during the course of the Jutland engagement. The British fleet had the advantage in both numbers and weight of fire over their German opponents.

received severe punishment. *Lützow* reeled out of the line and subsequently had to be sunk. Ordering his battle-cruisers to hurl themselves against the enemy and his destroyer flotillas to come into action to cover the turn, Scheer once again retired westward at high speed.

The massed torpedo attack by the German flotillas obliged Jellicoe to turn away and the two fleets thus found themselves on opposite courses just as the mist was beginning to thicken and the light to fail. Again Jellicoe was not informed of the German movement and he believed that the disappearance of the enemy ships was due to the decreasing visibility. At 7.35 p.m. Jellicoe turned back to close with the enemy. Ten minutes later, Scheer, concerned at being driven so far away from his base, altered course to the southward, by which time the two fleets were 19km (12 miles) apart.

At 8.25 p.m. Beatty's battle-cruisers had a final encounter with their German opponents, when the latter bravely tried to carry out their orders but were driven back. During this engagement hits were scored on the pre-dreadnought squadron, which now led the German fleet. At 9.14 p.m. Scheer set course for home, while Jellicoe re-formed his fleet in night cruising order. The course of the German fleet led it astern of the British battle-fleet and right through the middle of the destroyer flotillas, which became heavily engaged with the German ships.

None of these actions was reported to Jellicoe and the German fleet got clean away reaching the Horns Reef lightship and safety at 3.30 a.m. the next day. The British losses included three battle-cruisers, three armoured cruisers, and eight destroyers, with 6097 officers and men killed. They were heavier than those in the German fleet, which totalled one battle-cruiser, one battleship, four light cruisers, five destroyers and 2551 officers and men, but nevertheless the German fleet was in no condition to continue the action.

Reinhard Scheer

1863–1928

On being appointed to the command of the German High Seas Fleet in January 1916, Admiral Reinhard Scheer initiated a more adventurous strategy which culminated in the clash with the Grand Fleet at Jutland some four months later.

Dramatic pictures of ships and the sea, in a book extolling the virtues of the then-tiny Prussian navy, convinced a German pastor's son that he would be a sailor, long before he ever saw the sea. Reinhard Scheer, born in 1863 at Obernkirchen, Hesse-Nassau, not only abundantly fulfilled his boyhood dream but commanded his country's fleet in one of the greatest sea battles of this century.

Scheer became a naval cadet at the age of fifteen, eight years after the proclamation of the German Empire at Versailles in 1871, and his first ten years in the imperial German navy were associated with the foundation of Germany's colonial empire both in Africa and the Pacific. This period came to an end in 1888 with Scheer earning a decoration for his leadership of an attack on a native fort near Dar-es-Salaam. When he returned to Germany in the same year, Scheer attended the naval torpedo school.

To small navies with little or no chance of approaching the massive size of the British or other leading fleets, the invention of the Whitehead torpedo in the late 1860s was a godsend. Here was a weapon small enough to be carried by a small steam launch, but which was feared by even the strongest battle-fleet. The torpedo was bound to become a key weapon of the German navy, and for five years Scheer applied himself to torpedo tactics as captain of a torpedo-boat. By 1900 he commanded the German fleet's 1st Torpedo-boat Flotilla.

Scheer then made a name for himself as a naval theoretician; he translated his expertise onto paper and wrote a textbook on the tactical use of the torpedo. Advancement soon followed: command of a battleship after a spell at the Admiralty in Berlin, and in 1909, promotion to rear-admiral and the appointment as chief of staff to the High Seas Fleet. By the outbreak of war in August 1914, Scheer had moved up to the post of vice-admiral commanding the 2nd Battle Squadron. The torpedo expert had become a battleship admiral, in a fleet confronted with acute strategic difficulties.

There had never been any chance that the High Seas Fleet would win the pre-war shipbuilding race with the British, who had too great a start. The original German naval war strategy was to build up a navy big enough to deter Britain from attacking it for fear of losing so many ships that she became a second-rate naval power. At the beginning of the war it was hoped that the Royal Navy would attempt a close blockade of German ports. This would have enabled the Germans to whittle down the British superiority with mines and torpedoes. Seeing that the British were declining to risk such a war of attrition, Scheer argued that the High Seas Fleet should be used more aggressively. Weak German forces should put to sea and invite attacks by detachments of the British Grand Fleet. These detachments could then, given the right circumstances, be ambushed by the whole weight of the High Seas Fleet.

Scheer got the chance to initiate this more active role for the High Seas Fleet when he became its third commander-in-chief of the war on 24 January 1916. However, Scheer never knew that the British could locate the source of German radio signals, which told the British Admiralty whenever the High Seas Fleet put to sea. This British advantage, plus improved deployments of the Grand Fleet, brought on the one event which the German naval high command had always dreaded – a collision of the rival fleets in full strength – off the coast of Jutland on 31 May 1916.

Because of mist and smoke from a forest of guns and funnels, Scheer and his British opposite number Jellicoe were virtually fighting blind; it was Jellicoe who out-guessed Scheer, however, twice laying the Grand Fleet fairly across the head of the German line. Scheer neatly extricated the High Seas Fleet from the first collision but was badly let down by his scouting cruisers and ran straight into Jellicoe's line when he tried to feel for its flank. So dangerous was this second encounter that at one point Scheer ordered his battle-cruisers into a 'death-ride' against the British line, but this proved unnecessary as the High Seas Fleet managed to retire in disorder. Though twice out-manoeuvred and cut off from his base, Scheer did well to exploit the coming of night and the ensuing confusion in the Grand Fleet to steam through the British rear and make it home, having lost fewer ships than the British.

The narrow escape of Jutland convinced Scheer that the German navy only had one chance of victory left: unrestricted submarine warfare, although this only accelerated the United States' entry into the war on the Allied side. In 1918 Scheer left the High Seas Fleet to take control of the construction programme, but the naval mutinies of October, prefacing revolution and Germany's final acceptance of defeat, came as a crowning humiliation. Scheer died in 1928.

John Rushworth Jellicoe

1859–1935

Pictured aboard HMS *Iron Duke*, Sir John Jellicoe emerged with some credit from the battle of Jutland to become First Sea Lord in 1916.

John Rushworth Jellicoe, son of a master mariner, was born in 1859; he entered the Royal Naval training ship *Britannia*, passing out top of his term, in 1872. He first showed his mettle as a young lieutenant during the Arabi Pasha revolt of 1882, disguising himself in native garb and carrying a message through the enemy lines to General Wolseley. The course of his career was set when he returned to England to qualify as a gunnery specialist in HMS *Excellent*, the gunnery school at Whale Island.

Again qualifying with distinction, Jellicoe received his first appointments afloat as a gunnery officer in the *Monarch* and the battleship *Colossus* (1886) before returning to the experimental staff in *Excellent*. He had already attracted the favourable attention of two officers destined to revolutionize British naval gunnery by 1914: John Fisher and Percy Scott, respectively captain and senior staff officer in *Excellent*. Fisher thought highly of Jellicoe, and when Director of Naval Ordnance he chose Jellicoe to help him put through the 1889 Naval Defence Act.

After his promotion to commander in 1891, Jellicoe was fortunate to survive one of the most notorious naval tragedies of the age. He was executive officer of the Mediterranean Fleet flagship *Victoria* when she was accidentally rammed and sunk by the *Camperdown*, with the loss of half her complement including the commander-in-chief,

Admiral Tryon. Jellicoe was ill with Malta fever at the time of the disaster but managed to escape.

Jellicoe did not receive an immediate seagoing command. He returned to the Admiralty to serve a year on the Ordnance Committee before being appointed flag captain to Admiral Seymour, British commander in the international operations against the Boxer Rising in China. During the land operations Jellicoe distinguished himself again; one of the French officers noted that: 'He seemed to be everywhere at once: *where* he should have been *when* he should have been'. He was badly wounded by a bullet through the lung, however, and was lucky to survive.

After recovering from his wound, Jellicoe briefly commanded the cruiser *Drake* before being recalled to the Admiralty by Fisher, now First Sea Lord. Fisher's patronage and Jellicoe's own talents took the latter rapidly to the top: Director of Naval Ordnance (1904–7), rear-admiral and second-in-command of the Atlantic Fleet (1907–8), then Controller and Third Sea Lord in 1908. In the immediate pre-war years Jellicoe commanded the Atlantic Fleet and the 2nd Division of the Home Fleet, gaining final experience for the role Fisher had planned for him: 'Admiralissimo when Armageddon comes'.

As commander-in-chief of the Grand Fleet from August 1914, Jellicoe's tactical responsibilities were far outstripped by his strategic ones. He correctly refused to take any risk which might expose the fleet to decimation, and hence possible eclipse and defeat, by the German High Seas Fleet. Though wretchedly fed with information by his subordinate commanders, Jellicoe's initial deployment of the Grand Fleet at the battle of Jutland remains a model of instinctive brilliance.

After Jutland Jellicoe spent a year as First Sea Lord from 1916 to 1917, grappling with the U-boat menace. His obsession with keeping the Grand Fleet strong led him to oppose the adoption of the convoy system until America's entry into the war provided sufficient warships. After considerable friction with Prime Minister Lloyd George, Jellicoe was dismissed at the end of 1917.

After the Armistice Jellicoe toured the empire, advising Commonwealth governments on naval defence, and was a popular and successful governor-general of New Zealand from 1920 to 1924. He died in 1935.

PART SIX

World War II and After

After World War I the great powers attempted to limit the size of capital ships and the total naval tonnage allowed to each country. This was necessary because Japan began a massive shipbuilding programme in an attempt to gain control of the Pacific, and the United States were determined to prevent this. Britain was especially concerned because the proposed US shipbuilding effort posed a serious threat to British naval supremacy.

The Washington Treaty of 1921–2, whose signatories were Great Britain, the US, Japan, France and Italy, was followed by a number of further meetings to regulate the size and structure of the world's great navies, the most notable being the London Naval Conference of 1930. Although Japan's position was strengthened she demanded naval parity with Great Britain and the US. The refusal by both Britain and America to accede to Japan's demands and the growing international tension of the 1930s ensured the breakdown of the naval treaty system. In 1934 Japan announced her intention of withdrawing from the Washington Treaty.

Germany also resented the harsh restrictions imposed upon her by the Western powers and in 1935 Hitler repudiated the terms of the Treaty of Versailles and committed Germany to a rapid programme of naval and military rearmament. The naval race was, in fact, renewed by all the great powers during the 1930s and particular emphasis was given to battleship development.

The battleship was still accorded pride of place in the fleet but the success of the German U-boat campaign in World War I and the introduction of the first aircraft-carrier in 1918 steadily reduced its battle-worthiness. Doubts continued in conservative naval circles as to the merits of the aircraft-carrier and in Great Britain the RAF was slow to develop a strong carrier force despite the fact that the Royal Naval Air Service (RNAS) was a pioneer of naval aviation. When the RNAS was absorbed into the RAF in 1918, naval aircraft became a secondary consideration because of the RAF's view that bombers would win the next war. More surprisingly, no real improvements were made to submarine design until after the outbreak of World War II and overall numbers remained small in all the navies. New technical developments in warship construction including electro-welding soon became widespread, though perhaps the most far-reaching invention was that of radar, which, though only rudimentary in the 1930s, by 1940 was beginning to transform the conduct of naval warfare.

By the terms agreed at the Washington Conference it was laid down that battleships should not exceed 35,000 tons in displacement and that guns should not exceed 406mm (16in) in calibre. Rebuilding was to be limited to alterations for defence against aircraft and submarines. One of the results of the treaty was that Britain built two ships, *Rodney* and *Nelson*, which followed the Italian plan of big guns mounted in triple turrets. These were placed forward, in an attempt to bring the weight of the ship below the 'Washington limit' of 35,000 tons.

Germany's battleship programme was centred around the superb *Bismarck* and *Tirpitz* which with displacement of 41,700 and 42,900 tons respectively and an armament of eight 15-inch guns were a match for anything afloat. These ships were 'declared' at 35,000 tons to conform to the treaty limit, but were built much bigger in the hope that the fact would not be noticed.

The Italians retained a formidable navy, as did the French. The Italian battleships *Littorio* and *Vittorio Veneto* were among the finest looking and fastest men-of-war of their time. They mounted nine 15-inch guns and could carry four aircraft. The French had two handsome ships, *Dunkerque* and *Strasbourg*, which were termed light battleships. The battleship *Richelieu*, completed after war had broken out, was given the strongest protection of any warship designed up to that time. She had armour plate over 40cm (15.7in) thick, and she carried eight 15-inch guns in two quadruple turrets. All the naval powers made great efforts to improve battleship gunnery; sophisticated fire-control systems were introduced and ranges were extended up to 27,500m (30,000yd).

By the beginning of World War II, Britain was just bringing the 'King George V' class of battleships into service. Displacing 35,000 tons, mounting ten 14-inch guns in two quadruple and one double turret and with a speed of nearly 30 knots, they were a valuable asset in the war to come. The US had the 'Washington' class with ten 16-inch guns. As the war progressed, radar was introduced for rangefinding. At first it proved no more accurate than optical rangefinders, but it gradually improved and of course it was invaluable in low visibility and at night.

An example of good long-range shooting was when *Warspite* (eight 15-inch guns) straddled the Italian fleet flagship at 23,800m (26,000yd) off Calabria in July 1940. *Warspite* scored a hit seven minutes after opening fire and the Italians were forced to withdraw. Benefiting from the use of radar at night, Admiral Cunningham with three 'Queen Elizabeth' class battleships, each with eight 15-inch guns, got to within 2750m (3000yd) of two unsuspecting Italian heavy cruisers off Cape Matapan and blew them out of the water. In another night action in December 1943 Admiral Fraser in *Duke of York* (ten 14-inch guns) got to within 11,000m (12,000yd) of *Scharnhorst* (nine 11-inch guns) with the help of radar. *Duke of York* fired starshell to illuminate the scene and enable the director's crew to see the target. *Scharnhorst*'s guns were in the fore-and-aft position, so she was obviously completely surprised. She was repeatedly hit by *Duke of York*'s guns and finally sunk by torpedoes fired by British cruisers and destroyers.

The Americans had a number of night encounters with the Japanese, which were mostly somewhat indecisive. However, in November 1942 there was a full-scale duel between battleships when USS *South Dakota* and USS *Washington* (each with nine 16-inch guns) met the Japanese battleship *Kirishimo* (eight 14-inch guns). *Washington* fired seventy-five 16-inch shells at the Japanese battleship and scored nine hits in eight minutes at 7700m (8400yd).

During the battle of Leyte Gulf in October 1944 the Japanese battleships *Yamashiro* and *Fuso* (both with twelve 14-inch guns) in company with many cruisers and destroyers attempted to enter the Surigao Strait, but were heavily damaged by torpedo attack by American patrol boats. *Yamashiro*, one cruiser and one destroyer pressed on alone and met four American battleships. *Yamashiro* was overwhelmed by their combined gunfire and finally *Missouri* (nine 16-inch guns) finished her off with a salvo of 16-inch shells at 18,100m (19,790yd). This was the last full-calibre salvo to be fired in a naval engagement during World War II and given the demise of the big-gun battleship will probably remain so.

Ironically, at the very same time that the aircraft-carrier was being shown to be the most important class of surface vessel, both the Americans and the Japanese were building monster battleships – the death throes of a constructive effort which had begun several years before. It was effort wasted. When the Japanese *Yamato* and *Musashi* appeared, the type reached its apotheosis. These ships had a displacement of 65,000 tons, carried nine 18-inch guns, had seven aircraft, and a designed speed of 27 knots. They were considered unsinkable and were indeed very strong, but an unsinkable ship has not yet been built, and they succumbed to American bombs. The USS *Iowa* and *New Jersey*, smaller but faster than their rivals, with 48-cm (19-in) armour

Pictured here in a Norwegian fjord, the German battleship *Bismarck* was hunted and destroyed in 1941 by a force of no less than forty-eight surface ships.

and nine 16-inch guns, and with helicopters as part of their equipment, survived the war in triumph, and were later employed as floating fortresses around which task forces could be operated.

The fate of the battle-cruiser, which had played such an important role at Jutland, was decided even earlier and by 1920 this type had generally been abandoned in favour of the fast battleship. Built just after World War I, HMS *Hood* was a super battle-cruiser (and the last built for the Royal Navy). With a displacement of 42,000 tons and an armament of eight 15-inch guns she was one of the most impressive warships in the Royal Navy at the time, but her lack of adequate protection was to have fateful consequences when she met the battleship *Bismarck* in 1941. The inability of the battle-cruiser to withstand anything but light punishment, despite heavy armament, excluded them from the line-of-battle and their reconnaissance role was taken over by naval aircraft. The 31,850-ton German warships *Scharnhorst* and *Gneisenau*, which mounted nine 11-inch guns in triple turrets and had a speed of over 31 knots, were classed by the British as battle-cruisers, but their very heavy armour protection placed them among the fast battleships.

The aircraft-carrier which replaced the battleship as the capital ship of the navy owed its origins to the American aviator Eugene Ely who, in 1910, succeeded in flying off in his Curtiss biplane from a platform erected over the forecastle of USS *Birmingham*. Two months later Ely made history again by landing successfully on a similar platform above the quarter-deck of USS *Pennsylvania*, with the aid of primitive arrester gear consisting of sandbags between which a series of wires were stretched across the deck.

The year 1917 began a new chapter in the history of aircraft-carriers with the commissioning of a ship whose career was to span thirty years of carrier development. This was HMS *Furious*. Designed originally as a 19,000-ton cruiser, *Furious* had a 70-m (228-ft) flight-deck built from her bridge to her bow from which the fighter planes of the day had no difficulty taking off. The fact that at full speed *Furious* could steam into the wind at 31 knots inspired pilots to experiment with landing on the flight-deck. It entailed a difficult side-slipping approach around the superstructure, but Squadron Commander E.H. Dunning landed his Sopwith Pup successfully on deck on 2 August 1917. However, further trials were suspended when he was killed in a later attempt.

On the other hand, when the unfinished hull of the Italian liner *Conte Rosso* was converted into the carrier HMS *Argus*, it was a prime requirement that aircraft should be able to land on deck as well as take off. She was to have an unobstructed flight-deck 170m (560ft) long and 19.5m (64ft) wide. Below was a hangar for stowage and maintenance of aircraft which were transferred from one deck to the other by lift. However, by the time *Argus* was operational World War I had ended. Unlike *Argus*, where funnel smoke was ejected from the stern below the flight-deck, the next new carriers, *Eagle* and *Hermes*, had 'island' superstructures and funnels on the starboard side – an arrangement which became standard.

The conventional arrester system at this time, consisting of wires running fore-and-aft along the deck, proved unsatisfactory as heavier types of naval aircraft joined the carriers and was withdrawn in 1924. For the next eight or nine years British naval aircraft, though they had neither brakes nor steerable tail wheels, landed without the benefit of arrester gear.

In the US the first 'air admirals' foresaw and planned for an ocean war in which the carrier would be the decisive weapon. Consequently equipment and tactics were developed by which the aircraft gradually eclipsed the conventional warship. A more controversial view of the impact of air power on sea warfare was advanced by General 'Billy' Mitchell of the Army Air Corps. He claimed that warships would be unable to operate within range of land-based bombers. He buttressed this assertion with practical demonstrations in which obsolete capital ships were sunk by bombing.

The lethargy that gripped British naval aviation had so far confined the service to ancient and outmoded ships with equally outmoded aircraft. It was not until 1935 that steps were taken to acquire carrier tonnage to the limit permitted by the 1922 Washington Treaty, in the shape of the 23,000-ton *Ark Royal*, which had a speed of 32 knots and could operate sixty aircraft. This was the first British carrier to adopt the style, introduced earlier by the American *Saratoga* and *Lexington*, of incorporating her double hangars and flight-deck in the main hull structure.

With the expiry of the limitations on carrier tonnage imposed by the Washington Treaty at the end of 1936, the British laid down the first of four 23,000-ton ships, *Illustrious*, *Victorious*, *Formidable* and *Indomitable*. These ships were designed with an eye to the danger of bomb attacks and incorporated stoutly armoured flight-decks as well as armour-clad sides, which effectively made their hangars into armoured boxes.

When war with Germany broke out in September 1939, *Illustrious* was still under construction. The Royal Navy had to make do with only a single modern carrier, *Ark Royal*, for the first year of the war and had to employ outmoded aircraft for even longer. However, operating with Force 'H' based on Gibraltar after the entry of Italy into the war, *Ark Royal* played a leading part in Mediterranean operations, enabling convoys to be run to Malta in spite of the overwhelming enemy land-based air power flanking the route. When the great battleship *Bismarck* broke out into the Atlantic in May 1941, it was a torpedo from one of *Ark Royal*'s Swordfish biplanes that finally brought her to bay.

Prior to this, the newly commissioned *Illustrious* had joined the Mediterranean Fleet based on Alexandria, and in November 1940 her Swordfish torpedo-planes had neutralized the Italian battle-fleet lying in Taranto harbour. Damaged by German dive-bombers two months later *Illustrious* was sent to America for repair and her place was taken by *Formidable*, which played the key role in the battle of Matapan. But when Crete fell into German hands the waters of the eastern Mediterranean became too heavily ringed by enemy airfields for a carrier to operate. Badly damaged, *Formidable* followed her sister across the Atlantic. Before the end of 1941 *Ark Royal* was sunk by a U-boat near Gibraltar.

Carrier-based aircraft also played an important part in protecting transatlantic shipping. Pre-war naval plans had assumed that surface escort craft equipped with ASDIC (a sound-ranging device for locating a submerged submarine) would cope with any submarine offensive against merchant shipping. Consequently the navy was ill-equipped to meet concerted attacks on convoys by surfaced U-boat wolf packs. Shore-based aircraft equipped with radar and depth charges helped to master this threat by patrolling in the vicinity of convoys and forcing down any surfaced submarine in the area. However, there was an area of the mid-Atlantic which could not be covered even by the very long-range Liberator patrol aircraft.

In 1943 German submarines operating in mid-ocean came perilously close to severing Britain's life-line to America. A decisive factor in overcoming this menace was the introduction of the escort carrier. Their Swordfish and Avenger aircraft attacked U-boats with depth charges, rockets and homing torpedoes. Initially they gave direct protection to convoys. Then they extended their offensive to the U-boats' refuelling areas. By the end of May 1943, the combination of escort carriers, long-range patrol bombers and improved surface escort tactics had given the Allies the upper hand.

TOP The Fairey Swordfish torpedo bomber achieved notable success at Taranto, despite its obsolescent design.

ABOVE Squadron Commander Dunning became an early casualty in the attempts to perfect deck-landing techniques in the final years of World War I.

LEFT Commissioned late in 1918, HMS *Argus* was the first flush-decked carrier.

During World War II naval aircraft largely replaced the battleship-mounted heavy gun as principal weapon in the set-piece naval battle. In the European theatre, though ships' guns administered the *coups de grâce* at the battle of Matapan and during the chase of the Bismarck, aircraft were the decisive factor. It was in the Pacific, however, that the primacy of naval air power was most convincingly demonstrated.

The Japanese began the Pacific war with a dramatic example of the offensive power of carrier-based aircraft. They sank four American battleships and damaged three others, as well as destroying 164 aircraft on and above their airfields in the course of a two-hour attack on Oahu Island and the Pearl Harbor navy base on 7 December 1941. Attacking without warning, they caught the US ships at their moorings, which made their bombing much more effective. Unfortunately for the Japanese, all three of the US Pacific Fleet carriers were at sea at the time of the attack.

In the war in the Pacific that ensued, the dominant factor and main protagonists were the American and Japanese aircraft-carriers. The battles of Coral Sea and Midway in 1942 and the battles around the key Solomon Island of Guadalcanal saw the loss of two American carriers and five Japanese.

By the middle of 1944 the Japanese had been forced onto the defensive and the Americans were strong enough to exploit their advantage. The Japanese navy assembled a force consisting of three large carriers and six converted ships, with 430 aircraft between them. The American fast carrier task force consisted of fifteen ships with 895 aircraft, of which half were fighters. On 19 June 1944, the Japanese carriers launched most of their aircraft in a series of attacks on the American fast carrier force. The outcome was a massacre in which American fighter pilots, flying Grumman Hellcats, destroyed 346 Japanese aircraft in the greatest defensive air battle of the war. Japanese shipborne air power was broken for ever in this action – known officially as the battle of the Philippine Sea and to the pilots who took part as the 'Marianas Turkey Shoot'.

The Japanese reacted to successive defeats in conventional combat by resorting to suicide attacks on American naval forces. 'Kamikaze' tactics sought to overcome the enemy's superior material resources by harnessing the greater spiritual motivation of the Japanese. The kamikaze effort inflicted

BELOW A pilot's-eye view of USS *Essex* on his final approach. The carrier steams upwind to facilitate a slow touchdown speed.

INSET USS *Lexington* burns in the Coral Sea in May 1942, after sustaining severe damage through internal explosions.

considerable losses during the campaigns which followed in the northern Philippines, Iwo Jima and Okinawa but they were a last desperate attempt to stave off defeat and ultimately were unsuccessful. By the end of the war Allied carriers were roaming at will in the waters around Japan.

While the period between the world wars saw the gradual decline of the battleship relative to the aircraft-carrier, another important development of these years was the progress made in cruiser design. The Washington Treaty of 1922, in an attempt to prevent a repetition of the cruiser competition of the 1890s, had set limits on cruiser building for each navy. A new category, the 'heavy' cruiser, was created, which was not to exceed 10,000 tons in displacement nor to have guns larger than 8-inch calibre. Light cruisers were simply defined as having guns of 6-inch calibre or less and limited to 10,000 tons.

An unforeseen result of the Washington Treaty was the tendency for all navies to build up to the limits. This meant large costly ships, which usually sacrificed protection for speed. The British 'Kent' class, the French 'Tourville' and the Italian 'Trento' classes were all lightly protected and far too expensive to be built in large numbers. The Japanese achieved success with the 'Aoba' class by sensibly reducing the armament to six 8-inch guns, whereas other navies insisted on having eight, nine or even ten guns, which absorbed too large a proportion of the displacement. The only exception to this was the American 'Salt Lake City' class, which achieved a reasonable balance.

The London Naval Treaty of 1930 halted the development of the big cruiser for a while by allotting total tonnage figures to each navy, out of which they could build according to their individual requirements. The European naval powers favoured ships of about 7000 tons with eight or nine 6-inch guns and a series of well-designed ships resulted. The British 'Leander' and the French 'La Galissonnière' classes were two good examples of the balanced designs which were typical of the 1930s. To achieve greater numbers of cruisers from her allotted tonnage, Great Britain went to the logical extreme and designed the smallest possible cruiser for commerce protection. This was a new 'Arethusa' class, which displaced only 5000 tons and mounted six 6-inch guns.

The Americans and Japanese, however, above all needed endurance for operating in the Pacific. As this meant greater size, they built even their light cruisers up to the 10,000-ton limit. First came the Japanese 'Mogami' class, with fifteen 6-inch guns, to be followed by the American 'Brooklyn' class with a similar armament. As these cruisers so obviously outclassed their own 7000-tonners, the British reluctantly followed suit in 1937 with the 'Southampton' class, which mounted twelve 6-inch guns in four triple turrets.

Italy had long enjoyed a great reputation for building fast, handsome ships and the cruisers built between the two world wars proved no exception. *Trento* reached 38.7 knots in 1925, while *Alberico da Barbiano* maintained the incredible speed of 39.74 knots for eight hours.

In 1919, Germany had been limited by the Versailles Treaty to building warships of 10,000 tons armed with 11-inch guns, the idea being to force Germany to build only coast defence battle-

A German U-boat is pictured under depth-charge attack from a US B-25 Mitchell bomber off Ascension Island in the South Atlantic.

ships. However, German ingenuity overcame these restrictions. By adopting welding and an advanced form of diesel propulsion, the so-called *panzerschiff* or armoured ship turned out to be a powerful commerce-raiding armoured cruiser with great endurance, six 11-inch guns and a speed of 26 knots. The new German armoured cruisers were so obviously superior to all the 8-inch-gun cruisers built under the Washington Treaty, to say nothing of smaller cruisers, that the newspapers dubbed them 'pocket battleships'. As it was obvious that *Deutschland* of 1933 could outrange any cruiser afloat, it was argued that she could only be brought to action by the British battle-cruisers *Hood*, *Renown* and *Repulse*.

As we now know, the reputation of *Deutschland* was exaggerated, for her sister *Graf Spee* was outfought by one British 8-inch-gun cruiser, HMS *Exeter*, and two 7000-ton ships, *Ajax* and *Achilles*. The answer to a solitary powerful cruiser was, as it always had been, a concentration of smaller cruisers. As secrecy and surprise were essential to any commerce-raiding cruiser she had to decline action against all but the most feeble of warships. The main function of a commerce raider was to confuse the enemy by sinking unescorted merchantmen over a wide area for as long as possible. Any risk of damage or of being sighted by cruisers had to be avoided.

In the last years before the outbreak of World War II the threat of aircraft attack led to the conversion of some old British cruisers to anti-aircraft cruisers. As these vessels were stripped of all surface guns, there was no question of them serving in anything but a subsidiary role as escorts for fleets or convoys. The next step was to build the 'Dido' class, which mounted ten powerful guns (5.25-inch calibre) in a dual-purpose mounting. This enabled them to take part in surface actions on equal terms with 6-inch-gun cruisers and they proved highly successful in the Mediterranean. The Americans built a similar type of cruiser, the 'Atlanta' class, armed with twelve or sixteen 5-inch dual-purpose guns, but no other navies copied this interesting development during the war.

Cruisers played a major part in World War II. As escorts for battleships and aircraft carriers they were always a welcome addition to a fleet's strength and they were vital to the defence of any convoy threatened by enemy surface ships. In the Far East Japanese cruisers proved tough opponents in battle, while the Italian cruisers in the Mediterranean always had a decisive margin of speed over British cruisers and this enabled them to avoid trouble.

The cruiser also fulfilled a function hardly envisaged before the war. Her powerful gun armament made her extremely useful for shore bombardment and for providing anti-aircraft fire to protect an invasion fleet. Anti-aircraft cover was also an important requirement in the Mediterranean and the Pacific; American cruisers could provide a volume of fire only exceeded by battleships.

In 1941 the Germans initiated a new phase in their war on British commerce. Adapting an idea they had used in a limited way in the previous war, they created the disguised *hilfskreuzer* or auxiliary cruiser. This was a fast cargo vessel fitted with a concealed armament of 5.9-inch guns and torpedo tubes, which was disguised to avoid detection while she sank unescorted merchant ships in remote waters. For a while these raiders proved most effective and it was estimated that each one took fourteen British cruisers to find her. One of these ships, *Kormoran*, was caught by the Australian cruiser *Sydney* and both ships suffered so much damage in their duel that they both sank some hours later.

During World War II the belligerents did not produce many startling changes in cruiser design. The Italians, as was to be expected, built a new class of ultra-fast small cruisers, which were capable of 40 knots. The British concentrated on the 'Dido' type, the 'Fiji' type – a more compact version of the 'Southampton' class – and a very large type of 15,000 tons designed for the Pacific, known as the 'Neptune' class, which was cancelled in 1945. The Japanese revived the idea of the torpedo-cruiser by converting two old light cruisers, *Oi* and *Kitakami*, to carry no fewer than forty 24-inch 'Long Lance' torpedoes – by far the heaviest torpedo armament ever mounted in a warship. Their wartime cruiser programme was cancelled with the exception of five grossly under-armoured light cruisers.

The US laid down three classes of cruisers before the war and this programme was simply extended through to 1945 to speed construction. The 'Atlanta' anti-aircraft type has already been mentioned. The other types were the 8-inch-gunned 'Baltimore' class (13,600 tons) and the 'Cleveland' class (10,000 tons) which mounted twelve 6-inch guns. Late in the war an enlarged 'Atlanta' type was laid down, with automatic 6-inch dual-purpose guns in place of the 5-inch.

The destroyer is best remembered as an escort

HMS *Dido*'s 5.25-inch guns could be employed against either surface or aerial targets.

OPPOSITE PAGE
ABOVE HMS *Mauritius* named a class of cruisers developed from the 'Southampton'-class design. Their armament was twelve 6-inch guns, but one turret was removed from both *Mauritius* and *Kenya* after the war to make way for anti-aircraft guns.

BELOW *Mauritius* leads HMS *Danae* and *Arethusa* to the Normandy beaches in June 1944.

TOP The Japanese cruiser *Mogami* was heavily armed and had a top speed of 37 knots. The damage she sustained at Midway, however, put her out of commission for a year.

ABOVE The destroyer HMS *Jupiter* is shown here in the early days of World War II, with the smaller HMS *Garland* in line-astern.

vessel during World War II but it successfully filled a variety of roles and its versatility ensured it a central place in the naval war. Besides carrying out its old dual function of protecting the main battle-fleet against torpedo attack and acting as a torpedo-launching vessel, the destroyer acquired a number of new tasks.

The development of naval aviation gave the destroyer a new role as an air-direction vessel, coordinating the movements of ship- and shore-based aircraft. The increasing danger of the sub-marine demanded that the destroyer act increas-ingly as a convoy escort. For this role, the destroyer was equipped with ASDIC and depth charges as well as its primary armament of 4- or 5-inch guns.

The German navy introduced a series of heavy destroyer classes in the years leading up to World War II which were well armed and equipped with powerful engines. A good example of German destroyer design was the Type 1936 which had a displacement of 2411 tons, a maximum speed of 38 knots and was armed with five 5-inch guns, four 3.7-cm AA guns, eight 21-inch torpedo tubes and sixty mines.

During the inter-war years the Royal Navy had fallen behind in destroyer development so that Britain entered the war with ships which were underpowered and under-gunned. The diminutive 'S'-class destroyer had a displacement of 905 tons, a top speed of 36 knots and carried three 4-inch guns, one 2-pounder AA gun and four 21-inch torpedo tubes. Efforts were made to increase the size and strength of the Royal Navy's destroyers and the 'Battle'-class ships had a greatly increased displace-ment (2315 tons), a top speed of 34 knots and were armed with 4- and 5-inch guns, one 4-inch dual-purpose gun, twelve 40-mm AA guns and eight 21-inch torpedo tubes.

During the course of the war the destroyers' anti-aircraft armament increased considerably in re-sponse to the growth of air power. This was especially apparent in the Pacific theatre where the US navy deployed heavily armed destroyers. The 'Porter' class had a maximum speed of 37 knots and was armed with eight 5-inch guns, eight 1.1-inch AA guns, two 0.5-inch AA machine guns and eight 21-inch torpedo tubes.

The Japanese 'Fubitii'-class destroyers completed in 1929 were the most advanced of their type in the world and when armed with the 24-inch 'Long Lance' torpedo were amongst the most formidable. The 'Fubitii' class, which formed the basis for later Japanese designs, had a displacement of 2090 tons and were equipped with two turbine engines giving

a maximum speed of 34 knots and were armed with six 5-inch guns, two 13-mm guns and nine 24-inch torpedo tubes. Towards the end of the war anti-aircraft armament was increased as much as possible.

Although the destroyer acted as an escort vessel, Britain never had sufficient quantities and so a smaller and cheaper type was introduced just before World War II known as the 'escort vessel' and used almost exclusively for convoy protection. Under this one generic name, three new types of escort were developed during the next four or five years – the frigate, the sloop and the corvette. Of these, the largest was the frigate, first introduced in 1940, a ship of around 1500 tons displacement with a speed of 20–26 knots, fairly long endurance, and an impressive array of anti-submarine weapons in the shape of 4-inch guns and depth charges. The sloop, smaller and slower, did not have the range required for full ocean convoy duty, but was a valuable ship in anti-submarine warfare, particularly for forming support groups to reinforce the escort group of a convoy coming under actual submarine attack. The last of the trio was the corvette, a small vessel of 860–900 tons based on the design of the whale-catcher, sturdy ships of great endurance and able to stand up to the stormiest weather. They were simple, easy to build, and were produced quickly in very large numbers. With a maximum speed of only 16 knots, they were too slow to catch a submarine escaping on the surface, but nevertheless did good service in escort work until the larger and more powerful frigates and sloops were built. Their crew of eighty-five had only a 4-inch gun and a multiple AA 'pom pom' with which to defend themselves. In some cases this armament was augmented by depth charges. Being based on the whale-catcher design with its rounded hull sections, they rolled badly in a seaway, and were uncomfortable ships in rough weather, but they performed their escort duties with great distinction.

Alongside the aircraft-carrier, it was the submarine which emerged as the other most significant weapon in naval warfare. Apart from an increase in size and more sophisticated methods of torpedo fire control, there had been little basic development between the wars. The submarine of 1939 was still limited when submerged by the capacity of its electric batteries for propulsion, and when the batteries were exhausted she had no alternative but to come to the surface and recharge them with her diesel engines, driving her electric motors as dynamos. And a submarine on the surface is highly vulnerable to attack, for being low in the water her range of visibility is restricted, and it is difficult to identify enemy craft and evade them. What was recognized as the true submarine, a vessel completely independent of the surface of the sea at all times, had been dreamed of for years, but in the current state of research and development there appeared to be no way of supplying energy without burning up oxygen.

During the war, German scientists came near to it. They had a piece of good fortune, when Holland was overrun in 1940, in coming across a Dutch invention, a long breathing tube which, fitted to a submarine, enabled the diesel engines to be run while the submarine was submerged. Development was completed by 1944, and the first operational submarines using it put to sea in that year. This was still not the ultimate submarine, but it was a step in the right direction as it enabled the submarine to recharge her batteries without having to come to the surface, and even enabled her to use the diesel engines for propulsion when submerged. The depth at which this could be done was limited by the length of the tube, or 'schnorkel' as it was named. It had a disadvantage, too, in that the

HMS *Spey*, a frigate of the Royal Navy, escorts a convoy of merchantmen. The frigate was defined during World War II as a vessel larger than a corvette, but smaller than a destroyer.

exhaust fumes of the diesels also had to be discharged up the schnorkel, and more than one submarine was sunk because its diesel smoke betrayed its presence near the surface.

Although the schnorkel was not the final answer, it went some way towards making the submarine invisible for longer periods, particularly at night – the normal time for surfacing and recharging – when radar was sweeping the darkness. Having developed the schnorkel, German scientists went a step further in the evolution of the submarine by providing oxygen for the diesel engines while submerged, without using the oxygen in the submarine's atmosphere, all of which the crew needed to breathe. They did this by designing a closed-circuit diesel installation, using a catalyst with liquid hydrogen-peroxide to provide the gaseous oxygen to mix with the diesel fuel, thus making combustion possible without using the boat's atmosphere. Later, this was changed to a closed-circuit gas-turbine installation, which was more efficient and produced a very high underwater speed. They were known as Walther boats, from the name of their designer Dr Walther. It was, perhaps, fortunate for the Allies that the war came to an end before this new design of submarine became operational, for it would have posed tremendous problems for the anti-submarine units.

The Type VIIC was one of the more successful early German submarine designs and had a surface speed of 17 knots reduced to around 7 knots when underwater. Armament consisted of one 3.5-inch gun, one 3.7-cm AA and two 2-cm AA guns and five 21-inch torpedo tubes capable of launching fourteen torpedoes. The effectiveness of Allied air patrols over the Atlantic made an increase in anti-aircraft armament essential (despite the schnorkel the U-boat spent the vast majority of time above water) and some later models were equipped with as many as eight 2-cm AA guns. The most advanced of the conventional diesel/electric propulsion submarines was the Type XXI which, with an improved schnorkel apparatus, gave the submarine a maximum underwater speed of 12 knots. There were twenty-three 21-inch torpedoes, and an auxiliary armament of four 3-cm (or 2-cm) AA guns.

An important technical development which was introduced during World War II was the acoustic homing torpedo. Germany developed this device for use against Allied convoy escorts, which were taking an ever-increasing toll of her U-boat fleet. It was intended to pick up the distinctive, high-pitched noise generated by the warship's propellers and to home onto the source of the sound. This potentially devastating weapon was neutralized by a noise-making machine, which was codenamed 'Foxer'. This was towed behind Allied escorts to attract the homing torpedo and it proved to be a thoroughly effective countermeasure.

Despite sinking 2828 merchant ships (a total of over 14 million tons) the U-boats were finally overwhelmed by the steady application of anti-submarine techniques by the Allies.

In the Pacific theatre it was the Americans who were most successful in submarine warfare, although the Japanese produced a number of interesting designs including the massive 'I-400' class with a displacement of 5223 tons and a radius of surface action of nearly 50,000km (31,000 miles). Armament comprised twenty torpedoes, one 5.5-inch gun, ten 25-mm AA guns and space for three aircraft (the carriage of aircraft on submarines was a Japanese speciality). American designs were more modest and the well designed 'Gato' class had a surface/submerged speed of 20.25/8.75 knots and was armed with twenty-four 21-inch torpedoes plus one 1-inch gun and four AA guns. All told, the US navy submarine arm sank more than 5 million tons of Japanese merchant shipping.

The miniature submarine with a crew of between two and four men was also used during World War II. This usually took the form of a longer-range motorized torpedo whose crew sat astride it. The most famous exploits were the Italian attack on British ships berthed in Alexandria Harbour in December 1941 which crippled the *Queen Elizabeth* and the *Valiant* and the British midget submarine attack on the *Tirpitz* on 23 September 1943, which successfully immobilized her for seven months.

Nations such as Great Britain and Japan, who relied on well-regulated maritime trade for the import of vital raw materials, were particularly vulnerable to the depredations of the submarine. Great Britain had gained valuable experience in dealing with German submarines during World War I and had instituted the convoy system as a means of safeguarding merchant shipping. At the outbreak of World War II the convoy system was swiftly reintroduced but a desperate shortage of escort vessels led to heavy losses. The US lend-lease scheme made available large numbers of destroyers which helped make up the deficit.

Initially the British placed too great a reliance on sonar detection (ASDIC), not realizing that in war conditions it was not completely reliable and that skilful U-boat commanders could evade detection. Radar was soon installed on escort ships but it was not until March 1941 with the introduction of the special 10-cm radar that an effective means of surface detection was found. Its accuracy was such that a submarine periscope could be spotted at 1200m (1300yd). ASDIC and radar used in conjunction with powerful starshell and 'snowflake' illumination not only made discovery of lurking U-boats an easier task but inhibited the U-boat commander from moving within the convoys which had become an area of great danger for him.

The most potent weapon that was used against the submerged submarine was the depth charge which was in effect an explosive-filled canister which detonated at a predetermined depth. The techniques of depth-charge attacks were improved through the development of the 'squid', a device for launching depth charges forward of the ship (instead of more usually from the ship's stern) so that sonar contact could be maintained with the enemy submarine until the depth charge exploded. Another useful weapon was the 'hedgehog' which, like the 'squid', fired ahead of the escort and consisted of a 24-barrelled mortar which fired a barrage of 16-kg (35-lb) charges. These would explode on contact with the submarine's hull.

An even more important weapon, however, was long-range aviation protection. The ability of aeroplanes to scour the seas made it dangerous for

U-boat commanders to surface near convoys in daytime, forcing the U-boat to submerge, which in turn drastically reduced its speed and effectiveness. At the outset of the battle of the Atlantic, aircraft were only able to cover the coastal waters of Canada and Great Britain (the US joining the war only late in 1941), leaving the mid-Atlantic open to German submarines. This problem was solved in two ways. First, aircraft range was greatly increased by the introduction of specially prepared B-24 Liberators and Short Sunderland flying boats which proved highly effective as submarine spotters and hunters. Secondly was the development of small, quickly built aircraft-carriers which sailed with the convoys, known as 'light fleet carriers' and 'escort carriers', and what they lacked in aircraft capacity they more than made up for in numbers. They began to become operational in 1942 – an incredibly short building time for ships of that size – and by 1943 they were appearing in a steady stream. Inevitably, they became known as 'Woolworth' carriers. The simultaneous application of new fast building techniques and a large measure of prefabrication which produced the aircraft-carriers required also held immense promise for rapid ship production in the years to come.

In 1940 and 1941, before the small American carriers arrived on the scene, the British had produced a partial solution to the problem by the adaptation of merchant ships. In 1940 convoys were being attacked by German long-range aircraft, as well as by submarines, and to protect them some merchant ships were fitted with a small launching platform and a catapult, and carried a fighter aircraft

LEFT A torpedo is loaded into the forward tubes of a World War II Dutch submarine.

BELOW A Japanese midget submarine (Type A), seen beached on the Hawaiian island of Oahu shortly after Japan's entry into the war in 1941.

on board. They sailed in convoy in the normal way, and on the appearance of an enemy aircraft the fighter was catapulted into the air. On completion of its task, and being unable to land on deck, it ditched itself alongside the nearest ship and the pilot was picked up. They were known as 'camships' (Catapult Armed Merchantmen). A more sophisticated conversion was the 'macship' (Merchant Aircraft-Carrier). These ships, usually tankers or grain ships because they were longer and had an uncluttered deck, were fitted with a temporary flight-deck above the superstructure, where fighter aircraft could take off and land. When, as a result of these measures, attacks by German aircraft ceased, macships were used with naval Swordfish aircraft, adapted to carry depth charges instead of a torpedo, and used in an anti-submarine role. They lasted until the American escort carriers arrived to take over the task and, although they were only makeshift and temporary substitutes for the real thing, they filled the gap.

The battle of the Atlantic was finally won by the Allies through the intelligent application of new weaponry, well-coordinated organization between Britain and the US and by the determination of the crews of the escorts and merchantmen alike. The Japanese in contrast paid scant regard to merchant-ship protection and consequently were punished heavily. The Japanese code of *bushido* emphasized the virtue of the offensive and Japanese naval officers were contemptuous of defensive warfare in general, a contempt which included convoys. It was only in the face of enormous and mounting losses that in 1943 a convoy system was introduced, but by then it was too late.

The submarine was probably the most deadly weapon of World War II. For a relatively modest outlay small groups of highly trained and courageous submariners almost brought Britain to her knees. On the other hand, US submarines played a large – if unsung – role in bringing about the fall of the Japanese Empire.

World War II brought into prominence amphibious warfare, a branch of warfare that was transformed by the construction of new, specially designed ships. Once on the offensive a major problem facing the Allies in both the European and Pacific theatres of war was the transportation and landing of large numbers of men against well-guarded and hostile shores.

During World War I the use of amphibious attacks had fallen into disfavour. The ill-fated Allied landings at Gallipoli in 1915 – made from an assortment of commandeered merchantmen, barges and lighters – resulted in the principle of military strategy that attacks should not be made on a well-defended coast, even if one possessed absolute naval superiority. As a result comparatively little attention was paid to the building of specialized assault ships until the inter-war years, when both

Britain and the US developed amphibious warfare techniques.

In 1926 the first 'motor landing craft one' (MLC1) of 16 tons was built. This vessel could carry about a hundred troops. The Admiralty continued experimenting on its own, and just prior to World War II introduced MLC50 and 51, of alloy and wooden construction respectively.

Following the collapse of France, the Germans found themselves hampered in their plans for the invasion of Britain by their complete lack of any suitable craft in which to transport their armies across the Channel. In fact, the German navy was relieved when the operation was cancelled as they considered it certain to be a failure. The lesson that a seaborne assault required long-term planning was shown again by the failure of the Allied Dieppe raid in 1942.

Meanwhile, in England, plans were being drawn up for a fleet of liberation which would require very specialized ships and craft. Soon small commando raids on Hitler's European fortress were organized. Originally the raiders were landed from motor launches and ships' boats. However, it was not long before many different types of landing craft became available, and each had its specialized funtion. There was the simple 'landing craft infantry' (LCI) which could be hoisted on the standard davits of naval ships. Then there was the more robust 'landing craft assault' (LCA) which offered greater protection to the troops. Disembarkation from the LCIs was usually by ladder over the bow, while craft carrying vehicles had a bow ramp which was lowered to allow them to disembark onto the beaches. One of the most successful LCIs built in the US was capable of carrying 200 fully equipped troops at a maximum speed of 17 knots.

Landing ships were originally distinct from landing craft in that the latter were at first incapable of reaching an invasion area under their own steam. But with more advanced designs LCIs became more seaworthy and the distinction became one purely of size. Larger landing ships, commencing with the 'landing ship infantry' (LSI), were initially converted merchantmen, carrying landing craft on their davits.

It was soon realized that one of the prime needs of an assault landing would be to land supporting armour and artillery ashore as quickly as possible. Experiments therefore began in 1940 with the conversion of two tankers, the *Bachaquero* and the *Misoa*. Their bows were modified to allow a ramp to be lowered so that tanks, lorries and other vehicles could be driven from their storage position in the hold directly on to the shore. As these two ships had been originally designed with a special shallow draft for passing over the sand bars of Lake Maracaibo in Venezuela, they were therefore suited to such landings. It was from this experiment that the highly successful 'landing ship tank 2' (LST2) was developed.

Among the smaller craft many were adapted to give specialized close support to the troops in their landings. The LCA(FT) was equipped with a flame-thrower, while the LCA(OC) was specifically designed for clearing beach obstructions. Other vessels were also capable of performing a multitude of functions, ranging from the rocket-launching LCT(R) to the LCCS, which was a floating casualty clearing station to give assistance to the wounded.

The climax in the development of an amphibious force was the D-day invasion of France, known as 'Operation Overlord'. This proved to be the greatest amphibious undertaking of the entire war. On 6 June 1944, 5298 warships, landing ships and craft, and merchant ships took part supported by 2200 aircraft. Due to meticulous planning and execution, the operation was highly successful; 133,000 troops with tanks, stores and equipment having been disembarked by the evening of the first day.

The other important theatre of war where assault ships played a leading role was in the Pacific, where the Americans were fighting to regain control of the Japanese-held islands. Here many developments in landing-craft design were originated to assist in this 'island-hopping' warfare. Among these was the forerunner of one of the most successful assault craft – the landing ship dock. This was basically a self-propelled, floating dock with a ship's bow and stern, designed to accommodate a waterproof door. When the ship reached the invasion area the rear doors would be opened, the dock area flooded and the landing craft floated out.

The rapid developments of World War II confirmed the trend that was just becoming apparent in the 1920s and 1930s that naval warfare would be fought less on the ocean's surface but more under and over it. Thus this period can be described as the age of the submarine and the aircraft-carrier. But in addition there loomed the threat of the mushroom clouds hanging over Hiroshima and Nagasaki. It was obvious that a new concept in warfare had been born, and one that was to change dramatically the design and function of warships.

World War II left certain definite clues as to the future nature of naval warfare. The V2 rocket developed by the Germans towards the end of the war was the prototype of the intercontinental ballistic missile (ICBM), with a one-ton warhead and a range of 320km (200 miles). Atomic fission having been accomplished by US scientists, the way ahead to nuclear fusion was clear – and promised a massive increase in explosive power. The German Walther boat, which could stay submerged for long periods, led US scientists to aim for even further endurance, using the principle of nuclear fission. In 1945 there were few who could foresee the marriage of these three developments to produce the long-range submarine-launched nuclear missile, but with

hindsight the progression is easy to chart.

Other wartime inventions which were to affect the design of warships were the influence mine and target-seeking weapons such as homing torpedoes and depth charges. These all obviously increased the risk to the warship and greatly perplexed the leaders of the world's navies in their task of planning a post-war building programme. An additional problem was to determine where the dividing line between conventional and nuclear warfare would fall. The US was the first nation to harness nuclear power as a means of propulsion, and the keel of the submarine USS *Nautilus* was laid in 1952. The world's first nuclear-powered submarine was large for her day, displacing 3630 tons, and she was launched in January 1954 and commissioned in September of that year.

The principle of nuclear propulsion is not dissimilar to that of the steamship engine except that its power derives from controlled nuclear fission. This process, carried out in a reactor, produces great heat without using any oxygen whatsoever. This heat is

A depth charge explodes astern of a submarine-hunting convoy escort. Later in the war, anti-submarine weapons were devised that could be thrown ahead of the ship, so that sonar contact could be maintained with the target until the moment of detonation.

used in a submarine to produce steam, and the steam is used to drive a turbine. As no air is required in this process, a submarine need never come to the surface – provided that she has an air purification system which cleans and renews the internal air breathed by her crew. Nuclear propulsion brings an added dividend in that atomic fuel is virtually inexhaustible and one reactor charge will produce motive power for years at a time. So at last, the true submarine made her appearance – a vessel with an unlimited radius of action submerged, with no need to come to the surface, and with an endurance that is limited only by what her crew can stand. With nuclear propulsion has also come further technical development of hull strength and shape, giving the submarine a submerged speed of well over 30 knots and the theoretical ability to operate at up to 900m (2950ft), though claims to have reached this depth are so far unconfirmed. New weapons – particularly long-range rockets with nuclear warheads which can be launched from beneath the surface – have made the modern nuclear submarine the ultimate fighting vessel. Indeed, the ability of the submarine to remain virtually undetectable on the floor of the ocean and yet fire a nuclear missile to almost anywhere on the globe makes it arguably the most formidable weapon in the armoury of the superpowers.

Submarine competition between the Soviet Union and the US has been fierce. The Soviet Union was the first to introduce submarine nuclear missiles in the late 1950s, to which the Americans replied by developing Polaris-armed submarines, the first coming into service in 1960. The numbers of nuclear-armed submarines have increased rapidly in the past two decades; in 1978 it was estimated that the Soviet Union was able to deploy over 160 nuclear submarines, half of them armed with strategic missiles. The range of weapons had increased too. The A-3 Polaris missile has a range of 4000km (2500 miles) and the more powerful Poseidon missile can carry twice the payload up to 4800km (3000 miles). The Trident 1 system has a range of 7400km (4600 miles) and is able to deliver eight independently targeted warheads and the newer Trident 2 has a range of 9700km (6000 miles).

The United States has been making important progress with its ULMS (Undersea Long-range Missile Systems) programme. The strength of the submarine has been greatly improved allowing it to operate at great depths and the range of the missiles carried is such that the submarine need be nowhere near the intended target. The Soviet navy, meanwhile, has been quick to develop the cruise missile as a submarine weapon. The cruise missile is guided by computer to hug the ground contours at under 30m (100ft) and so is normally able to avoid radar detection. The other great advantage of the cruise missile is its pinpoint accuracy; even at long range it will land within a few metres of its target. The

SSN-7 cruise missile with a range of 48km (30 miles) was first introduced in 1968. Ranges of cruise missiles increased considerably during the 1970s and the Soviet SSN-13 cruise missile is estimated to have a range of 720km (450 miles) and a speed of up to Mach 4.

There is of course a great advantage in being able to launch a missile from a submarine as the enemy would have no idea of the presence of a hostile vessel and may well be caught completely unawares. The short-range missiles are ideal for attacking convoys or task forces from outside their protective sonar screens of ships and helicopters.

The modern submarine has made full use of the flexibility of missile systems so that besides long-range nuclear weapons it can be armed for local tactical operations against targets on land and sea and in the air. One of the more advanced of these systems is a British development called SLAM (Submarine Launched Air Missile) and consists of a small missile named Blowpipe which was originally developed for infantry use in the field. The launcher carries six missiles and is retractable, as it is fitted to a telescopic mast inside the submarine. It carries a television camera which is remotely controlled in the submarine's control room where the television screen is also fitted. When an aircraft is sighted through the periscope, the launcher is raised and automatically aligned with the periscope. The operator elevates the television camera until he sees the aircraft on his monitor. He then trains his camera to keep the aircraft picture in the centre of his television screen and, when the aircraft is within range, he selects one of the missiles and launches it. He sees it on his screen and directs it by radio commands from his joystick until it hits the target.

In spite of the great power, accuracy and range of missiles the torpedo still remains the standard weapon of the modern submarine. Even ballistic-missile submarines, such as the Royal Navy's 'Resolution' class, carry torpedoes in addition to their Polaris missiles. Since World War II, the torpedo has become primarily an anti-submarine weapon, although it remains effective for use against surface ships. The modern torpedo is generally electrically powered and it is fitted with acoustic-homing equipment. Typical of the most advanced torpedoes currently in service is the American Mark 48, the West's only such weapon capable of tackling the Soviet 'Alpha' attack submarine. The Mark 48 Model 1 is a high-speed (55-knot), long-range (46-km/29-mile) and deep-diving (910-m/3000ft) torpedo with an acoustic-seeker head. Unless otherwise directed, the Mark 48 carries out a preset target search pattern and, after acquiring a target, carries out multiple attacks until successful.

A weapon as formidable as the nuclear submarine has demanded counter-measures in the form of anti-submarine warfare (ASW). There are two separate elements in ASW: detection and destruction. The principle of ASDIC is still used in modern sonar

detection, which has now been divided into passive and active sonar. Passive sonar consists of highly sensitive devices capable of picking up the sound of the submarine's engine or propeller while in active sonar a series of pulses is transmitted from a source which is reflected back if a solid object such as a submarine hull comes into its path. Both passive and active sonar can be laid on the sea-bed and the NATO Sound Surveillance System (SOSUS) is a passive system stretching across the Atlantic between Greenland, Iceland and Great Britain. In addition to fixed sea-bed systems, sonar is used directly from surface ships, from sonobuoys and from helicopters which trail sonar sets in the water from low altitudes.

Despite technical refinements sonar has a number of inherent problems and is particularly susceptible to changes in water temperature and density. Thus highly sophisticated surveillance planes such as the British *Nimrod* are also used in ASW and can deploy a variety of devices to detect submarines both submerged and on the surface. By using a Magnetic Anomaly Detector (MAD) it is possible to detect the presence of a submarine through changes in the earth's magnetic field. Surfaced submarines are detectable through radar and the fumes from conventional diesel-engined submarines can be 'sniffed-out'. Surfaced submarines are also vulnerable to the 'eye' of spy-satellites.

Once discovered the submarine can be dealt with in a number of ways. Depth charges are not yet obsolete but new missile systems are coming into operation. Two ship-to-submarine missiles are used by NATO: Ikara, originally developed by the Australians and now adopted for use in the Royal Navy, and the American Asroc. They are both rockets which carry homing torpedoes or depth charges. They are launched in the direction of a submarine which has been detected by sonar. When they are over the position, the rockets drop their torpedo or depth charge. Ikara can be guided by radio commands when in flight and the British and Australians claim that this gives it a great advantage over Asroc which cannot be so guided. They argue that the modern nuclear submarine can attain

The British Aerospace Nimrod is one of the most advanced maritime reconnaissance aircraft of the 1980s.

OPPOSITE PAGE
TOP Converted merchantmen known as 'camships' were equipped with a single Hurricane fighter to deter convoy raiders.

CENTRE Troops disembark from an assault landing craft on D-day.

BOTTOM Stores are unloaded during the early stages of the Allied invasion of Sicily in 1943.

underwater speeds of 35 knots or more and is capable of altering its position considerably after the missile's launch. Submarines themselves are also used in an anti-submarine capacity, some equipped with wire-guided torpedoes. The US has developed a special submarine-to-submarine missile called Subroc which has a maximum range of 48 km (30 miles).

Progress in ASW has been impressive, but even with every modern technical development, the odds must always remain heavily in favour of the submarines. The oceans in which she can remain virtually invisible are vast and deep, and her range, endurance, and speed increase with each decade.

Missiles have largely replaced the gun on modern warships, their greater range and accuracy rendering the conventional shell obsolete except in a few special instances. The ability of the missile to be 'guided' onto its target makes possible an extraordinary degree of precision. A guided missile is simply a self-propelled shell with an explosive warhead, fitted with equipment which can alter the direction of the shell. The change of direction can be achieved either by radio command from the launching ship, or by the shell sensing the position of the target and automatically guiding itself. The first naval missiles were designed for use against aircraft. This occurred largely because aircraft speeds were much higher than those of ships and because they could change direction and height very rapidly.

The sinking of the Israeli destroyer *Eilath* on 21 October 1967 by a Russian-made Styx (the NATO codename) missile launched from a small Egyptian patrol boat made the Western world aware that missiles could also be extremely effective against ships. After this NATO started to develop ship-to-ship missiles. Thus there are now three types

of ship-launched missiles, ship-to-air, ship-to-ship
and ship-to-submarine.

Ship-to-air missiles can be broadly divided into
two types, long-range missiles for defence against
high-altitude bombers and close-range missiles for
use against high-speed low-level bombers or approaching missiles. The long-range missiles are
known as area-defence weapons, since they are used
to protect a force at sea before the attack actually
materializes. The close-range missiles are referred to
as point-defence weapons, since they are used to
defend an actual point of attack.

Long-range air-defence missiles can be guided in
a number of different ways. In the semi-active-
radar-homing method, the launching ship's radar
illuminates the aircraft target. The missile carries a
radar receiver in its nose. As the ship's radar waves
are reflected from the aircraft target, the receiver
picks them up, notes their direction and uses them
to guide the missile to hit. In the beam riding
method, the ship illuminates the target with its radar
as before. However, the missile is launched along
the radar beam which guides it towards its target,
holding it on course by delicate movements of the
ailerons and rudder. The missile can also be guided
directly from the launching ship by radio commands, transmitted by human operator or by a
computer. Both the missile and the target must be
'visible' from the ship and the sensors needed for this
can be radar, television cameras or the human eye.
Where an operator is used he has a small joystick
which he moves in the direction he wants the missile
to go. Movements of the stick automatically transmit radio commands to the missile and the system is
dependent on the skill of the operator.

The ranges of modern area defence missiles vary
widely. Britain's latest missile, the Sea Dart, has a
range of about 40km (25 miles). The Sea Dart was
fitted to a number of Royal Navy vessels during the
campaign for the Falklands in 1982 and was responsible for shooting down eight Argentinian
aircraft, but it was unable to provide a comprehensive area air defence. An improved version of this
missile is now being developed. Area-defence missiles measure between 4.5 and 8.5m (15–28ft) in
length and weigh anything from 500kg/1110lb (Sea
Dart) to 1850kg/4070lb (the French Masurca).
Propulsion is by jet motor and there is usually a
booster to get the missile off the deck and a sustainer
to keep it in flight.

The shorter-range missiles for point defence are
guided by the radio command of an operator,
though the latest models can be automatically
guided by radio commands generated by a computer. Their ranges are quite small, 3–5km (2–3
miles). One of the best known of these missiles is the
British Sea Wolf, a small but highly effective
weapon which was also used in the Falklands
conflict and proved to be capable of shooting down
both aircraft and missiles in flight.

At present most of NATO's ship-to-ship mis-

USS *Long Beach* launches a Talos missile. The vessel carries an eight-tube Asroc launcher in addition to six twin anti-aircraft missile launchers.

OPPOSITE PAGE Built before World War II and refitted as a guided-missile cruiser in the late 1950s, *Guiseppe Garibaldi* carries a mixed gun/missile armament.

siles are designed for use when the launching ship has spotted the enemy target on her radar. In other words the missiles' ranges are not much greater than the average radar ranges obtained on ships. These ranges depend upon the height at which the radar is mounted in the ship and the size of the target. Generally the maximum range for a radar reading on another ship is about 40km (25 miles), therefore missile ranges tend not to exceed this distance, although there are variations which are mentioned below.

The normal ship-to-ship missiles, fired at targets whose positions have been obtained by ship's radar, are guided by a two-stage method. Initially the missile is guided towards the target by an inertial navigation system. Inertial navigation simply means that the present position of the launching ship and the target's estimated course and speed are set on a computer which in turn transmits a course and distance to the missile's navigation equipment. The missile sets off on a course which will take it to the target's future position, provided the target does not alter course and speed during the time of flight. To allow for any alteration, the missile also has a radar fitted in it which, on nearing the target, opens up and searches an arc until it picks up the target. It then locks onto the target and guides the missile onto it.

It could be asked why the missile's radar does not operate from the start and thus do away with the inertial navigator. There are two reasons for retaining the inertial navigator. The first and most important reason is that if the missile's radar were transmitting during the whole of the flight, the enemy would have plenty of time to pick up the transmissions and jam them. Ship-to-ship missiles are subsonic in speed, about 965km/h (600mph), though supersonic missiles are being developed. At 965km/h and with a range of 32km (20 miles) a missile's time of flight would be two minutes, which is ample time to initiate jamming measures.

On the other hand, if the radar only opens up for the last 8km (5 miles) of flight, the enemy has only thirty seconds in which to take counter-action. The other reason is that the missile's radar would have to be much larger and more powerful if it had to detect the target at 40km (25 miles) and the limited space in the missile could not hold the larger radar and its power supplies.

Another method of missile homing is for the missile to lock onto the target's radar transmissions. Ships would be loath to switch off all their radar in the presence of an enemy, and yet the oncoming missile may be using them to guide itself.

Finally there is the television-guided missile with a camera in its nose. The camera can automatically steer the missile to keep the picture of the target in the centre of a monitor screen, or it can transmit a picture back to an operator in an aircraft who steers the missile by radio command, keeping the picture in view until impact. This system relies on good visibility, and bad weather can dramatically affect performance. On a clear day, the ship's defence is to make herself invisible by hiding behind a smokescreen.

For some years the Soviet Union has employed a ship-to-ship cruise missile called Shaddock, which has a range of about 320km (200 miles). It is launched on reconnaissance information received either from aircraft or possibly submarines, and it requires an aircraft in the vicinity of the target to carry out final guidance. NATO authorities are not particularly worried by it since they consider that the guidance aircraft would be an easy target to shoot down, either by a missile or by fighter aircraft if available. Despite this, America developed a similar though more advanced missile called Tomahawk which could be launched either from a surface ship, a submarine or an aircraft. After launch, the torpedo-like Tomahawk deploys its wings and tail surfaces; at the same time, its small turbofan engine is started for the cruise phase of the flight under the control of an inertial platform. For attacks on land targets, the Tomahawk would be fitted with a 200-kiloton nuclear warhead, and guided in the final stages of its attack by the inertial platform aided by TAINS (TerCom-aided inertial navigation system). The Terrain Comparison (TerCom) system of matching a radar image in the guidance computer ensures a high degree of accuracy. For attacks on ship targets, the Tomahawk would be fitted with a 450-kg (1000-lb) high-explosive (HE) warhead, and guided in the final stages of its attack by a two-axis active radar seeker. Both models would cruise at about 885km/h (550 mph), with a range of 3700km (2300 miles) for the land-attack model and up to 560km (350 miles) for the ship-attack model.

The Americans have also developed the composite Harpoon missile, which can be launched from a ship, an aircraft (including a helicopter), or from a submarine. This idea saves a great deal of money by having just the one missile for all types of launch. It has an air breathing turbo-jet engine with a solid propellent and a booster motor. Its range is at least 80km (50 miles). Like most ship-to-ship missiles it is inertially guided and has active terminal radar homing. Its radar is what is known as 'frequency agile' which means that it is constantly changing frequency (within limits), making it very difficult to jam. In addition it makes a number of evasive 'pop-up' manoeuvres during the later stages of its flight to render it more difficult to shoot down. The submarine version of the Harpoon was fitted to the British nuclear submarine HMS *Courageous* in 1981, and subsequent trials by the Royal Navy have proved it to be a highly effective weapon. An improved model, the very low-flying Harpoon 1B, came into service in June 1982.

France, Britain, Germany, Greece and Argentina, plus a number of other navies, have all adopted the French Exocet missile and it has been fitted in a variety of ship types as well as some aircraft. It has a two-stage solid propellent motor which gives it a speed of 1110km/h (690mph or Mach 0.9) and a range of 37km (23 miles). Like Harpoon, it is also a wave skimmer: after launch it goes right down to just above the sea and continues its journey at this height, making it more difficult to detect by radar. It has the standard two-stage inertial navigation and active terminal radar homing system. The Exocet achieved considerable fame (or notoriety) during the Falklands campaign when the British destroyer HMS *Sheffield* was sunk after being hit by an air-launched Exocet missile. An Exocet was also responsible for the sinking of the *Atlantic Conveyor*, and the 'County'-class destroyer HMS *Glamorgan* was damaged by a land-launched missile.

There are a number of other ship-to-ship missiles being produced in Europe. The Italians and the French, working together, have completed development of Otomat, a very similar missile to Exocet, but with a range of 68km (42 miles) and

Information from an American warship's air search radar is plotted to provide essential input for the vessels' anti-aircraft missile batteries.

designed to be launched onto its target through aerial reconnaissance as well as by ship's radar. The Italians also have the Sea Killer, again similar to Exocet, whilst the Norwegians have the Penguin, a much shorter-range missile designed for use by their patrol boats. Of the major seafaring nations, only Britain has failed to develop her own ship-to-ship missile and instead has bought from France.

Another missile to have seen war service is the Israeli Gabriel which performed extremely well in the Yom Kippur war in 1973, sinking a number of Egyptian patrol boats. There are two versions, one with a range of 20km (13 miles) and the other with approximately double that range.

The latest Russian missiles include the SSN-9 (an American term as no NATO codename has been issued), a cruise missile with a range of possibly 265km (165 miles); the SSN-10, a supersonic missile with a range of about 43km (27 miles) and fitted in the 'Kresta II' class of cruiser and the

'Krivak' class of destroyer; the SSN-11, similar to the SSN-10 but for use in patrol boats; and the SSN-13, a new cruise missile with a range of up to 7200km (4500 miles) and a speed of up to Mach 4.

The modern trend is to convert all ship-to-ship missiles so that they can be launched from ships' helicopters, because the height that can be gained by a helicopter will increase the missile's range. Britain has developed the helicopter-launched Sea Skua missile for use against small craft and this will be lighter and cheaper than Exocet.

Defence against missiles is one of the largest problems facing the navies of the world. Electronic counter-measures, such as jamming, do exist but new types of homing device are now possible which would render them useless. For example, one could have a missile which homed onto the infra-red rays given off by a ship. Such a system is already in use against aircraft, particularly in air-to-air missiles which home onto the hot exhaust gases emitted by jet aircraft. Any object which is at a higher temperature than its surroundings emits infra-red rays. Given a sensitive infra-red receiver in the missile, it is possible to pick up these rays and home onto them. No amount of electronic jamming will have the slightest effect. The only known counter-measure is to produce a more attractive infra-red source than the target itself. This can be done by dropping flares which emit strong infra-red rays or by firing them out of guns.

Although the guided missile has transformed the modern warship, naval guns have not been dispensed with in their entirety. The reason for retaining guns is because there are certain types of action for which a missile is quite unsuitable. For example, it would obviously be impracticable to launch a missile across the bows of a pirate junk to order her to stop and equally impracticable and uneconomical to use a missile to sink such a ship. Furthermore, missiles are not designed for shore bombardment and the gun is still the most effective naval weapon in this role, although bombardment rockets are now being introduced.

Another use for the gun is for close-range, fast-moving actions against small craft, such as fast patrol boats, hovercraft and hydrofoils. They are also used for providing illumination by firing starshell. The shells are set to burst on the far side of the target and they provide sufficient light for identification purposes. A more sophisticated use of guns is to distribute 'chaff', the tinfoil radar reflectors used to confuse enemy radars.

The gun therefore remains in use and most navies fit their ships with one gun capable of carrying out all these functions. The Royal Navy's single 4.5-inch gun, known as the Vickers Mark 8, has a surface range of 20,000m (22,000yd) and a rate of fire of twenty-five rounds per minute. It can be used against aircraft and is fully automatic, requiring a crew of only four men. It can be started up and fired by one man from the operations room in the bowels of the ship with no crew in the gun turret. Other navies have similar guns. The Americans have also produced the Phalanx system, which uses the Vulcan gun with the tremendous rate of fire of 6000 rounds per minute, for use against incoming missiles. The object is to put such a hail of bullets in the path of the missile that some must hit and deflect it. It is in this function of point defence that the Phalanx system will supplement missiles like the Sea Wolf in being able to knock out oncoming missiles. One of the lessons of the Falklands was the importance of adequate point defence, and embodying this lesson is the Royal Navy's HMS *Illustrious* which is armed with Phalanx Vulcan guns. The European-built Sea Guard anti-missile defence gun is designed to perform a similar function.

The aircraft-carrier emerged from World War II as the most powerful vessel afloat, replacing the

battleship as the capital ship. Since the war, however, its position of eminence has become less secure. Its vast size has rendered it vulnerable to missile attack and the improved range of jet fighters has, to an extent, made its role as a floating airfield irrelevant. Despite these reservations the aircraft-carrier is still very much in evidence and the US has several times used them to good effect.

Although the Royal Navy underwent a phase of rapid contraction during the post-war years, Britain has made an important contribution to carrier development. On 3 December 1945, for example, the first deck-landing of a jet aircraft took place when a de Havilland Vampire touched down on HMS *Ocean*. It was several years, however, before jet aircraft became operational with the Royal Navy, whereas the Americans embarked a squadron of FD 1 Phantoms as early as May 1948. The slow acceleration of jet aircraft led to a greatly increased use of catapult launching and eventually it became the only method. Existing catapults were unable to cope with the ever-increasing weight of naval aircraft. A British invention, the steam catapult, solved the problem and was subsequently adopted on carriers of all navies.

Another British idea that was adopted by other nations was to align the flight-deck at an angle to the centreline of the ship. This permitted an aircraft which had failed to hook an arrester wire to take off again, rather than crash into the wire barrier that

Widely used in World War II, the 40mm Bofors anti-aircraft gun remains in use as a complement to modern anti-aircraft missile systems.

A Lockheed S-3A Viking anti-submarine aircraft prepares to launch from USS *John F. Kennedy*. The vulnerability of the aircraft-carrier can be combated to some extent by such aircraft.

had hitherto protected the parking area at the forward end of the flight-deck. This greatly reduced the number of accidents involving naval aircraft of increasing weight and landing speed. Equally important in this respect was the mirror landing-sight, which gave the pilot of an approaching aircraft a visual indication of his position relative to the correct flight-path.

Carriers of the American, Australian and British navies took part in the Korean War. Early in that war their role was particularly important because there were no airfields in South Korea capable of handling the American jet aircraft. The first air strikes in July 1950 were launched from the American 'Essex'-class carrier *Valley Forge* and the British light carrier HMS *Triumph*. For the landing operation at Inchon behind North Korean lines in September 1950, they were joined by two more 'Essex'-class carriers, *Philippine Sea* and *Boxer*. From then until the end of the war a carrier task force was in almost continuous operation.

At the time of the French operations against the Viet Minh forces in Indochina in the early 1950s aircraft from the French escort carrier *Dixmude* and the light carrier *Arromanches* (formerly HMS *Colossus*) played an important role. Later, in the Vietnam War, American carriers operated in the Gulf of Tonkin at various times, carrying out reconnaissance and strike missions deep into North Vietnam. Carrier-based aircraft also took part at the time of the Suez Crisis in 1956 when they neutralized Egyptian air power by strikes on her airfields.

In Britain, however, the whole concept of the aircraft-carrier came in for increasing criticism, owing to the cost of maintaining carriers and the RAF's contention that naval air support could be

cheaply and effectively provided by shore bases. Thus it was decided that conventional aircraft-carriers should be phased out during the 1970s. The last carrier sailing under the white ensign to operate fixed-wing aircraft was the *Ark Royal*.

The French navy, on the other hand, operates two 27,300-ton carriers, *Clemenceau* and *Foch*. The Australian, Argentinian, Brazilian and Indian navies each have an ex-Royal Naval light carrier, used principally in an anti-submarine role.

The Soviet Union – at one time contemptuous of aircraft-carriers – introduced the 'Kiev'-class aircraft-carrier in 1975. The *Kiev* with a displacement of 38,000 tons is the largest warship ever built by the Soviet Union and is capable of carrying around 35 V/STOL (vertical and short take off and landing) aircraft and helicopters.

Though much reduced in recent years, the US navy's carrier force is gigantic by comparison with those of other nations. It includes eight carriers of the 'Kitty Hawk' and 'Forrestal' classes of 60,000 tons, three smaller 'Midway'-class carriers, and fourteen of the modernized 'Essex' class. Pride of the fleet is the USS *Nimitz* with a displacement of 95,000 tons, the largest warship in the world.

In recent years naval aircraft have become increasingly regarded as 'platforms' for the carriage of a variety of equipment, stores and weapon packages, with aircraft of the US navy generally showing the way. In the strategic reconnaissance field, for example, the Rockwell (North American) RA-5C Vigilante has long-range Mach 2 performance, and is equipped with side-looking airborne radar (SLAR) and many other advanced sensors. For use against land targets there is the redoubtable Grumman A-6 Intruder, armed with guided 'smart' bombs, conventional 'iron' bombs and guided missiles, which also equip the Ling-Temco-Vought (LTV) A-7 Corsair II tactical fighter.

For attacks on sea-surface targets the A-6 is also a key weapon, carrying conventional guided missiles or sea-skimming guided missiles; for operations against submarines there are the Lockheed P-3 Orion and Lockheed S-3 Viking, fitted with highly advanced sensors and computerized tactical equipment, and carrying mines, depth charges and torpedoes. For fleet air defence there is the Grumman G-14A Tomcat with the AWG-9/Phoenix weapon control missile combination which allows up to six targets to be engaged simultaneously at ranges of over 160km (100 miles); for airborne early warning there is the Grumman E-2B/C with advanced radar and computer capability, while for electronic defence there is yet another Grumman aircraft, the EA-6B Prowler, derived from the A-6 but carrying two additional crew members to operate the ALQ-99 jamming system.

Though naval aircraft have generally lost any pretence of strategic capability, they have perhaps grown in importance as very flexible tactical weapons. This seems to be confirmed by the growing development of helicopter cruisers for anti-submarine warfare; the introduction of the first true Russian aircraft-carriers in the 'Kiev'-class and the introduction of variable-geometry and V/STOL aircraft to increase payload and range while enabling the aircraft to operate from smaller carriers. In this last category, the British Aerospace Sea Harrier, the McDonnell Douglas AV-8B and the Yakovlev Yak-36 'Forger' are the prime examples.

Since 1945 the general trend in warship design has been to build smaller ships with helicopter or V/STOL flight-decks and to arm them with guided missiles. A limited number of cruisers has been built since 1945 – usually by modifying incomplete hulls. The British 'Lion' class was given an automatic dual-purpose armament and the US navy produced the giant 'Des Moines' class, which was basically a wartime design expanded to allow for a fully automatic radar-controlled 8-inch gun armament. The French produced two interesting anti-aircraft cruisers, while the Russians caused great excitement in 1952 by completing the first 'Sverdlov'-class cruiser, a modification of a pre-war Italian design.

Many gun-armed cruisers, particularly those of the US, have been partially equipped with guided missiles. Most have the after gun turrets replaced by medium-range anti-aircraft missiles to enable them to provide cover for other warships. The retention of the forward gun turrets means that they can also be used for shore bombardment, but the US has altered a few large cruisers to all-missile ships by gutting them completely and fitting them with launchers forward and aft.

Naturally conversions have been followed by new ships built with an all-missile armament. The US developed an enlarged destroyer type in the early 1950s which was rated as a 'destroyer leader' or 'frigate' and this size of hull was selected as the best for the new range of guided-missile ships. The medium-range surface-to-air missile is bulky and heavy and requires complex guidance equipment. A large hull of 5000 tons or more is needed to accommodate a useful number of missiles and to give the vessel a good radius of action. The term 'guided-missile cruiser' is now commonly used to describe these ships, but it is only a convenient way of indicating that they are larger than destroyers.

Commissioned in 1961, the USS *Long Beach* was the first nuclear-powered surface warship and the first warship to have a guided-missile main battery. Displacing 14,000 tons, she was the biggest guided-missile cruiser in the world for many years – but

Aboard each US navy carrier are several air wings with attack, electronic warfare, early warning, anti-submarine, reconnaissance and fleet-defence responsibilities. The Grumman F-14 fulfils the latter role.

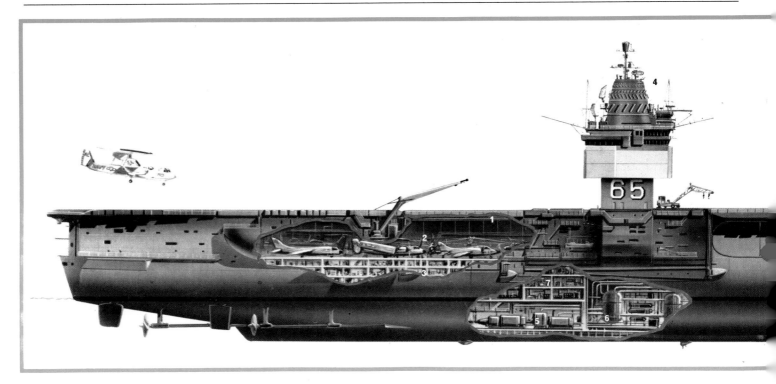

even she has now been dwarfed by the new Soviet 'Sovietsky Soyuz' class of 32,000 tons, the biggest such design yet contemplated, which appeared in 1979.

Since 1960 the Italian navy has built three handsome guided-missile cruisers and in 1979 laid down a new helicopter carrier. The versatility of these ships is shown by the fact that the *Vittorio Veneto* was suitable for the deck-landing trials of the British Aerospace Harrier VTOL aircraft. In addition to their missile armament, they carry anti-aircraft guns and from four to eighteen helicopters.

The French produced the prototype of the helicopter-cruiser in 1968: this was *Jeanne d'Arc* (formerly *Résolue*), which is capable of acting as a training ship in peacetime and as a helicopter-carrier in wartime. The British cruisers *Blake* and *Lion* surrendered half their main armament to provide space for a hangar and flight-deck to operate four large helicopters. This gave the ships a dual capacity to mount anti-submarine operations and to move a limited number of troops in an emergency. The chief disadvantage of such an ambitious conversion is that it provides – at vast expense – a hybrid warship which is only half a cruiser, but carries too few helicopters to qualify as a carrier.

The modern guided-missile cruiser may bear little resemblance to the cruiser of the last eighty years, but she does hark back to the old days of 'cruising' inasmuch as she is able to operate independently. Like the old sailing cruiser, her name indicates a function rather than any easily defined standard of armament. Her role of commerce-protection has been taken over by cheaper and less

One of the world's largest warships, the United States' aircraft-carrier *Enterprise*. Launched in 1960, she was the first aircraft-carrier to be nuclear-powered. *Enterprise* has eight nuclear reactors which power four steam turbines; her four screws produce a speed of 35 knots. Despite her gigantic overall size – 336m (1123ft) long with a displacement of 75,700 tons – *Enterprise* is characterized by her comparatively small superstructure. Although she is built to a modified 'Forestal'-class design, nuclear propulsion eliminates

the need for smoke stacks and boiler air intakes and hence the size of the island structure can be greatly reduced. *Enterprise* has a complement of 3100 plus 2400 members of the attack air wing. Key: **1** officers' state rooms; **2** aft hangar space; **3** crew living quarters; **4** radar array; **5** steam turbines; **6** nuclear reactors; **7** magazines; **8** forward hangar space; **9** avionics workshops; **10** store rooms and freezers; **11** anchor chain storage; **12** windlass room and capstan; **13** ballast.

LEFT USS *Enterprise*, the world's first nuclear-powered aircraft-carrier.

FAR LEFT An angled flight-deck allows an aircraft to land at the same time as another is being launched by the steam catapult in the bows.

sophisticated warships, but she still retains the vital function of escorting and protecting more vulnerable ships.

In 1969 the British announced a new type of warship called a 'through-deck command cruiser', which is a helicopter-cum-V/STOL-carrying guided-missile cruiser of 19,000 tons. The first of these, *Invincible*, was launched in May 1977 and proved itself a most successful design during the Falklands conflict. A second 'Invincible'-class carrier, HMS *Illustrious*, came into service following the end of hostilities in the South Atlantic.

The Russians had already caused considerable uneasiness in NATO by sending two powerful helicopter-carriers, *Moskva* and *Leningrad*, into the

Mediterranean. The later development of this design into the 38,000-ton 'Kiev'-class carrier, with all forms of guns, missiles and both helicopters and V/STOL aircraft, has now far outrun the title of 'cruiser'. Indeed, it would be more accurate to consider vessels like the *Kiev* and the *Invincible* as small, flexible aircraft-carriers.

World War II saw the decline in importance of the battleship in favour of the aircraft-carrier, to which destroyers transferred their services as escorts. In navies which continue to operate carriers, notably the US navy and, as a new development, the Soviet Union, this role will continue to be a prime one for the comparatively small, fast warships which are

The addition of missiles to the warship's armoury since World War II has multiplied its destructive potential. Here the British frigate HMS *Leander* fires an Ikara missile.

now classified as destroyers or frigates. The majority of such ships are now primarily armed with missiles – either surface-to-air (SAM) or surface-to-surface (SSM) – as well as anti-submarine weapons. Destroyers of the post-war period have mostly replaced their anti-ship torpedoes with anti-submarine homing torpedoes.

Modern frigates normally have a displacement of between 1000 and 3000 tons and as in World War II their primary function is still as escort. Indeed in the US, Russian and French navies they are classed, more logically, as 'escorts'. Some are specialized in the anti-submarine role, in which case they may carry a helicopter deploying submarine detection gear – sonar – in a hangar aft. The frigates are armed with anti-submarine torpedoes or depth charges, with perhaps two light automatic anti-aircraft guns and one heavier automatic gun on the forecastle – usually 4.5-inch – with a high rate of fire, which can be used against aircraft, missiles or for support bombardment ashore. In the anti-aircraft role the helicopter landing area and hangar is replaced by automatic anti-aircraft guns and the torpedo or depth-charge installation forward of the bridge is supplanted by a guided-missile launcher – all systems being backed up by linked radar and 'action-data' computer. More numerous than these specialized

types are the general-purpose frigates which combine both the anti-submarine and anti-aircraft roles.

Perhaps the most significant recent advance in frigate design is the development of the high-powered marine gas-turbine engine. The most modern classes have a dual engine installation of diesels for cruising at about 18 knots and gas turbines for fast spurts up to 40 knots. These may have a radius of up to 10,000km (6000 miles) at cruising speed, which is less than a destroyer or cruiser, but considerably more than a corvette or patrol boat.

The importance of the corvette, patrol boat and other small craft has risen relative to the introduction of the missile, which because of its light weight has given these vessels a new and potent punch. The sinking of the Israeli destroyer *Eilath* in 1967 by the diminutive 70-ton 'Komar'-class missile boat proved this fact to the world.

Following the end of World War II many landing ships and craft were broken up, but a large number were taken into mercantile service, and were used all over the world to ferry cars, lorries and passengers. But the outbreak of the Korean War in 1950 saw the need for a fleet of varied ships and craft. These were used to especially good effect at Inchon, where the seaborne assault was so successful that it could have ended the war had it not been for the intervention of China.

Later, in the Vietnam War, the Americans developed many new types of small craft which were used to support patrols along the waters of the Mekong Delta, while sea-going ships were used to support landings at different points along the coast of South Vietnam. The majority of these craft were modern developments very similar to the 'landing ship tanks' (LSTs) of World War II.

With the advent of the helicopter a new method of getting troops ashore has been made available. The Americans have adapted some of their older and smaller aircraft-carriers to this task, but they have also built a new class of ship which is able to carry both landing craft and troop-carrying helicopters.

The Royal Navy, suffering from financial restrictions, has made use of some of its light aircraft-carriers left over from World War II. These vessels were converted during the early 1960s to carry and maintain helicopters and accommodate troops. They were also able to carry on their flight-deck a number of military vehicles and were fitted with davits for four LCAs. These carriers were used mainly to support the British policing activities in a dissolving Commonwealth.

In recent years the Royal Navy has been able to build two specialized assault ships, HMS *Fearless* and HMS *Intrepid*, which were laid down in the early 1960s. These have been designed to transport tanks to a beachhead, a task for which the converted aircraft-carriers were inadequate, and also to serve in the role of a headquarters ship with a highly sophisticated communications system. *Fearless* and *Intrepid* are each capable of carrying 350 troops with sixteen main-battle tanks, and six helicopters can operate from their flight-deck. The tanks can be lowered into a docking space and loaded into

Although the term has largely been replaced by frigate, corvette and escort in other navies, the US still describes its fast, missile-armed ships as destroyers; the *England* is shown here.

HMS *Sheffield* ablaze off the Falklands after being hit by an air-launched Exocet missile (above). The French-made Exocet (below) was used with some success by the Argentines in the Falklands War of 1982.

landing craft, of which four are carried. They and the troops are then ferried ashore when watertight doors at the stern are opened and the docking area flooded. The value of this new type of ship was proved by the major part they played in the British assault at San Carlos Bay during the Falklands campaign.

Another new invention that has lent assistance to waterborne assaults is the hovercraft or, as the whole range of this type of transport is now designated, 'air-cushion vehicle' (ACV). Despite the interest of the British army, it is in the US that the most concentrated development of the hovercraft is being carried out following their successful deployment in marshy areas of the Mekong Delta during the Vietnam War. An amphibious assault craft is now being designed which will be capable of carrying a load of 150 tons at a speed of 50 knots. This will enable tanks and armour to be landed well inshore, beyond the dangerous beach area of a hostile coast.

The post-war years have seen a transformation of naval warfare. The guided missile has brought about the demise of the big-gun warship and its replacement by the light missile cruiser. Naval aviation continues to play an important role, although there is growing debate as to the value of the aircraft-carrier. Increasingly the world's navies are developing small 'through-deck' carriers which provide a launching pad for aircraft but are less vulnerable and much cheaper than the traditional carrier.

Helicopters have proved an ideal naval weapon,

and all but the smallest vessels can carry at least one. They are particularly valuable in an anti-submarine capacity, being able both to detect and destroy submarines. The nuclear submarine has forced all the naval powers to develop sophisticated counter-measures, though their effectiveness has yet to be proved in war conditions. The nuclear submarine is not only a great threat to surface shipping but now acts as a submerged strategic-missile platform.

The rapid strides in naval weapon technology have been matched by the post-war expansion of the Soviet navy. During World War II Soviet naval forces were of little consequence and most naval personnel fought on land, and yet over a period of two decades the Soviet navy has established itself as the second navy in the world and a close rival of the US. During the 1950s and 1960s the Soviet Union allocated a great portion of its military resources to its navy, and not only does it now outnumber the US in some classes of vessels but it has achieved a qualitative superiority as well. Today the Soviet Union is a dominating force in the Mediterranean, the North Atlantic and the Indian Ocean and has established a network of bases throughout the world.

The rise of the Soviet navy has been matched by the contraction of the British Royal Navy which has surrendered its commitments as a global naval power and concentrated on building up a smaller navy in keeping both with Britain's national requirements and her NATO commitments.

Until the Falklands campaign in 1982 few of the many naval advances of the post-war years had seen serious action. The Falklands campaign emphasized the central role of air cover in naval warfare: the two Royal Navy carriers *Hermes* and *Invincible* were the core of the task force; their Sea Harriers and Sea King helicopters not only protected the force at sea but made possible the landings at San Carlos Bay. The disaster during the landings at Bluff Cove, when British troops were caught unprotected by Argentine warplanes, only proved the absolute necessity of aerial protection for ground troops during amphibious operations.

In the field of aerial surveillance the conflict stressed the importance of airborne early warning (AEW). Although the naval vessels themselves were well equipped with radar, its limited range became only too apparent. Had a British AEW aircraft been deployed over the Falklands, the Super-Etendard aircraft that sank the *Sheffield* would have been spotted long before it could have released its Exocet missile, and would have been dealt with accordingly. The Royal Navy's usual field of operations within NATO is in the North Atlantic, where AEW duties are fulfilled by long-range land-based aircraft and by carrier-borne AEW aircraft of the US navy. In order to solve the problem of a crisis such as the Falklands a possible long-term solution could be the development of

STOL aircraft flying off 'through-deck' carriers.

The Falklands campaign brought to the world's attention the way in which missiles have become the main weapon in naval warfare. The Exocet, sinking both the *Sheffield* and the *Atlantic Conveyor*, revealed itself as an effective anti-ship missile. In the area of air-defence the British Sea Wolf was highly effective, being able to knock out missiles in mid-flight, though it was the US-built Sidewinder missile carried on the Harriers that knocked out most Argentine aircraft.

As for the ships themselves, the Type-22 frigate proved an effective design: although lacking any main gun, its seaworthiness and Sea Wolf armament made it an excellent escort. A major criticism of naval ship design was the combustibility of the smaller vessels: neither fire-proofing nor fire-fighting equipment was sufficient to prevent fire from engulfing those ships hit by missiles.

Although these and other lessons of the Falklands war will be digested over time, the main determining factors of naval warfare in the 1980s remain constant. The guided missile and the nuclear-powered and armed submarine are the two most important weapon developments of the modern age, and the importance of air power over the sea remains paramount.

The larger 'County'-class destroyer HMS *Antrim* was also part of the task force despatched to the Falklands in 1982. Her Seacat and Seaslug missile systems are augmented by a Westland Wessex helicopter.

The Sinking of the *Royal Oak*

AN UNSOLVED RIDDLE OF THE SEA

Lieutenant Günther Prien, who pressed home the attack to win a notable propaganda victory.

Shortly after 0100 hours on 14 October 1939 the British battleship *Royal Oak*, at anchor in the theoretical safety of the Home Fleet anchorage at Scapa Flow in the Orkneys, shook to four explosions, rolled over to starboard, and sank with the loss of twenty-four officers and 809 men of her crew. Within a few days German propaganda was trumpeting the news of a truly amazing feat: a German U-boat had daringly penetrated Scapa Flow, sunk one of the Royal Navy's mightiest battleships, and escaped unscathed. Lieutenant Günther Prien and the crew of *U-47* were fêted as national heroes of the Reich, while the British ruefully sealed the gap in the Scapa defences.

Karl Dönitz, commander-in-chief of Germany's U-boat arm, with the rank of commodore at the outbreak of war, was a former submariner himself. From study of airborne reconnaissance photographs of Scapa Flow he came to believe that, choosing a night from the dark phase of the moon, and timing entrance and exit for either side of slack water in order to cope with the sluicing tides pouring between the islands, a lone U-boat stood a good chance of squeezing past the incomplete line of blockships in Kirk Sound. Lieutenant Prien of *U-47* accepted the mission and sailed on 8 October. He made a stealthy approach to the Orkneys and spent most of 13 October on the sea-bed, planning to enter the Flow and make his attack on the night of the 13th–14th.

Though there can be little doubt that Prien *did* get into Scapa Flow and attack the *Royal Oak*, the account of the exploit published from *U-47*'s log bristles with inconsistencies and many of the survivors who read this account firmly believed that Prien was lying through his teeth. Prien asserted that his attack was made under a sky bright with a display of northern lights, which made the interior of the Flow 'disgustingly light'. He also claimed a hit on the battle-cruiser *Repulse*, but his most purple patches were about the *Royal Oak* attack.

According to Prien, *Royal Oak* was blasted out of the water by a sequence of terrible, blinding explosions suggesting that her magazines and shell-rooms had gone up after the torpedoes struck. He wrote dramatically of the whole bay 'springing to life' as he retired, with destroyers and patrol boats dashing to and fro, sweeping the surface with searchlights and making panicky depth-charge attacks. He even claimed that *U-47* was sighted 'by the driver of a car which stopped opposite us, turned round, and drove off towards Scapa at top speed'.

Even allowing for the extreme tension in which entries in a submarine's log are made during an attack, Prien's account hardly stands up. The northern lights were flickering over the Orkneys that night, but there was no moon, and it was intensely dark. *Repulse* was not in the Flow that night, though she had been, and in the position reported by Prien, two days before. *Royal Oak* was not blown apart by magazine explosions, she rolled over to starboard and sank. And the bay certainly did not 'spring to life' after the attack; there were no racing destroyers or patrol boats, and no depth-charge attacks. Above all, Prien could not have torpedoed *Royal Oak* from the direction he said he did, hitting her fairly on the starboard side, without having been about 2km (1.5 miles) inland!

The stories of the *Royal Oak* survivors naturally varied according to where each survivor happened to be at the time, but they are unanimous in rejecting the above points in the German story.

Prien's attack seems to have proceeded as follows, as seen from the receiving end. The first explosion occurred right up in the bows at 0104 hours. As divers later confirmed, this blew away *Royal Oak*'s stem and caused the anchor cables to run out. This explosion was so unlike that of a torpedo that most who heard it believed it to be a spontaneous explosion in the ship's CO_2 and paint stores. About twelve minutes later came a second and much more violent explosion. One eye-witness reported the distinctive column of spray thrown up by a torpedo, in line with 'B' turret. Seconds later came two more explosions of even greater violence, close together, after which *Royal Oak* started to heel rapidly to starboard. It took her between seven and ten minutes to capsize and sink, trapping hundreds of men below decks as she went to the bottom.

The attack sequence recorded in *U-47*'s log, setting aside this document's other errors and distortions, fits with the pattern of explosions recalled by *Royal Oak* survivors. Prien claimed that he began by firing a salvo of three torpedoes from his bow tubes. Two missed but one hit the bows of the non-existent *Repulse*. He then turned about and fired his stern torpedo, which also missed. Retiring towards Kirk Sound to reload the bow tubes, Prien then returned to a point near his original firing

point and fired three more torpedoes, all of which hit *Royal Oak* and, as he claimed, blew her out of the water in a sequence of blinding explosions.

Making allowances for minor discrepancies in Prien's firing times, and for vivid imagination, understandable excitement and gross exaggeration for propaganda purposes, the pattern of Prien's attack therefore fits. What makes less sense is the nature of the rending explosions suffered by *Royal Oak* deep within her hull, the outside of which was extensively 'blistered' to give anti-torpedo protection. It is hard to credit the indifferent torpedoes with which the German U-boat arm went to war with such penetrating power. At the time there was worry about possible sabotage, for *Royal Oak* had taken on stores two days before the attack. A submarine attack in the Flow was generally believed to be out of the question; no U-boat had been sighted, and there was no tangible evidence of one having got in. (Even the torpedoes from *U-47* that missed were never recovered.) It was almost with relief that the Admiralty received the German story and confirmed it in substance if not detail. Even after the war there could be no question of raising *Royal Oak* for an official post-mortem as the sunken battleship was a mass war grave, desecration of which was strongly opposed.

It hardly seems possible that German agents managed to smuggle into *Royal Oak*'s stores time-bombs triggered to explode on sympathetic detonation. Some unknown freak in the laws of physics, combined with careless stowage of *Royal Oak*'s stores, seem to have given Prien's torpedoes far more effect than they would normally have had.

As for the dramatic exaggerations of Prien's own story, these can be put down to a small percentage of human error during the actual attack, and a large percentage of attempted 'cover-up' afterwards. The attacking scheme was sound, but German air reconnaissance of the Flow was bad and it was left to Prien to discover that the only British capital ship there was the elderly and by no means vital *Royal Oak*. Inventing the *Repulse* made the attack sound more worthwhile, but it is particularly significant that Prien chose *Repulse* as his mythical second target. At the time of the attack, the German pocket-battleships *Deutschland* and *Graf Spee* were still at large, and the only warships believed capable of catching and destroying these raiders were the Allies' five battle-cruisers: *Strasbourg*, *Dunkerque*,

Hood, *Renown*, and *Repulse*. By claiming to have damaged one of these battle-cruisers, thereby taking her out of the hunt for the German raiders, Prien might have been trying to attract extra favourable notice from the German Admiralty.

As for the other items of Prien's story – the brightness of the northern lights, being spotted by a car (where no car could have been) and the equally fabricated speed of the British reaction after the attack on *Royal Oak* – these, too, helped atone for a sense of anticlimax on the German side. After all, Prien had ventured into Scapa Flow only to find the cupboard virtually bare, and the melodramatic published version of his report suppressed any tendency to ask why he had left the British Home Fleet base with five torpedoes still unexpended.

It is regrettable that neither Prien nor his crew survived to clear up these points after the war: *U-47* was lost with all hands on the night of 8 March 1941, while attacking Atlantic convoy OB-293. Nothing, however, can detract from the audacity of the attack as conceived by Dönitz and executed by Prien. And Germany's strategic gain far outweighed the comparatively modest tactical achievement of the sinking of *Royal Oak*; the British Home Fleet was to be deprived of its best base for six months until the defences of Scapa Flow had been rendered secure.

ABOVE *U-47*, the German submarine which sank the *Royal Oak* at anchor.

BELOW The *Royal Oak*, pictured at the outbreak of war. Note the 'blistered' hull, designed to give protection against torpedoes.

The River Plate

THE SCUTTLING OF THE *GRAF SPEE*

Fought on 13 December 1939 between the German pocket-battleship *Graf Spee* and a grossly out-gunned trio of British cruisers, the battle of the River Plate and its extraordinary aftermath gave the Allies a heartening naval victory after weeks of fruitless search for the elusive German raider.

Germany's pocket-battleships *Deutschland*, *Admiral Scheer* and *Admiral Graf Spee* were magnificently equipped for the role of commerce raiders. They were super-cruisers armed with battleship-sized guns: two triple 11-inch turrets with a secondary armament of eight 5.9-inch guns. Their high-endurance diesel engines gave them an enormous range of 30,500km (19,000 miles) at 19 knots and an impressive top speed of around 26 knots. Thus, at least in theory, a pocket-battleship could out-gun any Allied cruiser of superior speed, and outrun any Allied battleship in service in 1939. It was believed that the only Allied warships able to catch and out-gun the pocket-battleships were the Allies' five battle-cruisers, but only three of these could be spared to join the hunt for the German raiders in 1939.

Deutschland and *Graf Spee* were chosen to open the German surface-raiding programme and sailed for the Atlantic in the last ten days of August 1939. Each pocket-battleship was allotted a supply-ship, *Westerwald* for *Deutschland* and *Altmark* for *Graf Spee*, with a careful selection of prearranged 'waiting areas' and rendezvous points. Captain Hans Langsdorff of *Graf Spee* was the first to score, sinking the British SS *Clement* off Pernambuco on 30 September.

For the British and French Admiralties, the problems in tracking down the raiders were immense. 'Surface raider' attack reports by the latest victims (those messages that got through) were often incomplete or incorrect. The raider in question, thanks to constant changes of disguise (at which Langsdorff of the *Graf Spee* was adept) was repeatedly identified as any of the three pocket-battleships. After the news of the sinking of the *Clement*, the Allies formed eight raider hunting-groups in October (five British and three French) to operate from the West Indies to the Cape of Good Hope, and from the south-east coast of South America to Ceylon. But it was not until 21 October that they realized that two pocket-battleships were out, confirmed by the crew of *Lorentz W. Hansen*, *Deutschland*'s first victim in the North Atlantic.

By 22 October Langsdorff had sunk five ships in the South Atlantic before he threw the Allies completely off the track and headed east into the southern Indian Ocean. There *Graf Spee* sank the tanker *Africa Shell* in the Mozambique Channel on 15 November before promptly doubling back into the South Atlantic and returning to her former hunting-ground. More success followed: *Doric Star* on 2 December and *Tairoa* on the following day. But *Doric Star*'s distress signal was picked up and passed on.

Thousands of kilometres away from the spot where *Doric Star* went down, Commodore Henry Harwood of the British 'Force G', patrolling the south-east coast of South America, had always believed that the River Plate, trade outlet for Argentina and Uruguay, would sooner or later serve as a powerful lure for the German raider. When he heard of *Doric Star*'s sinking, Harwood sensed that the German captain would now decide to stop working the central South Atlantic and head west to South American waters, where he had not ventured since the sinking of the *Clement*. Harwood thereupon ordered a concentration of his force 240 km (150 miles) east of the Plate for the morning of 12 December, the day on which, according to his calculations, the raider would have had time to arrive from the Central Atlantic. As an example of 'placing oneself in the enemy's shoes', Harwood's guesswork was brilliant: he had anticipated Langsdorff by twenty-four hours.

Harwood's planning for battle with a pocket-battleship was based on the Nelsonic premise: 'Attack at once by day or night.' If the action took place by day, he planned to group his cruisers into two divisions in order to split the pocket-battleship's fire. On the morning of the 13th, Harwood was flying his broad pennant in the light cruiser *Ajax* (eight 6-inch guns under Captain Woodhouse). The rest of Harwood's force consisted of Ajax's sister-ship *Achilles* (Captain Parry), with her New Zealand crew, and *Exeter* (six 8-inch guns, Captain Bell). Harwood's other 8-inch-gun cruiser, *Cumberland*, was far to the south in the Falkland Islands. He nevertheless stuck to his plan, with the lone *Exeter* operating as one division and *Ajax* and *Achilles* as the second.

At 0614 hours on the morning of the 13th, the three cruisers were steaming in line when smoke was sighted to the north-west, and Harwood

The captain of the *Graf Spee*, Hans Langsdorff, is pictured with members of the pocket-battleship's crew. Langsdorff was to commit suicide three days after scuttling his ship.

signalled *Exeter* to leave the line and investigate. Two minutes later, back came the electrifying signal: 'I think it is a pocket-battleship.' As *Exeter* headed in to engage, *Ajax* and *Achilles* began to work up to full speed, drawing away to take the pocket-battleship in the flank.

Langsdorff had been pleased to sight masts and smoke over half an hour earlier. Berlin had briefed him that a British merchant convoy was due to sail from the Plate, and this was why he steamed confidently towards the British force. When the strange ships turned out to be warships no superior would have blamed Langsdorff if he had turned and run, because a force of three Allied cruisers possessed enough joint firepower to damage his ship and make it impossible to continue his cruise even if he sank the lot. At first, however, Langsdorff believed that he was only up against a single cruiser and a couple of destroyers, opposition which he seems to have assessed as easy meat. Long before Langsdorff realized that he was up against a British heavy cruiser and two light cruisers, it was already too late for him to give his enemies the slip for they had the superior speed.

But it would still have been far better for Langsdorff to have reversed course and retired at full speed, forcing the British cruisers to overhaul him as best they could, and thus giving *Graf Spee's* gunners ample time to pick off the pursuing cruisers one by one. By heading straight into action Langsdorff threw away his most powerful card, namely the long reach of his 11-inch main battery. Instead, *Graf Spee's* head-on entry into the battle of the River Plate rapidly brought down the range to a level at which the 6-inch and 8-inch shells of Harwood's force could hurt.

Langsdorff's worst mistake, however, was that once committed to action he failed to concentrate his fire on his three enemies one at a time. He kept switching target and dividing his fire between *Exeter*, *Ajax* and *Achilles* – precisely what Harwood was trying to make him do.

Exeter, the heaviest British cruiser, naturally attracted the heaviest weight of German shell. *Graf Spee* opened fire at 0617 hours and straddled *Exeter* with her third salvo at 0623; *Exeter's* return fire was no less accurate, but almost at once the cruiser began to suffer appalling damage. At about 0625 a direct hit wrecked *Exeter's* 'B' turret and bridge, forcing Captain Bell to con his ship from the after control position, using a boat compass and a chain of messengers relaying orders. Two minutes later came another couple of 11-inch direct hits up in the bows, causing extensive flooding; but Bell tena-

Graf Spee settles in the water after being scuttled on the evening of 17 December 1939. Langsdorff was convinced by propaganda that a powerful British squadron was waiting for him outside Montevideo, though none in fact existed.

ciously kept *Exeter* in the battle and fired three of his starboard torpedoes at 0632.

All three went wide, for at this moment Langsdorff decided that *Exeter* was so badly damaged that he could afford to head north and switch his 11-inch guns onto *Ajax* and *Achilles*. Scarcely had *Graf Spee* executed her turn, however, when Bell swung *Exeter* to starboard and fired a second spread of torpedoes, this time from the port tubes. These also missed, but caused *Graf Spee* to reopen fire on *Exeter* with her 11-inch guns and land three more crippling direct hits. This time *Exeter* lost her 'A' turret, switchboard and forward dynamo rooms, suffering additional flooding which eventually cut all power to 'Y' turret, the last 8-inch turret able to fire. But her engines were intact and Bell stayed in the fight, his gunnery officer standing on top of 'Y' turret as long as the power lasted, braving the muzzle blast and shouting spotting corrections to the gun crew down through a hatch.

By 0700 hours the first phase of the battle was over. *Graf Spee* was now running west, with *Ajax* and *Achilles* following to starboard and the savaged *Exeter* still valiantly keeping pace to port. *Ajax* had catapulted off her Seafox spotter plane at 0637 and its reports gave Harwood a useful but hardly encouraging overview of the battle. The British cruisers had headed *Graf Spee* back towards the mainland but had inflicted no serious damage on her armament; Harwood's biggest worry now was that the German would ignore *Ajax* and *Achilles* and head south to finish off *Exeter*.

To prevent this, Harwood decided to snatch the initiative by pressing a point-blank attack with *Ajax* and *Achilles*. At 0710 hours he turned towards *Graf Spee* and over the next half-hour sliced the range down to a mere 7000m (7700yd), finally crossing *Graf Spee*'s wake. The price of keeping *Graf Spee*'s undivided attention was heavy; just after 0725, both the after turrets of *Ajax* were knocked out, and about twelve minutes later she lost her topmast and radio aerials. Harwood was now left with what amounted to one and a half cruisers to pit against *Graf Spee*, and the British ammunition was running dangerously low. Bitterly commenting 'We might as well be bombarding her with a lot of bloody snowballs,' Harwood broke off the action at 0740 and fell back to the east to shadow the pocket-battleship. At about this time *Exeter*'s 'Y' turret fell

silent at last, and Harwood ordered Bell to head for the Falkland Islands for repairs and medical attention for *Exeter*'s wounded.

When he broke off the action Harwood had no impression of having won a victory – but by 0740 hours Langsdorff was in no mood to press his advantage and win the battle. Early in the action he had been knocked unconscious and slightly wounded in the head when a shell burst on *Graf Spee*'s control tower; and this, plus the continued ferocity of the British attacks, seem to have affected his nerve. With thirty-five of his crew dead and another fifty-seven wounded, he now assessed the material damage to his ship in deep pessimism. The galley was wrecked, a range-finder and two 5.9-inch guns were out of action, and there was a hole above the waterline in the bows measuring 2m (6½ft) square. None of this damage should have prevented *Graf Spee* from finishing off *Ajax* and *Achilles*, but instead the shaken Langsdorff made the fatal decision to head into Montevideo and win as much time as he could from Uruguay's neutrality laws. The rest of the 13th was spent in a long chase to the west, punctuated by frequent exchanges of gunfire, with *Graf Spee* finally anchoring in Montevideo harbour shortly after midnight.

The next four days saw the British, determined to prevent Langsdorff from fighting his way out to the open Atlantic, win a great victory on the propaganda front. By Sunday 17 December Langsdorff had been led to believe that the British aircraft-carrier *Ark Royal*, the battle-cruiser *Renown* and a destroyer force had joined Harwood outside Montevideo (when all Harwood had were the battle-scared *Ajax* and *Achilles* and *Cumberland*, which had raced north from the Falklands). Faced with apparent annihilation at sea and internment if he stayed in port, Langsdorff took *Graf Spee* out of Montevideo and scuttled her at sunset on the 17th. Three days later he committed suicide.

A spirited postscript to the River Plate action was written on 17 February 1940, when *Graf Spee*'s supply ship *Altmark*, trying to return to Germany with 299 prisoners taken by the pocket-battleship, was trapped in a Norwegian fjord by the British destroyer *Cossack*. Captain Vian of the *Cossack* refused to be deterred by Norway's neutrality and boarded *Altmark*, liberating the prisoners and bringing them home to Britain in triumph.

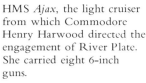

HMS *Ajax*, the light cruiser from which Commodore Henry Harwood directed the engagement of River Plate. She carried eight 6-inch guns.

Narvik

THE NAVAL BATTLE FOR NORWAY

Although the winter of 1939–40 was certainly no 'phoney war' for the Allied and German navies, the Norwegian campaign of April–June 1940 produced the most intense sea fighting in the first year of World War II. This campaign was a unique event, and for two reasons. It was the world's first combined land/sea/air operation; and it saw the tiny German surface fleet defy the power of the strongest navy in the world, thanks to surprise and the striking-power of the Luftwaffe on one side and a string of mistakes on the Allied side.

The crestfallen Allied retreat from Noway in June 1940 was accompanied by the greatest German naval victory since Coronel in 1914: the sinking of the aircraft-carrier *Glorious* and two destroyers. Never had conventional sea power been so completely flouted. Yet the heavy losses suffered during the Norwegian campaign made the German navy utterly incapable of taking a major role when the time came to plan the invasion of Britain; and the

biggest single concentration of German naval losses took place during the struggle for Narvik in April 1940.

This was no accident. Narvik was the key to the Norwegian campaign, for it was from this small northern port that Swedish iron-ore exports reached the North Sea. As long as Norway stayed neutral, the Germans planned to continue shipping the bulk of their essential iron ore imports from Narvik and sailing their freighters home to Germany in the safety of Norwegian territorial waters.

This the Allies planned to stop by means of 'Operation Wilfred', a plan to lay minefields across the German iron-ore route and, if this should provoke Germany into invading Norway, to land troops for the defence of Norway. 'Wilfred' was scheduled for the night of 7–8 April 1940, but the Germans had anticipated this plan by launching their own invasion twenty-four hours earlier.

Weserübung ('Exercise Weser'), the German plan,

A German merchantman burns in Narvik Bay, the victim of a British attack. Allied successes against merchant shipping, however, were few and far between.

envisaged simultaneous naval landings at Narvik, Trondheim, Bergen, Kristiansand, and Oslo, plus paratroop drops and air landings to seize the airfields at Stavanger and Oslo, so as to give the Luftwaffe a firm base in southern Norway. Each seaborne assault force was transported and screened by warships, with the battle-cruisers *Scharnhorst* and *Gneisenau* acting as a separate battle-squadron which, it was hoped, would keep the British Home Fleet fully occupied until the troops were safely ashore.

In order to assure virtually simultaneous landings on the morning of 9 April, the five assault groups sailed from German waters between 6 and 8 April. It was an unprecedented gamble, exposing every available warship in the German surface fleet – but it was a calculated risk. The basic premise of *Weserübung* was that the Allies would be totally unprepared for German naval operations on such an extensive scale, and would not react fast enough. In fact the British naval forces covering the 'Wilfred' minelaying operation were also at sea at the same time, which meant that the British and German navies were in action a day before the first German troops landed in Norway. This stroke of luck for the British was largely wasted by ill-judged and confusing orders from the British Admiralty under Winston Churchill, which made the Germans' task in Norway far easier than it might have been. Feint attacks against Norway, the Admiralty reasoned, could have been cover for a breakout by *Scharnhorst* and *Gneisenau*. Thus, unwilling to secure the Norwegian ports by tying naval forces down to the threatened coast, and at the same time unable to ignore *Scharnhorst* and *Gneisenau*, the British got the worst of both worlds. The Germans beat them into the Norwegian ports by a short head, and *Scharnhorst* and *Gneisenau* were not intercepted and destroyed.

The first confrontation of the two navies came on the morning of 8 April, when the British destroyer *Glowworm* encountered the German heavy cruiser *Hipper* of the Trondheim force. *Glowworm*'s sighting report reached the Admiralty but she was never heard from again. She was in fact smashed to a wreck by *Hipper*, but rammed and severely damaged the German cruiser before she sank. *Glowworm*'s signal resulted in the Admiralty's decision to disembark British troops from the cruisers waiting to take them to Finland (which was being invaded by Russia) so that the cruisers could join the fleet. This ill-judged move meant that the British had no troops ready for a counter-attack in Norway on the 9th and 10th.

Throughout the 8th, other omens continued to be ignored or misinterpreted by the British. An aircraft sighted the German Trondheim force at sea but reported a battle-cruiser in company, thus bringing on stage the spectre of an Atlantic breakout by *Scharnhorst* and *Gneisenau*. The Polish submarine *Orzel* sank a German troop carrier in the

Skaggerak, but the assertions of the surviving troops that they were bound for Bergen were disbelieved. But worse was to come in the early morning of the 9th. The British battle-cruiser *Renown*, only 80km (50 miles) west of the Vestfjord approach to Narvik, sighted *Scharnhorst* and *Gneisenau* at 0337 hours and had no option but to give chase. Using their superior speed the German ships escaped to the north after a running fight, but they had done their work well. Narvik now lay open to the approaching German assault force carried in Commodore Bonte's ten destroyers.

The dramatic events of 9 April revealed the full audacity of the German plan. Bonte's destroyers landed General Dietl's mountain troops, who took Narvik with no opposition. The Trondheim landing was also unopposed, but at Bergen the light cruiser *Königsberg* was badly damaged by shells from Norwegian coastal guns before the German troops landed and secured the area. Kristiansand, too, had been secured by noon – but while approaching Oslo the heavy cruiser *Blücher* was sunk by Norwegian gunfire and torpedoes with heavy loss of life and the Germans did not take the capital until later in the day.

Throughout the 9th, unaware of every detail in this prodigious German *fait accompli*, Admiral Forbes kept the bulk of the British Home Fleet off southern Norway in hopes of intercepting any further seaborne forces which might be coming from Germany. But he also sent north Captain Warburton-Lee's 2nd Destroyer Flotilla to reinforce Vice-Admiral Whitworth in *Renown*, up in the Narvik sector. By the evening of the 9th the Admiralty had intervened and was communicating directly with Warburton-Lee. From the Norwegian pilot station at Tranöy in the Vestfjord, Warburton-Lee had learned that six German destroyers had been sighted that morning heading up Ofotfjord on the way in to Narvik, and signalled, 'Intend attacking at dawn high water.' The Admiralty left it up to Warburton-Lee to decide what action to take.

Warburton-Lee's decision to attack at dawn on the 10th was a gallant one. He would be attacking a hornet's nest of a size unknown, except that it was certainly larger than his own force (the destroyers *Hardy*, *Hotspur*, *Havock*, *Hunter* and *Hostile*). But he also knew that the longer he stayed outside Ofotfjord waiting for reinforcements, the more chance there was of losing the element of surprise. Warburton-Lee told his captains to watch for German warships anchored in the side-fjords branching off the central spine of Ofotfjord, but the mist and driving snow showers which screened the British approach made this impossible. As it was, Bonte and the five German destroyers off Narvik town were caught napping by his attack.

With gunfire and torpedoes the British destroyers sank *Wilhelm Heidkamp* (killing Bonte in the process) and *Anton Schmidt*, badly damaging

German warships inside Ofotfjord. He entrusted the task to Whitworth and the Home Fleet's 15-inch gun battleship *Warspite*, a screen of nine destroyers and cover by Fleet Air Arm Swordfish from the carrier *Furious*. At 1230 hours on the 13th, this irresistible force surged into Ofotfjord where the surviving German destroyers put up what resistance they could before succumbing. The British destroyers *Punjabi* and *Eskimo* were badly damaged, but all five of the German destroyers were beached or sunk. In addition, a German submarine (*U-64*) was caught on the surface in Herjangsfjord by a floatplane from *Warspite* and sunk with bombs.

This second battle left Narvik wide open to the Allies and completely isolated Dietl's mountain troops but instead of an immediate move against Narvik the Allies tried to recover Trondheim and a foothold in central Norway. Landings were made at Namsos and Aandalsnes to take Trondheim by a pincer movement, but the plan never stood a chance in the face of the Luftwaffe's unchallenged command of the air. By 3 May both Namsos and Aandalsnes had been evacuated, together with King Haakon and his government plus Norway's gold reserves.

Thanks largely to the excessive caution of the British military commander, a decisive Allied drive to take Narvik was not launched until after the opening of the great German offensive against the Low Countries and France on 10 May. By the time Narvik fell to the Allies on 28 May, orders for its evacuation had already gone out; and by midnight on 7 June the last Allied troops had finally abandoned Narvik to the Germans.

Eager to wreak havoc amid the Allied troopships retreating to Britain, *Scharnhorst* and *Gneisenau* made another joint sortie on 5 June. Three days later they encountered the British aircraft-carrier *Glorious*, encumbered with RAF fighters and short of fuel for flying-off operations, escorted by the destroyers *Ardent* and *Acasta*. The German battlecruisers sank *Glorious* and both destroyers with ease, though the doomed *Acasta* damaged *Scharnhorst* with a torpedo hit. *Scharnhorst* therefore joined the long list of German warships which were still *hors de combat* when the time came to scrape together an invasion force for the proposed conquest of Britain. This was the sole Allied strategic gain from the otherwise calamitous Norwegian campaign.

For the Royal Navy, the campaign began and ended with the gallantry of single destroyers, hitting back to the last while staring destruction in the face. The brief-lived but bright gleam of success won at Narvik on 10 and 13 April remains a classic missed opportunity. But even the culminating tragedy, the loss of *Glorious* (the only occasion in World War II, apart from Leyte Gulf in October 1944, when battleship sank carrier) was not in vain. The vital troop convoys escaped, leaving the Germans robbed, as at Dunkirk, of the total destruction of their defeated foe.

Dieter von Roeder, *Hans Lüdemann* and *Hermann Künne*. A second attack an hour later (0530 hours) sank a total of six German supply ships, and Warburton-Lee decided to withdraw. As he did so, however, his force was engaged by the *Wolfgang Zenker*, *Erich Giese* and *Erich Koellner* out of Herjangsfjord and the *Georg Thiele* and *Bernd von Arnim* out of Ballangenfjord. *Hunter* was sunk, *Hardy* was so badly damaged that she had to be beached, and Warburton-Lee was killed; but none of the five German destroyers escaped damage or stopped *Havock*, *Hostile* and *Hotspur* from fighting their way out to sea, as they did so sinking the supply-ship *Rauenfels*, which had been bringing the ammunition for Dietl's troops in Narvik.

Also on the 10th, Fleet Air Arm aircraft finished off the damaged *Königsberg* in Bergen and the submarine *Truant* torpedoed *Karlsruhe* off Kristiansand, damaging her so badly that she was later sunk by the Germans. But the successes of the 10th were offset by the return to Germany of *Scharnhorst* and *Gneisenau* after a rendezvous with *Hipper*, though *Lützow*, retiring from Oslo, was so badly damaged by the submarine *Spearfish* that she was out of the war for the next twelve months.

By 12 April Admiral Forbes had moved the Home Fleet north, determined to eliminate the last

LEFT Narvik Harbour displays the evidence of visitations from two Royal Navy destroyer flotillas, with wrecked and burning ships littered around.

Taranto

A TRIUMPH FOR THE FAIREY SWORDFISH

As the second year of World War II opened, champions of the aircraft-carrier as the new arbiter of naval warfare had virtually nothing on which to base their claims. Aircraft-carriers had no great victories to their credit; on the contrary, they had proved eminently vulnerable to submarine, surface and air attack. But the British Fleet Air Arm's carrier raid on Taranto on the night of 11 November 1940 provided a resounding reply to the carrier critics. For the first time in naval history, units of a powerful battle-fleet, in the apparent safety of one of their strongest bases, were sunk or crippled while the solitary enemy warship responsible was 290km (180 miles) away.

The summer of 1940 found Admiral Sir Andrew Cunningham's British Mediterranean Fleet facing an acute crisis. In August the Italian battle-fleet had been reinforced by the new 15-inch-gun battleships *Littorio* and *Vittorio Veneto*, and the heavily-renovated 12.6-inch-gun battleships *Caio Duilio* and *Andrea Doria*. This left the ships of Cunningham's battle-fleet outnumbered by six to four, and decisively outpaced by the higher speed of the Italian battleships.

In early September, however, the odds improved slightly for the British. Cunningham was reinforced by the battleship *Barham*, anti-aircraft cruisers *Calcutta* and *Coventry*, and the brand-new aircraft-carrier *Illustrious* to join the old carrier *Eagle*. These welcome reinforcements arrived at Alexandria on 5 September.

With the Italians apparently unwilling to exploit their advantages in a fleet action to decide the mastery of the central and eastern Mediterranean, Cunningham planned to exploit the advantage conferred on him by the long-range strike power of the aircraft-carrier, and launch an attack on the Italian battle-fleet where it lay in Taranto harbour.

As worked out by Cunningham and Rear-Admiral Lyster, commanding the aircraft-carriers, 'Operation Judgement' was a complex venture. It had to be fitted in with the overall movements of the Mediterranean Fleet, which sailed regularly to receive reinforcements coming out via Gibraltar and to escort convoys carrying weapons and supplies to Malta. 'Judgement' would have to be carried out in a suitable moon-phase to give the Fleet Air Arm's slow and vulnerable Swordfish aircraft maximum protection as well as visibility; and it would depend completely on accurate air reconnaissance of the Italian fleet's movements.

The latter vital element was provided in time in the form of three American Martin Maryland reconaissance aircraft purchased for the RAF, which arrived in Malta in early October. These fast and high-flying 'eyes' kept regular watch on Taranto and the other Italian naval bases, and their photographs provided Cunningham and Lyster with all the information they needed.

'Judgement' was originally scheduled for 21 October, but a series of mishaps rendered this impossible. *Illustrious* was damaged by a fire in her hangar; *Eagle* was dropped from the strike force because of damage caused by earlier Italian air attacks; a number of Swordfish transferred from *Eagle* to *Illustrious* were lost because of contami-

A reconnaissance photo of Taranto Harbour after the Fleet Air Arm's raid. The fuel oil on the water tells its own story of the damage caused.

nated petrol in their tanks. Eventually 'Judgement' was re-scheduled for the night of 11 November.

Because of recent aircraft losses only twenty-one Swordfish were available instead of the thirty originally planned, but the attack was most carefully worked out from study of Taranto's defences. The Italian battleships lay in the outer harbour, or *Mar Grande*, protected by arcs of barrage balloons and torpedo nets. While flare-dropping Swordfish lit up the *Mar Grande* from the east, the main torpedo strike force would attack from the west in two waves. Diversionary bombing attacks on ships in the inner harbour or *Mar Piccolo* were included, to keep the Italian searchlights busily sweeping the skies instead of dazzling the torpedo-dropping force.

The operation began on 6–7 November when the Mediterranean Fleet sailed on yet another of its typically complex assignments. Cunningham left Alexandria with the battleships *Warspite*, *Valiant*, *Malaya* and *Ramillies*, and Lyster in *Illustrious*, covered by a skimpy destroyer screen. The fleet was escorting a convoy to Greece and Crete, plus another small Malta convoy, and taking charge of four empty supply ships sailing from Malta to Alexandria. In addition it was standing by to receive another reinforcement from the western Mediterranean: the battleship *Barham*, cruisers *Glasgow* and *Berwick*, and six destroyers carrying over 2000 troops for the Malta garrison. Only when this intricate pattern was completed would *Illustrious* be free to launch 'Judgement'.

For three tense days, until all the convoys had sailed or arrived in safety and the reinforcements had joined from the western Mediterranean, the British Mediterranean Fleet manoeuvred within 560km (350 miles) of Taranto. During this time a sortie by the Italian battle-fleet under Admiral Campioni could have ruined 'Judgement' at any time. In contrast to the excellent British air reconnaissance conducted from Malta, Campioni was badly served by the Italian air force; yet many of his warships carried spotter planes and he could easily have put to sea and carried out his own air reconnaissance. Instead he unwittingly played into the hands of the British by staying in Taranto harbour with his fleet. By 11 November Cunningham had welcomed the reinforcements from Gibraltar and the latest air pictures from Malta showed five Italian battleships lying snugly in Taranto. A sixth was spotted on the afternoon of the 11th, returning to Taranto and completing the line-up of targets for the 'Judgement' strike force.

Illustrious parted company with the Mediterranean Fleet at 1800 hours on the 11th. Cunningham sped her on her way with the following message: 'Good luck then to your lads in their enterprise. Their success may well have a most important bearing on the course of the war in the Mediterranean.' By 2030 hours *Illustrious* had reached her flying-off point and was preparing to despatch

the first strike wave. This consisted of twelve Swordfish led by Lieutenant-Commander Williamson. Six carried torpedoes, the other six bombs; two of the bombers were equipped with magnesium flares for illuminating the *Mar Grande*. The second wave, commanded by Lieutenant-Commander Hale, was even smaller: nine Swordfish, of which five carried torpedoes. For the first time, a new type of pistol was fitted to the torpedoes: the 'Duplex', featuring a magnetic as well as a contact pistol. A direct hit would detonate the torpedo in the usual way; if the torpedo ran too deep and passed beneath the victim's hull, the shift in magnetic field would also detonate it.

Williamson led the first wave into the air, formed up and headed north-west for Taranto, followed an hour later by Hale with the second wave. Shortly before 2300 the bombing and illuminating aircraft

The strike at Taranto was delivered by Fairey Swordfish torpedo-bombers of the Fleet Air Arm. A torpedo-bomber is shown here seconds after launching its weapon.

Completed a mere three months earlier, the Italian battleship *Littorio* lies sinking at her moorings, the target of four torpedoes.

left formation to carry out their diversionary mission while the torpedo aircraft circled away to the west to take up position for their attack.

Though the bombers and flare-droppers did their work well and the immobile Italian ships were perfectly illuminated, Williamson's strike wave had to fly through intense anti-aircraft fire thrown up by the shore batteries and the guns of the warships. As the Swordfish pilots came weaving down through the flak, dropping to about 9m (30ft) for their final run, they found two unexpected advantages. Recent storm damage had grounded about ten of the Italian barrage balloons, creating

useful gaps; and the anti-torpedo net defences were not fully deployed. (Believing that the British fleet had headed back to Alexandria, Campioni had planned to take the Italian fleet to sea on the 12th and bombard the Allied base at Suda Bay in Crete.) But the biggest help for the British pilots was the inaccurate fire of the anti-aircraft gunners, though Williamson was shot down as he launched his torpedo at the *Conte di Cavour* (Williamson and his observer being taken prisoner). Two other pilots managed to hit the *Littorio*; all the others missed. Meanwhile the bombing force, attacking targets in the *Mar Piccolo*, started fires which the second wave found a useful beacon. No other aircraft was lost, and by 0115 hours the Swordfish of the first wave had returned safely to *Illustrious*.

Though one of the bombers from Hale's second wave failed to take part in the attack, the other Swordfish reached the target area at 2350. Using the same tactics as the first wave, they put two more torpedoes into *Littorio* and one into *Caio Duilio*. *Andrea Doria* and *Vittorio Veneto*, however, escaped, as did the cruiser *Gorizia*, which shot down the Swordfish attacking her, killing the crew. The other seven Swordfish were all back aboard *Illustrious* by 0250 on the 12th.

'Manoeuvre well executed' was Cunningham's laconic signal when *Illustrious* rejoined the fleet. It was one of the biggest understatements of the war. For the loss of only two Swordfish, the Fleet Air Arm had made *Cavour* a total loss (she never went to sea again) and knocked *Littorio* and *Duilio* out of the war for five months. The naval balance in the Mediterranean had been overturned: Campioni was left with only two serviceable Italian battleships.

Apart from the obvious and devastating blow at Italian morale, the effects of the Taranto raid were no less dramatic than the attack had been, but, nonetheless, were to be shortlived. Taranto meant that the Italian fleet was unable to interfere with the flow of troops and supplies sent by the British to Greece; it freed Cunningham of the danger of an untimely action against a superior Italian force, and enabled him to release two battleships (*Malaya* and *Ramillies*) for vital convoy escort duty in the battle of the Atlantic. As they left the eastern Mediterranean they escorted another supply convoy to Malta.

The benefits of Taranto were dramatically ended in January 1941, however, when the Luftwaffe arrived in Sicily and established complete air supremacy over the central Mediterranean. Yet the Taranto raid was the first decisive proof, thirteen months before the stunning confirmation at Pearl Harbor, that naval strike aircraft had replaced the battleship as the overriding force in naval warfare.

Matapan

SHOCK DEFEAT FOR THE ITALIANS

In January and February 1941 a new factor entered the war in the Mediterranean: German military intervention on the side of Italy, first in the form of Luftwaffe squadrons based on Sicily, then in the despatch of the Afrika Korps to save Tripoli for Mussolini. Welcome though it was, this German military aid exposed the Italian High Command to increasing German pressure for all three of the Italian armed forces to put more energy into the Axis war effort; and as far as the Italian navy was concerned, the battle of Matapan (28 March 1941) was the depressing consequence of yielding to this German pressure.

After gaining complete air control of the central Mediterranean and suppressing the British strike forces on Malta, the trouble-free transfer of Rommel's Afrika Korps to Libya was secured. The next problem faced by the Germans was the continuing flow of British troops and supplies from Egypt to Greece and Crete. The Germans wanted the Italian fleet to strike at the British convoy routes to Greece, promising the full air support of their Fliegerkorps X based in Sicily.

On 16 March Fliegerkorps X played a persuasive card, claiming to have attacked and crippled two of the three battleships of the British Mediterranean

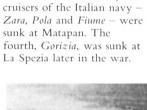

Three 'Zara'-class heavy cruisers of the Italian navy – *Zara*, *Pola* and *Fiume* – were sunk at Matapan. The fourth, *Gorizia*, was sunk at La Spezia later in the war.

Fleet. In the event, this was untrue, but it provided the Italians with the stimulus for action. There now seemed little reason why the Italian navy should not give way to German urgings, for the battleship *Vittorio Veneto*, if supported with the numerous Italian light and heavy cruisers available, should prove more than a match for the last British battleship and the handful of British cruisers left in the western Mediterranean.

Fighter cover would, however, be essential to fend off attacks by the British carrier-borne torpedo-bombers which had done so much damage at Taranto on 11 November 1940, and this protection was guaranteed by Fliegerkorps X and the Italian air force. Admiral Arturo Riccardi, Italian chief of naval staff, thereupon agreed to send a naval task force to sweep the Aegean and the south coast of Crete as far east as the island of Gávdhos. Little or nothing, however, had been done to ensure smooth air/sea liaison between the German and Italian airmen and the Italian task force when Admiral Angelo Iachino took the latter to sea on the evening of 26 March.

On the basis of the false information which sent it to sea, Iachino's fleet was indeed formidable. He sailed from Naples in *Vittorio Veneto* with a screen of

four destroyers, plus Vice-Admiral Sansonetti's 3rd Division of heavy cruisers: *Trieste, Trento* and *Bolzano,* with three destroyers. Vice-Admiral Cattaneo's 1st Division (heavy cruisers *Zara, Pola* and *Fiume*) sailed from Taranto and Vice-Admiral Legnani's 8th Division (light cruisers *Garibaldi* and *Abruzzi*) from Brindisi. When all three forces rendezvoused east of Sicily on the evening of the 26th, Iachino's fleet consisted of one battleship, six heavy cruisers, two light cruisers, and thirteen destroyers.

In Alexandria, Admiral Sir Andrew Cunningham of the British Mediterranean Fleet had sensed that a foray was about to be made by the Italian fleet because of a sudden intensification of Axis air reconnaissance; and in the afternoon of 27 March a Sunderland flying-boat sighted the outliers of Iachino's fleet steering towards Crete. Reckoning that the Greek convoys were an obvious target, Cunningham had already suspended further sailings and ordered Vice-Admiral Pridham-Wippell south from the Aegean with the cruisers *Orion, Perth, Ajax, Gloucester,* and four destroyers. With an intuition strongly reminiscent of Harwood's interception of *Graf Spee* in December 1939, Cunningham ordered Pridham-Wippell's ships to be off Gávdhos at 0630 hours on the morning of the 28th. Cunningham himself sailed from Alexandria on the evening of the 27th with the battleships *Warspite, Barham* and *Valiant,* the aircraft-carrier *Formidable* and nine destroyers.

Though the planned foray into the southern Aegean was cancelled on the morning of the 27th, Iachino continued on course for southern Crete and at 0630 on the morning of the 28th *Vittorio Veneto*'s spotter plane located Pridham-Wippell's cruisers south of Gávdhos. The Italian fleet worked up to full speed to engage this puny force — unaware, thanks to the lack of the promised German and Italian air cover and reconnaissance, that Cunningham's battle-fleet was approaching head-on from the south-east.

Though aircraft from *Formidable* sighted Italian cruisers as early as 0722, Pridham-Wippell's force did not sight *Trieste, Trentino* and *Bolzano* until about 0800. Declining to court destruction by engaging this formidable trio of 8-inch-gun cruisers, the British cruisers sped off to the east, luring their pursuers in the direction of the oncoming battle-fleet, by now only 145km (90 miles) away. Opening fire at 0812, Sansonetti's cruisers gave chase, but had scored no hits before Iachino, suspecting a trap, recalled them at 0855.

Pridham-Wippell promptly reversed course and followed the retiring Italian cruisers, but now it was Cunningham's turn to fear that his cruisers were being lured into a trap. At 0939 he ordered *Formidable* to fly off a strike force consisting of six Albacores, escorted by two Fulmar fighters, to attack the first enemy warships they sighted.

Iachino had meanwhile altered course to catch

the British cruisers between his own retiring cruisers and *Vittorio Veneto,* which *Orion* sighted at 1058. Pridham-Wippell tried to break away to the south but his cruisers attracted a hail of ninety-four rounds from the Italian battleship (all misses, but some uncomfortably close) for the next half-hour. At this tense moment the aircraft from *Formidable* appeared on the scene and promptly went in to attack *Vittorio Veneto.* All six of the Albacores' torpedoes narrowly missed, but the attack was enough to persuade Iachino to break off and retire to the north-west at full speed.

The first phase of the battle ended at 1230 hours, when Pridham-Wippell's cruisers joined up with Cunningham's battle-fleet. The combined British forces now settled down to a long chase, some 105 km (65 miles) behind *Vittorio Veneto* and the Italian cruisers, while Cunningham's aircraft tried to determine the precise composition of the enemy force. This was by no means easy as the Italian warships were retiring in three groups, and some of the British air reports mistakenly identified the two Italian light cruisers as 'Cavour'-class battleships. But at 1510 hours the second air strike from *Formidable* located and attacked *Vittorio Veneto,* the strike leader (Lieutenant-Commander Dalyell-Stead) scoring a hit before he was shot down and killed. This hit dropped *Vittorio Veneto*'s speed to under 15 knots. Further air strikes, twenty-four sorties all told, were made throughout the afternoon by RAF bombers based in Greece, but they scored no further hits as the Italian force stood on towards the west.

It was not until 1830 hours that further air reconnaissance told Cunningham that *Vittorio Veneto* was making about 12 knots 80km (50 miles) ahead of the British battle-fleet, with the Italian heavy cruisers closed up around the limping battle-ship. A third air strike from *Formidable* attacked at dusk but was met with dense smokescreens and a blinding array of searchlight beams. However, the Italian cruiser *Pola* was hit. The retiring Fleet Air Arm pilots could not know that this single success would shortly bring forward the climax of the battle.

As darkness fell, Cunningham made the crucial decision to continue the pursuit, accepting the risk of a possibly damaging Italian cruiser/destroyer attack. By morning, he knew, the Italian fleet would otherwise be safely under the air umbrella of shore-based Axis bomber forces. What he did not know was the wildly inaccurate estimate Iachino had made of the British battle-fleet's position. Furious with the lack of support from the Axis air forces during the day, he rejected a belated air reconnaissance report which put the British within 80km (50 miles) of him. Instead he chose to believe a dubious radio direction fix, relayed to him from Italy, which placed the British fleet about 275km (170 miles) away.

Iachino therefore had no qualms in ordering

BRITAIN'S SEA POWER

Maintain it with your SAVINGS

This poster of destroyers in line-ahead was used to encourage war savings. Destroyers were used at Matapan to deliver the *coups de grâce* to two Italian heavy cruisers.

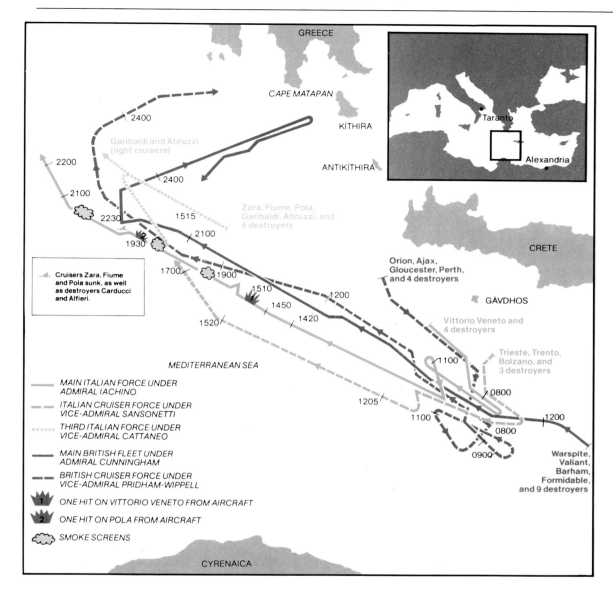

GREECE

CAPE MATAPAN

KITHIRA

ANTIKITHIRA

2400

Garibaldi and Abruzzi
(light cruisers)

2200

2400

2100

1515

2230

Zara, Fiume, Pola,
Garibaldi, Abruzzi, and
6 destroyers

2100

1930

CRETE

1700

1900

Cruisers Zara, Fiume
and Pola sunk, as well
as destroyers Carducci
and Alfieri.

1510

1200

Orion, Ajax,
Gloucester, Perth,
and 4 destroyers

1450

GÁVDHOS

1520

1420

Vittorio Veneto and
4 destroyers

MEDITERRANEAN SEA

1100

Trieste, Trento,
Bolzano, and
3 destroyers

1205

0800

1100

1200

MAIN ITALIAN FORCE UNDER
ADMIRAL IACHINO

0800

ITALIAN CRUISER FORCE UNDER
VICE-ADMIRAL SANSONETTI

0900

THIRD ITALIAN FORCE UNDER
VICE-ADMIRAL CATTANEO

Warspite,
Valiant,
Barham,
Formidable,
and 9 destroyers

MAIN BRITISH FLEET UNDER
ADMIRAL CUNNINGHAM

BRITISH CRUISER FORCE UNDER
VICE-ADMIRAL PRIDHAM-WIPPELL

1 ONE HIT ON VITTORIO VENETO FROM AIRCRAFT

2 ONE HIT ON POLA FROM AIRCRAFT

SMOKE SCREENS

CYRENAICA

Taranto

Alexandria

Admiral Cattaneo to turn back with *Zara* and *Fiume*, plus four destroyers, to rescue the stricken *Pola*, which by 2015 hours was lying dead in the water. Pridham-Wippell's cruisers, pressing westward in pursuit of Iachino, located the immobile *Pola* by radar and reported her to Cunningham, who closed to investigate with the battle-fleet. *Valiant*'s radar had just picked up *Pola* when on to the screen crept the ships of Cattaneo's force.

The ensuing action was a personal triumph for Cunningham, who swung his battleships into line-ahead and opened fire with devastating effect at 2228 hours, only three minutes after locating his approaching victims. As the three battleships opened fire the destroyer *Greyhound* lit up the Italian ships with her searchlight. It was all over in four and a half minutes: *Zara* and *Fiume* were reduced to blazing wrecks, while the destroyers *Vittorio Alfieri* and *Giosuè Carducci* were blown out of the water. *Fiume* blew up and sank around 2300; *Zara* and

Pola were torpedoed and sunk by destroyers.

Cunningham called off the pursuit to avoid accidental engagements between his own ships and retired to the north-east, returning at dawn to pick up survivors. This had to be cut short by the appearance of German aircraft, but Cunningham courteously signalled the position of Italian survivors still in the water to their Admiralty before leading his fleet back to Alexandria.

The battle of Cape Matapan rendered the sea-lanes to Greece safe from Italian naval attack throughout the approaching Balkans campaign. It had cost the Italian navy one battleship damaged, three heavy cruisers and two destroyers sunk, and the loss of 2400 officers and men. The only British loss was Dalyell-Stead and his aircraft during the attack on *Vittorio Veneto*. Apart from this unique imbalance in casualties, Matapan stands out as the first fleet action of the technological era: a triumph for naval aviation and radar.

The course of the engagement at Matapan. Only the escape of the battleship *Vittorio Veneto* marred Cunningham's triumph.

The Sinking of the *Bismarck*

THE GREATEST SEA-HUNT OF WORLD WAR II

Admiral Günther Lütjens, commander of the German navy's ill-fated 'Operation Rhine' which ended in the loss of his ship, the *Bismarck*.

By the spring of 1941, Nazi Germany controlled the entire coastline of Europe from the Pyrenees to the North Cape. Britain stood alone, without an ally in arms on the Continent. Her air victory in the battle of Britain in the summer of 1940 had, however, won Britain a reprieve from the danger of a cross-Channel invasion. Without the domination of the Channel sky by the Luftwaffe, the small but powerful German Navy dared not undertake the seaborne descent on southern England which the invasion plan – 'Operation Sea Lion' – demanded.

Hitler had, therefore, postponed 'Sea Lion' indefinitely and concentrated instead on plans for a powerful offensive against the Soviet Union. By January 1941, the 'Barbarossa' plan, as this colossal gamble was known, was already under way and German army units and air force and fighter wings had begun their eastward trek to refit and re-group before massing along the German frontier. Of the three arms of the German Wehrmacht – the army (Heer), the air force (Luftwaffe) and the navy (Kriegsmarine) – the initiative in continuing the war against Britain now passed to the German navy.

Germany's naval policy in World War II had two main aims: to destroy British merchant shipping with the U-boat force, and to pin down Britain's vastly superior surface battle-squadrons with the carefully judged dispositions and sorties of Germany's outnumbered surface warships. But the role of the surface craft was not purely strategic, and the German pocket-battleships *Lützow* and *Admiral Scheer* – despite the loss of their sister ship, *Admiral Graf Spee*, in the battle of the River Plate in December 1939 – had proved their nuisance value and efficiency as commerce-destroyers before the end of 1940.

On 22 March 1941, the tough new battle-cruisers *Scharnhorst* and *Gneisenau* sailed into Brest harbour after a triumphant cruise in the North Atlantic in which they had sunk 115,622 tons of British shipping. Grand-Admiral Raeder, commander-in-chief of the German navy, now planned the greatest gamble of the German battle-fleet – 'Operation Rhine'. This was to be another commerce-smashing cruise carried out by *Bismarck*, the strongest battleship then afloat, escorted by the heavy cruiser *Prinz Eugen*.

Bismarck was the pride of the German navy and her powerful offensive armament and superb defensive strength were impressive. The battleship's main armament consisted of eight 15-inch guns in four turrets, while secondary firepower was provided by twelve 5.9-inch, sixteen 4.1-inch and sixteen 3.7-inch anti-aircraft guns. Defensively, she had a 32-cm (12.6-in) belt of armour on the hull, 35cm (14in) of armour on her turrets and decks 20cm (8in) thick. In addition *Bismarck*'s great beam of 36m (118ft) and large number of watertight compartments gave her a high degree of underwater protection. Commissioned on 24 August 1940, she went through nine months of intensive exercises and then made ready for her first and last sortie.

Admiral Günther Lütjens, fresh from his success with *Scharnhorst* and *Gneisenau*, was given command of 'Operation Rhine'. In contrast to the orders for his previous foray, Lütjens would this time be allowed to attack escorted convoys, with *Bismarck* taking on an opponent of equal strength to allow other members of the squadron to get at the merchantmen. However, attacks on a warship were to be undertaken only when the success of the mission depended on it; excessive risks were to be avoided. The original plan envisaged *Bismarck* sailing with *Prinz Eugen*, *Scharnhorst* and *Gneisenau*. However, as the two battle-cruisers were undergoing repairs at Brest and were unable to rendezvous with *Bismarck*, the plan proceeded without them.

Lütjens sailed from the Baltic on 18 May 1941, his first task being to slip past the British naval blockade on German home waters and break into the North Atlantic. Luck was with him all the way. Although Royal Air Force reconnaissance planes had spotted the two ships refuelling in a Norwegian fjord, on 21 May, the weather had broken, thus favouring the Germans. Lütjens put to sea at once and sped north, heading for Iceland and the Denmark Strait, the narrow channel between Iceland and Greenland which he had selected as his route to the North Atlantic.

The news that two German warships had left the Baltic soon reached London and Admiral Sir John Tovey, commander of the British Home Fleet, was convinced of a second German naval sortie against the Atlantic convoys. He ordered the battle-cruiser *Hood* and the battleship *Prince of Wales* to sail from Scapa Flow to Hvalfjord on the west coast of Iceland in the hope of preventing the Germans from reaching the Atlantic. On 23 May at 1922 hours the cruiser *Suffolk* spotted *Bismarck* and her companion.

She then dodged into a patch of fog to avoid being fired upon and sent out a report of the German ships' positions, while shadowing them by radar. Soon afterwards, *Norfolk* also made contact with *Bismarck*.

At 0535 the following morning, using the information provided by *Suffolk*, the British squadron sighted *Bismarck* and *Prinz Eugen* off the starboard bow. On paper, the firepower of *Hood* and *Prince of Wales* was superior to that of the German ships, but in practice the advantage was with the latter. *Hood*, for all her 42,100 tons displacement and 262-m (860-ft) length, was beginning to show her age. She had been commissioned in 1920 and reflected World War I ideas of naval warfare. In particular, her deck defences against plunging fire left much to be desired. Thus, although firing the same broadside as *Bismarck* – eight 15-inch guns – *Hood*'s woeful lack of armoured protection was to prove fatal. On the other hand, *Prince of Wales* was so new that she drastically lacked battle-readiness. She was so unprepared that she had sailed with civilian engineers still on board and without all her guns fully operational.

Battle commenced at 0552 and within minutes the crisis was reached. Just as *Hood* was about to open fire on *Bismarck* a salvo of 15-inch shells landed on the British battle-cruiser, smashing through her frail armour and exploding in her magazine. *Prinz Eugen*'s gunnery officer described the scene:

. . . the salvo seemed to crush everything under it with irresistible force. Through huge holes opened up in the grey hull, enormous flames leaped up from the depths of the ship, far above the funnels, and blazed for several seconds through an ash-coloured pall of smoke, which spread terrifyingly towards the ship's bows.

Hood sank almost immediately and so rapid was her destruction that there were only three survivors.

Having disposed of *Hood*, *Bismarck* and *Prinz Eugen* turned their attention to *Prince of Wales*, which had not as yet been fired on. Within minutes the German ships landed four 15-inch and three 8-inch shells on the British battleship. With increasing breakdowns in her gun turrets, she was soon forced to retire.

In a mere twenty minutes, *Bismarck* had won the German navy's most sensational victory of World War II. But she had paid a price. One of her precious fuel-oil tanks had been pierced and vital fuel was

BELOW AND BOTTOM The *Bismarck* under way in the Baltic, seen from *Prinz Eugen*. The two ships sailed from Gdynia (Gotenhafen) on 20 May en route for Norway and the Atlantic.

ABOVE HMS *Hood*, pictured at anchor in Scapa Flow. Her limited armoured protection as a battle-cruiser was to prove her undoing.

BELOW *Bismarck* unleashes a 15-inch salvo before her eventual destruction. *Prinz Eugen* had by that time made her escape, arriving at Brest on 1 June.

lost or contaminated by sea water. Now 'Operation Rhine' had to give place to 'Operation Hood', as Lütjens dubbed it. *Prinz Eugen* was ordered to carry out independent commerce warfare, while Lütjens took *Bismarck* into St Nazaire, the only port on the French coast with a dry dock big enough for repairs. The ships separated, and *Bismarck* set course for France, tracked by the radar eye of the British cruiser *Suffolk*.

The British reacted swiftly to the shock of the *Hood* disaster. Tovey called on the new aircraft-carrier *Victorious* to launch an air strike against *Bismarck*. Just before sunset on 24 May, eight Swordfish biplanes located *Bismarck* and attacked with torpedoes. Although a direct hit was scored, the German ship's thick armour belt prevented any

damage being caused. As night fell, *Bismarck* pressed on south, with Lütjens painfully aware of the British radar watch on his ship.

However, at 0306 hours on the following morning the shadowing cruiser *Suffolk* lost radar contact with *Bismarck*. Now the German battleship's chances of reaching France improved, for the British, unaware of the damage to *Bismarck*'s fuel tanks, were reduced to pure guesswork on position. The Admiralty had already ordered the battle-cruiser *Renown*, the aircraft-carrier *Ark Royal* and the cruiser *Sheffield* – Force H – to leave their bases at Gibraltar and head north-west. This force was to head off the *Bismarck* from the east. The battleships *Rodney* and *Ramillies* were also detached from the convoys they were escorting to join the hunt while Tovey, in the battleship *King George V*, came down from the north-east. But where would *Bismarck* go? Tovey's first guess was that she would make for the British Atlantic convoys in the area east of Newfoundland, where *Scharnhorst* and *Gneisenau* had done such damage months before, and this was where the British concentrated their first air search. Naturally they found nothing, for *Bismarck* was far to the east.

Then *Bismarck* betrayed herself. Lütjens, unaware that he was in fact free of the British radar eye, sent a long signal back to Germany describing his triumph over *Hood* and *Prince of Wales*. British radio-location could now pinpoint *Bismarck*'s position. Unfortunately, an error in plotting put the German ship to the north-east of her actual position, and the British reversed course to chase this false position.

On 26 May, however, a patrolling Catalina flying boat of Coastal Command spotted *Bismarck* heading south-east about 1110km (690 miles) from Brest. As the pilot described it later:

George [the automatic pilot] was flying the aircraft at 500 feet when we saw a warship. I was in the second pilot's seat when the occupant of the seat beside me, an American, said: 'What the devil's that?' I stared and saw a dull shape through the mist which curled above a very rough sea. 'Looks like a battleship,' he said. I said: 'Better get closer, go round its stern.' I thought it might be the *Bismarck*, because I could see no destroyers round the ship and I should have seen them had she been a British warship. I left my seat, went to the wireless table, grabbed a piece of paper and began to write a signal.

The situation did not look good for the British; because of the earlier plotting error Tovey was not in a position immediately to intercept the German ship. Only Force H was close enough to be effective and a strike force of Swordfish planes was sent out from *Ark Royal*. If they could succeed in slowing down *Bismarck*, the battle would be won; otherwise *King George V* and *Rodney* would be forced to turn back through lack of fuel.

The first Swordfish strike was a total failure as the

planes mistakenly attacked the British cruiser *Sheffield*, which had been sent on ahead to keep track of *Bismarck*. Fortunately no damage was done, the episode only providing another demonstration of the inefficiency of British torpedoes. However a second strike located the *Bismarck*, scoring two hits. The first struck Bismarck's armour belt and caused no damage, but the second hit aft, damaging her propellers, wrecking her steering gear and jamming her rudders. The ship was now reduced to a speed of under 10 knots, and after desperate but unsuccessful attempts to free the rudders, Lütjens sent the following message: 'No longer able to steer ship. Will fight to last shell. Long live the Führer.'

After describing two complete circles, the luckless *Bismarck* limped slowly north-north-east, straight in the path of *King George V* and *Rodney*, pounding south at top speed. Before she met these two battleships, she ran into five destroyers led by Captain Vian, which had been taken off convoy duty to act as an anti-submarine screen for Sir John Tovey's main fleet. Seeing *Bismarck* so reduced in speed, Vian decided to attack. So accurate was *Bismarck*'s fire, however, that repeated attacks throughout the night made little impact.

Early the following morning, *King George V* and *Rodney* arrived on the scene. The last act began at

0847 hours when *Rodney* opened fire. Hopelessly out-gunned – her eight 15-inch guns pitted against *Rodney*'s nine 16-inch and *King George V*'s ten 14-inch guns – *Bismarck* fought gallantly but by 1000 hours had been pounded to a defenceless wreck.

Russell Grenfell has described the German battleship's end in vivid terms:

By 10 a.m. the *Bismarck* was a silent battered wreck. Her mast was down, her funnel had disappeared, her guns were pointing in all directions and a cloud of smoke was rising from the middle of the ship and blowing away in the

ABOVE An RAF Catalina on patrol sights the *Bismarck* at 1030 hours on 26 May heading south-east, some 1110km (690 miles) from Brest.

BELOW HMS *King George V*, from which Sir John Tovey, commander of the British Home Fleet, directed the interception of the German capital ship.

RIGHT The aircraft-carrier *Ark Royal*, flanked by HMS *Sheffield* (background) and *Renown*. These ships made up Force H despatched from Gibraltar to intercept *Bismarck* from the south-east.

BELOW HMS *Rodney*, the most modern British battleship at the start of World War II. Her nine 16-inch guns battered the *Bismarck*'s superstructure to a wreck.

wind. Inside, she was clearly a blazing inferno, for the bright glow of internal fires could be seen shining through numerous shell and splinter holes in her sides. Her men were deserting their guns, and parties of them could be seen running to and fro on the upper deck as the shells continued to rain in, and occasionally jumping over the side, to escape by a watery death from the terror on board.

Bismarck was still floating as the British cruisers closed in for the *coup de grâce* with torpedoes, but the hull remained intact and her crew fired demolition charges before abandoning ship. At 1036 *Bismarck* rolled over and sank.

The loss of *Hood*, Britain's proudest warship, had been avenged in full. *Prinz Eugen* fled back to Brest, having achieved nothing. The German tankers and supply ships sent out to support *Bismarck* and *Prinz Eugen* were hunted down and sunk. The greatest sea hunt of World War II was over.

Erich Raeder

1876–1960

Erich Raeder was the commander-in-chief of the German navy who had the impossible task of trying to educate Hitler in the realities and possibilities of sea power. Steeped in the lessons of naval history, Raeder tried to give his country the balanced navy that it needed. In the poisonous political atmosphere of the Third Reich, no man did more than Raeder to keep the German navy out of politics. For all this, Raeder ended his career in defeat and resignation, and was then sentenced to life imprisonment as a war criminal by the victorious Allies.

Raeder was born in 1876, a teacher's son from Wandsbeck in Hamburg, one of the foremost cradles of Germany's seafaring tradition. Until 1914, he had made his mark as a naval historian rather than as a man of action or professional weapons specialist, both at the Admiralty and at the Kiel Naval Academy. He was chief of staff to Admiral Hipper, commander of the High Seas Fleet's battle-cruiser force, from the outbreak of war until the autumn of 1917, serving at Dogger Bank and Jutland. Raeder ended the war as chief of the Admiralty's Central Department.

The careers of many German officers, army and navy, were jeopardized by unwise involvement in politics in the early years of the Weimar Republic in the 1920s, but Raeder wisely stayed aloof. At the Historial Section of the Admiralty, he produced the first two volumes of the official naval history of World War I, concentrating as these did on high-seas cruiser operations and commerce raiding. This only confirmed his belief that the imperial navy had not paid enough attention to this vital role.

Raeder became commander-in-chief of the German navy in October 1928 largely because of his apolitical views and a sound record of sea time and shore administration. The building of new warships for the small German navy permitted by the Treaty of Versailles had already begun under Raeder's predecessors, who had produced new torpedo-boats and the light cruiser *Emden*. Under Raeder, however, a revolutionary new class of high-seas cruiser was adopted: the 'Deutschland' class with its main armament of six 11-inch guns, warships better known by the originally derisive phrase 'pocket-battleships'.

Raeder naturally welcomed Hitler's accession to

Admiral Raeder (left), pictured with fellow admirals von Trotha (centre) and von Levetzow.

Raeder inspects the ranks on board the *Gneisenau*, one of the two battle-cruisers in his fleet at the outbreak of war in September 1939.

power in 1933 because of the latter's assurances that the German navy would be kept out of politics, and that an expanded fleet was part of the Nazi programme for reviving Germany from the humiliation of Versailles. He made it clear to Hitler that the reconstruction of the navy entailed a long-term building programme to produce a multi-purpose fleet. This would be capable of carrying out surface commerce raiding around the world, and have a powerful submarine force as well as a strong battle-fleet with the support of aircraft-carriers. When complete, the new German navy would be capable of tackling the British navy with confidence. He stressed, however, that this could not be before 1945 at the earliest. All this was embodied in the famous 'Z-Plan' of 1938–9, the product of assurances from Hitler that he had no intention of courting a premature war with the British.

When war broke out in September 1939 all Raeder had out of the total ruin of his methodical programme were the two battle-cruisers *Scharnhorst* and *Gneisenau*, three pocket-battleships, a handful of cruisers and seventeen sea-going U-boats; the first aircraft-carrier and a couple of battleships were launched but not yet completed. For all that,

Raeder initiated a damaging surface-raiding programme, using fleet warships and disguised merchant raiders, until sufficient U-boats could be built to undertake the main weight of commerce warfare.

Raeder's greatest strategic *coup* was his advocacy of the conquest of Norway, whose long coastline gave the German navy bases from which to outflank the British Isles. This boon, unknown to the German fleet in World War I, was largely negated by Hitler's timidity whenever the big ships put to sea. Furthermore, the jealousy of Göring ensured that the navy never got the full support it needed from the Luftwaffe, or aircraft for the only German carrier afloat, *Graf Zeppelin*.

Raeder's last great opportunity was the regular sailing of Allied convoys to Russia, each of them a target well within the range of the warships deployed in Norway. The humiliating failure of the Barents Sea battle of 31 December 1942, however, caused Hitler to order the entire fleet to be scrapped. Raeder resigned rather than issue the orders for this irrevocable step and spent the rest of the war in virtual retirement. Though condemned to life imprisonment at Nuremberg he was released in 1955 and died in 1960.

Pearl Harbor

JAPAN CATCHES THE US NAPPING

In the early morning of Sunday, 7 December 1941, a powerful Japanese aircraft-carrier task force swooped out of the blue on the American naval base at Pearl Harbor in the Hawaiian Islands and wiped out the eight battleships of the US Pacific Fleet. Planned with care and executed with skill and daring, the raid was one of the key events of World War II. It brought the US into the war after months of indecision; for a while, it eclipsed Allied naval power in the Pacific; but in the final analysis it turned out to have been one of the emptiest victories in the history of war at sea.

The main reason why the Americans were surprised at Pearl Harbor was their belief that the Japanese would concentrate on the Philippines, Thailand, and Malaya, and would have their hands full there. In fact the Japanese offensive, when it came, embraced the Dutch East Indies, Hong Kong, Guam, Wake Atoll and the Gilbert Islands as well – with an initial smash at Pearl Harbor to prevent the US Pacific Fleet from intervening.

The Americans had plenty of evidence that Pearl Harbor was vulnerable to surprise attack. During the peacetime manoeuvres in February 1932, an American task force of two carriers launched air strikes at the base after a stealthy, long-distance approach across the Pacific – also early on Sunday morning. They inflicted massive symbolical 'damage', which the Japanese were to make a terrible reality nine years later. But on 7 December 1941 war had not been declared and Admiral Kimmel's battle-fleet was not on the alert. It was still completing a long-term training programme which involved the concentration of the fleet inside Pearl Harbor every weekend. General Short, the land commander, had worries of his own. His biggest headache was the possibility of sabotage by the large Japanese population on Oahu. For that reason the American planes were concentrated on their airfields, rather than safely dispersed to minimize damage from air attack, when the Japanese struck.

The Japanese had all the information that they wanted about the Pearl Harbor base. Admiral Yamamoto, commander-in-chief of the Japanese Combined Fleet, had ordered detailed planning for the attack to begin in January 1941. Intricate models were built to give the air-group commanders the

Japanese aircraft swoop low over Ford Island, part of the Pearl Harbor base, during their surprise attack of 7 December 1941 which brought the US into World War II.

ABOVE USS *West Virginia* (left) and *Arizona* (right) were prime targets for the aerial bombardment; USS *Tennesee* (centre) escaped.

BELOW The stricken USS *California* settles down in the water as her crew escape.

BELOW A6M Zero fighters line up in front of Aichi 'Val' dive-bombers on the deck of the Japanese aircraft-carrier *Akagi* prior to the attack.

most accurate data on the layout of the target. Special torpedoes were devised which could run true in the shallow waters of the anchorage. Air training – level bombing, dive-bombing, and torpedo drops – was carried out in Japanese home waters. Vice-Admiral Nagumo, commander-in-chief of the First Air Fleet, was given the job and he formed a strike force of six carriers – *Zuikaku, Shokaku, Kaga, Akagi, Hiryu,* and *Soryu.* The total force, carriers and escorts, numbered thirty-one warships, and by 22 November they had been concentrated in Tankan Bay, at Etorofu in the Kurile Islands. The carrier force was to be supplemented by a submarine flotilla of sixteen submarines, five of which carried two-man midget submarines, which were intended to penetrate Pearl Harbor.

The strike force sailed from Tankan Bay at 0900 hours on 26 November, and headed due east through storms, fogs, and foul weather, before altering course on its final run-up to the launching-point. Just after midnight on 5–6 December, while the force was on the final leg, Nagumo received the message that the two American carriers, *Lexington* and *Enterprise*, were not in Pearl Harbor with the battleships. After a staff conference Nagumo decided to go ahead with the attack in the hope that the carriers would have reached the target area by the time it went in.

Apart from the American warships in Pearl

Harbor, the Japanese strike-force pilots were briefed to attack two other targets – American air bases on Oahu and the dockyards and oil-storage facilities. Wiping out the American aircraft on the ground would enable the attack to proceed without interruption and blowing up the dockyards and oil tanks would complete the task of neutralizing the Pacific Fleet. Two heavy assault waves were prepared, with a third held in reserve.

At 0630 hours on 7 December the first wave lifted from the decks of Nagumo's six carriers. It comprised fifty 'Kate' bombers armed with armour-piercing bombs, seventy torpedo-carrying 'Kates', fifty-one 'Val' dive-bombers, and forty-three Zero fighters for air cover and ground attack.

Meanwhile, the Japanese submarine attack had got off to a bad start. The US destroyer *Ward* sank one of the midget submarines at 0645 hours after a periscope had been sighted earlier. Admiral Kimmel's duty officer was not alerted until 0725 hours, and, because of congestion on the telephone lines, Kimmel himself had only just started for his office by 0750 hours, when the first bomb crashed down on Ford Island in the middle of the harbour.

An off-duty trainee radar operator, fiddling around with his set, had actually picked up the big 'blip' of the incoming Japanese formation. After considerable difficulty he found an officer and reported the sighting, but it was assumed that these aircraft must be from the US, as a flight of

American bombers was expected that morning. Drowsy preparations for the Sunday morning routine – flag-raising, breakfast, church service – were shattered when Commander Fuchida's first wave swept in and launched its attack. At 0758 hours the message crackled out: 'Air Raid, Pearl Harbor – This is no drill!'

Satisfied that surprise was complete, Fuchida radioed 'Tora-tora-tora!' ('Tiger-tiger-tiger!'), the assault order, at 0750 hours. The dive-bombers hammered the American air bases at Wheeler Field, Hickham Field, Keneohe, and Ewa, and in the wake of the dive-bombers came the strafing Zeros. The torpedo 'Kates' obtained hits on the battleships *West Virginia*, *Arizona*, *Nevada*, *Oklahoma* and *California*. The old target battleship *Utah* was also hit, capsized, and sank. The bombing 'Kates' also hit *Tennessee*, *Arizona*, *Maryland* and *California*.

At about 0825 hours the last planes of the first wave were droning back to their carriers. After the initial shock the Americans reacted quickly and the second wave, arriving an hour later, met a hotter reception from the guns of the surviving warships. USS *Nevada*, the only American battleship which had managed to raise steam and head for the open sea was nevertheless forced to beach rather than sink in mid-channel.

The first wave had done its work well in eliminating the American aircraft and only a hand-ful of planes managed to take off during the two attacks. The second wave retired at about 1000 hours, leaving behind four battleships sunk, one more beached and three crippled. American casual-ties were 2403 men dead and 1176 wounded. Out of a total force of 354 planes, the Japanese lost only nine Zero fighters, fifteen 'Vals' and five 'Kates'.

Nagumo decided against launching a third strike. He refused to order a sweep to search for the missing carriers and the American oil tanks and dockyards survived. His action effectively forced the US navy to rely on aircraft-carriers, and these, ironically, were the weapons which eventually wiped out the Japanese naval supremacy won at Pearl Harbor.

Pearl Harbor was not a unique operation in the annals of naval warfare. The British carrier strike at Taranto in November 1940 had crippled the Italian battle-fleet, although it had not eliminated the Italian navy. However, both actions confirmed the lesson learned in Norway in April 1940 that the battleship could only play its traditional role if it was provided with an 'air umbrella' by carriers.

Pearl Harbor was more than a battle. The fact that the attack was carried out while the two nations were at peace made it a military phenomenon, like Bunker Hill, the bombardment of Fort Sumter, and the sinking of the *Lusitania*. It forced the US into war and stiffened that country's determination. The effect of the Pearl Harbor attack upon American morale was, in the final analysis, a boon for the Allies which more than compensated for the material damage suffered.

Isoroku Yamamoto

1884–1943

Admiral Isoroku Yamamoto believed that a protracted war would not favour Japan's chances of victory, and it was this thinking which inspired Pearl Harbor.

It was inevitable that Admiral Isoroku Yamamoto, commander-in-chief of Japan's Combined Fleet, should immediately be branded as America's 'Public Enemy Number One' in the traumatic aftermath of his attack on Pearl Harbor – inevitable, but deeply ironic. No other Japanese military or naval commander had done more to oppose Japan's drift towards war with the US, a country which Yamamoto held in the highest respect as an enemy whom Japan could never hope to beat in a protracted war. It was precisely this belief which framed the Pearl Harbor attack and Yamamoto's subsequent attempts to destroy the US Pacific Fleet.

He had been born Isoroku Katano, son of a village schoolmaster of remote samurai descent, in 1884, and grew up in the perplexing but exciting years of the Meiji Restoration (Japan's rejection of traditional isolation and her energetic transformation into a modern world power). One of the most significant elements in this transformation was the creation of a modern navy on the best European models.

Isoroku entered the Naval Academy in 1900. When the Russo-Japanese War broke out in 1904 he was appointed ensign in the cruiser *Nisshin* and served at Tsushima, suffering a leg wound and losing two fingers. In 1914, already a respected figure in his home district, Isoroku was adopted by the Yamamoto family and took their name.

Yamamoto's connection with the US began in 1917 when the Japanese navy sent him to Harvard for a two-year university course. He became a devotee of aviation and in 1923 became executive officer of the new Japanese naval aviation school at Kasumigaura. This was one of the most decisive appointments of his career. Learning to fly himself, Yamamoto championed the development of the aircraft-carrier as a vital extension of the battle-fleet's hitting-power.

Yamamoto's rise was rapid. After two years as naval attaché in Washington he was promoted rear-admiral in 1930, attended the London Naval Conference as a delegate, and was appointed commander of the First Air Fleet. With the rank of vice-admiral he headed the Japanese delegation to the second London Naval Conference in 1934 and was the prime mover behind Japan's rejection of any further treaty limitations on the size of her fleet.

Yamamoto opposed Japan's military alliance with the Axis powers in 1938, and his 'pro-American' leanings earned him the hatred of the powerful and much-feared secret Black Dragon Society. His appointment as commander-in-chief of the Combined Fleet in August 1939 was richly deserved, but was also partly a move to save him from assassination.

Faced with the inevitability of war with the US, Yamamoto's forecast was bleak. 'I shall run wild for the first six months', he said, 'but have utterly no confidence in the second or third years.' Yamamoto knew that the only chance of a favourable peace for Japan was the earliest possible destruction of the US Pacific Fleet, which Pearl Harbor failed to achieve.

Shocked by Doolittle's carrier-borne raid on Tokyo in April 1942, Yamamoto planned the campaign to seize Midway and force a decisive fleet action with the remnants of the US Pacific Fleet. His assumption that the Americans would follow a set pattern of reactions was dangerous, however, and his belief that the Japanese forces would enjoy complete surprise was fatal. It was Yamamoto's own extensive deployment of the Combined Fleet which made it impossible to reverse the loss of the four carriers at Midway, retrieve the situation and go on to destroy the American fleet.

Yamamoto hoped that the ensuing Guadalcanal campaign would give the Japanese fleet the chance it had missed at Midway, but this murderous battle of attrition merely continued the destruction of the Combined Fleet. Most serious of all was the steady loss of the superb aircrews on which Japanese naval supremacy depended.

After the land defeats in New Guinea and the Solomons, Yamamoto prepared a massive naval air counter-strike – 'Operation I' – to contain the Allied advance in the South-West Pacific. Again, Japanese air losses were heavier than could be afforded, and Yamamoto was only deceiving himself when he claimed that 'Operation I' was achieving its object.

Yamamoto did not live long enough to realize his failure. In April 1943 American intelligence discovered the details of a flight Yamamoto would be making from Rabaul to Bougainville; his aircraft was ambushed by US fighters and shot down. Yamamoto proved to be an irreplaceable war leader. His death did nothing to diminish the steadily growing catalogue of Japanese defeats, and relieved the Allied commanders in the Pacific of their most formidable opponent.

The Sinking of
Repulse and *Prince of Wales*

ADMIRALTY BLUNDER IN THE FAR EAST

The catastrophic defeats inflicted on Britain by Japan in 1941–2 – Hong Kong, Malaya, Singapore, Burma – were far more than the latest in a long line of military setbacks for the Allies. These defeats helped shatter the myth of Britain's invincibility as an imperial power, and brought forward the dissolution of the British Empire. The first of these defeats was at the expense of the Royal Navy, for over a hundred years the prime instrument and enduring symbol of Britain's imperial might. This was the sinking by Japanese air attacks of the battleship *Prince of Wales* and the battle-cruiser *Repulse* on 10 December 1941. Never before had aircraft succeeded in sinking battleships at sea. It seemed the most bitter of ironies that the British, whose Fleet Air Arm had been demonstrating the vulnerability of the battleship since Taranto thirteen months before, should expose two of their own capital ships to such a fate at this stage of the war.

Though there is a case for putting most of the blame on Winston Churchill, there is no single 'reason why' *Repulse* and *Prince of Wales* went to court disaster off the Malayan coast. Before the war and in 1939–41, Churchill firmly believed that Japan had no intention of going to war with Britain and the US, that is until Japanese intentions became apparent in the late summer of 1941. He was certainly not alone in believing that Japan's armed forces were of indifferent quality, a delusion fondly held by many high-ranking British and American servicemen until it was exposed to the reality of war. But even if Churchill had understood Japan's military ambitions, there was little he could have done to combat them. The naval demands of British home waters, the Atlantic and the Mediterranean would still have prevented the British from setting up a powerful eastern fleet, with carrier-borne as well as shore-based air cover in time to meet the Japanese assault of December 1941.

When in the second half of 1941 the time came to grasp the nettle and commence the reinforcement of the Far East, Churchill argued from the experience of the Royal Navy in home waters. There the handful of German capital ships – *Scharnhorst* and *Gneisenau*, *Bismarck* and *Tirpitz* – had tied down large number of British warships ever since the outbreak of war. Churchill believed that the British could use this inhibiting factor against the Japanese by sending a small number of heavy warships out to Singapore as a deterrent to Japan's naval ambitions. Given time, this deterrent force would act as the nucleus for a full-blown Far East Fleet as soon as further reinforcements could be spared. But to be a genuine deterrent it must, Churchill argued, include one of the newest British battleships of the 'King George V' class.

The Admiralty tried in vain to persuade Churchill that the parallel was false. Germany's warships

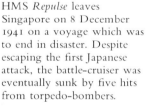

HMS *Repulse* leaves Singapore on 8 December 1941 on a voyage which was to end in disaster. Despite escaping the first Japanese attack, the battle-cruiser was eventually sunk by five hits from torpedo-bombers.

were a deterrent because, if unwatched, they could break out into the Atlantic and run amok on the British convoy routes. But the idea of sending battleships to the Far East was not to threaten Japan with a similar breakout into the Pacific: it was to ensure the defence of Malaya and Singapore. For this a larger force of older battleships would be more appropriate, leaving all three of the 'King George Vs' in home waters to contain the German capital ships. In any event, no battle-fleet of any size could be sent east without the protection of at least one aircraft-carrier.

Though Churchill overruled the Admiralty and got his way, he had to accept a compromise. The decision (20 October 1941) laid down that the 'King George V' battleship chosen (*Prince of Wales*) should proceed no further than Cape Town until the current situation had been assessed and a final decision on her destination taken in London. The orders for the battle-cruiser *Repulse*, already on her way to join the East Indies station in Ceylon, were allowed to stand.

The choice of commanding admiral for this new eastern fleet had already been made by the time of the 20 October discussion over *Prince of Wales*. Sir Dudley Pound, the First Sea Lord, had selected the vice-chief of the naval staff, Vice-Admiral Sir Tom Phillips. This was a particularly fateful appointment because Phillips, having spent the entire war in Whitehall, had no experience of modern naval warfare. He had not been to sea since 1939, and had no experience of air attack. Moreover, he believed that the firepower carried by a battleship was enough to 'see off' any air attack, and he held to his views with a dogged obstinacy which delighted Churchill, who shared Phillips's belief and certainly made no objection to his new appointment.

Phillips sailed from the Clyde in *Prince of Wales*, with the destroyers *Electra* and *Express*, on 25

October 1941, but the battleship was not even halfway to Cape Town when the first note of doom sounded from across the Atlantic. On 3 November the new carrier *Indomitable*, completing her working-up in the West Indies before heading east to join Phillips's command, ran aground and was severely damaged. As there was no other carrier to send – the small and aging *Hermes*, in the Indian Ocean, was scheduled for refit in South Africa – this changed matters completely.

Though Churchill and the Admiralty still hoped that *Repulse* and *Prince of Wales* would help deter Japan from going to war, it would now hardly be possible for the warships to use Singapore as a permanent base if war did, in fact, break out. On 16 November *Prince of Wales* arrived at Cape Town and Phillips paid a flying visit to Field-Marshal Smuts in Pretoria. Notifying Churchill of the visit by cable, Smuts added his own fears about the enormous distance between the Americans in the Pacific and the new British force in Singapore, both of which could be defeated in turn by the Japanese in between them. His cable included the immortal words: '*If the Japanese are really nippy there is here an opening for a first-class disaster.*'

Churchill reacted to this warning from his old friend not by recalling *Prince of Wales* but by agreeing with Pound that Phillips and his 'Force Z' must regard Singapore as a springboard for cruising further to the east. *Prince of Wales* duly went on to Singapore via Colombo, arriving on 2 December with *Repulse*, *Electra*, *Express* and the destroyers *Jupiter* and *Encounter* from the Mediterranean. Even before Force Z arrived at Singapore, Phillips was being advised by the Admiralty to keep his ships there as briefly as possible. Though never formally debated and certainly not ordered before the Japanese struck, a move of Force Z to northern Australia was belatedly agreed between Churchill and Pound in Whitehall. *Repulse* had actually sailed for a visit to Port Darwin before she was recalled, on 6 December, by ominous news. American air reconnaissance from the Philippines had sighted a Japanese troop convoy at sea, heading straight for the Malayan coast.

This was precisely the sort of Japanese move which Force Z had been sent east to deter. If, in the last forty-eight hours of peace, *Repulse* and *Prince of Wales* had raced north from Singapore and placed themselves in the path of the Japanese invasion fleet (for so it was), Malaya could well have been saved. But the American sighting could not have been made at a more inopportune moment. Phillips was actually in Manila, whither he had flown to confer with the Americans. *Repulse* was at sea with two destroyers, heading for Australia. By the time both Phillips and *Repulse* had returned to Singapore on the 7th, the weather over the Gulf of Siam had deteriorated and no further accurate evidence of the Japanese movements could be gleaned. Naturally unwilling to provoke war by precipitate action,

The battleship *Prince of Wales* was the flagship of Vice-Admiral Sir Tom Phillips. He went down with his ship.

Phillips decided to wait for a clearer picture on the following day.

The news on the 8th was catastrophic: the US battle-fleet wiped out in Pearl Harbor; Japanese attacks on the Philippines and Hong Kong; Japanese landings at Singora and Kota Bharu from the Gulf of Siam; and, most ominous of all, a bombing raid on Singapore itself. So far from being 'deterred' by the news of *Prince of Wales*'s arrival, the Japanese had reinforced their air strength in southern Indo-china to an awesome total of ninety-nine bombers, thirty-six fighters and six reconnaissance aircraft, all reserved to cover the invasion of Malaya.

Though British intelligence estimates of the Japanese air strength were surprisingly accurate, it was not realized that the Japanese Naval Air Force was highly trained in torpedo attacks against shipping, and this was soon to prove one of the most disastrous of all the British miscalculations.

At 1230 hours on the 8th, Phillips called a conference of his officers aboard the flagship. He outlined the three choices open to Force Z: stay in Singapore, retreat to the east, or head north into the Gulf of Siam and try to disrupt the Japanese landings. Hazardous though it undoubtedly was, the third choice at least offered a chance of joining in the defence of Malaya. Phillips sailed at 1730 hours with *Repulse*, *Prince of Wales*, *Electra*, *Express*, and the destroyers *Vampire* and *Tenedos* of the Singapore naval force.

Having learned that the Japanese had laid mines across the direct route north out of Singapore, Phillips planned a wide detour to the north-east, north, and finally west to arrive off Singora around 0600 on the 10th, when RAF fighter cover was promised. Early on the 9th, however, he learned that the fighter cover would not be available. Phillips nevertheless decided to continue, provided that Force Z was not sighted by the Japanese during the 9th.

In fact the British force was spotted twice during the run north on the 9th: by the Japanese submarine *I-65* early in the afternoon and by three Japanese seaplanes at dusk. This persuaded Phillips that he had lost all chance of surprise, and at 2015 hours he reversed course to head back to Singapore having already detached *Tenedos*, which was running low on fuel.

Shortly before midnight on the 9th Phillips received an 'Immediate' signal from his chief-of-staff in Singapore reporting a Japanese landing at Kuantan, 240km (150 miles) north of Singapore. Phillips immediately decided to head south-west and attack this landing-force. He has been criticized for not requesting fighter cover over Kuantan, but he must have been aware that the only fighters in Malaya were antiquated Brewster Buffalo biplanes, which were no match for Japanese Mark 22 'Nell' bombers. As a result the British warships were without fighter protection when the Japanese bombers appeared the following morning.

Phillips's squadron had been sighted by a second Japanese submarine, *I-58*, but her signal reporting the change of course towards Kuantan did not get through. As a result the bombers and torpedo aircraft of the '*Genzan*', '*Mihoro*' and '*Kanoya*' attack groups missed Force Z on their first long sweep to the south and a reconnaissance aircraft did not locate the British ships until 2215. By this time Phillips had checked the beaches off Kuantan, found that the reported 'invasion' was a false alarm, and was heading east to return to Singapore.

The Japanese onslaught, carried out in *ad hoc* fashion as each formation appeared on the scene, fell into two main attacks: a first attack from about 1100 hours to noon, a twenty-minute lull, then a second attack from 1223 to about 1245. *Repulse*, having escaped virtually unscathed from the first attack, was overwhelmed by five torpedo hits in the second; *Prince of Wales*, crippled in the first attack, suffered six torpedo hits all told. *Repulse* went down at 1233 and *Prince of Wales* at 1320 hours, the combined loss of life being 840 officers and men. The action was a complete triumph for the Japanese air torpedo attack: only three torpedo aircraft and no bombers were shot down.

Amongst the casualties was Admiral Phillips, who went down with his ship. Throughout the action he had continued to display his lack of experience, first trying to manoeuvre his fleet as a unit instead of instantly releasing his ships to take independent action, then failing to order smoke-screens. The main mistake, however, had been made some time before, in exposing valuable ships to the might of Japanese naval air power, with no air cover of their own. The result of the action had been a foregone conclusion from that moment on.

Seamen abandon the sinking *Prince of Wales* after being hit by six torpedoes. The Japanese victory was complete, with only three aircraft lost.

Battle of the Atlantic

THE BITTER STRUGGLE AGAINST THE U-BOAT

The convoy routes most frequently used in the Atlantic. Note the large danger areas beyond the limits of the escorts' ranges. From the end of 1941 convoys had continuous escorts and Iceland was used as a refuelling base.

The battle of the Atlantic – the campaign fought out around the Atlantic convoys mainly between the U-boat fleet of Nazi Germany and the sea and air escorts – received its name from Winston Churchill in a directive issued on 6 March 1941. The battle had been in progress since the first day of World War II when the passenger liner *Athenia* was torpedoed and sunk by the submarine *U-30*. Its intensity was to increase steadily.

The hostilities had begun on quite a small scale because Hitler had prematurely involved Germany in war with Britain and France. Instead of 250 U-boats as planned, there were only twenty-seven ocean-going and thirty of the coastal type in commission. The Allies had not entirely forgotten the lessons of World War I and a convoy system had been immediately established – albeit with a totally inadequate number of escorts. But these few U-boats were able to find all the targets they needed among the ships which sailed independently. One hundred and twenty-four ships had been sunk by the end of March 1940, when all U-boats were recalled to take part in the invasion of Norway, and there was a lull in hostilities until June.

When France was overrun and a submarine base was established at Lorient, the steadily growing U-boat fleet posed a mortal threat to Allied shipping and the vital life-line between Britain and America. U-boats could now probe further out into the ocean and remain longer on patrol. They could thus operate beyond the point where outward convoys were dispersed and homeward-bound convoys were met by their escorts. This forced the extension of escort protection from longitude 15 degrees west to 17 degrees west – the first move of a continual spread westwards of the battle until ships were eventually to sail in escorted convoys throughout their voyages.

U-boat captains had soon discovered that, with their low silhouette, they ran small risk of being sighted on the surface at night and there was no shipborne radar available to the escorts as yet. They had further learned that the British submarine detector – the sonar ranging device ASDIC – could only detect them when submerged. Opposed by two or three slow sloops or corvettes, which were all that could be provided at that time, convoys held few terrors for them.

They took to attacking by night with an impunity made almost total by the new tactics of gathering in packs. A pack would be spread across the anticipated route of a convoy. The first boat to make contact would signal U-boat headquarters, which would transmit instructions to the remainder to bring them simultaneously into the attack. The few slow escorts would soon be overextended by the intensity of the attack and reduced to picking up survivors while ships sank all around them.

Such disasters overtook two homeward-bound

Atlantic Ocean

Pacific Ocean

Sydney
Halifax

SOUTH AMERICA

AFRICA

MALTA

Liverpool
Gibraltar

Freetown

Cape Town

PRINCIPAL CONVOY ROUTES:
SEPT. 1939 TO MAY 1940
JUNE 1940 TO MID-MARCH 1941
LIMITS OF CLOSE SUPPORT FOR CONVOYS:
① SOUTHBOUND – 47°N.
② EASTBOUND – 56°W. & 53·5°W.
③ WESTBOUND – 15°W. (SEPT. 1939 TO JUNE 1940).
– 17°W. (JULY 1940 TO OCT. 1940).
– 19°W. (OCT. 1940 TO APRIL 1941).
OPERATIONAL LIMITS OF SHORE-BASED AIRCRAFT:
JUNE 1940 TO MARCH 1941
ANTI-U-BOAT AIR PATROLS: JUNE 1940 TO MARCH 1941.
NORTH SEA AIR PATROLS

convoys, in particular, in October 1940. Convoy SC7 lost seventeen out of thirty ships in two nights; HX79, following, lost fourteen in a single night. The U-boats escaped unscathed. Fortunately for the British the number of U-boats available was still too small for attacks on such a scale to be kept up continually throughout the winter months.

In November the pocket-battleship *Admiral Scheer* intervened briefly in the battle of the Atlantic. Breaking out past Iceland she encountered Convoy HX84 whose solitary escort, the armed merchant cruiser *Jervis Bay*, gallantly engaged her in hopelessly unequal combat, delaying the *Scheer* long enough for the convoy to scatter. By the time the *Jervis Bay* had been destroyed, the convoy was so scattered that only five out of the thirty-seven ships could be caught and sunk.

Meanwhile Germany's two battle-cruisers, *Scharnhorst* and *Gneisenau*, had also reached the Atlantic. Avoiding escorted convoys, they sank a total of twenty-one ships from convoys which had been dispersed. Then they sailed for Brest. It was intended that they should await the arrival in the Atlantic of the splendid new battleship *Bismarck* and the cruiser *Prinz Eugen*. Combined, these would form a formidable force. In the event, the two latter ships were located as they passed through the Denmark Straits and after a long running battle the *Bismarck* was sunk by the British Home Fleet. *Prinz Eugen* evaded her pursuers and later reached Brest.

With the coming of spring 1941 the number of U-boats increased as the building programme got fully under way. So also did the number and quality of the convoy escorts, however, and the experienced U-boat commanders found that their period of unbroken success had ended.

The strength and organization of the British Western Approaches Command, directly responsible for the Atlantic convoys, were being constantly improved under the leadership of Admiral Sir Percy Noble. Destroyers, released from defensive duties as the likelihood of a German invasion attempt receded, and the many new 'Flower'-class

ABOVE A convoy is viewed from the anti-aircraft position of an escort. Convoys proceeded at speeds of between 7 and 11 knots and some numbered up to 100 ships.

BELOW A convoy tanker goes down.

This German coastal U-boat was operationally employed around Britain's east coast and in the Channel to disrupt commercial sea traffic.

corvettes, were being welded into trained groups. Radio to improve communications and cohesion, and primitive radar, to give some degree of night 'vision', were installed. Commanders were becoming more experienced and competent.

Thus it was that in one week in March the careers of three German U-boat aces were brought to an end. Günther Prien – who had so skilfully penetrated Scapa Flow in October 1939 to sink *Royal Oak* – and Joachim Schepke went down with their craft. Otto Kretschmer and his crew of *U-99* were taken prisoner.

Throughout 1941 fortune favoured one side and then the other. The main battle area shifted as Dönitz – the commander of the U-boat fleet – sought for a weak link in the convoy chains, either the transatlantic system or that running north and south between Sierra Leone and Britain. In September he found it – in the western section of the Transatlantic route. A convoy of sixty-three ships lost sixteen to the U-boat 'wolf packs'. But before Dönitz could take full advantage of the situation he was ordered – against his strong protests – to send many of his operational boats to the Mediterranean and the approaches to Gibraltar. Although these achieved some notable successes, including the sinking of *Ark Royal*, the shift gave the British a slight respite during which to reorganize.

The new deployment of the U-boats brought a particularly severe threat to the convoys running between Gibraltar and Britain. To combat this, an escort group commanded and trained by Commander F.J. Walker, who was to become the most feared enemy of U-boats, was formed; and the first of a new type of warship – the auxiliary (or escort) aircraft-carrier *Audacity*, operating six Grumman Martlet fighter planes – came into action.

With Walker's group reinforced for part of the voyage by several destroyers and *Audacity*, Convoy HG 76 left Gibraltar in December 1941. From the 16th to the 22nd a running fight developed round the convoy in which four U-boats and two German Condor aircraft were destroyed and others damaged while only two ships of the convoy were torpedoed. Though *Audacity* and one of Walker's escorts were sunk, this was adjudged by both sides to be a notable victory for the escorts. One of the chief lessons learned was the immense advantage acquired by a convoy which had its own close air escort even when, as on this occasion, the aircraft were not equipped with weapons lethal to a submarine. A building programme for a number of escort carriers was under way in Britain and the US, and the products of this programme were to play a vital part in the defeat of the U-boats.

With the improved equipment, new methods

and greater expertise of the escorts at this time, and, on the other hand, the continuing expansion of the U-boat fleet, the year 1942 would have seen the struggle reach its decisive peak. But a transformation was brought about by the entry of the US into the war.

A state of undeclared, though limited, war between Germany and the US had in fact been in existence since July 1941 when the US navy had begun to escort convoys to the American garrison in Iceland – convoys to which Allied merchant ships might attach themselves. Two months later American destroyers were escorting transatlantic convoys over the western part of the route. These operations resulted in an indecisive skirmish between the USS *Greer* and a U-boat, and in the torpedoing of the destroyers *Kearney* and *Reuben James*, the latter being lost with most of her crew. In spite of this state of affairs Hitler had shrunk from provoking the US into full-scale hostilities by deploying U-boats along the shipping routes of the American east coast. But now, suddenly, this vast shipping traffic, carrying the oil, cotton, sugar, iron, steel and bauxite vital to the British war effort, was exposed, completely unprotected, to U-boat attack.

In spite of full knowledge of British experience in two wars which had so convincingly proved that convoy was the only effective form of defence for merchant ships, the American navy was neither ready to implement such a system nor convinced of its necessity. Dönitz took immediate advantage and over the next six months his U-boats caused havoc along the routes between the Caribbean and New York. In June 1942, no less than 121 ships were sunk. In the whole six months American ships and aircraft on patrol accounted for only four U-boats.

At last at the end of June the Americans were finally able to establish a convoy system along the whole route. Sinkings of merchantmen fell away to almost nothing and four U-boats were destroyed in the area during July. Dönitz switched the U-boats back to the transatlantic convoys, around which the decisive final scene of the battle was to be played out.

In the Atlantic the majority of the escorts had been increasing in quantity and in efficiency. The little 'Flower'-class, mass-produced corvettes, had been coming to sea in large numbers, making up for their low speed of 14 knots (less than that of a surfaced U-boat) by their seaworthiness and ubiquity. They and their bigger sisters, the destroyers and sloops, were being fitted with a war-winning British development – the 10-cm radar – which was to stultify the U-boat tactics of surface attack by night.

Destroyer escorts were being fitted with another British-produced device – the High-Frequency Direction Finder – which betrayed the bearing of any U-boat transmitting to headquarters, and so often enabled the assembly of a wolf pack to be nipped in the bud. With improved ASDIC sets and depth charges, escorts were able to hunt U-boats at the great depths to which they could descend and at which they had been previously immune from attack.

But most crucial to the outcome of the battle of the Atlantic was the absence of air escort in the mid-Atlantic 'black gap'. The remedy existed in the shape of Liberator aircraft adapted for very long-range operation (VLR); but priority was given to RAF Bomber Command for the bombing offensive on Germany, and few were being allotted to Coastal Command – a mere ten by the end of 1942.

So in the 'black gap' even well-equipped convoys

Many merchant vessels were pressed into wartime British service, as was this depth-charge-armed trawler pictured in action.

ABOVE A convoy is seen from the bridge of a World War I-vintage US-built destroyer in Royal Navy service.

RIGHT British officers approach *U-570* to take possession after the submarine surrendered to a Hudson aircraft.

were sometimes assailed by wolf packs, which, though they might be made to pay heavily, still managed to sink large numbers of ships. Throughout the winter the battle raged inconclusively; but in March 1943 three convoys were set upon and massacred, losing thirty-four ships between them. But steps which were to make this the last of the U-boats' triumphs were already being taken. Support Groups under experienced commanders such as Captain Walker had been formed, which could be sent to reinforce the escorts of a convoy under threat of attack.

There was to be one final, massive confrontation before a decision was reached. It took place about the slow outward-bound Convoy ONS5 whose escorts fought a running battle from 29 April to 6 May 1943. At first, in stormy weather which favoured the swarm of U-boats which gathered around, twelve ships of the convoy were torpedoed and sunk. Then storm gave way to calm; the convoy became shrouded in thick fog, transferring the advantage of invisibility to the radar-fitted escorts. In quick succession five U-boats were sent to the bottom; others, attempting to attack, were again and again driven off and damaged. Another was destroyed by an aircraft of the Royal Canadian Air Force and in addition, two U-boats racing to intercept the convoy collided and sank.

Dönitz called off his pack; but it was the loss both of tactical superiority and morale by the U-boat commanders, when they returned to attack some homeward-bound convoys during May, which convinced him that the battle of the Atlantic was lost. During that month no less than forty-one of Dönitz's boats were destroyed, twenty-five of them by the sea and air escorts of the convoys. Dönitz therefore decided to recall his whole fleet from the convoy routes.

Karl Dönitz

1891–1980

Though he ended World War II as grand admiral and *Führer*, head of the German navy and state, Karl Dönitz is almost certain to go down in history as the German officer who came closest to defeating Britain when commanding the U-boat force of the Third Reich. In contrast to his rival Göring, who commanded the Luftwaffe, Dönitz was a master of his profession and fully understood its potential.

Born in 1891, Dönitz entered World War I as a lieutenant in the light cruiser *Breslau* when she made her epic escape from the western Mediterranean, with the battle-cruiser *Goeben*, to Constantinople. Later in the war he entered the submarine service and was commanding *U-68* when she was sunk in the Mediterranean on 4 October 1918. At the time, *U-68* was carrying out a joint attack with *U-48* against a convoy. Though not the inventor of the U-boat wolf-pack technique, Dönitz was one of the first to put it into practice and, within twenty-five years, he was to direct it with terrible effect.

Captured with the other survivors, Dönitz spent the last weeks of the war in British captivity and in the following summer returned to Germany on the grounds of ill-health. Though his country was banned from adding U-boats to the small coastal navy permitted by the Treaty of Versailles, Dönitz never lost his faith that one day the U-boat arm would be rebuilt. He spent the 1930s training future submariners under cover of the official anti-submarine school.

In June 1935, after Hitler had publicly repudiated the restrictions of Versailles, the new U-boat arm began its official existence. The preparatory work of Dönitz was acknowledged by his appointment as officer commanding U-boats. The U-boat fleet built under the aegis of Dönitz between 1935–9 would probably have been far more ambitious if Grand-Admiral Raeder, commander-in-chief of the navy, had been a submariner himself instead of a High Seas Fleet staff officer. Dönitz set the ideal figure of U-boats needed for a future war with Britain at 267, but only 126 were envisaged in Raeder's 'Z-Plan' of 1938–9. This aimed at the completion by 1944–5 of a balanced German fleet capable of tackling the Royal Navy with confidence. In the summer of 1939 Raeder belatedly agreed to raise the 'Z-Plan' U-boat total to 300, but it was far too late. Germany entered World War II with a mere fifty-seven U-boats, of which only twenty-seven were ocean-going, though the thirty

Admiral of the Fleet Karl Dönitz, pictured at Flensburg after his elevation to become the Third Reich's last head of state on the death of Adolf Hitler.

coastal vessels could operate in the North Sea and British coastal waters.

Over the first eleven months of the war U-boat construction was almost exactly matched by U-boat losses, but the U-boat arm received many benefits in this period. For example, its torpedoes were provided with efficient pistols (in the opening months of the war many German torpedoes had failed to explode on contact). Combat experience showed up the most important weakness of Britain's ASDIC submarine-detector, which was that it was unable to locate submarines travelling on the surface. Above all, the fall of France gave Dönitz the unique opportunity of basing his U-boat force on the Atlantic ports of occupied France, with a clear run out to the patrol areas across Britain's North Atlantic convoy lifeline. He set up his headquarters at Lorient in August 1940.

The battle of the Atlantic began in earnest in September–October 1940. The still-small U-boat force put into effect Dönitz's speciality, the surfaced night attack which avoided the risk of detection by the convoy escorts' ASDIC. Results were both immediate and dramatic. In October 1940, eight U-boats sank sixty-three ships totalling 352,407 tons within the month.

Despite this initial success, Dönitz was never able to concentrate his entire forces on the vital North Atlantic battle zone for long. As the war expanded U-boats were constantly withdrawn from the Atlantic, some to the Mediterranean and some to the Arctic to strike at the Allied convoys to Russia. Furthermore the British and Americans steadily perfected a system of air/sea cooperation, bridging the former 'black gap' in the central Atlantic where once the U-boats had ruled supreme.

The New Year of 1943 carried Dönitz to the supreme rank of grand-admiral when Raeder resigned rather than carry out Hitler's enraged order to scrap the battle-fleet after the Barents Sea fiasco. A practised and subtle courtier, Dönitz soon persuaded Hitler that the surface fleet still had a role to play, while in March 1943 the U-boat force achieved its highest level of sinkings in the war. In May, however, U-boat losses reached a point which Dönitz accepted as suicidal for a continuation of the offensive, and the surviving U-boats were withdrawn. Though revolutionary new U-boats capable of reversing the course of the war at sea were produced in the last year of the war, not nearly enough were completed to have any worthwhile effect. Finally, the Allied liberation of France robbed Dönitz of his invaluable Atlantic bases.

Dönitz's last naval 'campaign' of the war was a splendid achievement: the evacuation by sea of some two million refugees from East Prussia and the eastern Baltic before the remorseless advance of the Red Army. Hitler formally nominated Dönitz as the next head of state before committing suicide on 30 April 1945. The new *Führer* tried to spin out the surrender talks in order to allow as many servicemen and refugees as possible to escape to the West, but this was cut short by the unconditional surrender on Lüneberg Heath on 3 May. Dönitz and a rump government continued to function in Flensburg, guarded by armed German troops, until outraged Russian pressure led to their arrest by the British on 23 May. At Nuremberg Dönitz received the surprisingly light sentence of ten years (compared with the life sentence meted out to Raeder), served his time in Spandau and was released in 1956. He died in 1980.

From left to right, Albert Speer, Dönitz and Colonel-General Jodl after their arrest by the Allies. It is as a naval commander rather than as a politician that Dönitz will be remembered.

The Channel Dash

RED FACES AT THE ADMIRALTY

In early 1942 Britain's navy was fighting a three-ocean war. The Mediterranean campaign was still being fought, and battleships and carriers had been sent to the Far East to hold the Japanese advance. Only three battleships and a carrier could be spared for the Home Fleet, the main task of which was the blocking of any German attempt to send heavy ships against the Atlantic convoys. In this endeavour, the initiative lay with the Germans. They not only had ships which could be sent through northern waters, but also a strong force at Brest.

This French Atlantic port contained the fast battleships *Scharnhorst* and *Gneisenau*, and the cruiser *Prinz Eugen*. Because the British did not have sufficient ships to cover this force, it was attacked by bomber aircraft almost every night. In 300 raids the RAF flattened the town, but hit the ships only three times. However, the Germans realized that one day the bombers might cause serious damage. The German naval staff were in favour of sending the ships back into the Atlantic. Knowing how much of Britain's strength had been diverted to the Indian Ocean, the staff realized that there could be no better time for attacks by surface warships on the vital British convoys.

Hitler, however, thought differently. For some weeks he had been convinced, quite wrongly, that the Allies intended to invade Scandinavia. He therefore ordered the transfer of the ships from Brest to Norway. He insisted that, given surprise, it would be possible to send the ships through the English Channel. His naval staff were less optimistic, but preferred this route because the alternative, to the north of Scotland, seemed even less inviting.

The final plan for the 'Channel Dash' specified departure at nightfall. This would enable the ships to leave undetected, but it meant a daylight passage past Dover. The sortie was planned for 11 February, as it promised a moonless night and a strong spring tide. This tide would bring the ships' speed up to 30 knots and, by raising the water level, would marginally reduce the danger from mines.

The British Admiralty, as early as 2 February, had issued a warning to local commanders, that the passage of the German ships through the Channel was imminent. Even without secret intelligence reports, the activity of German minesweepers in the Channel, sweeping and buoying a route for high-speed ships, would have been sufficient indication of what was planned. However, there seemed little that the Admiralty could do. It would have been risky to bring the battleships down from their base at Scapa Flow to fight an action within easy range of German bomber bases, and such a move might have allowed other German units to slip into the Atlantic, through the northern passages. As only one modern submarine was available, mines, aircraft, and perhaps torpedo craft seemed the only practicable counter-measures.

The German ships had been inactive for months, so for a week preceding the breakout they ran trials near Brest, closely escorted by fighter aircraft. On 11 February, delayed three hours by an air raid, they left late at night. The first British air-patrol line, off Brest, was maintained by a single aircraft, but its radar failed shortly before the ships left harbour. A second patrol line, off Ushant, failed to sight the Germans for the same reason and, to make matters worse, this failure was not reported to the naval authorities. A third patrol line, off Le Havre, was never in radar range of the German units. Finally, well into the morning of 12 February, three Spitfires sighted the heavy ships, with their strong escort of destroyers, minesweepers, motor torpedo-

Despite sustaining serious damage from two mines, the battleship *Scharnhorst* (shown here) survived the Channel Dash. Although *Gneisenau* also made it home, she never returned to service.

Fairey Swordfish torpedo-bombers were deployed against the German battleships, but all six aircraft were shot down without causing any damage.

boats, and fighters. However, it was not until the Spitfires landed that they reported what they had seen. By then it was nearly midday, and the Germans had almost reached the Straits of Dover.

Instead, therefore, of the planned series of coordinated attacks, the British had to send in whatever ships and aircraft could be made ready in time. Coastal guns and motor torpedo-boats scored no hits. Then, six Swordfish torpedo bombers attacked, but they were shot down by gunfire and fighters before they could do any damage. The leader of this ill-fated attack, Lieutenant-Commander Esmonde, was awarded a posthumous Victoria Cross for the action.

By 1430 hours the Germans had arrived unscathed off the Dutch coast, and were steaming at full speed towards the German bases. Some days before, British aircraft had dropped mines in these waters and *Scharnhorst* struck one of these, but after stopping for some minutes, she was able to continue at 25 knots. The next attack came from six old destroyers, which were despatched from Harwich. These pressed home their attack, through heavy gunfire, but the Germans were able to evade all their torpedoes. One destroyer, HMS *Worcester*, was badly damaged by gunfire from *Prinz Eugen*, but managed to crawl home. After this attack, the battle was left to the RAF.

However, by 1942, the RAF had already devoted most of its offensive strength to night bombing and neither by technique nor training was

it suited for attacks on warships at sea. It had a few torpedo bombers, but torpedoes were not readily available for all of them. Its bombers, designed for high-level bombing, were confronted on this day by low cloud, and navigational shortcomings meant that most of its aircraft never found the target. Those that did made lone attacks, instead of the mass attacks which were needed to penetrate the strong defence. When night fell the air attacks ceased, having achieved nothing.

After dark *Gneisenau* struck a mine, but was able to continue. Soon afterwards *Scharnhorst* struck a second mine which seriously damaged her, but she was able to reach the River Elbe. The British knew nothing of the mine damage, so the apparently unscathed passage of the German ships, within sight of the English coast, was a great propaganda victory for Germany. Even the British press, which had loyally supported the government through much more serious setbacks, condemned the evident mismanagement of the British counter-measures. Nevertheless, although the Germans had won a tactical and psychological victory, it was the British who reaped the strategic benefit. The departure of the German ships from Brest removed a threat which had been difficult to counter. Moreover, this was the last voyage of *Gneisenau*, which was heavily bombed by the RAF at Kiel and never returned to service. Her consort *Scharnhorst* survived until Boxing Day 1943 when she was sunk off the coast of Norway.

Java Sea

A HEROIC BID TO SAVE THE ISLAND

Though one of the least celebrated actions of World War II, the battle of the Java Sea (27 February 1942) deserves investigation as the first Allied attempt to defeat the triumphant Japanese navy with combined naval forces. And it stands out as an example of what friendly naval powers can expect if, having made no joint defensive preparations in peacetime, they hastily assemble a multi-national force and send it into action against a powerful and well-trained enemy.

By New Year's Day 1942, three weeks after the opening of the Pacific war, the Japanese offensive was still proceeding and the harried Allies were beginning at last to discern its pattern. The Pearl Harbor raid had ensured that the American Pacific Fleet could make no move to impede a four-pronged Japanese assault on Malaya, Borneo, the southern Philippines and the Moluccas. Having seized airbases on these initial objectives, the Japanese could then 'leap-frog' south and attack the southernmost arc of the Dutch East Indies: Sumatra, Java, Bali and Timor.

In their efforts to counter the Japanese attack the Allies set up 'ABDA' – the American/British/Dutch/Australian joint command. At first it was hoped that Singapore would serve as the ABDA base, but the continuing pace of the Japanese advance throughout January soon made it clear that Singapore, far from serving as an anchor point for holding and counter-attacking the Japanese, would soon be totally besieged. ABDA headquarters were therefore set up on 3 January 1942 at Bandoeng on Java, which was itself already becoming an obvious future objective for the Japanese.

The ABDA warships gathered in Javanese ports (Batavia and Surabaja on the north coast, Tjilatjap on the south coast) amounted to a motley collection of heavy and light cruisers and destroyers. They had no battleships, no aircraft-carriers, and precious little in the way of land-based reconnaissance, strike or fighter aircraft. As long as there was a glimmer of hope that Singapore could be saved, every available fighter was being sent there instead of being hoarded on Java. Lavishly supplied with land-based and naval aircraft, the Japanese held all the cards.

This they exploited to the full when the assault on Java began in the third week of February. It began by cutting off Java from any hope of reinforcement or relief whether from west or east. On 14 February the Japanese landed in southern Sumatra, investing

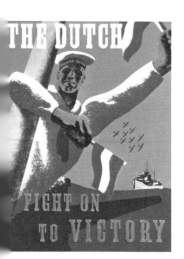

ABOVE A poster for the Free Dutch navy. The service fought valiantly, but was overrun with its allies by the sheer speed of the Japanese advance.

Java from the west. Five days later they attacked Bali and Timor in the east. At the same time (19 February) the Japanese carrier strike force which had wrought such havoc at Pearl Harbor devastated Port Darwin in northern Australia, the only Allied base capable of sending reinforcements to Java. Singapore had fallen, wasting all the belated efforts to save it, on 15 February; by the 20th it was clear that nothing could save Java from the same fate. While ordering Java to be held to the last (21 February) the Allied chiefs of staff also agreed that no further attempts should be made to reinforce the island.

With the formal dissolution of ABDA Command (25 February) the surviving land, sea and air forces on Java reverted to overall Dutch command. The naval commander-in-chief, Admiral Helfrich, decided that the eastern threat to Java would materialize first and concentrated a 'Combined Striking Force' at Surabaja under the sea-going command of Rear-Admiral Karel Doorman. This consisted of two 8-inch-gun cruisers (the British *Exeter* and the American *Houston*, the latter with her after turret inoperable since a bomb hit on 4 February) and three 6-inch-gun cruisers (the Dutch *De Ruyter* and *Java*, and the Australian *Perth*). To work with the cruisers, Doorman could call on a total of ten destroyers.

On paper this was quite an efficient-looking strike force, but only on paper. Any air reconnaissance it received was accidental rather than deliberate; communications were patchy; the Allied ships had never worked together as a combined force; all the ships of the force were either old or in urgent need of repairs or refit after weeks of non-stop combat service; and the crews were desperately tired.

These disadvantages more than cancelled out the Combined Striking Force's nominal superiority over the enemy. This was the squadron of Rear-Admiral Nishimura, escorting the transports of the Eastern Java Invasion Force: the 8-inch-gun cruisers *Nachi* and *Haguro*, the 5.5-inch-gun cruisers *Jintsu* and *Naga*, and fourteen destroyers. The Japanese also carried a 'secret weapon' about which the Allies were ignorant: the 'Long Lance' torpedo propelled by liquid oxygen, leaving virtually no track and with a range of 40,000m (44,000yd) at 36 knots.

No sooner had the last ships of the Combined Striking Force assembled at Surabaja on the 26th than a large Japanese invasion force was sighted about 305km (190 miles) to the north-east, and Helfrich promptly ordered Doorman to sail and intercept. After twenty-two hours of fruitless search, Doorman was returning to Surabaja to refuel his destroyers when the Japanese force was sighted again, this time only 130km (80 miles) away. Doorman headed back out to sea, leading the line of Allied cruisers in *De Ruyter* with the British destroyer *Electra* scouting ahead; and at 1620 hours on 27 February *Electra* signalled 'One cruiser, unknown number large destroyers, bearing 330, speed 18 knots, course 220.'

Though Doorman's mission was to sidestep escorting warships and get through to destroy the Japanese transport fleet, *Electra*'s report indicated a moderate enemy strength well within the doubtful capacity of the Combined Striking Force. Doorman therefore turned the Allied line to steam parallel to the Japanese force and give battle but he soon found out that *Electra* had only sighted the left-flank Japanese warships (*Naga* and six destroyers) which were soon joined by *Nachi*, *Haguro*, *Jintsu*, and eight more destroyers. With *Machi* and *Haguro* firing a combined broadside of twenty 8-inch guns and *Exeter* and *Houston* only able to reply with twelve, Doorman's line soon found itself out-gunned as well as out-ranged.

Disaster for Doorman's fleet began at 1708 hours when *Exeter* was hit in the boiler-room by an 8-inch shell. Spewing steam and smoke she reeled out of line; *Houston* turned to port to avoid *Exeter*; and *Perth* and *Java* followed *Houston*, thinking this to be

a move ordered by the admiral. As the Allied line fell apart in confusion the Japanese destroyers launched a torpedo attack, hitting the Dutch destroyer *Kortenaer*, which sank at once. To retrieve the situation Doorman ordered *Electra* to counter-attack while he took *De Ruyter* in a wide circle to the east to re-form the line.

Gallantly attempting to comply with Doorman's order, *Electra* found herself under the rapid and effective fire of three Japanese destroyers and was shelled to a wreck, finally sinking at 1800 hours. The British destroyers *Jupiter* and *Encounter*, however, drove back the Japanese destroyers trying to finish off the *Exeter*, and screened the stricken cruiser with smoke. Meanwhile, Doorman had re-formed his line by 1730 hours, heading east with *Perth*, *Houston* and *Java* astern of *De Ruyter*, having ordered *Exeter* to make her own way to Surabaja escorted by the Dutch destroyer *Witte de With*.

As night fell Doorman, still determined to get through to the troop transports, tried to circle round the Japanese warships. Shortly after 1930 hours, however, he sighted *Jintsu* and her destroyers in his path, and after safely avoiding a torpedo attack he broke away to the south, closing the Javan coast before turning to try again. During this run to the south, Japanese seaplanes dropping flares accurately reported every Allied move to the Japanese force, which stayed in position between Doorman and the transports.

Before he reversed course to return to the north Doorman detached the four elderly American destroyers (*John D. Edwards*, *Alden*, *Ford* and *Paul*

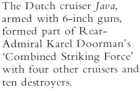

The Dutch cruiser *Java*, armed with 6-inch guns, formed part of Rear-Admiral Karel Doorman's 'Combined Striking Force' with four other cruisers and ten destroyers.

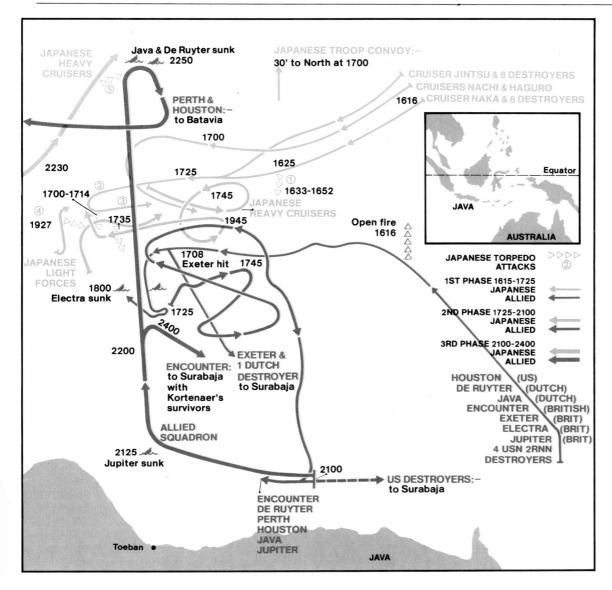

Java & De Ruyter sunk 2250

JAPANESE TROOP CONVOY:— 30' to North at 1700

CRUISER JINTSU & 8 DESTROYERS
CRUISERS NACHI & HAGURO
1616 CRUISER NAKA & 6 DESTROYERS

JAPANESE HEAVY CRUISERS

PERTH & HOUSTON:— to Batavia

1700

2230

1725

1625

1700-1714 ②

1745

1633-1652

④

1735

1945

1927

JAPANESE HEAVY CRUISERS

Open fire 1616

Equator

JAVA

AUSTRALIA

JAPANESE LIGHT FORCES

1800 Electra sunk

1708 Exeter hit 1745

1725

2400

2200

1725

JAPANESE TORPEDO ATTACKS

1ST PHASE 1615-1725 JAPANESE ALLIED

2ND PHASE 1725-2100 JAPANESE ALLIED

3RD PHASE 2100-2400 JAPANESE ALLIED

ENCOUNTER: to Surabaja with Kortenaer's survivors

EXETER & 1 DUTCH DESTROYER to Surabaja

ALLIED SQUADRON

HOUSTON (US)
DE RUYTER (DUTCH)
JAVA (DUTCH)
ENCOUNTER (BRITISH)
EXETER (BRIT)
ELECTRA (BRIT)
JUPITER (BRIT)
4 USN 2RNN DESTROYERS

2125 Jupiter sunk

2100

US DESTROYERS:— to Surabaja

ENCOUNTER DE RUYTER PERTH HOUSTON JAVA JUPITER

Toeban

JAVA

Jones) to refuel at Surabaja. The run north began with another calamity. At 2125 hours the British destroyer *Jupiter* blew up and sank; almost certainly on one of the mines laid that afternoon, unknown to Doorman, by a Dutch minelayer. Thirty-five minutes later what was left of the Combined Striking Force passed over the spot where *Kortenaer* had sunk, and Doorman was obliged to sacrifice his last destroyer (*Encounter*) to pick up the men in the water.

At 2255 there was another irony. One of the last American Catalina flying-boats operating on Java sighted Doorman's objective, the Japanese invasion convoy, and radioed an accurate fix. This Doorman never received. Instead, five minutes later (2300 hours), he ran straight into *Nachi* and *Haguro*. The Japanese heavy cruisers had been steaming south, but they reversed course and opened fire as cover for a devastating torpedo attack. *Java* was sunk at 2332 and *De Ruyter* was fatally damaged, sinking

two hours later and taking the gallant Doorman with her. *Perth* and *Houston* were left with no alternative but to obey the admiral's last order and head for Batavia.

None of the Allied ships which escaped the Java Sea action survived for longer than forty-eight hours. On the evening of 28 February *Perth* and *Houston*, retiring through Sunda Strait, fell in with the Japanese Western Invasion Force and most courageously attacked. They sank one transport and forced three others to beach themselves before being sunk by the escorting Japanese warships. But they hit out to the last and succeeded in damaging a cruiser and three destroyers. On the following morning (1 March) the crippled *Exeter* and her escorting destroyers, *Pope* and *Encounter*, were sunk by four cruisers and three destroyers. The last elements of naval opposition to the Japanese invasion force had been swept away and Java now lay open to conquest.

The battle of the Java Sea, in which the Japanese completed the invasion of Java despite Allied resistance in the shape of Doorman's ill-assorted multinational fleet.

War in the Mediterranean

A HARD-WON ALLIED VICTORY

In the hundred years before the outbreak of the war in 1939 the waters of the Mediterranean Sea had been dominated by the presence of the Royal Navy. Since 1869, when the Suez Canal was opened, the sea had been, in effect, a short cut to India, and to guard it the Royal Navy had three bases: Gibraltar in the west, Alexandria in the east, and Malta, roughly halfway between the two. The other prime concern of the British Mediterranean Fleet in 1939 was to guard the two-pronged pipeline of oil from Iraq, one prong which emerged at Haifa, through the British Mandate of Palestine, and the other at Beirut, in Syria – a French mandate.

Naval strategy in the Mediterranean would be largely governed by the security of Egypt – with whom Britain had signed a 'Treaty of Friendship' – and the Suez Canal, as well as the oil pipelines.

Although King Farouk's government had not officially declared war on Germany, it had expelled the German ambassador and asked for British aid.

In 1939 the Mediterranean was securely under Allied control: France had a powerful fleet based at Toulon and Mussolini's Italy was neutral. The possibility of Italy coming into the war on the Axis side, however, did cause the Allies some concern and for that reason a strong British force was maintained in the Mediterranean. To oversee this situation, Admiral Andrew Browne Cunningham was given command of the Mediterranean Fleet, and although he flew his flag in the old battleship *Warspite*, he retained the flamboyance of the destroyer captain he had been for much of his sea-going life – a quality which was to stand him in good stead in the next few years.

The aircraft-carriers *Victorious*, *Indomitable* and *Eagle*, pictured from top left to bottom right, were the cornerstones of British naval strength in the Mediterranean.

Cunningham arranged his forces soundly; a British destroyer force closed off the Straits of Gibraltar, while the French undertook to sweep the western basin between Gibraltar and Malta. Cunningham himself sat with his main fleet of heavy ships in the harbour at Alexandria.

On 10 June 1940, with northern France in the hands of the Germans, Mussolini declared war on France and Britain. The British reply was to augment the Mediterranean Fleet with cruisers from the East India station, the aircraft-carrier *Eagle*, and a number of submarines and small gunboats from the China station. At Alexandria, Cunningham was joined by three battleships, four cruisers and a number of destroyers from Gibraltar. For a month he scoured the eastern Mediterranean without sighting a major enemy vessel, though his destroyers sank a number of Italian submarines and a flotilla of minesweepers was shelled in the harbour at Tobruk. Towards the end of that month, however – on Sunday 23 June – Cunningham received word that the French were to sign an armistice with Germany. Units of the French fleet in the western Mediterranean were recalled to Toulon and other French bases in the Mediterranean.

Italy's entry into the war on the German side coupled with the French surrender transformed the strategic situation in the Mediterranean. Now the British were faced by the strong Italian fleet and in addition feared that the ships of their former French allies would be used against them. Gone too were the former 'friendly' bases that facilitated Britain's Mediterranean strategy, leaving only Egypt, Palestine, Malta and Gibraltar as refuges for Cunningham's forces. Even then, Malta was being hammered by enemy bombers, and convoys of supplies between Malta, Alexandria and the Suez Canal were being badly damaged despite the activities of British destroyers.

With the French gone, a new British force was sent to operate out of the Mediterranean. Known as Force H, it was commanded by Admiral Sir James Somerville and consisted of the aircraft-carrier *Ark Royal*, with a group of capital ships and destroyers. Somerville's first task was a tragic one; the bulk of the French fleet was lying in the Algerian harbour of Mers-el-Kébir, near Oran, and made its intention of returning home quite clear. Once there its capture and possible use by the Germans seemed to the British most probable. Therefore, after delivering an ultimatum to the French to immobilize their vessels (which was rejected), Somerville took Force H into Mers-el-Kébir on 3 July and opened fire, sinking several French ships, including a battleship, badly damaging the battle-cruiser *Dunkerque*, and killing 1000 French sailors. This attack on the

An escort ship flying the Royal Navy's white ensign, with one of its charges in the background. Despite the armed escorts convoy losses in the Mediterranean were considerable.

HMS *Penelope*, launched in 1935, served in both the Mediterranean and Home Fleets. She is shown here entering Valletta Harbour, Malta, in October 1941.

French fleet, followed by a similar incident at Dakar, was a great blow to Anglo-French relations and turned many Frenchmen away from the Free French cause of General de Gaulle into the arms of the collaborationist regime of Pétain's Vichy government.

The first fleet action of the war in the Mediterranean took place on 9 July 1940 off the Italian coast of Calabria, when a British force escorting a convoy from Malta to Alexandria encountered an Italian convoy bound for North Africa. The engagement was inconclusive, however, and little damage was inflicted on either side.

So far Cunningham had been hampered in trying to bring the main Italian fleet to battle by the necessity of maintaining escorts for the vital Malta convoys. The arrival of the carrier *Illustrious*,

however, materially altered the odds in his favour. Scouts reported that a large part of the Italian battle-fleet was lying in harbour at Taranto, and Cunningham decided that if he could not engage the Italian navy on the high seas, he could, using the Fleet Air Arm, destroy it at anchor. The planes of the Fleet Air Arm, including the famous Fairey Swordfish, met with little resistance and the raid was a great success. By first light RAF reconnaissance was able to report that supply and ammunition dumps in Taranto were ablaze, with three battleships heavily damaged and beached. Later it was established that half the Italian battle-fleet had been crippled by eleven aircraft torpedoes, for the loss of two aircraft.

Taranto was a moral and material triumph for the Royal Navy; it sapped Italian resolve but more

dockyard were four Sea Gladiator biplane fighters awaiting shipment to the carrier *Eagle*.

None of the R A F pilots on Malta had ever flown single-engined fighters before, but they unpacked the Gladiators and took to the air. One was nearly lost early in the defence of the island, but the remaining three took on flights of ten or fifteen Italian bombers as a matter of course: the fighters were dubbed 'Faith', 'Hope' and 'Charity' by the islanders. With the respite granted by the British victory at Taranto Hurricane fighters were flown in and damaged defences repaired. Later, King George VI was to bestow the George Cross for gallantry on the people of Malta as a whole.

Despite his problem in bringing the Italian fleet to battle, Cunningham still hoped to bring about a decisive naval engagement that would tilt the naval balance in Britain's favour. On 28 March 1941, the possibility of such an opportunity presented itself. Two separate squadrons of Italian cruisers and the battleship *Vittorio Veneto* were sighted by British air reconnaissance west and south-west of Crete. A squadron of British cruisers set off after them, attempting to lure them towards Cunningham's main battle-fleet, but perceiving their danger the Italians turned and began to run for home. Aircraft from the *Formidable*, the carrier which had replaced the *Illustrious*, pursued them, and managed to damage the battleship sufficiently to slow it down; when dusk came the cruiser squadron was still in pursuit. Another torpedo hit the Italian cruiser *Pola*, which dropped out of line and then stopped engines off Cape Matapan. The Italian admiral made the mistake of sending back a squadron to help *Pola*, and Cunningham set upon the Italian ships in a fierce night-battle. Three heavy cruisers and two destroyers were sunk, for no British losses.

The balance of forces in the Mediterranean turned in favour of the British in the winter of 1940–41; the convoy system was working in spite of the efforts of the Italian air force and navy while Italy, on the other hand, was suffering a series of military reverses both in Africa and in the Balkans. Mussolini appealed to Hitler for help and the German dictator reluctantly despatched a number of bomber and fighter squadrons to bases in Italy in January 1941, to be followed a few months later by army units which were then ferried to Libya to become the famous Afrika Korps.

The situation in the Mediterranean was further complicated by the British promise of aid to the Greeks who were engaged in a fierce struggle with the Italian army. As part of his preparation for the coming offensive against Soviet Russia, Hitler was determined to safeguard his southern flank and on 6 April 1941, launched a *blitzkrieg* campaign against Yugoslavia and Greece; both countries fell in a matter of weeks. Germany had been dragged into the Mediterranean but her contribution was to be far from negligible, as the British were to discover.

The greatest problem for the Royal Navy posed

importantly it relieved pressure on the beleaguered island of Malta. Around 275,000 people were crammed into the 300 sq. km (115 sq. miles) of Malta and its small neighbouring island of Gozo; and at the best of times the island's own agricultural resources were only capable of feeding one-third of the population. By early 1940 the rest of the island garrison's supplies could only be supplied from Britain via the Suez Canal in the east. The Governor, Sir William Dobbie, and the flag officer in charge of Valetta Harbour, Vice-Admiral Sir Wilbraham Ford, had the job of feeding the people while simultaneously defending the island with outdated anti-aircraft guns manned by the Royal Malta Artillery and the King's Own Malta Regiment. There were also an R A F squadron and a few obsolete 'London' flying-boats; still crated in a

by the Germans was the quality of her air force which took a terrible toll of the Malta convoys and at times put the entire convoy system into jeopardy. Dangerous too were the U-boats, but fortunately for the British there were never enough of them to affect the outcome at the strategic level. The now deteriorating position of the Royal Navy in the Mediterranean was accompanied by a series of disasters in the autumn of 1941.

On 14 November the *Ark Royal* was torpedoed, and although taken in tow she sank in the Mediterranean. The cruiser *Sydney*, detached from Cunningham's Alexandria-based fleet to operate in Australian waters, was also torpedoed – though she managed to sink her attacker before going down. On 25 November the old battleship *Barham* was sunk by a U-boat. On 7 December the Japanese launched their devastating attack on Pearl Harbor, and vessels which might have aided the Mediterranean campaign were sent to the Far East to shore up the situation there; two of the mightiest of these, the *Prince of Wales* and the *Repulse*, were sunk by aircraft attacks together on 10 December.

On 19 December, Cunningham suffered what must have been his greatest personal setback when the Italians launched an original and courageous attack on Alexandria. For this they used their newly developed 'human torpedo' – a large torpedo guided by two men sitting astride it and controlling the fins and the electric motor. The nose was packed with explosive, and was attached by the operators to an enemy vessel. In this case the targets were the battleships *Queen Elizabeth* and *Valiant*, which were crippled in Alexandria Harbour. With his flagship *Warspite* undergoing a refit after damaging her steering gear, Cunningham was down to three cruisers and a handful of destroyers and submarines without any hope of immediate replacement.

The Italian 'human torpedo' attack was one of the most daring exploits of the war and was in marked contrast to Italian naval policy which was in general characterized by extreme caution. An inhibitory factor was the chronic shortage of fuel oil, although it can be argued that the Italian navy underestimated its strength and was too easily put off fleet engagements.

All through 1942 the German U-boats and land-based aircraft tightened the noose around Malta, making the life of a seaman in the Gibraltar-Malta-Alexandria convoys a nightmare, particularly in

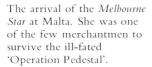

The arrival of the *Melbourne Star* at Malta. She was one of the few merchantmen to survive the ill-fated 'Operation Pedestal'.

view of the fact that surface ships were in almost certain danger of being bombed while refuelling on the island. In all a total of nineteen merchantmen were destroyed on the convoys between February and August, while at least two were sunk at their berths while being unloaded. But 'Operation Pedestal' – the August convoy drive – proved to have strengthened Malta just in time to allow the island's new air power to strike hard at the Axis forces, who were flagging in North Africa in the late summer.

Towards the end of 1942 the material strength of the American armed forces began to be felt in the Mediterranean. The steady stream of supplies and munitions was vital to British success and on 7 November 1942, the tide turned decisively in the Allies' favour with 'Operation Torch', the Anglo-American invasion of North Africa. 'Torch' met with little opposition, landings being made at Casablanca, Oran and Algiers. The combined forces of Britain and the US were to prove too much for the Axis and after a bitter campaign all Axis forces surrendered to the Allies on 12 May 1943.

Much of the Allied success in the later stages of the Mediterranean campaign stemmed from their ability to secure air superiority in selected areas, making possible the amphibious assaults on Sicily in July 1943 and then against the Italian homeland in September. The experience gained by the Royal Navy in more than three years of war ensured that,

from a naval point of view, the landing operations went without a hitch.

The overthrow of Mussolini and the surrender of Italy to the Allies on 8 September 1943 brought the naval war, as such, to a virtual close in the Mediterranean. The Allies held the strategic initiative forcing the Germans to fight a defensive war in Italy and the Balkans. The strategic importance of the Mediterranean declined steadily after 1943 as plans were made for the invasion of France from Great Britain. Convoys sailed virtually unimpeded from Alexandria to Gibraltar and so the British naval policy of keeping the Mediterranean open as a mercantile life-line had been achieved.

For the remainder of the war the Royal Navy acted in support of land operations. The guns of the Mediterranean Fleet played a significant role as an offshore battery in protecting the beach-head at Anzio. The amphibious landing in the south of France in July 1944 was the last naval action of any consequence in the Mediterranean with the Royal Navy again providing offshore bombardment.

The war in the Mediterranean saw the destruction of both the powerful French and Italian fleets. The Allied victory was not bought cheaply, for 167 warships were lost on the British and Commonwealth side, including one battleship, two aircraft-carriers, fourteen cruisers and fifty destroyers.

ABOVE LEFT The six 5.25-inch guns paired in the turrets of this British light cruiser could be used against both ships and aircraft.

ABOVE A lookout scans the horizon from this Italian motor torpedo-boat. Such vessels were used with considerable success against Allied merchantmen in the Mediterranean.

Andrew Browne Cunningham

1883–1963

Admiral Sir Andrew Cunningham commanded the Mediterranean Fleet on the outbreak of World War II. Despite strategic and logistic difficulties, he quickly proved himself more than equal to the challenge of the Italian navy.

Though Cunningham's parents were Scottish, he was born in Dublin in 1883 and joined the navy as a *Britannia* cadet in 1896. He first saw action ashore with the Naval Brigade in the Boer War (1899–1902) and received his first independent command, a torpedo-boat, as a lieutenant in 1908. Most of Cunningham's service over the next ten years was spent in destroyers. For seven of those years he commanded the coal-burning destroyer *Scorpion*, taking part in the pursuit of the *Goeben* and *Breslau* in 1914. At the Dardanelles in 1915, Cunningham was promoted commander and decorated with the Distinguished Service Order. In April 1918, serving with the Dover Patrol, he helped support the Zeebrugge Raid. Two bars to the DSO followed in 1919 and in the following year, when serving with Admiral Cowan's squadron in the Baltic.

In the early 1920s Cunningham continued to command destroyers until promoted flag captain to Admiral Cowan on the America and West Indies station between 1926 and 1928, commanding the cruiser *Calcutta*. In the last decade of peace he commanded the battleship *Rodney* and served at the Admiralty as deputy chief of the naval staff before succeeding Sir Dudley Pound in command of the Mediterranean Fleet in the summer of 1939. The action started in earnest as soon as Mussolini declared war on 10 June 1940.

One of Cunningham's most immediate problems was posed by the French warships in Alexandria, technically subject to the armistice with Germany. Cunningham's direct approach and excellent relationship with the French Admiral Godfroy prevented a duplication of the tragedy of Oran and Mers el Kébir, where the British bombarded the French fleet rather than risk its capture by the Germans. Securing the peaceful demobilization of the French ships in Alexandria was a diplomatic triumph of the highest order.

It also released Cunningham to take the early offensive action with which he planned to seize and hold the initiative in the eastern Mediterranean. Within a week of his settlement with the French at Alexandria, Cunningham was at sea with his fleet, winning the first of a sequence of actions against the Italian navy. From Cape Spartivento on 9 July 1940 to Cape Matapan on 28 March 1941, the Mediterranean Fleet repeatedly humiliated the Italians, who never attained the aggressive spirit which Cun-

ningham radiated throughout his command. Also in this period, Cunningham ordered the devastating Fleet Air Arm strike at the Italian battle-fleet in Taranto on 11 November 1940.

In the spring of 1941 Cunningham showed that he had unshakable courage in the bitterest adversity as well as in the attack. After the disastrous campaigns in Greece and Crete, he steadfastly exposed his shrinking fleet to possible decimation by the Luftwaffe in order to keep faith with the army and bring the troops off the beaches. 'It takes three years to build a ship,' he replied to protests about the losses; 'it takes three hundred years to build a tradition.'

All Cunningham's fortitude was needed throughout 1941 and the first half of 1942, as his fleet was brought to the verge of destruction by U-boat, air and human-torpedo attacks. But under Cunningham the Mediterranean Fleet helped Force H, under Admiral Somerville, to keep the Malta garrison supplied, and as long as Malta held out the German and Italian forces in North Africa were denied the supplies they so desperately needed.

In 1942, with the outcome of the Mediterranean war still hanging in the balance, Cunningham was sent to Washington as head of the British Admiralty Delegation to the Combined Chiefs of Staff Committee. In the preliminary discussions over 'Operation Torch', the projected Anglo-American descent on North Africa, Cunningham rapidly established a sound working relationship with General Eisenhower, the designated commander of 'Torch'. It fell to Cunningham to direct the entrapment of the Axis forces in Tunisia with the signal: 'Sink, burn and destroy. Let nothing pass.' In July 1943 came a great triumph, when Cunningham received the surrender of the Italian fleet and saw it anchored, as he proudly signalled to the Admiralty, 'under the guns of the Fortress of Malta'.

Cunningham richly deserved his advancement to First Sea Lord in October 1943, although he could not disguise his distaste for administration and staff work which had first become apparent in Washington. He held this post until his retirement after the defeat of Japan. In the last two years of the war he duly attended the summit conferences at Quebec, Yalta and Potsdam. For many years after his retirement he continued passionately to defend the interests of the Royal Navy as a viscount in the House of Lords. He died in 1963.

Coral Sea

BATTLE OF THE CARRIERS

At the beginning of May 1942 Japan had taken every one of the initial war objectives of December 1941: Hong Kong, Malaya, the Philippines, and the Dutch East Indies. The Japanese army was well on the way to another victory in Burma, and there seemed no reason why the tide of Japanese conquest should not roll on to engulf New Guinea, Australia, New Zealand, the entire South Pacific, and finally the Hawaiian Islands.

But in the second week of May 1942 something extraordinary happened. After winning a tactical naval victory in the Coral Sea, the Japanese for the first time accepted a strategic defeat, calling off their planned seaborne invasion of southern New Guinea. This alone would qualify the battle of the Coral Sea for a special place in naval history without its other unique claim to fame: that, also for the first time, aircraft-carrier had fought aircraft-carrier without the rival fleets ever sighting each other.

American carriers checked the Japanese in the Coral Sea largely because the Pearl Harbor attack left the US Pacific Fleet with no alternative but to rely on carriers; the 'flat-tops' which escaped Pearl Harbor and the subsequent Allied defeats were the only instruments of Allied long-range sea power left in the Pacific by the spring of 1942. The timely despatch of the American carriers *Yorktown* and *Lexington* to the Coral Sea came about because Commander Joseph Rochefort's Combat Intelligence Unit had cracked the Japanese navy's war-

time code three days after Pearl Harbor. By late April 1942 Rochefort's team had warned Admiral Chester Nimitz, commander-in-chief of the US Pacific Fleet, that the next Japanese invasion would be aimed at Port Moresby in southern New Guinea. For once, the Allies had advance notice of a Japanese assault and the resources with which to meet it; also for once, the Japanese would be going into battle without undisputed control of the air.

The two American carriers each formed the core of a task force (TF): TF 11 for *Lexington*, TF 17 for *Yorktown*. The overall commander, Rear-Admiral Fletcher in *Yorktown*, also had the aid of the British Rear-Admiral Crace with the Australian cruisers *Australia* and *Hobart*, the American cruiser *Chicago* and two American destroyers. The carrier task forces were to rendezvous in the Coral Sea on 1 May and Crace's force was to join Fletcher's command three days later.

Flushed with their recent successes, the confident Japanese planned another complex operation from widely separated bases, once again assuming that the Allies would be caught totally by surprise. From Rabaul in New Britain, a small force would set up a seaplane base at Tulagi in the Solomon Islands (3 May). The Port Moresby invasion force would then sail, covered by a task force with the light carrier *Shoho* and four cruisers from Truk in the Caroline Islands. To keep off any attempt by the Americans to intervene with their carriers, the Japanese heavy

The Japanese carrier *Shoho*, was sunk by US aerial attack in the Coral Sea engagement.

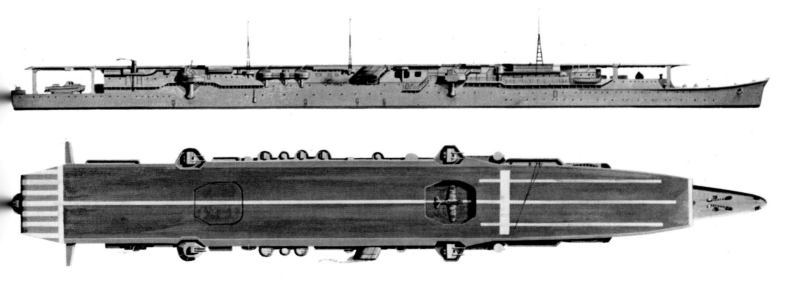

ABOVE Commander-in-chief of the US Pacific Fleet, Chester Nimitz was the architect of his country's victories at Coral Sea and Midway.

ABOVE Two bombs and two torpedoes were enough to account for the US carrier *Lexington*, the loss of which cancelled out the Americans' previous destruction of *Shoho*.

carriers *Shokaku* and *Zuikaku* would also sail from Truk and sweep into the Coral Sea from the east.

Though the resultant collision was later dignified with the title 'battle of the Coral Sea', it was admittedly a thoroughly confused sequence of air searches and air strikes spread over six days (3–8 May). The Americans and Japanese each spent the first three days in discovering the opposition's true strength and objectives before the rival carrier forces attacked each other on 7–8 May. And as no battle like this had ever been fought before, it was not surprising that grave mistakes were made by both sides. In addition to Japanese over-confidence, the American and Commonwealth forces had one advantage which they had not enjoyed before: long-range air reconnaissance by B-17 bombers based on New Guinea and Australia. And it was information furnished by the B-17s which triggered off the battle's first phase on 3–4 May, as the Japanese made their opening moves.

The first Japanese ships sighted by the B-17s (2 May) belonged to the Tulagi force, and they puzzled Admiral Fletcher because they seemed to have no direct relevance to the expected Japanese thrust at Port Moresby. Then, at 7.00 p.m. on the 3rd, Fletcher heard that the Japanese were landing at Tulagi and raced north with *Yorktown* to attack. On the 4th *Yorktown*'s pilots carried out three air strikes against the Japanese on Tulagi, returning with confident accounts of widespread destruction caused. In fact all the air strikes had achieved was the destruction of the old destroyer *Kikutsuki*, three minesweepers and five seaplanes, for the loss of three American aircraft out of about forty. Confident that he had scotched this Japanese move into the Solomons, Fletcher headed south again and rejoined *Lexington* early on the 5th.

The 5th was a day of waiting for clearer inform-ation, sifting the constant sightings of Japanese shipping virtually from Rabaul to the Solomons, but by evening Fletcher was confident that the Port Moresby force was by now at sea. As he prepared to head north-east to hunt it down, however, Admiral Hara was already entering the Coral Sea from the east with *Shokaku* and *Zuikaku*.

On 6 May Hara's carriers closed to within 110km (68 miles) of *Yorktown* and *Lexington* without sighting them, before retiring north to fuel; a Japanese plane from Rabaul sighted Fletcher's carriers but the news failed to reach Hara; B-17s sighted the Port Moresby invasion force and the *Shoho* covering force. By the morning of the 7th, therefore, Fletcher was preparing to locate and attack the Port Moresby force without realizing that a large Japanese carrier force was in the offing; whereas the Japanese carriers had not yet located *Lexington* and *Yorktown*, but were hard on their heels.

The 7th began with both sides chasing wolves which turned out to be sheep. A coding error sent the entire strike forces of *Yorktown* and *Lexington* pursuing 'two carriers and four heavy cruisers', when air reconnaissance had actually reported 'two heavy cruisers and two destroyers'. Equally faulty Japanese air reconnaissance had the same effect on *Shokaku* and *Zuikaku*, sending their strike aircraft roaring off to attack 'a carrier and a cruiser', actually the American fleet tanker *Neosho* and destroyer *Sims*, both of which were duly sunk at 0930 hours. No sooner had Hara's aircraft taken off on this wasteful strike than the position of Fletcher's carriers reached him at last – but there was nothing that Hara could do until the aircraft returned.

Fletcher was suffering similar apprehension. Aware that his aircraft had left on a wild-goose chase but informed by now of the Port Moresby force's position and course, Fletcher could do no more than detach Crace's cruisers to lie in wait for the Japanese transports. But shortly after 1100 hours the Americans hit beginners' luck. Though most of the Coral Sea was patched with low cloud and rain squalls, the American strike force sighted *Shoho* and the Japanese covering force in clear weather and plunged to attack, overwhelming the little carrier with thirteen bomb hits and seven torpedo hits. 'Dixon to carrier!' radioed one of *Lexington*'s squadron commanders as *Shoho* sank; 'Scratch one flat-top!'

Shoho's sinking, plus the menacing presence of Crace and his cruisers, caused the Japanese to make a fateful decision: the Port Moresby force was withdrawn until its path could be cleared. But the final outcome of the battle still rested with the rival carrier task forces, each fully alerted now to the other's existence.

By mid-afternoon *Yorktown* and *Lexington* had recovered and re-armed their aircraft, but Fletcher decided against sending them out again to hunt for the Japanese carriers with evening approaching and the weather bad. Hara took the gamble, however, and launched another strike to attack the American carriers at dusk. It was a fiasco. The Japanese pilots searched fruitlessly until they had to ditch their bombs and torpedoes in order to make sure of returning to their carriers – then flew clean over the American force and its umbrella of F4F Wildcat fighters. Six Japanese pilots were so disorientated that they actually tried to land on *Yorktown*. Only seven Japanese aircraft returned safely; the other twenty were either shot down or forced to ditch in the sea. Hara's aggressive over-confidence had handed the Americans another easy victory.

The morning of 8 May 1942 saw the world's first true carrier battle, the American and Japanese task forces remaining 300km (186 miles) apart, but furiously and inexpertly attacked by each other's strike forces. The Americans drew first blood. While a rain squall shrouded *Zuikaku*, *Shokaku* was caught in the clear and badly damaged by two bomb hits which wrecked the flight-deck and started a petrol fire forward. Then it was the turn of the Japanese, who found the two American carriers in clear weather. *Lexington* was hit by two torpedoes

and two bombs; *Yorktown* suffered severe internal damage from a 400-kg (880-lb) bomb but was still able to operate aircraft. And yet Japanese losses in trained carrier aircrew were considerable: forty-two Japanese aircraft were lost, against thirty-three American.

By noon on 8 May the Americans could claim victory. They had forced the postponement of a Japanese invasion, sunk one Japanese carrier and knocked two others out of the fight, *Shokaku* with battle damage, *Zuikaku* with excessive aircraft losses. But *Lexington*'s fires were just being brought under control when she erupted with massive explosions caused by accumulated petrol vapour, and had to be abandoned. Though the postponement of the Port Moresby invasion soon became a cancellation, the destruction of *Lexington* enabled the Japanese to claim a tactical victory.

Much more important in the long term was the optimistic Japanese belief that *Yorktown* would be out of action for months – ample time, surely, for the Japanese navy, with its decisive carrier superiority, to win the Pacific war with the forthcoming operation aimed at Midway.

One of the last explosions aboard *Lexington*, caused by accumulated petrol vapour. A damaged carrier was always at risk from such explosions, often hours after being hit.

Midway

A US DEFENSIVE TRIUMPH

On 4 June 1942 the US navy, hopelessly out-numbered but forced to fight for an objective which could not be abandoned, won what must be regarded as one of the decisive battles of history: the battle of Midway. In a single day the Americans ended the Japanese navy's crushing superiority in aircraft-carriers, reducing the Pacific war to a battle of attrition in which superior shipbuilding capacity would give the US inevitable victory.

On the Japanese 'side of the hill', Midway was an attempt to lure the last heavy warships of the US navy out to destruction. Midway Atoll, western-most of the Hawaiian island chain, was an objective which, in Japanese hands, would ensure Japan's domination and rapid conquest of the rest of the Hawaiian islands. With their Hawaiian bases gone, the Americans would be pushed back to the west coast of the US, leaving the north and central Pacific a Japanese preserve and isolating Australia, New Zealand and the South Pacific islands. Midway was therefore essential for the Americans and they would throw every last ship they had into its defence – so calculated Admiral Isoroku Yama-moto, commander-in-chief of the Japanese Com-bined Fleet. But he rejected the possibility that American decoders would discover the Japanese preparations for the Midway attack. Nor did the Japanese plans cater for the Coral Sea battle reduc-ing the Japanese carrier strike force from six to four, while leaving the Americans with three carriers with which to counter-attack at Midway.

At Pearl Harbor, Commander Rochefort and his team of decoders had sensed that the Japanese were preparing a major operation in the central Pacific to follow the thrust at Port Moresby in New Guinea (catalyst of the Coral Sea battle). The new objective mentioned in Japanese radio messages was 'AF', and this was not pinpointed as Midway until 15 May – a week after *Lexington* went down in the Coral Sea. Admiral Chester Nimitz, commander-in-chief of the US Pacific Fleet, recalled his last three carriers from the south-west Pacific: Admiral Fletcher with *Yorktown* (in urgent need of repairs after Coral Sea) and Admiral Halsey with *Enterprise* and *Hornet*. Before Halsey's task force (TF 16) headed north of Pearl Harbor it had the luck to be spotted by a Japanese aircraft and duly reported to Japanese naval intelligence as still being in the southern Pacific. This added to the dangerous over-confidence which characterized the approach to the Midway attack on the Japanese side.

On 25 May Rochefort's team picked up their most vital windfall of the war: a long intercept containing virtually all the details of the Japanese forces involved in the Midway operation scheduled for around 3–5 June. Over the next ten days all available guns, ammunition, barbed wire, and strike aircraft were rushed out to Midway. *Hornet* and *Enterprise* reached Pearl Harbor on 26 May and *Yorktown* on the 27th. Working flat-out round the clock, the Pearl Harbor dockyard workers had *Yorktown* ready for action in an incredible three days, completing repairs which normally would have taken three months, in order to send her out to what was to be her last battle.

By 29 May, therefore, the Americans knew that a second Japanese invasion, in the western Aleutians, scheduled for the same time as the Midway attack was only a diversion. They knew that Midway would be softened up by Admiral Nagumo's 1st Carrier Striking Force of at least four carriers, backed by battleships and cruisers, before the Midway invasion force went in. They even knew that Nagumo's carriers would approach Midway from the north-west while the Japanese main body and invasion force came in from the west. But despite this advance knowledge of the Japanese plans, the odds against the Americans were enorm-ous. From the Aleutians down to Midway the Japanese would be sailing eleven battleships, eight heavy and light carriers and twenty-three de-stroyers. To save Midway and stave off utter defeat,

A Boeing B-17 Fortress takes off for a long-range sweep. The first Japanese attack on Midway failed to catch the US aircraft on the ground, in sharp contrast to the Pearl Harbor raid.

the US Pacific Fleet was committing no more than three carriers, eight cruisers, and fourteen destroyers.

In addition to the formidable surface fleet, twelve Japanese submarines, detached to form an arc-shaped patrol line west of Pearl Harbor, were supposed to locate and identify the US Pacific Fleet as it dutifully charged west from its base in response to the attack on Midway. Due to Rochefort's timely decoding work, however, *Enterprise* and *Hornet* sailed from Pearl Harbor on 28 May; thanks to the heroic efforts of the Pearl Harbor dockyard workers, *Yorktown* followed on the 29th. Thus the watching Japanese submarines formed their patrolling arc a day too late to sight the three American carriers on their way to a rendezvous at 'Point

Luck', a dot on the chart about 480km (300 miles) north-east of Midway. By 3 June *Yorktown, Enterprise* and *Hornet* were lying in ambush and the Japanese had no idea they were there.

Admiral Fletcher was in overall command in *Yorktown* (TF 17). Halsey, in hospital at Pearl Harbor with a skin disease, had been replaced as commander of TF 16 (*Enterprise* and *Hornet*) by his cruiser/destroyer commander, Rear-Admiral Spruance. Fletcher's plan was to hold back until air searches from Midway had identified the most important element in the Japanese fleet – Nagumo's carriers – and then do what he could to cripple Nagumo's force. If he could do this the Japanese would have to think twice about attacking Midway in the teeth of the strike aircraft based on the island.

The Japanese air strike against Midway found the Americans on the alert. Their bombers had already sortied to attack the Japanese aircraft-carriers when the first Japanese wave went in.

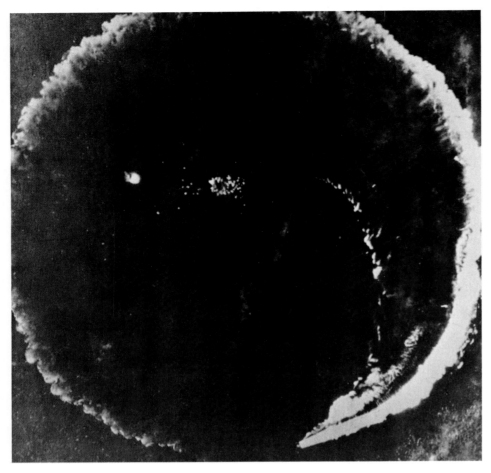

TOP The crippled Japanese carrier *Soryu* describes a 360-degree circle in a vain attempt to evade the deadly attentions of US navy bombers.

ABOVE The USS *Yorktown* being readied for action after having sustained severe damage during the Coral Sea battle.

Given the odds against him, there was little else that the American admiral could do.

Midway's PBY flying-boats made the first sighting at 0925 on 3 June, 1100km (685 miles) west of Midway, and as the morning wore on it became clear that this was the Japanese invasion force. Midway launched its first strike – nine B-17 bombers – at 1230. With 1000km (620 miles) to fly, they did not attack until 1638 hours, scoring no hits. A night attack by PBYs armed with torpedoes followed at 0130 on the 4th; one tanker was hit, but she was able to stay with the convoy as it plodded on to the east. The burning question now was the whereabouts of the Japanese carrier striking force.

By 0430 on the 4th, Nagumo's four carriers *Kaga*, *Akagi*, *Soryu* and *Hiryu* were ready to launch their softening-up strike against Midway's defences. Nagumo held back half his available aircraft, armed with torpedoes and armour-piercing bombs, for a possible attack against any American warships in the area. Such prudence was sound, and would have been even sounder if Nagumo had held back the air groups of two carriers instead of letting all four join in the Midway attack. He did take out insurance by ordering air searches by scout planes from *Kaga*, *Akagi*, and the cruisers *Chikuma* and *Tone*, but catapult trouble aboard *Tone* delayed her aircraft's launch for half an hour (until 0500). This delay, trifling at the time, was soon to prove fatal.

Reduced to its simplest essentials, the course of the battle over the following crowded four hours ran as follows. PBYs from Midway sighted Nagumo's carriers (0530) and the incoming air strike (0540). All available strike aircraft on Midway sortied to attack the Japanese carriers, with the result that none was caught on the ground when the Japanese air strike went in (0630–0730). The leader of the strike radioed back to Nagumo that a second strike was necessary. No sooner had Nagumo ordered his reserve aircraft to be re-armed with bombs for a second strike than *Tone*'s belated scout plane sighted Fletcher's cruiser/destroyer screen (0728); but it took another hour before Nagumo heard that the American force included at least one carrier. By the time all the aircraft which had attacked Midway had returned to their carriers, refuelled, and begun re-arming with anti-shipping weapons, it was 0917. Nagumo turned his force north-east to attack the American force but it was too late. Fletcher's strike aircraft were already on their way.

An hour after the first sighting of Nagumo's carriers had been reported to Fletcher at 0630, *Enterprise* and *Hornet* began launching aircraft while *Yorktown* stayed behind to recover her search aircraft. Spruance had taken the gamble of attacking at extreme range while Nagumo was still committed to the Midway attack. The US torpedo pilots became separated from their fighter cover and paid a terrible price for the valiant but inexpert attacks

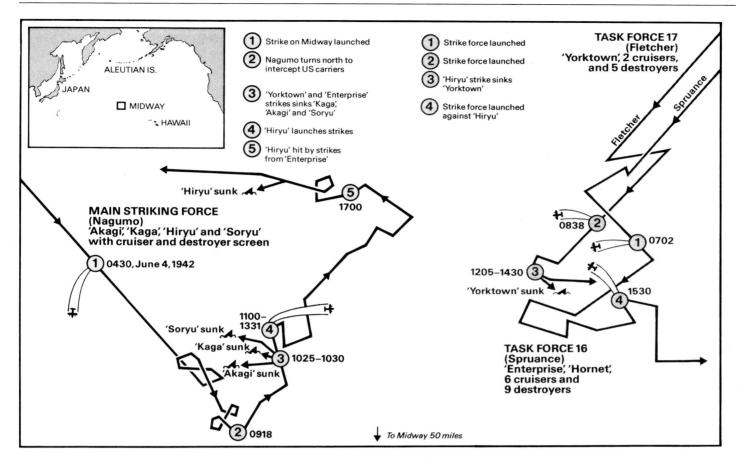

Legend:
- ① Strike on Midway launched
- ② Nagumo turns north to intercept US carriers
- ③ 'Yorktown' and 'Enterprise' strikes sinks 'Kaga', 'Akagi' and 'Soryu'
- ④ 'Hiryu' launches strikes
- ⑤ 'Hiryu' hit by strikes from 'Enterprise'

- ① Strike force launched
- ② Strike force launched
- ③ 'Hiryu' strike sinks 'Yorktown'
- ④ Strike force launched against 'Hiryu'

ALEUTIAN IS.
JAPAN
MIDWAY
HAWAII

TASK FORCE 17 (Fletcher) 'Yorktown', 2 cruisers, and 5 destroyers

Fletcher Spruance

0838 ②
0702 ①
1205–1430 ③
'Yorktown' sunk
1530 ④

MAIN STRIKING FORCE (Nagumo) 'Akagi', 'Kaga', 'Hiryu' and 'Soryu' with cruiser and destroyer screen

'Hiryu' sunk
1700 ⑤

① 0430, June 4, 1942

1100–1331 ④
'Soryu' sunk
'Kaga' sunk
③ 1025–1030
'Akagi' sunk

② 0918

To Midway 50 miles

TASK FORCE 16 (Spruance) 'Enterprise', 'Hornet', 6 cruisers and 9 destroyers

they made on the Japanese carriers: only six torpedo planes returned out of forty-one. But the three US torpedo attacks between 0918 and 1015 delayed the launching of Nagumo's strike at the American carrier force, a strike which had already been delayed by no less than five attacks by the Midway-based aircraft.

At 1020 hours, having now beaten off eight American attacks without having taken a single hit, Nagumo's carriers turned into the wind to launch aircraft. Precisely at this moment, undetected because of the Japanese lack of radar, the dive-bombers from *Enterprise* and *Hornet* arrived overhead. Nagumo's carriers could not have been more vulnerable, their decks packed with aircraft and strewn with petrol bowsers and hoses, plus piles of bombs left lying after the abandoned second strike at Midway. At 1025 Nagumo was commanding a veteran fleet; five minutes later *Akagi*, *Kaga* and *Soryu* were blazing wrecks, victims of the American air strike. Only *Hiryu* was left undamaged to carry on the fight.

At 1054 *Hiryu* launched the first Japanese counter-strike against the American force but it only caught *Yorktown*, temporarily crippling her with three bomb hits shortly after noon until the fires were put out and steam raised again two hours later. A second *Hiryu* strike with torpedoes at 1445 put *Yorktown* out of action again, this time for good.

The unscathed *Enterprise* and *Hornet*, however, launched a second American strike which wrecked *Hiryu* shortly after 1700 hours; Nagumo's last carrier burned all night and sank at about 0910 on the following morning.

Taking stock on the night of 4–5 June, Yamamoto was forced to accept that Nagumo's carriers had met the annihilation intended for the US Pacific Fleet. Though still possessing crushing naval superiority, Yamamoto could only use it if the Americans advanced within range of the Japanese navy's guns and torpedoes. Spruance, who had taken tactical command when Fletcher abandoned *Yorktown* at 1500 hours, avoided all rash moves and held back, waiting to strike if the Japanese attacked again. Conversely, Yamamoto could only proceed with the Midway attack by exposing his fleet to unopposed American air strikes. This he refused to do, cancelling the 'occupation of AF' at 0255 on the 5th.

Yamamoto's fleet was already in full retreat to the west when a last American strike caught the lagging cruisers *Mikuma* and *Mogami* (damaged in a collision early on the 5th) and sank *Mikuma*. The Japanese, however, denied the Americans the chance of saving *Yorktown*. Shortly after dawn on the 6th she was hit by two torpedoes from the Japanese submarine *I-168*, finally sinking at first light on the 7th.

The action at Midway was exceptional in that, as may be seen in this diagram, the two fleets involved did not actually meet.

Raymond Ames Spruance

1886–1969

Normally noted for his prudence, Raymond Spruance heeded his chief of staff's advice at Midway and launched a daring early air attack, which was successful.

Raymond Ames Spruance rose to fame when he was appointed commander of the US carrier Task Force 16 on the eve of the battle of Midway, ending that vital engagement in tactical command of the American fleet. His performance at Midway and in later carrier actions, most notably in the Philippine Sea two years later, testifies to the ability of Admiral Nimitz to pick men. Spruance was not a carrier specialist by training, however. Before Midway, he had been known only for the quiet, precise formality associated with gunnery specialists: a 'black-shoe' admiral, a battleship man, with none of the informality in dress or manner affected by the carrier officers.

Spruance was born in Baltimore, Maryland, in 1886 but was raised in Indiana, where he went to the US Naval Academy. He served in the battleship *Pennsylvania* in World War I, and came to Britain after the war on special duty to accelerate the US navy's adoption of director fire control. Between the wars Spruance became earmarked for high command, completing the senior instruction course at the Naval War College in 1927 before serving in the battleship *Mississippi* as executive officer. He was twice a member of the Naval War College staff, from 1931 to 1933 and 1935 to 1938. His service as a senior captain was rounded out with a spell in the Caribbean before he took command of a cruiser division in September 1941 with the rank of rear-admiral.

From Pearl Harbor to May 1942, Spruance commanded the cruisers and destroyers of Halsey's carrier Task Force 16. Hit-and-run attacks were made on the Japanese in the Marshall Islands, Wake Island and Marcus Island before the task force was urgently recalled to Pearl Harbor on 16 May with the Midway crisis looming large. On the return voyage Halsey went down with an incapacitating skin disease and was immediately placed in hospital on arrival at Pearl Harbor. When Nimitz asked Halsey to recommend a replacement Halsey had no hesitation in recommending Spruance. Though there were many other officers more technically qualified for this crucial appointment, Nimitz backed Halsey's hunch and gave Task Force 16 (the carriers *Enterprise* and *Hornet*) to Spruance.

Spruance sailed for Midway under the overall command of Admiral Fletcher, but his biggest asset in adjusting to the complex world of carrier operations was Halsey's excellent staff. Spruance's wise reliance on his staff's expertise can be said to have won Midway, for when Nagumo's carriers were finally located his own inclination was to launch the first American strike at 0900 hours. Spruance's chief of staff, Captain Browning, urged that the strike be launched two hours earlier, at extreme range, to catch the Japanese before they could locate and strike at the American force. With the entire weight of the Pacific war bearing on his shoulders, Spruance took Browning's advice: the result was the destruction of three of Nagumo's four carriers in under ten minutes. When he assumed tactical command from Fletcher, Spruance wisely decided not to pursue the retreating Japanese: he had fulfilled the near-impossible mission of defending Midway and refused to court destruction at the hands of Yamamoto's main battle-fleet.

After Midway Spruance served as chief of staff to Nimitz and became deputy commander-in-chief of the Pacific Fleet in September 1942. In August 1943 he was appointed commander of the Central Pacific Force, and from April 1944 he began his regular spells of command of the carrier-borne armada known as the 3rd Fleet under Halsey's command and the 5th Fleet under that of Spruance. Entrusted with covering the Marianas invasion force in June 1944, Spruance repeated the pragmatic approach to battle which had characterized his performance at Midway. He stood on the defensive, using his massive carrier fighter force to destroy Ozawa's air strikes in the battle of the Philippine Sea. Criticized for not having pursued the Japanese with more energy, he had nevertheless broken the back of the Japanese navy's most dangerous arm – its carrier force. The last operations he performed with the 5th Fleet were the assaults on Iwo Jima and Okinawa.

After the war, Spruance succeeded Nimitz as commander-in-chief of the Pacific Fleet before going to the Naval War College as President in March 1946 until his retirement in July 1948. He later served as US Ambassador to the Philippine Republic between 1952 and 1955, and died in 1969.

Guadalcanal

BATTLE OF ATTRITION IN THE PACIFIC

The struggle for Guadalcanal (August 1942–February 1943) has a unique place in naval history. This grinding six-month ordeal was the Stalingrad of the Pacific war, unique because the American and Japanese troops struggling for the mastery of the island were both completely dependent on sea power. From start to finish the outcome of the battle turned on which fleet would succeed in making it impossible for the enemy fleet to continue supplying and reinforcing its troops on Guadalcanal.

Thus Guadalcanal was a land battle governed by repeated clashes between warships whose movements were constantly imperilled by enemy land-based air attacks. As aircraft-carriers dared not remain for long in the battle zone, Guadalcanal was the focus of successive hit-and-run cruiser/destroyer clashes by night. Attempts to tip the vital air balance by using carriers brought on two carrier engagements; attempts to secure decisive firepower superiority by night brought on one of the rare battleship actions of the Pacific war.

The Guadalcanal sea battles repeatedly proved, to the Americans' cost, that the best technology in the world is useless without skilled operation and exploitation. Though lacking radar and voice-radio communication between ships, the Japanese scored time and again because of the excellence of their night-fighting technique and their lookouts' unassisted night vision. But Guadalcanal was first and

foremost a battle of attrition; both sides lost heavily throughout, and victory went to the fleet with the most reserves.

The sea fighting for Guadalcanal took the form of no less than seven 'set-piece' battles: Savo Island (9 August 1942); a carrier clash in the Eastern Solomons (24 August); Cape Esperance (11–12 October); Santa Cruz, the second carrier battle (26 October); the intervention of the battleships in 'First Guadalcanal' (12–13 November) and 'second Guadalcanal' (14–15 November); and finally Tassafaronga (30 November). After Tassafaronga the Japanese accepted that their navy was unable to guarantee land victory on Guadalcanal, and their subsequent naval efforts were aimed at evacuating the maximum possible number of troops from the island.

From Bougainville in the north-west to San Cristobal in the south-east, the Solomon archipelago is a double skein of islands some 1050km (650 miles) long, separated by a wide sound which the Americans called 'The Slot'. Virtually dominated by Japanese airbases in New Britain and the western Solomons, the Slot was the natural highway for the regular despatch of Japanese warships and supply ships to Guadalcanal which was known as the 'Tokyo Express'. During the long battle for the Solomons, however, the Americans received valuable information about Japanese shipping and air movements from the 'coast-watchers', gallant individuals and small teams of observers operating on Japanese-held islands with loyal native help.

The US Marines landed on Guadalcanal on 7 August 1942 to prevent the Japanese from setting up a new airbase on the island. This airbase would have ensured Japanese air domination of the Solomons and Coral Sea, and until the Americans seized and won the initiative on Guadalcanal it remained the most priceless objective in the South-West Pacific. The Marines took the airbase (to be called Henderson Field after a marine pilot killed at Midway) on the 7th, but their supply fleet was still unloading when the Japanese made their first bid to destroy the American landing-force on the night of 8–9 August. This brought on the battle of Savo Island.

On the 7th and 8th, prompt Japanese bombing attacks were made against the Marine beach-head on Guadalcanal by aircraft based on Rabaul in New Britain. Coast-watcher alerts enabled planes from the American carriers covering the landing –

The battleship *South Dakota* comes under attack from a Nakajima 'Kate' bomber of the Japanese navy.

Japanese destroyers in battle formation. Sea power was the crucial factor in the struggle to keep the troops of both combatants fighting on the island of Guadalcanal.

Enterprise, *Saratoga* and *Wasp* – to intercept the bombers, without the vital landing programme being seriously disrupted. But Vice-Admiral Mikawa, commanding at Rabaul, planned a night attack with four heavy cruisers, two light cruisers and a destroyer to surprise and destroy the American invasion force. His final approach would bypass Savo Island, lying in the Slot off Guadalcanal's north-western tip, to the south. Rear-Admiral Crutchley of the Royal Navy commanded the American and Commonwealth cruiser/destroyer force screening the landings. Alerted by reports of Japanese warships at sea (course and number unknown) he had posted radar-equipped destroyers to patrol west of Savo Island and divided his five American and three Australian cruisers into a Northern and a Southern Group, each east of Savo.

Mikawa's high-speed approach in line-ahead was not detected by the American destroyer *Blue*; by 0130 hours on the 9th the Japanese cruisers were sweeping past Savo with a spotter plane aloft. At 0145 the latter dropped flares to illuminate the transports and Mikawa's force fell on the unsuspecting Southern Group, scattered it, and swung north to repeat the process with the Northern Group. In just fifty minutes Mikawa's force, illuminating its victims with searchlights and attacking with gunfire and torpedoes, wrecked the Australian cruiser *Canberra* and the American cruisers *Astoria*, *Quincy* and *Vincennes*, all four ships sinking. But although Mikawa had destroyed the Allied screening force he decided to retire without re-forming his ships and attacking the transports. Such a move would have ensured that the Japanese warships would have had to return up the Slot in full daylight, courting annihilation by American carrier aircraft. As it was he lost the cruiser *Kako* to an attack by the American submarine *S-44* on 10 August.

The American landing on Guadalcanal was successfully completed, but Admiral Fletcher refused to keep the three American carriers within range of the Japanese airfields; and this withdrawal of close air support resulted in the temporary isolation of the Marines on Guadalcanal. From 17 August the Japanese began landing their own troops on the

island by night; by the 20th, US Marine fighters and dive-bombers were operating from Henderson Field, making the destruction or capture of the airfield the main Japanese objective. The next major clash at sea occurred on the 24th, when the Japanese commander-in-chief, Admiral Yamamoto, tried to succeed where he had failed at Midway and lure the American carriers to destruction. Yamamoto planned to use the light carrier *Ryujo* as a sacrificial offering with which to expose Fletcher's carriers to attack from *Shokaku* and *Zuikaku*, the Japanese carriers which had missed Midway. Meanwhile, Rear-Admiral Tanaka would land more troops on Guadalcanal.

The Japanese plan almost succeeded. On 24 August Fletcher attacked *Ryujo* before *Shokaku* and *Zuikaku* had been sighted. *Ryujo* was duly sunk, but the counter-strike from *Shokaku* and *Zuikaku* damaged *Enterprise* with three bomb hits. Well-alerted American air defences, supplemented by the massive firepower of the new battleship *North Carolina*, again cost the Japanese more aircrew than they could afford (seventy out of the eighty Japanese aircraft in the strike were lost). When both sides drew off at dusk the battle ended inconclusively.

Over the next month the American carriers covered more supply missions into Guadalcanal, but their patrol zone was dangerously predictable. *Saratoga* was crippled for three months on 31 August and *Wasp* was sunk on 15 September, both by Japanese submarines. With *Enterprise* still repairing the damage of the Eastern Solomons, this temporarily reduced the American carrier strength to *Hornet*. Meanwhile fresh cruisers and destroyers were arriving in the South Pacific and a new striking force was formed under Rear-Admiral Scott to challenge the Japanese mastery of the Slot by night. On the night of 11–12 October, Scott's force got its chance off Cape Esperance.

On the night of the 11th another 'Tokyo Express' headed for Guadalcanal with troops and artillery. Cover was provided by Rear-Admiral Goto with three cruisers and two destroyers, under orders to bombard Henderson Field after the landings had been made. Scott's force of four cruisers and five destroyers was perfectly placed to intercept Goto west of Savo Island, heading across the bows of the Japanese. But once again American inexperience threw away the advantage of radar. The cruiser *Helena*'s radar picked up the approaching force, but fifteen minutes were wasted before word was passed to Scott in his flagship. What should have been a battle of annihilation ended with the Japanese losing only the destroyer *Fubuki* and the cruiser *Furutaka*, with severe damage to the cruiser *Aoba*. The Americans needlessly lost the destroyer *Duncan*, while the cruiser *Boise* and destroyer *Farenholt* were badly damaged. To offset this narrow American tactical victory, all the Japanese reinforcements were landed in safety.

By the middle of October the Japanese had discovered the formula which brought them closest to victory on Guadalcanal: using their night control of the sea to bombard Henderson Field. Goto's bombardment mission was foiled at Cape Esperance, but on the next three nights Japanese heavy cruisers and the 14-inch-gun battleships *Hiei* and *Kirishima* virtually closed down Henderson Field with their devastating gunfire. Yamamoto now sent the full strength of the Japanese Combined Fleet to circle round the Solomons, keep off the American carriers from the east, and, once General Hyakutake's troops had taken Henderson Field, fly in aircraft to clinch Japan's victory on Guadalcanal.

This brought on some of the bloodiest land fighting of the campaign as the Marines repelled Hyakutake's fanatical attacks. And at sea it resulted in the desperate carrier battle fought north of the Santa Cruz Islands, east of the Solomons, on 26 October. The American Rear-Admiral Kinkaid, with only *Hornet* and *Enterprise*, was up against *Shokaku*, *Zuikaku* and the light carriers *Zuiho* and *Junyo*. Although the Americans damaged *Zuiho* and *Shokaku*, they were forced to retire when *Hornet* was reduced to a wreck. But this new tactical victory, thanks to the growing prowess of American pilots and the steady drain of experienced Japanese pilots, left the Japanese carrier arm with sufficient aircraft only for the light carriers *Junyo* and *Hiyo*. This, plus the Marines' defence of Henderson Field, made Santa Cruz an American strategic victory.

After Santa Cruz both sides resumed running in supplies by night, making inevitable further clashes in 'Ironbottom Sound', the strait between Savo Island and Guadalcanal (so named because of the number of ships sunk there). On the night of 12–13 November ('First Guadalcanal'), Admiral Callaghan's cruiser/destroyer force engaged Vice-Admiral Abe commanding the battleships *Kirishima* and *Hiei*. The Japanese wrecked the cruisers *Portland*, *Atlanta*, *Juneau* and the destroyer *Aaron Ward*, and sank four other destroyers, also killing Admirals Scott and Callaghan – but *Hiei*, damaged and forced to retire, was caught in daylight by aircraft from Henderson Field on the following morning, and so badly damaged that she had to be scuttled.

'Second Guadalcanal', on the following night,

came after a day of furious air activity against a new Japanese troop convoy escorted by Admiral Tanaka. Meanwhile, to fend off a return visit by Japanese battleships, the Americans had brought up the battleships *Washington* and *South Dakota*. For once the Americans, under Rear-Admiral Lee, made full use of their radar advantage. In the now-familiar cruiser/destroyer *mêlée* in Ironbottom Sound the Americans lost three more destroyers, but *Kirishima* was pounded to a wreck by *Washington*'s radar-guided guns. Another Japanese attempt had failed to get through and bombard Henderson Field. With great tenacity, Tanaka had managed to land 2000 troops and a handful of supplies, but only by beaching and writing off eleven invaluable troop transports. These were the last Japanese reinforcements to land on Guadalcanal. With Henderson Field soon secure, the initiative remained in American hands.

The last sea battle off Guadalcanal came at the end of November when Tanaka sailed for Guadalcanal with a 'Tokyo Express' of eight destroyers. His plan was to make a high-speed run past Tassafaronga Point, jettisoning buoyant supply containers to be washed ashore and picked up by the troops. Rear-Admiral Wright, with five cruisers and six destroyers, was waiting for Tanaka but was disconcerted by the speed of the Japanese advance. When the American cruisers tardily opened fire, Tanaka's veteran destroyer commanders whirled to attack with their 'Long Lance' torpedoes, crippling the cruisers *Minneapolis*, *Pensacola* and *New Orleans* and sinking *Northampton*. Tanaka escaped with the loss of one destroyer, *Takanami*.

Though the order to evacuate was not given until 4 January 1943, December was the month in which the Japanese accepted defeat on Guadalcanal. The Japanese had lost the equivalent of a peacetime fleet: two battleships, one carrier, five cruisers and twelve destroyers. Only their superiority at night enabled them to evacuate, in a series of night runs, 12,000 exhausted and fever-ridden troops (1–7 February).

USS *New Orleans* lies camouflaged at anchor after losing her bow in the battle of Tassafaronga on 30 November 1942, when Rear-Admiral Tanaka secured a minor victory.

Barents Sea

A CONVOY ACTION IN NORTHERN WATERS

When the Soviet Union was forced into World War II by the German invasion of June 1941, the British were already fighting for their lives in the battle of the Atlantic and were also hard-pressed in the Mediterranean. Britain's decision to send supply convoys to northern Russia therefore put an almost unbearable strain on the Royal Navy when it came to finding warships to operate in this new naval theatre. True to its traditions, however, the navy rose to the challenge, and conducted many operations which were classics of convoy escort, in difficult conditions and often against great odds. The battle of the Barents Sea is probably the best example of these operations.

The Russian convoys were faced by a number of hazards; amongst these was running the gauntlet of the Barents Sea, which features some of the most appalling weather conditions in the world. The convoy route was penned between the Arctic ice-edge to the north and the Luftwaffe's nearby airfields in northern Norway. Winter convoys, when Murmansk was the only ice-free port at journey's end, were forced 320km (200 miles) closer

A tanker in an Atlantic convoy falls victim to a German torpedo. When hit, tankers tended either to blow up immediately or burn for some time.

to the German airfield by the ice-edge; when the ice receded in summer, the midnight sun favoured non-stop German air attacks on convoys to Archangel in the White Sea. As if the weather, the Luftwaffe and the U-boats detached to attack the Russian convoys were not enough, the convoys and their escorts had to endure a fourth menace: the heavy warships of the German surface fleet, based in the northern Norwegian fjords.

The notorious 'PQ' convoys (September 1941–September 1942) had got off to an easy start because the German surface ships were still mostly deployed in southern waters. By the spring of 1942, however, the German air and naval build-up for attacks on the convoys was proceeding apace. In early July 1942 came the débâcle of PQ-17. Fears that the battleship *Tirpitz*, pocket-battleship *Scheer* and heavy cruiser *Hipper* had sortied to attack convoy PQ-17 caused the British Admiralty to order the convoy to scatter. Though the German ships never came anywhere near the convoy, the scattered merchantmen fell easy prey to Luftwaffe and U-boat attacks.

After P Q-18 arrived at Archangel on 20 September 1942, the convoys were temporarily suspended until the winter. All experience had shown that such large convoys (thirty to forty merchantmen) were almost impossible to defend properly, even with a fighting escort of destroyers to keep down U-boats and help beat off air attacks. Future convoys (redesignated 'JW' for security reasons) would be split in half, the second half sailing a week after the first. There were encouraging signs that the Germans were considerably reducing their air strength in northern Norway to meet the demands of the Eastern Front (this was the autumn and winter of Stalingrad). But it was the German warships that posed the biggest threat, though perhaps the most encouraging lesson of the PQ convoys had been that German surface forces tended to attack with notable caution, and had been outfaced by resolute manoeuvring by the escorts.

Grand-Admiral Raeder still believed that the Russian convoys offered the German navy unique opportunities. In December 1942, when the JW convoys started running, Raeder planned to attack them with the pocket-battleship *Lützow*, the *Hipper*, and six destroyers – Operation *Regenbogen* ('Rainbow'). The first of the new convoys, JW-51A, sailed from Iceland for Murmansk on 15 December, with seven destroyers and five smaller warships to escort the fifteen merchantmen, heavier support being available in the form of Rear-Admiral Burnett's cruisers *Sheffield* and *Jamaica*. This convoy went straight through to Murmansk without a hitch; but this alerted the Germans to the fact that the Russian convoys were running again.

JW-51B sailed on the 22nd: fourteen merchantmen escorted by Captain Sherbrooke's six destroyers, two corvettes, two trawlers and a minesweeper. All went well until the 27th, when the destroyer *Oribi* lost contact due to compass failure; and the same night the convoy was hit by a gale which scattered the convoy's port wing column. The minesweeper *Bramble* was detached to search for the missing ships, three of which rejoined on the 29th; the trawler *Vizalma*, also detached by the gale, found a fourth and escorted her independently; the fifth eventually reached Murmansk on her own. Meanwhile Burnett had headed west with *Sheffield* and *Jamaica* to help JW-51B past the North Cape; but the gale had forced the convoy further south and west than Burnett had expected.

On 30 December a U-boat sighted JW-51B and reported a convoy of six to ten ships with a weak escort – precisely the vulnerable target for which Raeder had hoped. At 1800 hours that day Vice-Admiral Oscar Kummetz sailed from Altenfjord, flying his flag in *Hipper*, with *Lützow* and the six destroyers in company. By 0830 a.m. on the 31st, as Kummetz headed north-east to attack the convoy from the west, the British forces were scattered. *Vizalma* and her merchantman were 72km (45 miles) north of the convoy and Sherbrooke's five destroyers in company. By 0830 on the 31st, as (15 miles) to the south-east, trying to find the convoy, which was 50km (31 miles) to the south; and *Bramble*, still looking for stragglers, was 24 km (15 miles) north-east of the convoy.

Kummetz meanwhile had divided his forces at 0240 hours, taking *Hipper* north with three destroyers to approach the convoy from the north while Captain Stänge came in from the south with *Lützow* and the other three destroyers. This was an admirable move which promised to exploit the German superiority in firepower to the full, even though Kummetz had been given specific orders not to risk his ships even against an enemy of equal strength.

On the British side, Sherbrooke had worked out a well-considered defence plan in the event of an attack by German surface forces. His destroyers were to concentrate on the threatened flank of the convoy, which was to make smoke and turn away while the destroyers engaged. When the time came, Sherbrooke's plan saved JW-51B from the *Hipper* but should have been quite incapable of stopping *Lützow* from racing up from the south and savaging the convoy like a tiger let loose in a flock of goats.

As it happened, *Hipper*'s destroyers were the first German ships sighted. At 0941 Sherbrooke sent off an enemy sighting report, but *Hipper* was sighted within minutes of the destroyers. From about 0940 to 1020 Sherbrooke in *Onslow*, accompanied only by *Orwell*, dodged in and out of a smoke-screen and kept *Hipper*'s attention fixed while *Obdurate* and *Obedient* moved back to join *Achates* in screening the convoy from any attack by the German destroyers.

TOP An Allied convoy to Russia sails through the twilight in October 1942, watched by a British seaman on board an escorting vessel.

ABOVE *Ayrshire*, a British armed trawler, prepares to join Convoy PQ-17. This vessel is typical of the deep-sea trawlers used as escorts.

Shortly after 1000 hours Burnett signalled to Sherbrooke that he was heading south with *Sheffield* and *Jamaica*, having taken until 0955 to deduce that two worrying radar contacts to the north (*Vizalma* and her merchantman) must in fact be stragglers from the convoy, which was lying much further south than Burnett had anticipated. *Sheffield* and *Jamaica* raced south, heading for the gun flashes from the one-sided action between *Hipper* and *Orwell*.

At about 1020 *Hipper* finally got *Orwell*'s range and crippled the British destroyer with a damaging series of 8-inch hits. Though severely wounded, Sherbrooke stayed on his bridge until he knew that command of the destroyers had passed to Lieutenant-Commander Kinloch in *Obedient* (1035). By this time the guns had temporarily fallen silent and the fast-approaching *Sheffield* and *Jamaica*

were hard put to tell friend from foe on radar alone. In thick weather with repeated snow squalls, this was a major problem for both sides during the battle. At 1036, however, *Hipper* ran across the solitary *Bramble* and sank her at close range; nine minutes later, *Sheffield* caught her first glimpse of *Hipper* through the snow and gave chase.

Leaving the destroyer *Friedrich Eckholdt* to make sure of *Bramble*, *Hipper* raced south at 31 knots with *Sheffield* and *Jamaica* on her tail. By 1100 hours *Lützow* was within 8km (5 miles) of the convoy with only the corvettes *Rhododendron* and *Hyderabad* in her path, but Stänge was holding back and hoping for better visibility before attacking. His delay robbed Kummetz of a resounding victory. As *Hipper* came down from the north she opened fire on *Achates* at 1115 and smashed her to a wreck; but *Orwell*, *Obdurate* and *Obedient* bravely moved out to intercept, threatening a torpedo attack which caused *Hipper* to retire north – straight towards *Sheffield* and *Jamaica*.

The intervention of the out-gunned British cruisers was decisive. Completely surprised, Kummetz took *Hipper* off to the west at 1145, having taken three 6-inch hits. *Hipper*'s escape was assisted by the sudden appearance of the destroyers *Friedrich Eckholdt* and *Richard Beitzen* on the flank of the British cruisers, which sank *Eckholdt* at point-blank range and forced *Beitzen* to retire. *Lützow* had briefly opened fire on one of the convoy's merchantmen, inflicting minor damage before being forced to shift his fire to the *Obdurate*; and almost at once *Lützow* received Kummetz's order to break off the action and retire. At the very moment that victory had been his for the taking, Kummetz had abandoned it to the British, whose battered ships sailed on and delivered JW-51B safely at Murmansk on 3 January 1943.

The aftermath of the Barents Sea action came close to being as big a German defeat as the battle could have been a German victory. Hitler raged at the indecision and timidity which he himself had instilled in his admirals and captains, denounced the surface fleet as a waste of good men, guns and steel, and ordered the fleet to be scrapped. Raeder resigned in protest, but his successor Dönitz soon persuaded Hitler that the German surface warships must be retained, if only to keep the British Home Fleet pinned in Scapa Flow. Thus the heaviest German warships still in commission – *Tirpitz* and the battle-cruiser *Scharnhorst* – survived to haunt the Russian convoys of 1943.

North Cape

SWANSONG OF THE *SCHARNHORST*

The battle of the North Cape (26 December 1943) was the last battleship action fought in European waters. It culminated in the sinking of the German battle-cruiser *Scharnhorst*, leaving the battleship *Tirpitz* as the last German capital ship capable of seriously inhibiting British naval strategy. Like the Barents Sea action of the previous year, the North Cape battle followed an attempted German naval strike at an Allied convoy bound for northern Russia.

The climax of the battle of the Atlantic combined with the bitter lessons of summer 1942 to cause the British Admiralty to insist on suspending the Russian convoys for the summer of 1943. By the end of March 1943 the Germans had concentrated a strong battle-squadron at Altenfjord in northern Norway: *Tirpitz*, the pocket-battleship *Lützow*, and finally *Scharnhorst*, long regarded as a 'lucky ship' in the German navy. These ships present the classic example of the 'fleet in being' and its role: an operational force which, despite its small size, pins down superior enemy forces by reason of its very existence; a threat which cannot be ignored and which must if possible be destroyed.

Once the Allies had gained the upper hand in the battle of the Atlantic (from May 1943) the British tried to eliminate the menace of the German force at Altenfjord by sending in an X-craft (midget submarine) attack on 22 September. The X-craft failed to locate *Scharnhorst* and *Lützow* because they were

C. E. Turner's painting entitled 'The Sinking of the Scharnhorst' reflects the destruction wrought by the shells and torpedoes of the British Home Fleet.

coming German naval movements than had been previously available. The first two convoys of the new cycle, J W - 5 4 A and J W - 5 4 B, caught the Germans by surprise and arrived in Murmansk without loss. But when Fraser heard that the Germans had sighted J W - 5 5 A, which sailed from Iceland on 12 December, he decided that a German naval sortie against the convoy was extremely likely. Fraser therefore took his battleship covering force all the way through to Murmansk, arriving without incident on 18 December.

Fraser was convinced that *Scharnhorst* would attempt a sortie against the next convoy, J W - 5 5 B. He therefore trained his ships for a night encounter (the most likely condition at that time of year), operating in two groups. 'Force 1' comprised Rear-Admiral Burnett's cruisers *Belfast*, *Sheffield* and *Norfolk*. These would sail west to cover R A - 5 5 A, the return convoy from Murmansk, and 'pick-up' J W - 5 5 B as it approached the longitude of North Cape. Fraser himself would follow J W - 5 5 B with 'Force 2': the battleship *Duke of York*, the cruiser *Jamaica* and four destroyers. If *Scharnhorst* were located, Fraser planned to close the range, illuminate her with starshell and open fire with *Duke of York*'s 14-inch guns, detaching the destroyers for torpedo attacks.

Fraser's plan would allow Force 2 to remain in the danger zone off North Cape for about thirty hours. He was ready to take the risk of leaving the convoy temporarily undefended in order to bring *Scharnhorst* to action; and he insisted that radio silence would be broken whenever necessary to keep the two British forces fully informed of each other's movements. Sacrificing radio silence for accurate information would, he believed, avoid much of the confusion which had marked the Barents Sea battle twelve months before.

On the German side, Dönitz was equally determined to demonstrate to Hitler that the German surface fleet still had a role to play. He wanted the battle group of *Scharnhorst* and six destroyers to make some kind of gesture to prove that the German navy was ready to fight in support of the hard-pressed armies on the Eastern Front. *Ostfront* ('Eastern Front') was, in fact, the codename coined for the operation. The German commander would not be Admiral Kummetz, who had come so close to success in the Barents Sea action but was now on sick leave. Kummetz would be replaced by Rear-Admiral Bey, his first independent command since his shattering defeat at Narvik in 1940.

On 22 December German air reconnaissance sighted J W - 5 5 B coming up from the west, having left Iceland on the 20th. Also on the 22nd, R A - 5 5 A sailed from Murmansk. On the following day Burnett left Murmansk with Force 1, and Fraser sailed from Iceland with Force 2. Worried about the distances separating J W - 5 5 B from Forces 1 and 2, Fraser broke radio silence for the first time at 1325 hours on the 24th. He ordered the convoy to reverse

TOP The *Scharnhorst* at sea. The turreted guns are the vessel's 5.9-inch secondary armament, with anti-aircraft guns above and in the foreground.

ABOVE HMS *Duke of York*, which opened fire at long range, disabling Scharnhorst with her 14-inch shells.

out on exercises, but badly damaged *Tirpitz*, the most dangerous of the three ships. Within a week of the attack, *Lützow* had been withdrawn to the Baltic. This completely changed the naval balance in northern waters, and plans went ahead to restart the cycle of 'J W' convoys to Russia.

Admiral Sir Bruce Fraser, commander-in-chief of the British Home Fleet, believed that *Scharnhorst* would sooner or later risk an attack on a convoy, and he was determined to bring her to action. He had the benefit of one technological advance which his predecessor had lacked: 'Ultra' intercepts of German coded signals, which gave British naval intelligence a much more accurate picture of forth-

course for three hours and increased his own speed to 19 knots. Twelve hours later he broke radio silence again, ordering R A-5 5 A to swing further north and detach four of its escorting destroyers (the 36th Division) to reinforce the escort of J W-5 5 B. Neither of these messages was intercepted and the Germans remained unaware that a British battleship force was at sea. At 1415 hours on the 25th Dönitz ordered 'Eastern Front – 1700', a message picked up by the British. So was a signal from *Scharnhorst* five hours after she sailed at 1900 hours on the 25th, reporting that she was entering the operation area. By 0339 on the 26th, Fraser knew that *Scharnhorst* was at sea.

Fraser broke radio silence again at 0401, this time ordering all forces to report their positions. It was now clear that Burnett's Force 1 would be the first to make contact with *Scharnhorst* if she made straight for the convoy. At 0605 Fraser therefore ordered the convoy to head further north, and Burnett to steer for the convoy and cover it. Shortly after 0700, Bey turned *Scharnhorst* to the south-west, ordering his destroyers to fan out ahead and search for the convoy. But at 0840 *Belfast*'s radar located *Scharnhorst*, and at 0921 the British cruisers sighted her for the first time. *Norfolk*, the only cruiser able to get into action, opened fire at 0925. Bey's reaction was to try and duck round the British force, swinging abruptly south, then north. The outpaced British cruisers tracked *Scharnhorst* by radar until they lost her shortly after 1000 hours. Fraser had meanwhile ordered the 36th Division to leave the convoy and join Burnett ahead of the convoy. This blocking move was complete by 1100, and at 1205 radar contact was regained.

The second cruiser action (1224–1241 hours) resulted in moderate damage to *Norfolk* but was decisive in causing Bey to swing *Scharnhorst* to the south-south-west, pursued as ever by Burnett. Fraser, doggedly ploughing east with Force 2, now knew that unless radar contact was lost again he had an excellent chance of intercepting *Scharnhorst* from the west. Meanwhile Bey had been passed a German air reconnaissance report that a second British force had been sighted to the west – but the message made no mention of a British battleship. For three hours, Bey unknowingly continued to steam on a converging course with *Duke of York*. He ordered his destroyers to abandon their abortive search for the convoy at 1418 hours and return to base. *Scharnhorst* was therefore on her own when *Duke of York*'s radar located her at 1617 hours at a range of about 35km (22 miles).

Excellent radar data and his own outstanding gunnery expertise allowed Fraser to position *Duke of York* perfectly for her opening 14-inch salvo, prefaced by starshell illumination from *Belfast* and *Duke of York*, at 1650. The first salvos from *Duke of York* and *Jamaica* scored hits, but as Bey turned and steamed east at 32 knots, a pace which only the fragile British destroyers could match, the range

began to open. Force 1 entered the fray at 1657 hours but by 1712 *Scharnhorst* was out of range of the cruisers. Had Bey refrained from yawing continuously south to fire broadsides at *Duke of York*, he might have contrived to outpace his pursuers. As it was, the lengthening range meant that *Duke of York*'s guns fired at bigger and bigger angles of elevation, giving her plunging 14-inch shells much more destructive power than they would have had at a shorter range. At 1820 hours *Scharnhorst*'s 'B' turret was knocked out and her speed was temporarily cut to 10 knots by a broken steam pipe, enabling the British destroyers to close and attack with torpedoes.

As *Duke of York* ceased fire, the destroyers *Savage*, *Scorpion*, *Saumarez* and *Stord* made the torpedo attack which sealed *Scharnhorst*'s fate. Four hits were scored, causing severe flooding and reducing *Scharnhorst*'s speed to less than that of *Duke of York*. Fraser and Burnett now came in for the kill, reopening fire from 1901 to 1930 hours. By 1915, *Scharnhorst*'s last 11-inch turret had been silenced, her speed further cut to less than 10 knots, and she had developed a list to starboard. In obedience to Fraser's terse signal 'Finish her off with torpedoes,' *Belfast*, *Jamaica*, and the destroyers *Musketeer*, *Virago* and *Opportune* of the 36 Division went in to deliver the *coup de grâce*. Having taken an incredible amount of punishment – eleven torpedo hits and about thirteen 14-inch shells, not to mention lesser hits from smaller ships – *Scharnhorst* sank around 1945 hours. Only thirty-six of her complement of 1840 were saved. J W-5 5 B sailed on to Russia without a single casualty, with Fraser paying a triumphant second visit to Murmansk in *Duke of York*.

The Royal Navy's light cruiser HMS *Sheffield* makes way in heavy seas. This vessel formed part of Rear-Admiral Burnett's 'Force 1'.

Philippine Sea

'THE GREAT MARIANAS TURKEY SHOOT'

The battle of the Philippine Sea was the greatest battle fought exclusively between rival fleets of aircraft-carriers. Taking place on 19–20 June 1944, two years after Midway, which saw the defeat of Japan's original peacetime carrier fleet, the Philippine Sea action repeated the process with Japan's reconstructed carrier fleet. After the murderous air losses suffered in the Philippine Sea fight, Japan was left with only a handful of empty carriers which were unable to pose an active threat to the US Pacific Fleet.

The battle came about when the Japanese navy attempted to disrupt the latest American landings in the Marianas Islands in the central Pacific. The Marianas were to serve as the base for the decisive American drive against the Japanese home islands, and the Japanese High Command was well aware that the islands were a likely target. But with General MacArthur's forces advancing steadily towards the Philippines along the north coast of New Guinea, it was not at first certain whether the Philippines or the Marianas would be the next major American objective after the fall of the Marshall Islands in February 1944.

By the summer of 1944 the Japanese fleet was in much better shape than it had been eighteen months before, after the cumulative ravages of the Coral Sea, Midway and Guadalcanal fighting. The re-styled 'Mobile Fleet' was commanded by Vice-Admiral Jisaburo Ozawa and formed three groups. Vice-Admiral Kurita commanded the 'Van Force' of four battleships, five cruisers and nine destroyers. Ozawa himself commanded 'Carrier Force A': light carriers *Chitose*, *Chiyoda* and *Zuikaku* with the new carrier *Taiho*, screened by three cruisers and nine destroyers. Rear-Admiral Joshima commanded 'Carrier Force B': carriers *Ryuho*, *Junyo* and *Hiyo*, battleship *Nagato*, one cruiser and ten destroyers.

The US navy's aircraft-carrier *Intrepid*. The Philippine Sea was the stage for one of the several battles fought by the US and Japanese carrier fleets.

The Japanese carriers together operated some 432 aircraft.

Ozawa's fleet was, however, dwarfed by the American forces. Vice-Admiral Turner's Expeditionary Force alone had five old battleships, eleven cruisers, and twelve escort carriers which could operate over 300 aircraft. And the Expeditionary Force was covered by Admiral Raymond Spruance's enormous 5th Fleet. Seven large and eight light carriers, in four powerfully screened task groups, made up Vice-Admiral Mitscher's Task Force 58, operating another 900 aircraft. In addition there was Admiral Lee's 'Battle Line': seven new battleships, four cruisers and thirteen destroyers.

Heir to the great Yamamoto as Japanese naval commander-in-chief, Admiral Soemu Toyoda drew up an elegant plan to cancel out the Americans' crushing superiority. The Mobile Fleet would hold back until the next major American invasion had been committed and the 5th Fleet had moved into position to cover the landings. Ozawa would then sortie in full strength, catching the American fleet between the hammer of the Japanese carrier strikes and the anvil of land-based Japanese air attacks. But this 'A-Go' defence plan was a paper tiger. Though it would stand or fall by command of the air, it ignored the fact that Japan had lost thousands of naval aircraft since Pearl Harbor and that most of the Japanese navy's crack airmen were dead. To counter the powerful new American combat aircraft – the excellent Hellcat fighter in particular – the Japanese carrier force was starved of the expert pilots who alone could have atoned in part for the Americans' technical superiority and combat expertise.

But the biggest weakness of the 'A-Go' plan was the under-estimation of the damage done by American 'softening-up' carrier strikes at the land airfields. These began four days before the landings on Saipan on 15 June and by the 19th American air superiority over the Marianas was complete, with only fifty Japanese aircraft left operational on Guam. And this depleted handful represented the land-based force which, in the 'A-Go' plan, was supposed to eliminate a third of the American carrier force before Ozawa came in from the west to deliver the *coup de grâce*.

When ordered to carry out 'A-Go' on 15 June, Ozawa had one advantage: the superior range of Japanese scout aircraft, which by the evening of the 18th had sighted parts of the US 5th Fleet 675km (420 miles) to the east. Spruance, on the other hand, had no up-to-date positive information on the whereabouts of the Japanese fleet. Three American submarines had sighted Japanese naval forces on the 15th and 17th and radio intercepts made it clear that a major Japanese counter-blow was imminent. Spruance therefore decided to play safe and stand on the defensive west of Guam, relying on the abund-

The *Intrepid* burns after Japanese bombers find their mark. The final result of the battle, however, was a resounding victory for the US navy.

A Japanese aircraft plunges on its final dive against a background of clouds and anti-aircraft fire. An American escort carrier stands by.

ant Hellcats of Mitscher's carriers to defend the American fleet against Japanese air attacks from either quarter.

Events on 19 June began with a whirling air battle over Orote Field on Guam, in which over thirty Japanese aircraft were shot down none getting clear to attack the American fleet. Unaware that the land-based air element of the 'A-Go' plan was being defeated with ease by the American carrier fighters, Ozawa launched his first carrier strike of sixty-nine aircraft at 0830 hours, followed just before 0900 by a second strike of 128 aircraft.

Ozawa's aircraft were still taking off when *Taiho* was attacked by the American submarine *Albacore*, which had been stationed in the anticipated path of the Japanese fleet with three other submarines. Of *Albacore*'s six torpedoes, one was exploded in a matchless act of self-sacrifice by Sakio Komatsu, a

Japanese pilot who spotted the incoming torpedo and dived his aircraft on to it. Another scored a hit which did not prevent *Taiho* launching her aircraft, but which started an insidious and ultimately fatal leak of petrol vapour.

American radar detected the incoming Japanese first wave when it was still 240km (150 miles) away, giving Mitscher time to recall the fighters operating over Guam and send up a massive air umbrella of fighters. Not a single Japanese aircraft of the first wave got through to attack, and by 1100 hours forty-two of the sixty-nine had been shot down. The second wave fared little better, though twenty Japanese aircraft got past the Hellcats and launched abortive attacks. One torpedo-plane smashed into the battleship *Indiana* on her waterline but the torpedo failed to explode, and not a single hit was scored on the American carriers.

The survivors of the Japanese first wave were landing on their carriers when *Shokaku* suffered three torpedo hits at 1220. The torpedoes were fired by the American submarine *Cavalla*, which had been chasing the Japanese task force ever since sighting it on the evening of the 17th. Desperate efforts were made to save *Shokaku* but she sank at 1624 after a final giant explosion caused by petrol fumes. Meanwhile, six hours after being torpedoed by *Albacore*, *Taiho* had become a floating bomb for the same reason. She blew up at 1532 hours and went down four minutes after *Shokaku*, having forced Ozawa to make a hasty shift of flag to the cruiser *Haguro*.

Haguro was not fitted for fleet command and her spartan communications prevented Ozawa from learning the full magnitude of the day's defeats in the air. Two more Japanese carrier strikes had been launched before noon, of forty-seven and eighty-two aircraft respectively. Half the first strike failed to find the American fleet and turned back; the other half made an ineffective attack, scoring no hits, before being driven off by the Hellcats at 1300 hours. The second strike had been guided too far south because of a scout plane's error. One group of thirty-three was shot down while attacking the southernmost American carrier group; the other forty-nine found nothing and headed for Guam. Throughout the day American carrier bombers had been plastering Orote field in order to leave their flight-decks clear for fighter operations and Orote's runways were unusable, but only a handful of the incoming Japanese aircraft survived to discover this. Thirty of them were shot down by Hellcats before they had even sighted the field.

All in all, Japanese aircraft losses on 19 June (including those based on Guam) came to 346 for a total of only twenty-nine American aircraft lost. What the Americans called the 'Great Marianas Turkey Shoot' had been one of the most decisive and one-sided air victories of the entire war. But Ozawa did not know it. He chose to believe the wild claims of his inexperienced surviving pilots that four American carriers had been sunk and many American aircraft had been downed. He also chose to believe that a good deal of missing pilots had flown on to Guam and would be ready to renew the battle on the 20th. Virtually isolated in the inadequate *Haguro*, he ordered a retirement north-west to a prearranged refuelling rendezvous. By the time he transferred to *Zuikaku* and restored order to his confused fleet, late in the afternoon of the 20th, it was too late to break off and escape from the pursuing Americans.

When Ozawa's fleet was sighted at 1605 on the 20th, it was almost too late for the Americans to take effective action against it. But Mitscher gambled on an all-out strike at dusk, accepting losses from ditching or crashes caused by aircraft retracing 480km (300 miles) of ocean to land-on in the dark. The strike went in at 1840 and left the carrier *Hiyo*

sinking, carriers *Zuikaku* and *Chiyoda*, battleship *Haruna* and cruiser *Mayo* damaged, and forty-nine Japanese carrier-planes, plus several reconnaissance aircraft shot down. It was another triumph for the Hellcat fighters, eighty-five of which accompanied the strike. Altogether 130 American aircraft were lost, mainly through lack of fuel on the return journey, but many ditched crews were recovered, bringing aircrew losses to only seventy-six men. Ozawa, however, was forced to make his way back to Okinawa with a mere thirty-five aircraft left in his entire fleet.

Spruance was heavily criticized for not having sought out the Japanese fleet more aggressively, but his main brief was the covering of the Saipan bridge-head. This was guaranteed by the 'Great Marianas Turkey Shoot', in which the prime battle honours had gone to the Hellcat fighter.

TOP Bursts of anti-aircraft fire cover the sky above an American task force.

ABOVE A 'Shokaku'-class fleet carrier (centre) turns to evade US bombs, with Japanese destroyers (foreground) taking similar action.

Chester William Nimitz

1885–1966

Admiral Chester Nimitz, commander-in-chief of the Pacific Fleet, is remembered for his cool handling of the Midway crisis in mid-1942.

Without question one of the greatest Allied commanders of World War II, Admiral Chester William Nimitz picked up the US Pacific Fleet from the shattering humiliation of Pearl Harbor, nursed it through the ensuing months of crisis when the outcome of the Pacific war hung in the balance and led it confidently to total victory over the imperial Japanese navy. Among Nimitz's many gifts as a commander-in-chief was his refusal to interfere continually with the operations of his subordinate task-force commanders. Nimitz believed that operations afloat were best left to the man on the spot carrying out a general assigment in the manner he thought best.

Nimitz was a Texan, born at Fredericksburg in 1885. Graduating from the US Naval Academy in 1905, his first naval duty and specialization was in submarines. When the US entered World War I in 1917, Nimitz served as chief of staff to the admiral commanding submarines in the Atlantic. This post led him, in the 1920s, to his first command afloat (a battleship), a return to submarines in command of a squadron, and a course at the Naval War College.

Throughout the 1930s Nimitz followed the usual alternation of shore and sea-going appointments. An important achievement was his establishment of one of the first reserve officers' training units at the University of California, in which he served as an instructor. During 1933–4 he served as flag captain in the Asiatic Fleet, followed by three years as assistant chief of the Bureau of Navigation. He moved up to rear-admiral in command of a cruiser division and then a battleship division before he became Chief of the Bureau of Navigation in 1939. Nimitz replaced Admiral Kimmel as commander-in-chief of the Pacific Fleet on 31 December, with his headquarters at Pearl Harbor.

Nimitz's first vital task was to restore morale at Pearl Harbor after the shock of the Japanese attack. In this his calm and down-to-earth manner worked wonders. His endorsement of the famous 'Doolittle Raid' on Tokyo stemmed not from love of easy publicity – a weakness of so many high-ranking commanders – but from the fact that the raid was the best way of showing the world that the US Pacific Fleet was still very much in the war. No publicity stunt, the Doolittle Raid was a most carefully calculated risk, accepting the virtual aban-

donment of trained aircrews and priceless aircraft at a moment when these were vitally needed elsewhere in the Pacific theatre. By contrast, the succeeding carrier strikes which Nimitz authorized – the Marshalls, Wake, and Marcus – were modest in scope, intended to sound out the Japanese strength.

The Midway crisis of May–June 1942 was Nimitz's finest hour. As if the responsibility he carried for repulsing the coming Japanese assault were not heavy enough, he somehow contrived to be everywhere in person, encouraging and heartening the Midway garrison and the sweating Pearl Harbor dockyard workers without any attempt to conceal the supreme peril of the hour. In the same vein, he ordered Admirals Fletcher and Spruance, the latter completely inexperienced in carrier combat command, to go out and save Midway, inflicting maximum damage for minimum risk as seemed best to them.

It was Nimitz's refusal to make over-hasty interventions or indulge in scapegoat selection that made him such a resounding success as a 'stand-off' fleet commander in whom his admirals had complete confidence. During the repeated early defeats of the Guadalcanal campaign between August 1942 and February 1943, Nimitz realized that genuine success could not be gained without vital if painful combat experience in the night operations at which the Japanese were adept. This did not, however, prevent Nimitz from intervening sharply in the middle of the battle of Leyte Gulf, cutting through the earlier confusion created by Halsey's pursuit of the Japanese carriers. Even then, Nimitz's curt request to Halsey to report the position of the all-important Task Force 34 came more as a reproving tug on the reins rather than as an initiative-crippling counter-order from base.

Nimitz was promoted fleet admiral in December 1944, on the eve of the decisive advance against the heart of the Japanese islands, and was present when the Japanese formally surrendered in Tokyo Bay. He succeeded Admiral Ernest King as Chief of Naval Operations in December 1945 and held this supreme post for two years. His last main service to the US navy was as special adviser to the Navy Secretary on Pacific and West Coast affairs. He died in 1966.

Leyte Gulf

THE GREATEST SEA-BATTLE OF ALL TIME

Leyte Gulf was the last fleet action between the American and Japanese navies in the Pacific war. It was also the greatest sea battle in modern history, involving a grand total of 244 warships of all types. (There had been about ten more ships at Jutland in 1916, but the combined warship *tonnage* at Leyte Gulf was nearly double that of Jutland.) The Leyte Gulf battle spanned three days – 24–6 October 1944 – and destroyed the Japanese Mobile Fleet as an effective combat force. From the start it had amounted to a colossal suicide operation on the part of the Japanese, foredoomed to defeat by the American carrier superiority, and yet a suicide operation which came perilously close to achieving its aim of halting the American invasion of the Philippines.

After their conquest of the Marianas in June–August 1944, the Americans planned to begin the reconquest of the Philippines with a daring

A Curtiss Helldiver bomber breaks formation prior to final landing approach, while the carrier crew on deck prepare to receive it.

amphibious bound from New Guinea to the island of Leyte. Until the airfields on Leyte had been captured and made operational, the invasion forces would be totally reliant on the carriers of the US navy for air cover. Vice-Admiral Kinkaid's 7th Fleet would cover the invasion forces during the assault-and-lodgement phase, with six battleships, eight cruisers, eighteen light escort carriers, and thirty-seven destroyers. Admiral Halsey's huge 3rd Fleet – eight fleet and eight light carriers, four battleships, fourteen cruisers and fifty-seven destroyers – would shield 7th Fleet and destroy any Japanese naval attempts at intervention. In the week before the landing on Leyte (20 October), the 3rd Fleet also had the key task of launching carrier strikes against the main Japanese airfields on Formosa and in the Philippines. These preliminary attacks cut the total strength of Japanese land-based aircraft available for the defence of the Philippines

to under 200, and destroyed most of the reserve which had been hoarded for the coming battle.

On 17 October 1944 a US cruiser/destroyer force began softening up the Japanese-held island of Suluan in the mouth of Leyte Gulf. On the following day Admiral Toyoda, the Japanese naval commander-in-chief, decided that Leyte must be the American objective. He therefore issued his executive orders for 'SHO': an intricate counter-offensive which would commit the entire Japanese fleet to the defence of the Philippines. At Lingga Roads, Singapore, Admiral Kurita's battle-fleet was divided into two parts. 'Force A', under Kurita himself, included the cream of the battleships: *Yamato*, *Musashi*, *Nagato*, *Kongo* and *Haruna*, twelve cruisers and fifteen destroyers. Vice-Admiral Nishimura commanded 'Force C': battleships *Fuso* and *Yamashiro*, a heavy cruiser and four destroyers. 'Force C' was to be reinforced from Japanese waters by Vice-Admiral Shima's '2nd Striking Force' of three cruisers and four destroyers.

'SHO' provided for Forces A and C to head east to Brunei, refuel, then separate for the hazardous approach to Leyte Gulf: an ambitious pincer-movement. Force A was to head north-east from Brunei up the deep-water Palawan Passage, swing east through the Sibuyan Sea, run through San Bernadino Strait and finally head south for Leyte Gulf down the eastern coast of Samar. Force C would take the shorter route east across the Sulu Sea and enter Leyte Gulf from the south via Surigao Strait, timing its approach in order to arrive at the same time as Kurita. As the ships would be most vulnerable when negotiating the narrows of San Bernadino and Surigao Straits, both passages were to be run simultaneously by night – the night of 24–5 October. Meanwhile Vice-Admiral Ozawa would bring the last four carriers south from Japan into the Philippine Sea and play decoy, hopefully drawing off the bulk of the American carriers and

The keynote of the US approach to Leyte Gulf was flexibility of planning, with the Joint Chiefs of Staff working together to open the way to the Philippines.

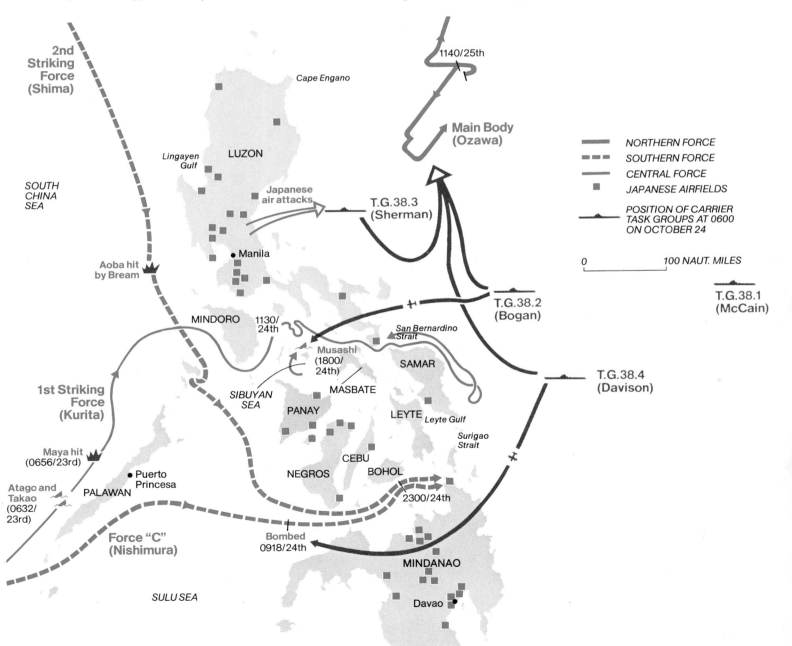

allowing Forces A and C to wreak havoc with the American invasion fleet in Leyte Gulf.

On 20 October the Americans finally landed on Leyte, and the Japanese forces began to move. Kurita and Nishimura arrived at Brunei and began refuelling; Ozawa and Shima set out from Japanese waters. Kurita sailed on the morning of 22 October; Nishimura followed that evening. But Force A was still steaming up the Palawan Passage when, at 0116 hours on the 23rd, it was detected by the radar of the American submarines *Darter* and *Dace*. Each submarine attacked one of the two columns in which Force A was steaming. *Darter* badly damaged the heavy cruiser *Takao* and sank her sister-ship *Atago* – the flagship of Kurita, who was forced to swim for his life with his staff while *Dace* sank a third cruiser, *Maya*. Despite this inauspicious start Force A raced clear of their attackers at 24 knots, remaining undetected, as was Nishimura, for the rest of the 23rd. Later that day, Kurita rehoisted his flag in *Yamato*.

The battle opened on the morning of the 24th. At 0812 scout planes from 3rd Fleet sighted Force A rounding Mindoro Island, but there was no time to launch a concerted strike before 3rd Fleet came under intense air attacks from the Japanese land-based aircraft on Luzon, supplemented by seventy-nine strike aircraft from Ozawa's carriers. In these attacks the carrier *Princeton* was set ablaze and later had to be abandoned with heavy loss of life.

These Japanese attacks prevented any sizeable American carrier strikes at Force A, still approaching across the Sibuyan Sea, until the early afternoon. Around noon, however, the super-battleship *Musashi* was hit by eight torpedoes and four bombs, suffered power failure and dropped out of the line. She became the main target for the afternoon attacks and was finally immobilized by another ten torpedo hits shortly after 1520. Even then, *Musashi*'s tough build and superb counter-flooding by her crew kept her from capsizing and sinking until 1935 hours.

The air attacks on the 24th persuaded Kurita to retire temporarily out of range of the American carriers and he reversed course at 1500 hours, resuming his original course four hours later. But this delay meant that Force A now stood no chance of arriving in Leyte Gulf simultaneously with Force C on the following morning.

As long as the battleships of Force A remained the sole target, Halsey continued to throw the full available weight of 3rd Fleet's air strength against them. He provided for a possible battleship action by concentrating his own battleships and cruisers into a new 'Task Force 34', commanded by Vice-Admiral Lee. But when Ozawa's carriers were finally sighted to the north at 1740 on the 24th, Halsey's instinctive reaction, that of every admiral since the Coral Sea battle back in May 1942, was to attack the enemy carriers.

In deciding to go for Ozawa's carriers (thus falling for the deception element of the 'SHO' plan) Halsey was not to blame for his ignorance that the Japanese carriers were now virtually empty. But he was unwise to conclude that Kurita could pose no further threat after the air strikes of the 24th, and was certainly to blame for leaving Admiral Kinkaid of 7th Fleet with the mistaken impression that Lee's Task Force 34 would be left to guard San Bernadino Strait. As it was, Kinkaid massed all 7th Fleet's battle units north of Surigao Strait to block Force C, which had been spotted heading across the Sulu Sea on the morning of the 24th. This left San Bernadino Strait wide open for Kurita but it also ensured the destruction of Force C, the southern jaw of the 'SHO' pincers.

The action in Surigao Strait began shortly before midnight with torpedo attacks by PT boats and destroyers against both flanks of Nishimura's line. Forewarned by reconnaissance and radar data, Rear-Admiral Oldendorf had laid a perfect ambush across the northern exit from the strait. His battleships and cruisers were deployed across the bows of the Japanese, 'firing over the heads' of the destroyers as they made their decisive torpedo attacks. By 0410 on the 25th it was all over. Nishimura had gone down in *Yamashiro*; *Fuso* and three of the four destroyers were either sunk or sinking. Only the destroyer *Shigure* and cruiser *Mogami* escaped, and the latter was abandoned and sunk after American air attacks on the following day. Shortly before daybreak Shima arrived on the scene of the disaster with 2nd Striking Force and made the prudent decision to retreat.

Exultation at Surigao Strait was immediately followed by consternation off the Samar coast 320 km (200 miles) to the north, when Force A headed south from San Bernadino Strait and caught the northernmost escort carrier group of 7th Fleet completely by surprise. Practically the first warning of acute peril for Rear-Admiral Clifton Sprague's six diminutive carriers came when enormous Japanese shells started exploding around them at 0659 hours. This was the first time that battleships had sighted an enemy carrier since *Scharnhorst* and *Gneisenau* had sunk the British carrier *Glorious* on 8 June 1940.

Granted the supreme opportunity for which the Japanese navy had longed since Midway, Kurita threw away much of his colossal gun superiority by ordering a devil-take-the-hindmost general chase. Frantic evasive action, smoke-screens and timely rain squalls gave Sprague's carriers half an hour to head across wind, just long enough to launch a handful of strike aircraft before fleeing south. By 0716, however, the leading Japanese cruisers were closing the range so fast that Sprague was forced to order the seven ships of his flyweight destroyer screen to counter-attack.

The next two hours saw what Admiral Nimitz later called the most 'glorious two hours of resolution, sacrifice, and success' in the history of the US

The flight-deck of the US navy light carrier *Cowpens*, with Grumman F6F Hellcat fighters queueing for take-off.

navy. The American destroyers attacked again and again, engaging the Japanese cruisers with gunfire when their last torpedoes were expended. *Hoel*, *Johnston* and *Roberts* were lost, but not before forcing the battleships *Kongo* and *Yamato* to shy away, torpedoing the cruiser *Kumano* and battering *Chokai* and *Chikuma* with shells. The aircraft launched at the start of the chase, aided by others from Rear-Admiral Stump's group to the south, attacked with equal gallantry and sank the cruisers *Suzuya*, *Chokai* and *Chikuma*. But by 0910 the rearmost carrier, *Gambier Bay*, had already been overwhelmed and sunk and three others had been badly hit. With the leading Japanese cruisers overhauling the labouring carriers to port, it seemed that nothing could save the whole of Sprague's force from destruction.

Nothing, that is, except Admiral Kurita, far astern in *Yamato*, who abruptly called off the chase at 0915. Already downcast by his own cruiser losses, the destruction of Force C and the absence of news from Ozawa, Kurita now believed that the retreating Americans were deliberately luring him within range of the main carrier fleet. Hardly able to believe their deliverance, the survivors of Sprague's battered 'Taffy 3' headed south to rejoin 7th Fleet.

But their ordeal was not over. The recently formed 'kamikaze' corps of Japanese suicide pilots made its first attacks on the shaken 7th Fleet on the morning of 25 October, damaging the escort carriers *Santee* and *Suwanee* of 7th Fleet's 'Taffy 1'. At 1100 hours a second kamikaze attack hit Sprague's 'Taffy 3'. *Kitkun Bay* and *Kalinin Bay* were damaged, but a plunging Zero smashed through the flight-deck of *St Lô*, exploded in her hangar and sank her in half an hour. But even the shock of the kamikaze attacks did not prevent Sprague's pilots from speeding the parting guest, damaging the battleship *Nagato* and cruiser *Tone* as Kurita retired north towards San Bernadino Strait.

The crisis off Samar prevented Halsey from achieving the total destruction of Ozawa's force, which he decided to attempt before racing south to answer 7th Fleet's appeal for help. When located at 0710 Ozawa's force was 230km (143 miles) ahead of 3rd Fleet and the first American strike did not arrive until 0830. Though consisting of 120 aircraft this achieved little, sinking only the carrier *Chitose*, crippling the cruiser *Tama*, sinking one destroyer and slowing *Zuikaku*, from which Ozawa transferred his flag. A second strike at about 1000 hours set the carrier *Chiyoda* on fire.

At 1115 Halsey reluctantly headed south with Task Force 34 and a single carrier task group, leaving the remainder of 3rd Fleet to finish the job, but the surface threat to 7th Fleet had already passed with Kurita's retirement, and Halsey arrived at San Bernadino Strait three hours after Kurita had escaped through it. Heavy air strikes from the 3rd Fleet carriers sank *Zuikaku* and *Zuiho*, finished off *Tama* and *Chiyoda* and sank the destroyer *Hatsuzuki*, though Ozawa's last two capital ships, the battleship-carriers *Ise* and *Hyuga*, escaped with the light cruiser *Oyodo* and five destroyers. The battle of Cape Engano (named for the nearest point of land in Luzon) was over. On the 26th a frustrated Halsey sent 3rd Fleet's aircraft after Kurita but achieved nothing more than sinking the light cruiser *Noshiro*, and by evening all surviving Japanese forces were out of range.

The three days of Leyte Gulf had cost the Japanese the loss of three battleships, four carriers, ten cruisers and nine destroyers. The two American fleets had lost one fleet carrier and two escort carriers and three destroyers. The battle was the last great naval engagement of World War II, and as such may well have been the last great naval battle of all time. In an age of nuclear weapons and guided missiles, it is unlikely that such huge forces will ever meet in combat again.

William Frederick Halsey

1882–1959

Colourful, extrovert, exuberant 'Bill' Halsey symbolized the US Pacific Fleet's will to avenge the 'stab in the back' by the Japanese navy at Pearl Harbor. His resounding slogan 'Kill Japs, kill more Japs,' was an invaluable boost to American moral.

William Frederick Halsey was born in Elizabeth, New Jersey, in 1882. After his graduation from the US Naval Academy in 1904, Halsey became a destroyer specialist and leading authority on destroyer tactics and strategy. Between the wars, however, Halsey realized that the aircraft-carrier would be the dominant naval weapon of the future. Halsey's conversion was total: he enrolled for flight training at Pensacola in Florida and qualified as a US navy aviator in 1935.

When the Japanese attacked Pearl Harbor in December 1941 Halsey, albeit unknowingly, had already made a sizable contribution towards winning the war. He had taken the Pacific Fleet's aircraft-carriers to sea for exercises, thus saving them from the destruction meted out by the Japanese to the American battle-fleet.

Despite the fitness of Halsey for carrier command and the thoroughness of his preparations, nearly three years were to pass before he got his chance to command a carrier fleet in battle. Commanding Task Force 16 in April–May 1942, Halsey narrowly

Admiral William F. Halsey commanded the US navy's 3rd Fleet at the battle of Leyte Gulf, the biggest sea fight in history.

missed the Coral Sea battle and was in hospital with an incapacitating skin disease on the eve of Midway. Despite this personal misfortune, however, Halsey's contribution to the Midway victory was considerable. Well aware of the teamwork he had built up in Task Force 16, he recommended his deputy, Spruance, to Nimitz as the best available replacement task-force commander. Spruance relied considerably on the advice and expertise of Halsey's fine staff for his victory at Midway.

On returning to active service, Halsey took command of naval operations in the South-West Pacific during the crucial battles for Guadalcanal and the rest of the Solomon Island chain. His resilience and energy were great assets in winning through against the damaging early successes of the Japanese. When the advance into the central Pacific began during 1943 and 1944, Nimitz turned to Halsey as the second commander-in-chief for the massed carrier fleet spearheading each new American offensive. This was styled '5th Fleet' when commanded by Spruance and '3rd Fleet' when commanded by Halsey.

It fell to Spruance to win the greatest carrier battle of the later Pacific war: the battle of the Philippine Sea, in June 1944. But it was Halsey, with his faith in far-ranging carrier strikes, who sensed that it would be possible to begin the all-important invasion of the Philippines in the autumn of 1944 instead of the New Year of 1945.

Halsey finally got his chance at Leyte Gulf in October 1944, which earned him a secure niche in naval history as the victor of the biggest sea fight in history. His controversial pursuit of the Japanese carriers, leaving Kinkaid's 7th Fleet exposed to the Japanese battleships, was possibly explicable, at least in part, by Halsey's earlier frustrations and inability to get to grips with the Japanese through no fault of his own.

It was fitting that 3rd Fleet anchored in Tokyo Bay to receive the Japanese surrender in September 1945. The fleet had already enjoyed the last 'Halsey-ism' of the war, over what procedure should be followed if suicide attacks were made by Japanese pilots after the surrender. 'They will be shot down in friendly fashion,' was Halsey's order.

Halsey finally left 3rd Fleet in November 1945 and undertook duty in the office of the Secretary of the Navy until he retired from the service in 1947. He died in 1959.

Falkland Islands

A TESTING-GROUND FOR NEW TECHNOLOGY

When the first detachment of Argentine soldiers landed by helicopter just outside Port Stanley on the morning of 2 April 1982, few realized then what a dramatic conflict was to ensue, and how significant the military and naval consequences of the campaign were to be. For over a hundred years Argentina had laid claim to the Falkland Islands (or Islas Las Malvinas) but until General Leopoldo Galtieri took power in Argentina in December 1981 such claims were little more than bluster, sops to popular nationalist aspirations. Galtieri realized, however, that the 'recovery' of the Falklands would tremendously increase the popularity of his tottering military government, which was faced by mounting economic and social problems.

The Argentine government instigated a diplomatic campaign to pressure Britain to relinquish its control over the Falklands and at the same time began to whip up a mood of nationalist chauvinism amongst its people. Behind the diplomatic wrangling at the United Nations – and elsewhere – and the anti-British demonstrations in the streets of Buenos Aires, the Argentine armed forces drew up plans for invasion.

The opening moves of the Argentine conquest occurred, in fact, 1300km (800 miles) south-east of the Falklands on the dependent island of South Georgia, when an Argentine scrap-metal crew – contracted to dismantle an old whaling station – raised their national flag and refused to accept British sovereignty. Pressure mounted as the Argentines refused to leave South Georgia, and on 29 March the Argentine fleet put to sea, ostensibly on naval exercises, but the true purpose of the move became apparent two days later when Argentine warships were reported off the Falklands coast.

The die was cast, and during the early hours of 2 April Argentine marines made a text-book amphibious landing around Port Stanley. Despite a fierce struggle by the Royal Marine garrison of seventy-nine soldiers, the Argentine forces proved to be overwhelming and by 1100 hours on the 2nd the Falklands were under Argentine control. The following day another Argentine force seized South Georgia.

The British response to this humiliating loss was surprisingly swift and determined. On Monday 5 April – only three days after the invasion – the first wave of a British task force set sail from Portsmouth under the command of Rear-Admiral J.F. 'Sandy' Woodward. The central element of the task force was provided by the two aircraft-carriers *Hermes* (28,700 tons) and *Invincible* (20,000 tons), which together carried the twenty Sea Harriers responsible for air support. Protecting the carriers were three 'County'-class destroyers, seven Type-42 destroyers, one Type-82 destroyer, three Type-22 frigates, six Type-21 frigates, three 'Rothsay'-class frigates and three 'Leander'-class frigates. The remainder of the naval force was made up of two amphibious assault ships *Fearless* and *Intrepid*, four sub-surface nuclear (SSN) submarines and a number of auxiliary vessels.

The vast distance of 13,000km (8000 miles) from the home base to the Falklands necessitated complex logistical support which was provided by the Royal Fleet Auxiliary and Royal Maritime Auxiliary, and by ships requisitioned from the merchant navy, which ranged from ocean-going tugs to the cruise ships *Canberra* and *Queen Elizabeth II*.

Although the Argentine navy had the advantage of short supply lines, nearby port facilities and, above all, the benefit of shore-based air cover, it adopted a low profile throughout the campaign. Even though the Argentines possessed an effective, though ageing, aircraft-carrier, the *Veinticinco de Mayo*, and a number of British-built Type-42 destroyers, it was no match for the task force and wisely remained in port.

During April – as the task force steamed southward – the politicians attempted to resolve the conflict without recourse to violence. But despite much diplomatic 'shuttling' by Alexander Haig, then the US Secretary of State, neither side would budge, and it became clear that force alone would decide the fate of the Falklands. Britain's determination to win back the islands was made clear with the declaration of a 320-km (200-mile) maritime exclusion zone (MEZ) on 7 April, to come into effect on the 12th, by which time British submarines would be in a position to interdict Argentine supply lines to the Falklands.

The first phase of the British military operation began on 25 April with the recapture of South Georgia. In a cleverly planned and well-executed operation, the British forces suffered no casualties and had the good fortune to sink the Argentine submarine *Santa Fé* while in harbour at Grytviken. With this success behind it the task force then turned its attention to the Falkland Islands themselves.

LEFT One guided-missile destroyer and three frigates of the Royal Naval task force, on their way to the Falkland Islands in April 1982.

BELOW A complete list of the ships of the Royal Navy that made up the task force. Two destroyers, two frigates and the container ship *Atlantic Conveyor* were sunk during the campaign.

Rather than attempt an immediate assault on Argentine positions the British declared a total exclusion zone (TEZ) on 30 April with the intention of wearing down the Argentine garrison by preventing any supplies reaching it by air or sea from Argentina. Now that the Royal Navy was in position off the Falklands, its duties were to enforce the blockade, protect the task force from aerial attack and lastly to put ashore the land force at the right place and at the right time.

Although only a few light vessels slipped through the British sea blockade the protection of the task force from Argentine air attack proved a far harder business. The Argentine air force could call upon sixty-eight A-4 Skyhawk and forty-three Mirage III and Israeli-built Dagger aircraft, flown by well-trained and dedicated pilots, while the task force had only its Sea Harriers and a further twenty-two RAF Harriers, which were also needed to support ground operations. While the Harriers were to distinguish themselves in air combat – their pilots able to out-manoeuvre the Argentine aircraft – they were numerically insufficient to provide comprehensive air protection. Thus the task force was destined to come under direct Argentine air attack.

The sinking of the Argentine cruiser *General*

Royal Navy Task Force

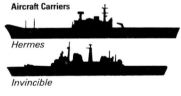

Aircraft Carriers

Hermes
Invincible

County Class Destroyers

Antrim
Fife
Glamorgan

Type 42 Destroyers

Sheffield
Glasgow
Coventry
Exeter
Cardiff
Birmingham
Southampton

Type 82 Destroyer

Bristol

Type 22 Frigates

Broadsword
Brilliant
Battleaxe

Type 21 Frigates

Antelope
Ardent
Arrow
Alacrity
Ambuscade
Active

Rothsay Class Frigates

Yarmouth
Plymouth
Rhyl

Leander Class Frigates

Bacchante
Minerva
Andromeda
Penelope

Submarines

Conqueror
Spartan
Splendid
Sceptre
Ocelot
Onyx

Amphibious Assault Ships

Fearless
Intrepid

Ocean Survey Ships

Hydra
Hecla
Herald

Fishery Protection Vessels

Dumbarton Castle
Leeds Castle

Ice Patrol Vessel

Endurance

Belgrano on 2 May came as a prelude to the main Argentine aerial offensive. The *Belgrano* was sunk just outside the MEZ and out of a crew of over 1000 men some 360 were lost at sea. Two days later it was Britain's turn when the Type-42 destroyer HMS *Sheffield* was hit by an Exocet missile fired at long range by an Argentine Super-Etendard bomber. The Exocet penetrated the *Sheffield* 1m (6ft) above the waterline and then exploded causing a major fire amidships that led to the death of twenty of the ship's crew and left a further twenty-four wounded. The spreading conflagration proved too much for the hastily assembled fire-fighting teams and five hours after the attack the ship was abandoned, eventually to sink on 10 May.

The raid against the *Sheffield* was followed by a full-scale assault on the task force as a whole. Flying Skyhawks and Mirage/Dagger planes the pilots of the Argentine air force reached the combat zone only to be faced by a barrage of surface-to-air missiles (which included Sea Dart, Sea Wolf and Sea Slug) and small-arms fire. The first missile kill recorded by the Royal Navy came on 12 May when four Skyhawks launched a low-level attack against two task-force vessels; two were shot down with Sea Wolf missiles while a third crashed in an attempt to take evasive action.

Also on the 12th, the *Queen Elizabeth II* left port at Southampton with 3500 men of the 5th Infantry Brigade that included the Welsh Guards, the Gurkhas and elements of the Household Cavalry armed with Scorpion light tanks. While awaiting the arrival of the *QE2* the Task Force kept up its pressure on the estimated 10,000 Argentines on the Falklands: Harriers, supported by Vulcan bombers

based on Ascension Island, bombed military bases while the warships of the Royal Navy shelled targets around Port Stanley. On 14 May twelve four-man SAS teams made a successful raid against Pebble Island, destroying radar installations as well as knocking out eleven Argentine light aircraft and blowing up an ammunition dump.

Besides being an exercise to soften up Argentine defences the assault on Pebble Island also helped the task force move towards the Falklands Sound – dividing East and West Falkland – unobserved by the Argentines. On the night of 20–21 May a series of all-out air strikes was launched against the Falklands while the British assault fleet sailed into the Sound. Spearheaded by Royal Marine commandos, British troops scrambled ashore in San Carlos Bay during the early hours of 21 May. After a short but fierce engagement the commandos routed the forty-strong Argentine garrison and a beach-head was swiftly established around San Carlos. During the day 1000 troops came ashore – commandos, paratroops, plus artillery, engineers and logistic support.

Relying again on their air force the Argentine's response to the British landings was to mount ferocious air attacks on the cluster of task force ships in the Falkland Sound. Known as 'bomb alley' the Sound became the scene of the fiercest ship–aircraft battles of the whole campaign. Sparing no effort the Argentines did their utmost to destroy the beach-head and the ships supplying it; in the biggest raid against the task force it was reported that up to eighty Argentine aircraft were employed. Faced by Sea Wolf and Sea Dart missiles from the warships in the Sound and Rapier and even man-portable

Men of the 1st Raiding Squadron, Royal Marines, in training for the invasion of the Falklands. In the background is the amphibious assault ship HMS *Fearless*.

Blowpipe missile launchers from the shore, Argentine casualties were heavy, but a considerable number of aircraft were able to make successful bombing runs. On 21 May the frigate HMS *Ardent* was sunk by a bomb from a Mirage fighter-bomber and two days later another frigate, HMS *Antelope*, was sunk after a 226-kg (500-lb) bomb exploded in her engine room. British losses mounted when the destroyer HMS *Coventry* was sunk and the container ship *Atlantic Conveyor* had to be abandoned after being hit by an Exocet missile. Although these losses caused consternation both at home and within the task force, the British were fortunate in not suffering even heavier casualties. The bombs used by the Argentine air force were of old ex-US World War II stock and the faulty fusing in many of them saved a number of British ships from a watery grave.

Despite all the efforts of the Argentine air force, the beach-head remained secure and British troops pushed inland. On 28 May the 2nd Battalion Parachute Regiment took the settlements of Darwin and Goose Green while the commandos pushed directly eastward towards Port Stanley. Although the centre of the conflict had moved away from the sea to the land, the Royal Navy continued to play a vital role in conveying supplies and munitions to the army as they prepared to assault the main Argentine positions around Stanley.

Bad weather during the first week in June gave the task force respite from the Argentine air force but on the 8th the weather cleared and Argentine warplanes were once again over the Falklands. The main target turned out to be the landing area around Bluff Cove and Fitzroy some 32km (20 miles) south of Port Stanley. Men and equipment of the 5th Infantry Brigade were being put ashore when Argentine Skyhawks and Mirages flew down into Bluff Cove bombing the two logistic landing ships, *Sir Galahad* and *Sir Tristram*. Lacking adequate air defence both ships were badly damaged and fifty-nine troops (forty-three from the Welsh Guards) were killed and a further seventy-four wounded.

The British build-up continued undeterred, however, and by 11 June forward units had secured the high ground near the Falklands' capital. Nevertheless the Argentines continued to resist and on the 11th, HMS *Glamorgan* – one of the destroyers engaged in bombardment duties against Port Stanley – was hit and damaged by a land-based Exocet, killing thirteen of the ship's crew.

On 13 May, after an intense artillery barrage, British troops captured Tumbledown Mountain, Wireless Ridge and Sapper Hill, the key positions looking down onto Port Stanley. The next morning Argentine forces were seen to be retreating from their battle positions into the town and at 2100 local time the 10,000 Argentine troops under the command of General Mendez surrendered to Major-General Moore, the British commander.

The whole campaign had lasted just under eleven weeks, and although relatively short, casualties on both sides had been far from light. The British had lost 255 men killed and over 600 wounded since 2 April and the Argentines over 1000 men killed.

The Falklands campaign was a remarkable venture by any standards, and for the British armed forces especially so. The degree of cooperation displayed between the three services was exemplary – in marked contrast with those of Argentina – and the role played by the Royal Navy and the Fleet Air Arm was central to the success of the whole operation. Not only did British naval and merchant ships endure the full brunt of Argentine air attacks, more significantly they prevented the Argentine navy from venturing away from its bases on the mainland. Thus the ability of the Royal Navy to control the sea lanes isolated the Argentines on the Falklands, converting them, in effect, from invaders to prisoners. The freedom of movement possessed by the task force allowed the land forces to be landed at will. Once ashore, the superior quality and equipment of the British army gave them a tremendous advantage over their more numerous Argentine adversaries, so that only three weeks after the landings at San Carlos the Union Jack was again flying over Port Stanley.

The Type-21 frigate HMS *Ardent* sinking in San Carlos Bay after being hit by à bomb from an Argentine Mirage aircraft.

Glossary of Naval Terms

Admiral The international term for the commander of a fleet, or a part of it.

ASDIC SEE **Sonar**

Barbette Originally a raised gun platform protected by armour; on modern vessels an armoured tube reaching down to the magazine in the lower decks, around the top of which the gun turret revolves.

Battle-cruiser Developed in the early years of this century as a heavily armed, high-speed reconnaissance ship. Sacrificing armour for armament and speed, they were widely used in World War I, but were very vulnerable to enemy fire and few remained in commission by the start of World War II.

Battleship The capital ship of the ironclad and steam-driven navies of the nineteenth century. The size of the battleship increased steadily from the original *Warrior* (1860) of 9200 tons to the 63,000-ton *Yamato* (1944). But it eventually proved too vulnerable to air and underwater attack, and by the end of World War II its position of eminence had been taken by the aircraft-carrier.

Bireme SEE **Galley**

Bow-chaser Gun fitted to the bows of a sailing vessel, enabling it to fire directly ahead.

Cannon General name for smooth-bore artillery used on naval vessels from the fifteenth to the nineteenth centuries. In the early period the various pieces were known by different names: cannon were of large calibre and medium range; culverins of smaller calibre and long range; periers were short guns of short range (usually firing a stone shot); and mortars were very short guns firing loose stones or bullets. From the seventeenth century onwards cannon became standardized and differed only in the weight of shot they fired – 12-pounders, 24-pounders etc. In the late eighteenth century the carronade was introduced, a small gun firing a heavy shot over a short range. Since World War II the term cannon has been applied to automatic weapons firing small-calibre shells, used especially for anti-aircraft defence.

Capital ship The most important class of vessel in a navy. Ships-of-the-line were the capital ships of the eighteenth century; in the late nineteenth century they were superseded by ironclads and in the early twentieth century by

dreadnoughts. During World War II the battleship was replaced by the aircraft-carrier as the capital ship; in the post-war period the vulnerability of all surface vessels to aircraft and missiles has elevated the missile-carrying submarine to capital-ship status.

Captain The international term for the rank below commodore; normally the commander of a ship.

Carrack A large European trading vessel of the fourteenth to seventeenth centuries, also used as a warship. The carrack was square-rigged on fore- and mainmasts, with a lateen sail on the mizen.

Carvel-built Method of wooden boat construction in which the side planks lie flush with each other, as opposed to clinker-built, in which they overlap.

Cathead Heavy timber structure projecting from each bow of a ship used for holding the stock of an anchor temporarily in position. Modern anchor design has made the cathead obsolete.

Cinque ports This confederation of Channel ports (originally made up of Dover, Romney, Hythe, Hastings and Sandwich but to which Winchelsea and Rye were added later) held rights from the king in return for the provision of a fleet in wartime.

Clinker-built SEE **Carvel-built**

Cog A small broad-beamed ship of the Middle Ages, usually with castles fore and aft.

Corvette In the seventeenth and eighteenth centuries a three-masted warship slightly smaller than a frigate. In World War II the term was re-introduced for small escort vessels brought into service as a stopgap measure in the submarine war.

Cruiser In the age of sail large frigates or fourth rates were called cruisers and were used for commerce protection. The designation continued into the steam age with the armoured cruiser (up to 15,000 tons) and the light cruiser (about 5000 tons). Their reconnaissance function has now been taken over by aircraft, though they retain a role in today's navies as missile carriers and general-purpose vessels.

Culverin SEE **Cannon.**

Degaussing The operation of neutralizing a ship's magnetic field so that it will not activate a magnetic mine.

Depth charge An explosive charge which can be detonated at a chosen depth of water. It was invented in World War I as an anti-submarine weapon.

Destroyer Developed towards the end of the nineteenth century as an anti-torpedo-boat vessel, the destroyer was a small ship around 250 tons armed with torpedoes and guns. Fast, well-armed and versatile, they were quickly adopted by all the major navies of the world. Today they remain an important part of any fleet, and range in size up to 5000 tons.

Dreadnought A class of battleship, the first of which, HMS *Dreadnought*, was launched in 1906; these vessels had a large uniform-calibre main armament, high speed and very strong armour.

Dromon A vessel used mainly as a transport or troopship in the Mediterranean during the Middle Ages. It was a large ship for its time, and was propelled by oars, with the assistance of a single mast and square sail.

Fighting Instructions A list of instructions imposing tactical discipline on the British navy. When originally issued in 1653 there were twenty-one; more were added later. Until amended in the late eighteenth century these instructions tended to cramp the initiative of commanders, with occasionally disastrous results.

Flag officer Officer of the rank of rear-admiral or above; officers of this rank have the right to fly a flag (rather than the commodore's broad pennant) on the ship they are commanding.

Fleet Either the total of ships which make up the naval strength of a nation, or a large collection of ships under a single command.

Flotilla Spanish word meaning 'little fleet'. In modern usage, a collection of small warships, especially destroyers or submarines.

Forecastle Originally a small raised platform – the castle – built on the bows of medieval sailing ships, upon which archers were stationed. Thus the short raised deck at the front of the ship became known as the forecastle.

Freeboard The distance from the upper deck to the waterline measured in the middle of the ship.

Frigate In the days of sail, fast lightly armed ships used for reconnaissance and escort work, classified by the British navy as fifth and sixth rates. The term was reintroduced during World War II for small convoy escorts and nowadays denotes a general-purpose naval vessel.

Galleasse Developed in the Mediterranean in the sixteenth century, the galleasse was based on the galley but was larger and carried a number of masts and sails, plus a light armament of guns.

Galleon Sir John Hawkins developed the galleon around 1585 by eliminating the high forecastle of the carrack, which made for a more seaworthy and weatherly ship. It was very successful and soon superseded the carrack as the main trading and fighting vessel of northern Europe.

Galley A long low-built warship driven with oars, widely used in the Mediterranean from early Classical times up to the eighteenth century. The simple galley with one bank of oars gave way through the centuries to the bireme and the trireme, with two and three banks of oars respectively. A ram was generally built on the bows as the galley's main armament.

'General chase' A British naval signal dating from the eighteenth century which freed commanders from the rigid line-of-battle. It authorized them to head straight for the enemy and attack the first unengaged ship they met.

Greek fire A highly inflammable liquid based on naphtha invented as a naval weapon by the Byzantines in the seventh century and used generally in the Mediterranean until the cannon rendered it obsolete. Its first and major success was at the siege of Constantinople in AD 678.

Gunwale (pronounced 'gunnel') The plank around the edges of a wooden ship which covers the heads of the hull timbers.

Influence mine Mine whose detonation depends on the magnetic, acoustic or water-pressure influence of a ship.

Letter of marque Commission to a non-naval ship authorizing it to attack merchant vessels of an enemy power, i.e. to become a privateer. A letter of marque was often regarded as a licence for piracy. Privateering was internationally abolished at the Convention of Paris in 1856.

Line-abreast Ships sailing parallel to each other.

Line-ahead This was for centuries the most usual battle formation, each ship sailing in the wake of the one ahead to enable the most concentrated broadside fire to be delivered.

Longship Single-masted vessel with one row of oars used by the Vikings for their raiding and exploratory voyages from the sixth to the tenth century AD.

Mach number The ratio of an aircraft's speed to the speed of sound, which is approximately 1234 km/h (767 mph). Therefore Mach 2 is twice the speed of sound, and so on.

Mortar SEE **Cannon.**

Nef Large French version of the cargo-carrying round ship.

Orlop deck The lowest deck of a ship, used for general storage. In sailing warships it held the powder magazines and anchor cable lockers as well as the junior officers' cabins.

Pocket-battleship The name given to the three heavily armed German cruisers built during the 1930s, of which *Admiral Graf Spee* is the most famous. They were designed along battleship lines, but had displacements of only 11,700 tons.

Privateer SEE **Letter of marque**.

Quarter-deck The section of a ship's upper deck aft of the mainmast, by tradition reserved for officers, and the point from which the captain used to command his ship in the days of sail.

Range-finding The science of estimating the correct angle of elevation of the guns in order to hit a given target. At the long distances and high speeds associated with twentieth-century naval warfare the optical range-finder has given way to radar.

Rates A means of grouping the ships of a navy according to how many guns they carried. This method was employed by most navies during the age of sail and was based on the Royal Navy's six-rate system introduced by Lord Anson in the 1750s. Although the system varied over the years, a first rate would normally have over 100 guns, a second rate 84–100, a third rate 70–84, a fourth rate 50–70, a fifth rate 32–50 and a sixth rate fewer than 32 guns. Only ships of the first three rates were deemed strong enough to take their place in the line-of-battle, and these were known as ships-of-the-line.

Round ship Medieval general-purpose sailing ship with a length-to-beam ratio of about 2½:1.

Sea Beggars Dutch Protestant sailors who played a prominent role in the War of Independence, fought against the occupying Spanish forces in the late sixteenth and early seventeenth centuries.

Ship-of-the-line SEE **Rates**.

Sloop A general term for an eighteenth-century sailing warship too small to be classified as one of the six rates.

Sonar Method of detecting objects (mines, submarines etc.) underwater, using high-frequency sound pulses. Originally known as ASDIC.

Squadron A small group of warships under a single flag officer.

Stern-chaser Gun fitted to the stern of a ship in the days of sail.

Submarine Vessel designed to travel under the surface of the water. It became a practical military proposition during the late nineteenth century, and proved its effectiveness in World Wars I and II when armed with torpedoes. Today's nuclear-powered submarines armed with nuclear missiles are the most deadly weapons in the armouries of the superpowers.

Trenails Oak pins used to fix a ship's planks to her timbers.

Trireme SEE **Galley**.

Truck Cap at the top of a ship's mast. Also a name given to the wheels of a gun-carriage in the days of muzzle-loading cannon.

Tumble-home The difference between the maximum beam of a ship and her width across the upper deck. Wooden warships of the fifteenth to eighteenth centuries had a very pronounced swelling of the beam just above the waterline. This was because all the heaviest guns were mounted on the lower and main decks, and the extra width was needed to operate them, and to allow for recoil on firing.

Weather gauge The position to windward. In the days of sailing sea-battles, the fleet in this position had the advantage.

Weatherly A ship is said to be weatherly when she is capable of sailing close to the wind.

Bibliography

Anderson, R.C. & Marshall, P. *Oared Fighting Ships: From Classical Times to the Coming of Steam* London 1962

Bennett, G. *Naval Battles of the First World War* London 1968

Brown, D.B. *Carrier Operations in World War II* 2 vols, London 1974

Casson, L. *Ships and Seamanship in the Ancient World* Princeton 1971

Clark, G.N. *The Dutch Alliance and the War against French Trade, 1689–97* Manchester 1923

Cowburn, P. *The Warship in History* London 1966

Cowie, J. *Mines, Minelayers and Minelaying* London 1949

Dönitz, K. *Memoirs* London 1958

Dull, P. *A Battle History of the Imperial Japanese Army* London 1978

Friedman, N. *Naval Radar* London 1981

Grant, R. *U-Boat Intelligence* London 1969

Humble, R. *Aircraft Carriers: The Illustrated History* London 1982

Ireland, B. *Warships of the World: Escort Vessels* London 1979

Ireland, B. *Warships of the World: Submarines and Fast Attack Craft* London 1980

Kemp, P. *History of Ships* London 1983

Kemp, P. (Ed.) *History of the Royal Navy* London 1969

Kemp, P. *The Oxford Companion to Ships and the Sea* London 1976

Kemp, P. *Victory at Sea, 1939–1945* London 1957

Lenton, H.T. *Navies of the Second World War* 2 vols, London 1971

MacIntyre, D. *The Naval War against Hitler* London 1971

McLachlan, D. *Room 39, Naval Intelligence in Action 1939–45* London 1968

Mahan, A. *The Influence of Sea Power upon History 1660–1783* London 1897

Mahan, A. *The Influence of Sea Power upon the French Revolution and Empire, 1793–1812* London 1897

Marder, A. *From Dreadnought to Scapa Flow* 5 vols, London 1965

Marx, H.F. *Battle of Lepanto* Cleveland, Ohio 1966

Mattingley, G. *The Defeat of the Spanish Armada* New York 1959

Moore, J.E. *Warships of the Royal Navy* London & New York 1981

Mordal, J. *Twenty-five Centuries of Sea Warfare* London 1959

Morrison, J.S. & Williams, R.T. *Greek Oared Ships, 900–322 BC* Cambridge 1968

Morrison, S.E. *The Battle of the Atlantic* Boston 1948

Padfield, P. *Guns at Sea* London 1973

Parkes, O. *British Battleships* London 1957

Preston, A. *Sea Combat off the Falklands* London 1982

Richardson, D. *Naval Armament* London & New York 1982

Rogers, P.G. *The Dutch In the Medway* London 1970

Rohwer, J. *The Critical Convoy Battles of March 1943* London 1977

Roskill, S.W. *The War at Sea 1939–1945*. Vols 1, 2, 3/1, 3/2. In *History of the Second World War*, UK Military Series, London 1954–61

Roskill, S.W. *Naval Policy between the Wars* 2 vols, London 1968–76

Ruge, F. *The German Navy's Story 1939–45* Annapolis 1957

Ruge, F. *Sea Warfare 1939–1945. A German Viewpoint* London 1957

Snyder, W.P. *The Politics of British Defense Policy 1945–1962* Columbus, Ohio 1964

Terzibaschitsch, S. *Aircraft Carriers of the US Navy* London 1980

Terzibaschitsch, S. *Escort Carriers and Aviation Support Ships of the US Navy* London 1981

Warner, O. *Nelson's Battles* London 1965

Wettern, D. *The Decline of British Seapower* London 1982

Willmott, H.P. *Sea Warfare* Chichester 1981

Wilson, C. *Profit and Power. A Study of the Dutch Wars* London 1957

Index

Acknowledgments
Photographs have been supplied by the following:
Associated Press   Bapty   BBC Hulton Picture Library   C. Bevilacqua   Biblioteca Nacional, Madrid   Bibliothèque Nationale, Paris   A. Bollo   British Library, London   British Museum, London   Buckland Abbey   Bundesarchiv, Berlin   C. Ciccione   COI, London   E. Conrad   Conway Maritime Press   G. Costa   G. Dagli Orti   Gordon Davies   René Dazy   C.M. Dixon   Essex Institute   Mary Evans Picture Library   Werner Forman Archive   Fox Photos   Michael Holford   Robert Hunt Library   IGDA   Imperial War Museum, London   Keystone   H. Le Masson   Library of Congress, Washington   Magdalene College, Cambridge   Mansell Collection   Marka   Marka/L. Coccia   F. Arborio Mella   Ministero della Marina Mercantile, Rome   Ministry of Defence, London   Musée de la Marine, Paris   Musée de Versailles   Musei Vaticani, Rome   Museo Archeologico Nazionale, Athens   National Archives, Washington   National Maritime Museum, London   Nationalmuseet, Copenhagen   National Portrait Gallery, London   Naval Photographic Centre   Novosti   HMS Osprey Personality Picture Library   Photri   Plymouth Guildhall   Popperfoto   Press Association   By gracious permission of Her Majesty The Queen   RAF   E. Ramsay   Rex Features   B. Richner   A. Rizzi   Roger-Viollet   Scala   Science Museum, London   Ronald Sheridan   Sivilgenir Jens Erik Werenskiold, Oslo   Stato Maggiore della Marina, Ufficio Documentazione e Propaganda   Submarine Museum   Süddeutscher Verlag Bilderdienst   Titus   US Airforce   US Navy   University of Chicago   J.N. Westwood   Woburn Abbey